Library of
Davidson College

Strands Afar Remote

International Studies in Shakespeare and His Contemporaries

Editorial Advisory Committee

Jay L. Halio, Chair
University of Delaware

Professor J. Leeds Barroll III
University of Maryland

Professor Ann Jennalie Cook
International Shakespeare Association

Professor Werner Habicht
Institüt für Englische Philologie
University of Würzburg

Professor Yoshiko Kawachi
Kyorin University

Professor Arthur F. Kinney
University of Massachusetts

Professor Jerzy Limon
University of Gdansk

Dr. Barbara Mowat
Folger Shakespeare Library

Professor Stanley Wells
The Shakespeare Institute
University of Birmingham

Professor George Walton Williams
Duke University

Strands Afar Remote

Israeli Perspectives on Shakespeare

Edited by
Avraham Oz

In Association with
The International Shakespeare Association

Newark: University of Delaware Press
London: Associated University Presses

© 1998 by Associated University Presses, Inc.

All rights reserved. Authorization to photocopy items for internal or personal use, or the internal or personal use of specific clients, is granted by the copyright owner, provided that a base fee of $10.00, plus eight cents per page, per copy is paid directly to the Copyright Clearance Center, 222 Rosewood Drive, Danvers, Massachusetts 01923. [0-87413-597-4/98 $10.00+8¢ pp, pc.]

Associated University Presses
440 Forsgate Drive
Cranbury, NJ 08512

Associated University Presses
16 Barter Street
London WC1A 2AH, England

Associated University Presses
P.O. Box 338, Port Credit
Mississauga, Ontario
Canada L5G 4L8

The paper used in this publication meets the requirements of the American National Standard for Permanence of Paper for Printed Library Materials Z39.48–1984.

Library of Congress Cataloging-in-Publication Data

Strands afar remote : Israeli perspectives on Shakespeare / edited by Avraham Oz.
    p. cm. — (International studies in Shakespeare and his contemporaries)
Some essays translated from Hebrew.
Includes bibliographical references and index.
ISBN 0-87413-597-4 (alk. paper)
    1. Shakespeare, William, 1564–1616—Criticism and interpretation. 2. Criticism—Israel. I. Oz, Avraham. II. Series.
PR2976.S765   1998
822.3'3—dc21   97-19193
                                                                                            CIP

PRINTED IN THE UNITED STATES OF AMERICA

To Tal
Omnia vincit

Contents

Contributors	9
Foreword	11
Innocent Arrows and Sexy Sticks: The Rival Economies of Male Friendship and Heterosexual Love in *The Merchant of Venice* ZVI JAGENDORF	17
The Rhetoric of Exclusion: Jew, Moor, and the Boundaries of Discourse in *The Merchant of Venice* ALAN ROSEN	38
"The Poor Sequestered Stag": St. Augustine Metaphor in *As You Like It* AHUVA BELKIN	51
"I See a Voice": The Desire for Representation and the Rape of Voice ELIZABETH FREUND	62
"War and Lechery Confound All": Identity and Agency in Shakespeare's *Troilus and Cressida* MICHAEL YOGEV	87
Motive and Meaning in *All's Well That Ends Well* RUTH NEVO	113
The Isolation of the Tragic Protagonist: Tragedy and *Richard III* BARUCH KURZWEILL	138
Prophecy as a Cultural Model: The Politics of *Tamburlaine* and *Julius Caesar* AVRAHAM OZ	151
Hamlet's Entrails DAVID HILLMAN	177
Othello and Woyzeck as Tragic Heroes According to Aristotle and Hegel YEDIDIA ITZHAKI	204

Coriolanus and the Compulsion to Repeat SHULI BARZILAI	232
Shakespearean Re-Generations in Hebrew: A Study in Historical Poetics HARAI GOLOMB	255
Afterword: "Prosper Our Colours": A Case/Noncase for National Perspectives on Shakespeare and his Contemporaries AVRAHAM OZ	276
Index	301

Contributors

SHULI BARZILAI is a Senior Lecturer in the Department of English at the Hebrew University of Jerusalem. She has written essays on literary theory, psychoanalytical criticism, and women writers for scholarly publications, including *American Imago, Diacritics, New Literary History, PMLA,* and *Yale French Studies.*

AHUVA BELKIN is a Senior Lecturer at the Department of Theatre Arts at Tel Aviv University. Her special fields of interest are history of the theater and Jewish theater.

ELIZABETH FREUND is a Senior Lecturer in the Department of English at the Hebrew University of Jerusalem. She is the author of *The Return of the Reader* (1987) and of many essays on Shakespeare. She has written several study guides on selected plays by Shakespeare for the Open University of Tel Aviv. Her most recent work is on the language of wit in Shakespeare's plays.

HARAI GOLOMB is a Professor at Tel Aviv University's Faculty of Arts, and has published and taught in the fields of literature, theater, musicology, and comparative art studies. His fields of interest include Hebrew linguistics and English literature. He is an active translator of opera librettos into Hebrew.

DAVID HILLMAN was educated at the Hebrew University of Jerusalem and is now a graduate student in English at Harvard, where he is writing a dissertation on the idea of the interior of the body in the Shakespearean corpus. He is the coeditor of *The Body in Parts: Essays on Early Modern Corporeality* and the editor of *Authority and Representation in Early Modern Discourse.*

YEDIDIA ITZHAKI was born in Jerusalem, 1929. He is an architect, as well as a Lecturer in Hebrew literature at Bar Ilan University and the editor of *Alei-Siah,* a Hebrew review of literature. Among his numerous publications on Hebrew and world literature and drama is *The Concealed Verses: Source Materials in the Work of A. B. Yehoshua* (1992).

ZVI JAGENDORF was born in Vienna in 1936, educated at Oxford, and then moved to Israel. He is a Senior Lecturer in the Department of English and a former head of the Department of Theatre History at the Hebrew University of Jerusalem. A former actor, a translator of poetry, and a critic, he is the author of *The Happy End of Comedy: Johnson, Molière, and Shakespeare* (1984).

BARUCH KURZWEILL was born in 1907 in Moravia, educated in German and Jewish schools in Frankfurt, Germany, and received his Ph.D. in 1933 from the University of Frankfurt for a dissertation on *Goethe's Faust and the Bourgeois Spirit*. From 1939 until his death in 1972, he was noted as one of the most controversial figures in Israeli literary criticism. Holding the Chair of Hebrew and Comparative Literature at Bar Ilan University since 1955, he published numerous books and articles on Hebrew and world literature and drama.

RUTH NEVO, educated in South Africa and England, is widely known for her major Shakespearean studies, including *Tragic Form in Shakespeare* (1972), *Comic Transformations in Shakespeare* (1980), and *Shakespeare's Other Languages* (1987). She is a member of the Israel Academy and Professor Emerita of English and former head of the Department of English at the Hebrew University of Jerusalem.

AVRAHAM OZ, born in Tel Aviv, was educated in Israel and England. He is head of the Department of Theatre at the University of Haifa and former head of the Department of Theatre Arts at Tel Aviv University. His books and articles on early modern drama and political theater include *The Yoke of Love: Prophetic Riddles in "The Merchant of Venice"* (1995). He is a former associate director of the Cameri Theatre and dramaturg of the Haifa Municipal Theatre, and the editor of the Hebrew edition of Shakespeare's works; his translations of Shakespeare, Brecht, Pinter, and of other plays and operas have been mounted by all major theaters in Israel.

ALAN ROSEN is a Lecturer in English Literature at Bar Ilan University. He writes on early modern drama and prose.

MICHAEL YOGEV teaches Shakespeare and English romanticism at the University of Haifa. He is currently working on a study of chivalry in the later plays of Shakespeare.

Foreword

I have chosen to comment in greater detail in a separate article on the invited concept underlying the present volume and its intriguing, but not entirely premeditated consequences. This article forms the afterword to this collection of essays by various hands. There is not much, however, to say generally at the outset by way of a preliminary agenda for this volume as a unified whole. To some extent it reflects, as may be expected, a tentative intersection of two national cultures, separated in time and location, although the implications of that kind of meeting point is not necessarily articulated by, or marked as the main stress of most of the following articles.

As the chapter by Harai Golomb that concludes the body of these essays may indicate, the modern Shakespearean project woven into the tissue of the nascent Israeli culture dates back to the latter half of the nineteenth century. It was the very juncture in the history of Judaism where the Jewish enlightenment, allegedly liberated, yet not fully dissociated from the cultural fetters of the strictly religious identity of Jewishness, appropriated the latter's long-established, imposed-upon otherness, in order to have it constructed as a fresh collective national identity. This was the movement that produced the Zionist project as a political/territorial implementation of Jewish cultural claims. In spite of the large interest in the canon, which has given rise to fine examples of theatrical interpretation and produced sophisticated and thought-provoking instances of Shakespearean criticism, there is hardly any evident correlation between that interest and any distinctive features, if such exist, of the constantly developing Israeli culture. Inspired by various intellectual traditions, and fostered in conjunction with different forms of personal involvement in a still-emerging and striving-for-recognition national project, the identification with which inevitably implicates one with some inherent presence of active desire, the cultural aspects of such a complex and problematic agenda hardly converge on any unified patterns or focused economy of approach to its ideological appropriations. Even the enunciating of a privileged Western cultural asset such as the Shakespearean canon as a distinctive vehicle and a charged channel whereby the newly formed organ of enlightened nationalism is to be related to the mainstream of European cultural heritage, not the least to prop the Zionist project to stand its own against a narrower claim of religious exclusivity, a point proclaimed by the forefathers of Zionism as a major part of its agenda, fails to embrace the entire compass of the intellectual or artistic interest in the canon as manifested in the intriguing harvest of Israeli critical involvement with Shakespeare over the last century: its predictable, subjective obsession with *The Merchant of Venice* is only one telling instance in which its ongoing confusion regarding its cultural sources are far from settled or well-defined. Nor does one of the most essential features of the Israeli national narrative, namely the extent to which the establishment of a positive Jewish-Israeli cultural entity depends on developing ancient-new patterns of otherness, necessarily find its reflection in the critical treatment of the creator of Shylock, Othello, or Aaron by writers permanently exposed to such phenomena in the cultural, let alone political, context within which their work is being carried out. In view of the charged, conflict-riddled history of the Zionist project, which has promoted the interest in Shakespeare within the Israeli culture, the reason why, for instance, fraternal feuds are often represented to date on the Hebrew stage rather by sugared versions of *Romeo and Juliet* than in terms of the more telling cases of *Troilus and Cressida* or *Henry V*, is one of several issues yet to be discussed by theater historians in Israel.

The present, representative, yet somewhat diffused gathering of Israeli Shakespearean criticism may still attest to the cultural pluralism constituting the elusive construct of modern Israeli culture, still struggling for self-definition. Whereas articles such as those by Baruch Kurzweill and Yedidia Itzhaki represent the significant influence of central European, especially German romantic notions, on the emerging national culture, others, such as those by Ruth Nevo, Zvi Jagendorf, Alan Rosen, or Michael Yogeve may represent the infiltration of Anglo-American thread of thought into its complex tissue. Thematically or methodically, however, there is hardly a local distinction to this collection. There are discussions of Shakespearean works against traditional concepts of tragic drama (Kurzweill, Itzhaki), medieval and Renaissance theology and iconography (Belkin), conventions of love and friendship (Jagendorf) or rhetorical and verbal practices inherent in the original texts (Freund, Rosen), or its Hebrew translations

(Golomb); some of the represented approaches are to various extents psychoanalytically bent (Nevo, Barzilai, Yogev, Hillman), or ideologically so (Oz). Perhaps this very multiplicity of approaches, stances, and methodologies is itself a telling account of the current state of Israeli national culture.

I would like to take this opportunity to thank the contributors for their patience in the long and tortuous way towards the production of this volume; particularly so to Professor Ruth Nevo, who gracefully turned a blind eye to my neglecting another project, more acutely touching her, while working on this volume. I thank Mrs. Kurzweill for kindly seeing to the translation of her late husband's article and Mrs. Ruth Pancer for translating two of the articles from the Hebrew. Jay Halio, chief editor for the University of Delaware Press, kindly and (almost) patiently absorbed all the delays caused by an overburdened editor involved in several projects at once. Most kind and loving, as always, was Tali, my wife, to whom this volume is offered, as ever, as a tribute of love.

Avraham Oz
University of Haifa and Tel Aviv University

Strands Afar Remote

Innocent Arrows and Sexy Sticks: The Rival Economies of Male Friendship and Heterosexual Love in *The Merchant of Venice*

ZVI JAGENDORF

ONE of the oddest things about *The Merchant of Venice* is the mixture of dry legalism and bawdry in its closing lines. Although it is common knowledge that the lovers in Shakespeare's comedies do not usually end up in the marriage bed but somewhere nearby with business to dispatch, still the ending of *The Merchant* is remarkable for its lack of romantic glow and anticipation. Portia's last words are more appropriate to legal than nuptial chambers:

> Let us go in,
> And charge us there upon inter'gatories
> And we will answer all things faithfully.
> (*The Merchant*, 5.1.297–99)[1]

It is almost morning we are told. So the last scene of the play, instead of being the prelude to the night's consummation, becomes the start of a day's debriefing led by Portia. It takes Gratiano, in the role of buffoon, to raise the priapic standard and remind us with talk of bed, and of Nerissa's ring and thing that lovers in comedies are meant to end up between the sheets untying more interesting things than the knots of a comic plot.

Sex is for servants, a cynic might say; money is what interests the gentlefolk in this play. This is an exaggeration, yet there is truth in it for clearly the search for money and the quest for love are the twin poles that sustain the world of the play and any interpretation has to deal with their interplay—indeed the commerce between them.

When Jane Austen wrote "It is a truth universally acknowledged that a single man in possession of a good fortune, must be in want of a wife" she is both mocking and affirming, through her cunning balance of possession against want, the market relations on the basis of which marriages were arranged in the society portrayed in *Pride and Prejudice*. Love does get mentioned in that memorable opening conversation, but it is Mrs. Bennet, "a woman of mean understanding" who does so. "But it is very likely that he may fall in love with one of them." Thus the trivial, hysterical mother utters the romantic piety and does obeisance to the totem worshiped by mothers and daughters in the teeth of observation and experience. The fact that Austen still makes love the credible foundation of a good fortune is one of the pleasures of reading her but unfortunately not the subject of this essay. Yet her lucidity on the embarrassment of genteel poverty and on the necessity of falling in love with four or five thousand a year might well serve as a benchmark for an interpretation of the much less lucid, more paradoxical, and sexually troubled Shakespearean inversion of the topic in our play where the opening situation might be stated as follows: It is a truth equally universally acknowledged that a single man *not* in possession of a good fortune must be in want of a rich wife.

The unspoken word is again love, also first mentioned in the play by a trivial person, Solanio, whose declaration, "Why then you are in love" is an attempt to find a cause for the merchant's inexplicable melancholy. Antonio's strange reply "Fie, fie!", as if love were some disease, is the first sign of trouble to come.

The ethos of love and of the need for money, kept in such judicious balance by Austen's prose, cannot be balanced so gracefully in the antagonistically violent, linguistically explosive, and paradoxical world of poetic drama. On the Shakespearean stage the controlled perspective that keeps money and love in steady focus is less apparent than the pressure and anxiety that force them together creating the unexpected combinations and reversals that are germane to all drama but that are at the very heart of *The Merchant*.

In spite of the traditional Christian praise of poverty and suspicion, to say the least, of riches and of the influential Aristotelian notion of gold as sterile when set against the natural fecundity of the body, the languages of wealth and love have always been interdependent. The question, "How much do you love me?" illustrates such contact in the most banal way. That is what Antony seems to think when he counters Cleopatra's opening question in *Antony and Cleopatra* with a challenge to the very notion of quantity as demeaning:

> There's beggary in the love that can be reckon'd
> *(Antony and Cleopatra,* 1.1.15)

We may instinctively assent to his brave contempt for measure but the question of how much, though it smells of the market and the countinghouse, cannot be excluded from love's discourse.

In the *Song of Songs* it appears as a strange turn in a passage that speaks of the power of love to withstand immense material weight and mass:

> Many waters cannot quench love, neither can the floods drown it.
> *(Song of Songs,* 8:7)

In this figure of fire against water, the single flame (love) outlives the onslaught of what is by grammatical character plural in Hebrew (*mayyim*). So the multiplication of waters fails to put out the flame and quantity surrenders to intensity. But the same verse, in a movement closely parallel to what happens at the opening of *Antony and Cleopatra,* goes on to note the social penalty to be paid when love's extreme demands are met in terms of property:

> if a man would give all the substance of his house for love, it would utterly be condemned *(Song of Songs,* 8:7)

Contempt, we remember, is what Philo has for Antony who is transformed by his dotage from "the triple pillar of the world" into "a strumpet's fool." On the one hand then, love is unmeasurable, on the other, a social measure of the extreme actions love provokes finds that the price the lover pays is excessive. All your wealth for love? A third of all the world for a strumpet? Is it worth it? Can love be reckoned after all?

Obviously, the question "how much?" is not at all out of place in the rhetoric of love. Ideally love is a simple and economically innocent exchange or barter: my love is mine and I am his. But as soon as this is sophisticated and subjected to analysis or more pertinently, when the intimate exchange of feeling is given a social setting, say in the context of an economy (in London or Venice) where value is dependent on the market, then anxiety about numbers becomes apparent. When Portia confesses to Bassanio:

> One half of me is yours, the other half yours
> Mine own, I would say;
> *(The Merchant,* 3.2.16–17)

she would dismiss calculation; she means to give herself entirely. But her language is caught up in the web of numbers, laboriously so, even dangerously when we remember that she is an heiress and the goal of Bassanio's voyage is her fortune, not half but the whole of it. Once love is thought of as a kind of sophisticated exchange, then notions of measure and quantity become pertinent, together with the language of debt and credit, borrowing and lending, even investment and return. When Falstaff answers Hal's "Sirrah do I owe you a thousand pound?" with

> A thousand pound, Hal? a million, thy love is worth a million; thou owest me thy love
> (1 *Henry IV*, 3.3.136–37)

he like Portia is measuring and defying measure at the same time. Speaking as someone who is chronically in debt, he clearly wants to turn the prince's love into realizable assets (a million). His hopes of riches and influence depend on such convertibility. At the same time a million, to a poor man, stands for infinity and Hal's love is therefore beyond reckoning. The specifics of financial calculation and the bravado of its dismissal are copresent here and we do not find it grotesque to see moneybags on one side of the scale and on the other the old man's vital claim to the prince's debt of love. There's beggary in the love that can be reckoned, implies Falstaff, yet he uses the astounding number theoretically, the way a reckless gambler does, as a spell to defy ill luck and to keep sober reality at bay.

If the language of how much colors the speech of Antony, the rich man, and Falstaff, the poor man, in plays that do not focus particularly on the workings of money, we would expect its presence to be doubly and insistently noticeable in *The Merchant*, which tracks the quest for love on a map busy with the flow of goods and money. Clearly the trajectories on this map must cross each other at many points, crossings we may take to be invitations to interpretation.

One of the most rewarding of such points is Bassanio's request for money from Antonio to finance his quest for Portia and her golden fleece. This is the point from which the play's lines of desire and indebtedness are projected. One trajectory leads from Antonio to Bassanio and to Portia, the other interpolates Shylock between Antonio and Bassanio. The first line is complicated by the implied competition between homosexual love characterized by debt and heterosexual love that releases treasure. The second line is complicated by the unpleasant involvement of Jewish usury as a catalyst and go-between in the amorous commerce between both men and women.

It has always seemed to me one of the more intriguing weaknesses of the play that Bassanio, patently a prodigal and a fortune hunter, should be proposed apparently without irony for the part of a beau ideal, ephebe, scholar, and Christian gentleman. While Shakespeare's darker comedies offer curious studies of shadowy, fallible young men of doubtful character but of handsome looks (like Bertram in *All's Well*) who are chosen as love objects by strong and energetic young women, *The Merchant* is different in its apparent acceptance of Bassanio on his own terms. We know what a Jonsonian treatment of a Bassanio would be like. He would have given us a desperate, sexually ambiguous, cynical, and misogynistic fortune hunter living off his wits and his sex in the manner of Truewit and Dauphine in *The Silent Woman*. In that play the young men's hunger for money and even for food is blatant as they struggle to survive in London society. It gives their wit a harsh, barking quality and it strips them of all pretense in our eyes just as they strip their victims to the bone with their savage analysis of every physical, mental, and social defect.

Bassanio is saved the fate of his Jacobean cousins because he is a protagonist in an apparently romantic fiction in which the golden cheese falls into the handsome fox cub's mouth because of his good breeding and healthy complexion. There is such a guarded flatness about Shakespeare's characterization of the young man that we might suspect the poet of defending him from suspicious inquiry. It is as if he is saying, leave the boy alone, he's only a breeder, a key to Portia's treasure chest. Bassanio's blandness is in fact the cause of desire in others, notably in Antonio and even in Portia, while the Jew's involvement sharpens and displaces the libidinal energy by directing it toward the suffering body of love's true victim, the merchant, Antonio. The play's strange, almost strangled, sexuality may then be approached through the young man whose blandness is the negative heart at the center of a series of positive desires. Neither wholly a man's erotic friend, nor truly a husband to a wife, he moves between them entangling both in the consequences of his debt with which the play starts.

Bassanio's initial request for money from Antonio bears close analysis because it goes to the erotic/economic heart of the play and conceals beneath the proclaimed innocence of its rhetoric a strong analogy between debt and its return and the homosexual bond. The young man is not in a good position at the beginning of the play. He is a profligate borrower asking his benefactor to throw good money after bad; like the commonest of gamblers caught in a losing streak all he needs is enough money for one last throw that will make him rich and redeem all his debts. The first thing one notices about the way he leads up to his actual request is its blurred and circuitous parlance:

> 'Tis not unknown to you, Antonio,
> How much I have disabled mine estate,
> By something showing a more swelling port
> Than my faint means would grant continuance.
> Nor do I now make moan to be abridg'd
> From such a noble rate, but my chief care
> Is to come fairly off from the great debts
> Wherein my time something too prodigal
> Hath left me gag'd.
>
> (1.1.122–30)

This follows the prattle of the Venetians Salerio, Gratianio, and Solario whose comic descriptions of social stereotypes and various hypothetical business disasters are aimed at filling the void of Antonio's undiagnosed melancholy. If their energetic babble makes Bassanio's speech sound dull that is because it is. And it is so because he is trying to describe the plight of a prodigal antiseptically without using any of the wounding caustic language of traditional moral assault on wastrels. The result is that Bassanio sounds like a mealymouthed lawyer speaking in defense of his good-for-nothing client whose desperate state he is trying to camouflage. We are meant to decipher the code of a proper young gentleman: the understatement, the good intentions, the stiff-upper-lip. Prodigality is made to look like a minor carelessness, a gentlemanly oversight, like not paying one's tailor. Yet the cosmetic phrasing cannot hide the cruel request at the heart of the speech:

> To you, Antonio,
> I owe the most in money and in love,
> And from your love I have a warranty
> To unburthen all my plots and purposes
> How to get clear of all the debts I owe.
>
> (1.1.130–34)

In other words, he needs more of Antonio's money in order to be free of Antonio's love. This is not a perverse reading, given the consistent and unresolved tension in the play between the love of men and the love of women, the former characterized by debt and sacrifice, the latter by treasure and its release.

Antonio's answer to Bassanio forces us, even if we have evaded it up to now, to contemplate the erotic aspect of debt:

> My purse, my person, my extremest means
> Lie all unlock'd to your occasions.
> (1.1.138–39)

The assonance could not be more assertive in this declaration of availability. "My purse, my person," which, echoed in Shylock's "my ducats and my daughter", can sound so grotesquely wrong in its juxtaposition of flesh and blood with gold, is when spoken by Antonio darkly dangerous in its blurring of the borders between the offering of gold and the offering of self. The prone openness of the unlocked, metonymic purse is embarrassingly linked with a defenselessness of person, making the availability of a sum of money a dangerous criterion for the vulnerability of a life.

We must remember that Bassanio's request still has not been made. This is all foreplay. When it does come, it is with his meditation on the caskets, his most important speech in the play. And compared with that safely orthodox reflection on lead and its virtues, it is as close to self-revelation as this bland character can be allowed to come. Like many important texts it is full of redundancy. It overloads the channels of communication for the message: lend me more money could have been easily understood without the parable of the arrows. Even the sympathetic Antonio is made uneasy by its evasiveness and criticizes its unnecessary rhetoric:

> You know me well, and herein spend but time
> To wind about my love with circumstance,
> (1.1.153–54)

What, we may ask, is this winding all about? Uncharacteristically, Bassanio speaks here in a kind of parable. He tells an exemplary story and then interprets it in case his friend has missed the point.

> In my school-days, when I had lost one shaft,
> I shot his fellow of the self-same flight
> The self-same way with more advised watch

> To find the other forth, and by adventuring both
> I oft found both. I urge this childhood proof,
> Because what follows is pure innocence.
> I owe you much, and like a wilful youth
> That which I owe is lost, but if you please
> To shoot another arrow that self way
> Which you did shoot the first, I do not doubt,
> As I will watch the aim, or to find both
> Or bring your latter hazard back again,
> And thankfully rest debtor for the first.
>
> (1.1.140–52)

This tale of two arrows aims at setting before the older man a picture of a presexual boyish game in which money is child's play and debt innocent and, like Peter Pan, never grows.[2] It is an argument for lending without profit or increase and, in a more secret way it is an allegory of homosexual commerce. The arrows whose flight the story tells are identical ("self-same"); they seek each other out through the air like the separated twins at the beginning of *The Comedy of Errors*. In the rhetoric of child's play the loss of the first arrow is hardly a fault. It is something that happens in a game and the remedy is at hand in the second shaft. The languages of play and commerce meet at the key word "adventuring" which is what boys do for fun and merchants for profit, unless they make a loss. The wiliness of the tale becomes apparent when Bassanio interprets it in "pure innocence" and shifts the identity of the archer from the willful boy (Bassanio) to the merchant. It is no longer I (Bassanio) who do the shooting but you (Antonio) who will shoot sums of money after each other while I cast myself in the responsible role of watcher and retriever of at least some of the debt.

Antonio is irritated by these rhetorical flights, the only moment in the whole play when he shows impatience toward his young friend. He finds all this talk circuitous and wasteful and he counters Bassanio's fiction of innocence with a statement of adult commitment devastating in its lack of reserve:

> you do me now more wrong
> In making question of my uttermost
> Than if you had made waste of all I have.
>
> (*The Merchant*, 1.1.155–57)

How much, Antonio is saying, is not a question even for a merchant when love is concerned. The two arrows with their implied calculation of debt and its repayment are swept aside by a lover's impatient extremism that would rather imagine disaster and sacrifice than weigh profit and loss. There's beggary in the love that can be reckoned.

Given the transparency, indeed the redundancy of Bassanio's parable as a strategy of raising money, it is nevertheless interpretable in a more subversive way as an allegory of male friendship and sexual identity placed at a point in the play where a male economy of indebtedness is about to give way to a female economy based on unlocked treasure. How then does Bassanio's tale speak of sexual identity? Essentially by stressing the sameness of the arrows in build, flight, and direction. Difference has no place in this story because that would prevent the arrows' finding each other. Sameness on the other hand is stressed and overstressed by the doubling of "self-same," the trebling of "self," the chiming repetition of both and even, to a reader, by the way *FEL* in "fellow" plays against *ELF* in "self-same." The arrows' sameness is an essential part of the boyish world of play that can be called innocent because it is undisturbed as yet by the difference of women. An analogy from *The Winter's Tale* will bear this out. That play also begins with two friends and when one of them, Polixenes, describes the boyhood he and Leontes shared, he talks of a paradisal state of innocence, an idyllic pastoral in which the boys are compared to:

> twinn'd lambs that did frisk i' th' sun,
> And bleat the one at th' other.
> *(The Winter's Tale, 1.2.67–68)*

There too the sameness of a pair of boys is the basis for a masculine Eden secure and sealed off in its closed circle by the exclusion of women. It is a world of play before sin in which sexual identity allows for the purest and simplest kind of exchange or barter:

> What we chang'd
> Was innocence for innocence;
> (1.2.68–69)

It is of course women who introduce temptation into this paradise and lead the boys into the dangerous world of sexual difference, experience, and the fathering of children.

Bassanio's tale of the twinned arrows does not posit the innocent game on the absence of women but it colors the borrowing and spending of money in a prelapsarian glow, economically and sexually. As well as ruling out disaster and loss Bassanio's parable rules out interest and profit, or in other words increase. And that is where women and Jews come in.

Enter Shylock, whose apologia for interest as increase in act 1, scene 3 is aggressively, even bestially, sexual in ways that create specific and pointed contrasts with Bassanio's celibate arrows. If we juxtapose Bassanio's apologia for lending with Shylock's for interest we contemplate a play of categories which holds true throughout the play. It is an opposition between innocence and experience, the former Christian, the latter Jewish, the one dependent on sexual similarity and profitless exchange, the other on sexual difference, breeding, and increase. Although the opposition is familiar, seen as a crux where money and sexuality meet, it moves our interpretation a step forward.[3]

Like Bassanio's tale Shylock's is a parable; it has a lesson although he, unlike the young Christian, does not bother to spell it out.[4] Its design on its audience (Antonio and Bassanio) is to defend interest by citing biblical precedent and perhaps also to offend Christian propriety by drawing an overly graphic picture of animal sexuality. Bassanio's tale we will remember was noteworthy for its denial of evil. Shylock's tale of Jacob's resourceful breeding methods is set in a web of tricks and stratagems aimed at amassing property and wealth by taking them away from others. Thus we know, though Shylock does not say so, that Jacob is the "third possessor" only because he tricked his father. We also know that Jacob's device of the sticks and the breeding ewes is a counterstratagem to foil Laban's plan to send him away with nothing:

> When Laban and himself were compremis'd,
> That all the eanlings which were streak'd and pied
> Should fall as Jacob's hire, the ewes being rank
> In end of autumn turned to the rams,
> And when the work of generation was
> Between these woolly breeders in the act,
> The skilful shepherd pill'd me certain wands,
> And in the doing of the deed of kind,
> He stuck them up before the fulsome ewes,
> Who then conceiving did in eaning time
> Fall parti-color'd lambs, and those were Jacob's.
> This was a way to thrive, and he was blest;
> And thrift is blessing if men steal it not.
> (*The Merchant*, 1.3.78–90)

Shylock's grotesque pastoral sexualizes interest as a kind of breeding and challenges with its farmyard realism and its subtext of cheating the prettified pastoral of the Christian.[5] The Jew's story smells of dung. Although the Bible does not tell him this, he knows that the ewes were in heat at the end of autumn and he talks approvingly as a farmer would of *the work* of generation. An active participant in this work is Jacob, whom we imagine moving among the woolly breeders wielding his wands with an energy for profit every bit as avid as the rams' for propagation.

The peeled wands are Shylock's version of the boyish arrows. Whereas these fly in pursuit of each other and can mirror each other but not reproduce, the wands are props in a scene of procreation. They are witnesses to conception but not passive ones, for they affect conception by controlling the color of the offspring. In the Bible the significance of the peeled branches is clear. In Shakespeare's version, because of the contrast with Bassanio, something less obvious may be understood. Bassanio's arrows are of a piece; innocent, unreproductive male identity is their message. Jacob's rods, on the other hand, are marked by and create difference. They are motley, white peeping through black and pied like the breed they induce. There are therefore sexualized, not only by being part of a scene of procreation but in bearing the marks of contrast, the cuts, and slashes that make for difference. They are therefore a factor in increase and generation and a figure for the energetic breeding of kind and money for which the Jew stands but that the Gentiles (or at least Bassanio and Antonio) profess to find unnatural.[6]

The connection between the flight of arrows and deep friendship between young men is at the heart of a biblical episode very different from Shylock's but analogous to Bassanio's tale. The episode of Jonathan and David, the arrows and the anger of Saul (1 Sam. 20) is the Bible's most poignant and detailed account of friendship between men. The episode has been the subject of much analysis and it is not my purpose here to attempt more commentary on its art. I just want to consider the arrows. Unlike Bassanio's, they are not "innocent" even though they are shot in sport. They are part of a stratagem and aim to deliver a message from Jonathan to the hidden David: flee or come back. While Bassanio's shafts are about the flight and return of money, Jonathan's mark the tragic divide between friendship and separation. They do not *stand* for the love between men; this is openly and directly expressed in the story, but they elaborate its peripety as it is posed between closeness and separation. Finding the arrows, for Bassanio, means the return of debts and the justification of friendship. In Sam. 20 the return of the arrows signals the dispersion of the friends. The boy who gathers them does not know this, but Jonathan does; the hidden David does and so does the reader. In the biblical story then, the arrows are not a figure of the friendship and its fate but they bear a message that it might be too dangerous to speak face-to-face. They are an authenticating detail because they make it possible for Jonathan to leave his father's house to practice archery in a rural scene, where David can hide. Yet the true beauty of the arrows lies in their retreat from foreground to background when the message they bear cannot contain the emotional pressure of the love between friends and when David comes out of hiding to embrace Jonathan and bid him farewell:

> And as soon as the lad was gone, David arose out of a place toward the south and fell on his face to the ground, and bowed himself three times; and they kissed one another, and wept one with the other, until David exceeded. (Sam., 20:41)

In their role as a rhetorical device, Bassanio's arrows trace out a message he chooses not to speak directly, a request for more interest-free credit colored by an ambience of innocent male friendship. Both stories occur at the separation of the ways for two loving friends. Between David and Jonathan stands the jealousy and anger of the violent father and king. Between Antonio and Bassanio comes the lady of Belmont whose treasure, once opened, makes the noble yet sterile love-debt of friendship recede into the background. It can hold its own neither financially nor erotically against heterosexual wealth and procreation.

Yet procreation is apparently not as simple for Christians as it is for rams and ewes. All kinds of things get in the way. One of the severest conditions of the law of the father in Portia's Belmont condemns choosers of wrong caskets to refrain from marriage for the rest of their lives, which translating from the language of romance is the doom of castration. The Prince of Morocco seems to realize this as he droops off the stage:

> Cold indeed, and labor lost:
> Then farewell heat, and welcome frost!
> (*The Merchant*, 2.7.74–75)

In the Italian novella *Il Pecorone* a probable source of Shakespeare's play, the Portia figure, a rich widow who can only be reached by sea, inverts the Shakespearean order. In *The Merchant* the wrong choice of casket leads to enforced celibacy; in *Il Pecorone* the widow demands proof of manhood *before* choosing the lucky suitor. Impotence on the crucial night costs the candidate not only his reputation but whatever wealth he has brought with him on his quest. Needless to say, the lady drugs the candidates with a doctored potion before they retire and remains so to speak impregnable until the Bassanio figure, after two defeats and a heavy loss of merchandise, tumbles to the stratagem, with the help of a maid encounters the lady, and wins the prize. Both in Shakespeare and in the Italian tale loss of manhood and loss of wealth are linked. In the more primitive version the phallic performance is the test; in the politer version the test is an apparently ethical one but failure unmans the suitor just as it denies him Portia's treasure.

The pleasant fiction of Shakespeare's play, that love releases money and makes children, is a way of imagining a profit motive that is legitimate, Christian, and natural as opposed to the Jew's unnatural ways with ewes and money. Portia's use of a rhetoric of multiplication when she dedicates herself to Bassanio after his successful choice is an unashamed embrace of number and market value as valid criteria of worth as well as integrity and virtue:

> yet for you,
> I would be trebled twenty times myself,
> A thousand times more fair, ten thousand times more rich
> That only to stand high in your account,
> I might in virtues, beauties, livings, friends,
> Exceed account.
>
> (3.2.152–57)

When the Lord said be fruitful and multiply, he was probably not thinking of the profit motive, yet marrying is a way of combining God's word with sound business practice. Increase is what the sex drive and the profit motive have in common and the play labors hard to keep clear the distinction between legitimate and illegitimate increase while, in the background, lurks the example of homosexual love that, valuing identity, offers neither profit nor increase, only debt and sacrifice.

Gratiano, Bassanio's buffoonish friend, spells out the simplest way to profit in the direct and bawdy way unavailable to polite people. He is also getting married in act 3, not to money but to money's maid, Nerissa, and true to Venetian mores he turns the conventional coincidence into a money-making proposition:

Gratiano. We'll play with them the first boy for a thousand ducats.
Nerissa. What, and stake down?
Gratiano. No, we shall ne'er win at that sport, and stake down.

(3.2.213–16)

Getting a male child is the goal in a competition and a gamble, a game that is played not only for pleasure but also for profit. This is neither the innocent play of boyish arrows nor the aggressive, hubristic interventionism of Jacob's peeled wands. It is a hazard (a word much used in the play) something like setting a merchant vessel on its journey without insurance and for security all Gratiano has is what every Christian merchant should have: faith in God and confidence in one's upright stake. But that, as we know from the traditions of comedy, is easier for servants and in our play consummation is delayed by more than two acts as both Antonio and the Jew intrude the obligations of friendship and debt into the space between the bride and bridegroom.

The dependence of the happy end on the Jew's claim for his bond is a major feature of the play's closing action and has been the subject of much commentary. My purpose in taking another look is to reconsider the all-important erotic/financial triangle that now comes into clear focus and weigh the implications of the intriguingly similar threesome who play out a plot of love, power, and debt in Sonnet 134.

When we listen to Bassanio telling Portia the bad news in the letter from Venice, we realize with a shock that these are the first passionate and urgent words we have heard from him in the whole casket scene:

> Here is a letter, lady,
> The paper as the body of my friend,
> And every word in it a gaping wound
> Issuing life-blood.

(3.2.263–66)

The subjection of his friend's very life to Bassanio's success gives the young man's speech a physical immediacy that was never apparent in the formal phrases he spoke as Portia's suitor. That was the language of literary love; this merges word and paper with a suffering, dying body. It substitutes a real sacrifice for the very literary one that Portia imagined herself enacting in the tense moment before Bassanio's choice.

> I stand for sacrifice
>
> (3.2.57)

she says, comparing Bassanio to Hercules and herself to the captive Trojan maiden of the legend. Antonio's body bleeding his debt is in no legend; it is going to happen and every minute brings the sacrifice nearer.

No one can doubt the emotion the play invests in the relationship between the older merchant and his young friend. What is intriguing is the position of Portia vis-à-vis the two male points of the triangle. In the plot, she is the savior of Antonio and the releaser of his bond. But the sad fate she succeeds in preventing bears a strong emotional emphasis. Antonio's sacrifice would be a *liebestod*, or a "martyrdom," a lover's willing acceptance of the mortal debt that proves his love's worth and raises it above the love of women. This is what Antonio's farewell speech in court to Bassanio implies:

> Commend me to your honorable wife,
> Tell her the process of Antonio's end,
> Say how I lov'd you, speak me fair in death;
> And when the tale is told, bid her be judge
> Whether Bassanio had not once a love.
>
> (4.1.274–77)

When Portia intervenes to make the happy end possible, she robs the male romance of its only possible public consummation—the shedding of blood, for Shylock's cut would have fulfilled Antonio's tragic promise of purse and person to his friend. Here then as in a tragedy the boast of the hero, his willingness to go to the extreme would become the cruel reality which vindicates his spirit and his integrity and his love even as it breaks his body. But a tragedy this is not.

As chief agent of the comic plot that is committed to happy endings, marriage beds, and the release of large sums of money, Portia does her job well. But she is not only an agent of resolution; for if we put the plot of *friendship* in the foreground she begins to look more like one of Frye's blocking characters whose function in comedy is to frustrate desire. Because of her, Antonio's love will not be remembered among the great love stories but will decline into a marginality best summed up by the merchant's pronounced singleness among the wedded couples who exit at the end.

The thoughts of this man so miraculously saved from death and penury but denied the enjoyment of his love cannot be put into words in the play. The enigma of the first scene's melancholy is never solved. But a reading of Sonnet 134 together with the play's closing movement offers a way of putting into words the feelings of the necessary loser in the struggle over the young man's love. If we think of the voice in the sonnet as Antonio, we may go on to say that he is addressing someone who is a composite of both his rivals, a woman and a usurer.

> So now I have confess'd that he is thine,
> And I myself am mortgag'd to thy will,
> Myself I'll forfeit, so that other mine
> Thou wilt restore to be my comfort still:
> But thou wilt not, nor he will not be free,
> For thou art covetous, and he is kind;
> He learn'd but surety-like to write for me
> Under that bond that him as fast doth bind.
> The statute of thy beauty thou wilt take,
> Thou usurer, that puts forth all to use,
> And sue a friend came debtor for my sake,
> So him I lose through my unkind abuse.
>   Him have I lost, thou hast both him and me,
>   He pays the whole, and yet am I not free.
>
> (Sonnet 134)

The sonnet's woman is an exaggerated Portia seen through the eyes of a defeated rival. She is a powerful woman who has the formidable assets of beauty, money, and the law at her command to wield in unequal battle against the loser, the weaker, the poorer, less resourceful male.[7] In the sonnet the woman's sexuality and wealth, kept apart decorously in the play (but not in *Il Pecorone*) coalesce in predatory and unacceptable ways. Like Shylock, she does not play by the Gentile rules of business but invests herself in erotic transactions that bring her profit and power, seemingly without risk. There is much anger in the "all" of "Thou usurer, that puts forth all to use" because it points to the available sexuality of a woman who can exploit it for her profit in the marketplace, as opposed to the inhibited sexuality of a man whose *all* in the love for a friend can only mean the surrender of everything in death. Antonio's total commitment of purse and person for Bassanio put forth all but expected no *use*. Giving up his life for his friend's debt would place Antonio in the act of exchange that belongs to the symbolic pattern of the arrows. There can be no profit; either the two find each other and rest content with a doubleness that can produce no increase, or one is lost and a debt remains. When profit is impossible, loss is more than likely.

The financial sexual battle is lost and not even the last desperate move of a bankrupt "Myself I'll forfeit" will achieve its purpose. The woman's wealth and sex give her complete control over the men who are clients for her services. Unlike Shylock's bond her statute of beauty is lawyer-proof for there is no appeal to any judge or legal precedent to restrain the reach of her sex.[8] She will take whatever its power incites her to take and the language of law in the sonnet is sarcastic because eros will have nothing to do with the rules and codes of society.

While the analogy between poem and play holds as long as we hear the resigned male voice of loss and the image it creates of the predatory, profiteering woman-usurer, his rival in business and love, yet it becomes harder to maintain when we consider the position in the erotic triangle of the younger man that "other self" with whose loss the sonnet tries to come to terms. Like the play's Bassanio, the young man here is something of a cipher. He is passive to the woman's predatory desire. She is "covetous" while he is merely "kind"; instead of willing *something* positively he "will not be free"; essentially therefore he is possessed and, to the discomfort of the speaker, acquiesces in this his slavish state.

The one aspect of the young man that contradicts his passivity is his activity as a go-between in the interest of his friend, an action that creates the entanglement in which he is content to rest. The language the speaker in the sonnet uses to describe this going-between, words like debt, bond, and surety, is the language of Antonio's erotic/financial commitment in the play. In the play the debt and the bond put the merchant at the mercy of the Jew-usurer; in the sonnet they put the young man in the power of the woman-usurer. Both men bind themselves out of friendship and are trapped by statute and law. But in substituting the law of sex and beauty for the legal practices of Venice the sonnet dramatizes the necessary defeat of Antonio, for the power of the covetous woman, limited by no rules, is also based on the willingness of her victim. He will not be free because being bound to a woman is *kind* (remember Shylock's description of Jacob's sheep engaged in " . . . doing of the deed of kind") or in other words the nature of sexual relations as God intended them. In the trial scene of the play it is Bassanio who declares his willingness to "pay the whole" (Portia's money of course) but is still not able to free Antonio from Shylock's grasp. In the sonnet what is imagined is not just an offer as in the play but the young man's actual payment of the whole that in the transactions of sex means the placing of his body at the service of a beautiful usurer.[9] Yet, as the last line says so explicitly, such a payment frees no one, which is what we might imagine to be the subtext of Antonio contemplating, in a jaundiced way, the union of Bassanio and Portia at the end of the play.

By postulating this hybrid *Jewoman*, part Portia, part Shylock, Antonio's loss of Bassanio to the heiress of Belmont, inevitable and natural in the plot of romantic comedy, becomes darker and more painful. The convention of the happy ending would have us believe that the characters have been freed of the threat of ruin and death, the burdens of poverty, and the unnatural state of virginity. The sonnet prompts us to view things differently. By twinning full payment of the debt with the continuation of bondage, the sonnet tells the adult story that hides behind the fairy tale. Profit in love always involves some loss. Love is not the equal exchange of either the homosexual paradise or the heterosexual innocence of "my love is mine and I am his." Rather it is a matter of debt and possession, lending and repayment with interest out of which the stronger party emerges possessing everything. The combination of usury and beauty is devastating because the risk is always the suitor's, never the creditor's.

In the play's last scene, Portia plays the Jew as well as the woman when the riddle of the rings is posed and the almost tragic entanglements of the past are recapitulated. When the impasse of the missing rings is at its crisis and everything hangs on Portia's lips, Antonio takes the action back to its very beginning, the forfeit of his body to the Jew in order to obtain credit for his friend. Seeking a way out of the impasse Antonio proposes repeating his catastrophic gesture by binding himself once again, this time to Portia, for Bassanio's welfare:

> I once did lend my body for his wealth,
> Which, but for him that had your husband's ring
> Had quite miscarried. I dare be bound again,
> My soul upon the forfeit, that your lord
> Will never more break faith advisedly.
>
> (*The Merchant*, 5.1.249–53)

Read one way, this gallant gesture, a form of words rather than a sinister contract, is a symbolic act of healing. It replaces the evil corporal bond to Shylock with a fortunate binding of soul. Portia's act of forgiveness and Bassanio's faithfulness as a husband will ensure that this forfeit is never brought to court. Yet despite the obvious differences, Antonio's replay of his fatal move places Portia firmly in the position once occupied by Shylock, even as Antonio, "the unhappy subject of these quarrels" comes once again between the young couple and the consummation of their marriage. On the surface, this is not his wish, though it has been the case since the arrival of his troubled letter in act 3. On the surface of it Antonio's credit is what enables Bassanio to undertake his venture in the first place. But beneath the surface, the radical stance of Antonio's commitment, his talk of "extremest means," his offer of everything, would reach its unnatural but logical conclusion in the surrender of his body for Bassanio and in his consequent usurpation of Portia's place as true lover.

So the benign if melancholic Antonio of the plot may be offset by the darker Antonio, the lover whose necessarily unrequited love can find release and expression only in death. It is this voice that speaks in the sonnet offering to tie himself in debt to the sex-wealth of a ruthless beauty but asking desperately for the young man, the quid pro quo that Antonio could never mention in the play. For a moment at the end of the play, when he turns to Portia with his new offer of forfeit, Antonio could have quoted the sonnet:

Him have I lost, thou hast both him and me,

Even in the final tableau when he has won back his wealth he is the sonnet's words still "not free." For his release from sacrifice is an anticlimax. He has nowhere to go. So although wealth is spread around liberally, like manna, at the end it is the unfinished business between the merchant and Bassanio that occupies the mind.

Because this business provides the only selfless motive in the play and because its burden is the only unrequited and unrequitable love, it sets up the contrasts between profit and sacrifice, interest and love as contrasts not only between Jew and Gentile but between woman and man. Both Jews and women are profiteers whose treasure grows with use, whereas the merchant can only give his purse and his person and hope for no return. Is it any wonder then that this figure who begins his part in the play by taking refuge in ignorance:

> In sooth, I know not why I am so sad (1.1.1)

approaches its end by taking refuge in silence:

> I am dumb. (5.1.279)

Notes

1. All quotations from Shakespeare are from *The Riverside Shakespeare*, eds. G. B. Evans et al. (Boston: Houghton, 1974).

2. W. H. Auden in his essay on the play *Brothers and Others* in *The Dyer's Hand* (New York: Vintage Books, 1968); 218–37, accepts Bassanio's rhetoric of innocence with no reservations. Bassanio, according to Auden "is one of those people whose attitude towards money is that of a child; it will somehow always appear by magic when really needed" (p. 232).

3. This conjunction is placed in its economic setting by Lars Engle in "'Thrift Is Blessing': Exchange and Explanation in *The Merchant of Venice*," *Shakespeare Quarterly* 37 (1986): 20–37. Engle sees that "A Christian merchant, preserving homosocial connection to a lord, cannot afford to understand the parable of economic relations offered by the Jew" (p. 32). But he fails to draw a precise parallel between the rival parables. For a thorough attempt to place the play in an historical, Venetian economic, and legal context (without emphasis on sexuality) see Walter Cohen, "*The Merchant of Venice* and the Possibilities of Historical Criticism," *English Literary History* 49 (1982): 765–89.

4. It is interesting to note how the economic implications of the biblical text so transparent to contemporary critics were of minimal importance to a scholar like Barbara K. Lewalski, who in a comprehensive article, "Biblical Allusion and Allegory in *The Merchant of Venice*," *Shakespeare Quarterly* 13 (1962): 327–43 gives little attention to the Laban/Jacob episode, seeing it as a move in an essentially moral conflict between Christian venture (good) and Jewish thrift (bad).

5. Yet as Ruth Nevo points out in *Comic Transformations in Shakespeare* (London and New York: Methuen, 1980), 127, the contrast is also between Jacob and Bassanio as different kinds of suitors. For all his cunning, Jacob labors for the hand of his bride. Bassanio, like the other young Venetians, is born into idleness. That is why he needs Portia.

6. The unnaturalness of the juxtaposition of friendship and breeding together with the undertone of barrenness (as a natural feature of friendship as well as an ideological feature of metal) is apparent in the scornful way Antonio challenges Shylock to lend him money: " . . . lend it not / As to thy friends for when did friendship take / A breed for barren metal of his friend?"

7. Writing about the sexual triangle in the sonnets in *Between Men: English Literature and Male Homosocial Desire* (New York: Columbia University Press, 1985), 28–48, Eve Kosofsky Sedgwick wishes that the sonnets were a novel so that the reader could seek refuge from their self-reflexive language in a fully

rendered and described set of social and sexual relations (p. 46). She wants to know just who these people are. My analogy with the play does not give an answer but helps to characterize the social and sexual scene.

8. But see the discussion of the sonnet in *Shakespeare's Sonnets*, ed. Stephen Booth (New Haven and London: Yale University Press, 1980), 463–66. In his commentary on "statute" Booth gives equal weight to the language of legal rights and limitations and to that of sexual bondage.

9. Joel Fineman, discussing the sonnet in *Shakespeare's Perjured Eye* (Berkeley: University of California Press, 1986), 285–86, argues that the pun whole/hole links the sex of the young man and the woman with the emptiness or disjunction within the poet and his project of writing sonnets. Fineman's point about the sound of "whole" as "pure languageness" which denies the univocity of traditional poetic language is finely made but his fierce emphasis on the rhetoric leaves the financial and legal language largely uninterpreted.

The Rhetoric of Exclusion:
Jew, Moor, and the Boundaries of Discourse in *The Merchant of Venice*

Alan Rosen

In the 1590s, both Jew and Moor remained for English Christians exotic infidels, whose obstinate unbelief and cultural difference continued to challenge, boldly or surreptitiously, Christian hegemony in Europe.[1] In Shylock the Jew and the Prince of Morocco the Moor, *The Merchant of Venice* presents these two kinds of infidels, and thus brings together within this problem comedy two groups for whom Renaissance England felt a special fascination and repulsion. That the play forges and exploits a link between the two groups is not self-evident, for Shakespeare assigns Shylock and Morocco to separate realms—Venice and Belmont respectively—and thereby seems to place in the background any meaningful association between Jew and Moor. I wish, however, to foreground this association, and to argue that the distinctive rhetoric of each character—for Shylock, plainness; for Morocco, eloquence—threatens in its own way to undermine the linguistic foundations of the play. Although this threat is contained, dramatic juxtaposition works to connect the two characters, blurring the boundaries between them. Once linked, shared aspects of their language challenge the play's discourse of insider/outsider while simultaneously reinforcing the threat that the infidels pose.

I

Despite varying assessments of Shylock's language, critics share two assumptions: first, Shylock is made by Shakespeare to speak differently from other characters in the play; second, he speaks more plainly than other characters.[2] This plain-speaking is evidenced particularly in Shylock's propensity to repetition.

The play foregrounds Shylock's repetitions from his first appearance on stage in 1.3. For the scene quickly establishes a pattern in which Bassanio initiates and Shylock repeats the financial terms of the proposed agreement. Moreover, the constant pattern of Shylock's repetition makes the audience retroactively aware that, although Shylock speaks the first words of the scene—"Three thousand ducats"—even these words echo an implied offstage proposal by Bassanio.[3] In the first eight lines of the scene, then, Shylock speaks words that are not his own.

This appropriation of another character's words at the moment of dramatic introduction blurs the distinctions that one expects to obtain between Bassanio and Shylock, noble Christian and miserly Jew,[4] frustrating at least for a time the expectation that Jews speak differently, that they have in Sander Gilman's phrase "a hidden language" uniquely their own.[5] By repeating Bassanio's words, Shylock also makes use of them. It is this aspect of use that, as Sigurd Burckhardt and Marc Shell have argued, is a defining characteristic of Shylock's approach to language as well as to money.[6] From the very first utterance, then, Shylock's role is to keep things (and words) in circulation.

Though Shylock continues to echo Bassanio, he also introduces a note of self-repetition, a mode of iteration that becomes conspicuous in Shylock's next scene, in which he calls for Jessica several times. Although the repeated call serves at first as an anxious summons for his daughter, it is soon taken up by Lancelot, parodying Shylock's earnestness.[7] In the next few scenes, as Jessica flees, this pattern of repetition and parody intensifies.[8] Solanio quotes Shylock repeating the features of his losses and Salerio notes that boys echo Shylock's repetitions (*The Merchant*, 2.8.12–24). As Shylock repeats himself with increasing frequency, seemingly in search of a language to express his loss, other characters parody his iterations, resulting in what one critic refers to as the denial of "the right to coherent speech."[9] Even as Shakespeare ritualizes Shylock's language, the choric procession of children simultaneously establishes a parody of that ritualization.

In act 3, the climax of Shylock's self-repetition, Shakespeare complicates the variations on this technique. To the Christians, Shylock responds to taunts with the "Hath not a Jew" speech, in which the repetitions are arranged in a complex rhetorical schema: "Hath not a Jew eyes? Hath not a Jew hands. . . ." (3.1.46–47)? To Tubal the Jew, by contrast, Shylock merely repeats words, bereft of this larger rhetorical framework:

> *Tubal.* Yes, other men have ill luck too. Antonio, as I heard in Genoa—
> *Shylock.* What, what, what? ill luck, ill luck?
> *Tubal.* —hath an argosy cast away coming from Tripolis.
> *Shylock.* I thank God, I thank God! Is it true, is it true?
>
> (3.1.77–81)

Shylock's repetitions embody language at a reduced and primitive level: "An even more primitive way than punning to strip words of their meaning," suggests Burckhardt, "is repetition. Say 'a rose is a rose is a rose' a few more times, and what you have is a meaningless sound, because you have torn the word out of its living linguistic matrix and so are left with nothing but a vile phonetic jelly."[10] Repetition emphasizes material corporeality, "mak[ing] the word malleable, ready to take the imprint the poet wants to give it."[11]

Burckhardt's emphasis on the corporeality of language enforces Shylock's association with the corporeal; a Jew, in other words, whose materiality symbolizes for Christians an unredeemed carnality, would fittingly speak a language itself carnal. Appropriately, Shylock reaches the climax of such "primitive" speech in the only scene in which he speaks at length with another Jew.

According to A. R. Braunmuller, however, the rhetorical strategies of Renaissance drama point in a different direction, not enforcing but subverting the conventional system of meaning.[12] Dramatists carried out this subversion by emphasizing "alliteration, repetition, echo, reversal,"—language that privileged sound over sense. "This similarity of sound," writes Braunmuller, "among words and phrases overrides the semantic, conventional, unthinkingly assumed difference between them."[13] While these rhetorical strategies informed other modes of public discourse in Renaissance England, the plotted nature of drama exploited "patterned speech" in ways that significantly undermined conventional systems of linguistic meaning, keeping audiences in "a continuous rhetorical anxiety," a linguistic limbo "puzzling and possibly terrifying."[14]

Braunmuller's comments suggest that Shylock's discourse is not only to be viewed as signifying a perverse materiality but also as concretizing the vertiginous aspects of Renaissance dramatic rhetoric. Made to speak an ever-more-heavily-patterned speech, Shylock embodies the unfamiliar system of meaning, the "continuous rhetorical anxiety," produced by this rhetoric. As he repeats more frequently, his idiom threatens to subsume the system of semantic difference that continues to inhere in the language of other characters. The repetitions of his repetitions—Solanio's account and the boys' cries—acknowledge the threat of Shylock's idiom but also keep it in check through parody. Seen in this light, the force of Shylock's meeting with Tubal is that, as Shylock comes to repeat almost every line, there is no parody, no repetition of his repetition, no policing of his alternative system of meaning. At this point, not only does Shylock's passion for revenge endanger Antonio, but his iterative language, multiplying without check, threatens to overwhelm all other languages.

But Shakespeare himself polices Shylock's phonic language. Just as the court scene defuses the danger that Shylock poses to Antonio's well-being, so it also constrains Shylock's language, compelling him to speak in proper rhetorical formulas.[15] Even if Burckhardt and other ironic readers are correct in claiming that Shylock's courtroom rhetoric outshines that of Antonio and Portia, it is also the case that Shakespeare eliminates the subversive repetitions. Indeed, the elimination of what had become an increasingly frequent sign of Shylock's distinctiveness is startling and perplexing. The answer may lie in the way the institution of the courtroom shapes the language spoken.[16] For, as the play implies, the courtroom represents the Venetian law, which allegedly applies equally to all. As the law applies to all equally, so, one may speculate, do all participants in the court proceedings share the same discourse. Hence, this legal discourse preempts Shylock's repetitions before they are set in motion.

If the courtroom eliminates the repetitions, there nevertheless remains an imagistic trace of the threat they posed. Telling the Duke why he cannot explain his passion for revenge, Shylock suggests that "Some men there are that love not a gaping pig; / Some that are mad if they behold a cat; / And others when the bagpipe sings in i'the nose / Cannot contain their urine: for affection / Masters oft passion, sways it to the mood / Of what it likes or loathes" (*The Merchant*, 4.1.48–52). Shylock's list—pig, cat, and bagpipe—enumerates what are generally benign aspects of culinary, domestic, or musical culture. But what is benign to most makes dysfunctional an idiosyncratic few. In the case of the bagpipe, the special sound causes the victim to lose control of natural functions. This association of unnerving sound and a threat to control recalls the "rhetorical anxieties" that confronted the audience faced with "patterned speech," that is, repetition. Braunmuller indicated that, by replacing semantic difference with phonetic identity, repetition subverted the conventional system of linguistic meaning, a subversion that occasioned a "possibly terrifying" feeling in the audience. Similiarly, the bagpipe foregrounds an unusual type of sound that assaults the listener, causing a breakdown of normal functioning. Both bagpipe and repetition figure in the play as sources of phonic subversion. Even though Shylock himself is no longer given to repetition, then, the analogy he chooses to represent his motivation continues to intimate the threat embodied by it. It is suggestive, furthermore, that the only other reference in the play to bagpipes comes in association with the creature most emblematic of repetition: "Now by two-headed Janus," says Solario, also trying to account for abnormal behavior, "Nature hath framed strange fellows in her time: / Some that will evermore peep through their eyes, / And laugh like *parrots* at a bagpiper" (1.1.50–53; emphasis added).[17]

II

The difference between Shylock's recursive speech and that of other characters has frequently been described in terms of plainness versus eloquence: where Shylock the Jew speaks unpoetically, realistically, plainly, the Christians in the play speak lyrically, beautifully, eloquently.[18] Most critics valorize eloquence, understanding Shylock's deviant plain-speaking as reinforcing his villainy. But the dichotomy drawn between plainness and eloquence has its proponents as well among those who see Shylock as the play's victim, a view culminating in Burckhardt's extended contrast between Antonio and Shylock. Suspicious of Antonio's flaccid grandiloquence, Burckhardt favors Shylock's plainness, supporting his reading by indicating that the play itself puts forth a hermeneutics of suspicion regarding eloquence. Additionally, Burckhardt argues that the plainness with which Shylock speaks registers Shakespeare's achievement as a dramatist: "But the qualities which make us rank Shylock's lines over Antonio's have long been accepted among the criteria by which we seek to establish the sequence of Shakespeare's plays, on the assumption that where we find them we have evidence of greater maturity and mastery."[19]

Though most critics have not shared Burckhardt's radical suspicion of eloquence in the play in general, they have shown a marked suspicion of the eloquence of one specific character: the Prince of Morocco. According to this view, Morocco's eloquence indicates his concern with appearances; just as his language is full of ornate rhetorical flourish, valuing surface over substance, so he chooses the gold casket, again valuing surface over substance.[20] Language reflects action, and vice versa. Besides testifying to Shakespeare's multilevel control of plot, this reading of Morocco's language often attempts to assign it a psychological or moral significance, confirming his unworthiness to win Portia.[21]

Initially, Shylock and Morocco seem as much separated by style as by setting, the rhetoric of the former shaped by the absence of ornament, that of the latter formed by the excess of it. But by associating Shylock with plainness and Morocco with eloquence, Shakespeare positions both outsiders at the opposite extremes of the rhetorical continuum, equally, if contrarily, pressing against the borders of legitimate discourse. On the one hand, this positioning allows the other characters in the play to speak comfortably within the limits that the Jew and Moor articulate. On the other hand, Shylock and Morocco are compelled linguistically as well as culturally to inhabit a place on the margins of discourse.

Having established this linguistic extravagance, glosses on Morocco amplify this suspicion of eloquence by indicating that his language recalls Marlowe's Tamburlaine, an intertextual resonance initially noted by M. C. Bradbrook and subsequently applied by numbers of readers.[22] Frank Whigham, for instance, sees Morocco

> handicapped by his race, his lack of sophistication and his outmoded style. The attribute of his style most relevant here is his lavish claims made for his own desert. In the early days of Elizabethan drama the non-European setting and character, presented with extensive rhetorical ornament, gave the exotic an incantatory power over Elizabethan audiences. In the courtly context, however, the imperialistic titanism of Tamburlaine is ill-adapted to purposes of wooing.[23]

This judgment implies that Shakespeare chose to outfit his suitor with a clumsy language, one more appropriate to conquest than romance. But the association with Marlowe also suggests that for Morocco's lines Shakespeare turned to a earlier, more primitive dramatic language. Morocco's eloquence, then, not only represents a psychological or moral flaw but also Shakespeare's parody of the bombastic vocabulary that Tamburlaine spoke and Marlowe wrote. Just as Bassanio displays his romantic merit by choosing the right casket, so does Shakespeare display his dramatic merit by surpassing his predecessors in the fit choice of language, not gaining the fortune of Belmont but rather containing the influence of his greatest competitor and asserting his authorial mastery.[24]

In his reading of the play, Freud also connects the casket scene with mastery, arguing that the choice of the caskets is actually the choice of a beautiful woman and that the scene dramatizes the attempt to master death—death here masquerading as its opposite, beauty.[25] The emphasis for Freud is on choice: "Choice stands in the place of necessity, of destiny. In this way man overcomes death, which he has recognized intellectually."[26] The casket scene registers the move from nonchoice to choice, from a passive relation to what is determined to an active mastery over it. The scene becomes the site where psychological overcoming works in conjunction with stylistic mastery. In both instances, mastery is achieved by containing what is other: on the one hand, death represents the metaphysical other; on the other hand, Morocco (and Tamburlaine and Marlowe) represents the cultural other. Even these realms converge, however, in Morocco's second appearance, in which, after a speech replete with images of burial and death, Morocco chooses the casket containing "A carrion Death" (*The Merchant*, 2.7.63). By having Morocco choose a death's head, Shakespeare links what is culturally other to what is metaphysically other, doubly enforcing repulsion while simultaneously mastering it.

While the play admittedly encourages the association of Morocco and Tamburlaine, it also questions the aptness of the parallel, and consequently provokes doubt in Morocco's position as an absolute other. Significantly, Morocco styles himself as a kind of Hercules, the Renaissance ideal of a warrior (and a prototype of Tamburlaine as well),[27] a self-identification that would seem to reinforce his "titanic" status. But the association does not promote his warrior status but rather undermines it, for the Hercules that Morocco invokes renounces acting as a warrior, consenting instead to "play at dice" and to be led by "blind Fortune" (2.1.36). Bassanio, moreover, is also identified with Hercules (3.2.53–62), and in this identification Shakespeare emphasizes the more familiar, martial side of the Greek hero. Tellingly, where Morocco's link to Hercules highlights an uncharacteristic submission, Bassanio's dramatizes a stereotypical aggression, provoking the audience to see not Morocco but Bassanio as the emblem of heroism, as the one who brings into the "courtly context . . . imperialistic titanism." This link to Bassanio via Hercules further destabilizes Morocco's status as Other, for it makes it difficult to clearly distinguish one suitor from another, effacing to a degree the difference between winner and loser and between familiar Venitian and exotic Moroccan.[28]

In the Prince of Morocco, Shakespeare represents a Moor who is liminal and transitional, chronologically and theatrically situated between the demonization of Aaron in *Titus Andronicus* and the heroic, if problematic, characterization of Othello.[29] The critical dispute concerning two pivotal traits, color and religion, attests to this liminal status. Morocco is described as *tawny*, a term that some critics argue indicates "light-skinned, as distinct from a 'blackamoor'";[30] others believe the linguistic and even dramatic evidence demonstrates that Morocco is black.[31] Morocco's religion is less subject to dispute; but the lack of an explicit religious designation has led at least one recent critic to assume that Morocco is Christian, a judgment which in essence qualifies his outsider status.[32] Morocco's position vis-à-vis stage and social history reinforces this transitional status. Significantly, Morocco is one of the first "non-villainous" Moors to appear on the English stage,[33] a stage that had previously dramatized Moors as villains and in which blackness served as an emblem of evil. Morocco as a noble suitor contravenes this stereotype. Nevertheless, the representation of Morocco as an exotic "tawny" Moor continues to reinscribe the alien traits of previous stage Moors (including Shakespeare's own Aaron in *Titus Andronicus*) and thereby to provoke suspicion, particularly suspicion concerning sexual propriety that would be aroused in watching a black alien attempt to marry a white heroine.[34]

Though the play eschews the direct representation of the Moor as villain, it recalls and enforces suspicion of Morocco by linking him dramatically with Shylock the Jew, a strategy that blurs the boundaries between one outsider and the other. At the beginning of act 1, scene 3 Shylock enters the play, a Jew in a Christian world; at the beginning of act 2, Morocco enters, a black in a white world. As Shylock intrudes upon the homogeneity of Christian Venice, so Morocco intrudes upon the homogeneity of white Belmont. The discomfort caused by the entry of one enforces the discomfort caused by the intrusion of the other. In addition, reference to Morocco's "complexion" frames Shylock's first appearance. In act 1, scene 2, Portia shows her repulsion of Morocco by quipping, "If he have the condition of a saint, and the complexion of a devil, I had rather he should shrive me than wive me" (*The Merchant*, 1.2.123); next Shylock has his scene (1.3); then act 2 begins by Morocco in effect answering Portia's quip: "Mislike me not for my complexion" (2.1.1).

Shylock's scene both postpones and substitutes for Morocco's. If we recall that prior to *The Merchant* black men on the English stage were conventionally villains, the postponement of Morocco's arrival intensifies anxiety over what kind of black man will appear on stage. Where Portia's racial strictures initially seem to apply only to marriage in contrast to religion ("rather he should shrive me than wive me"), the substitution of Shylock for Morocco problematizes this formula, exposing the way the discourse of exclusion governs religion as well as matrimony. The substitution of one intruder for the other also means that Shylock arrives in a drama whose discourse is already in place to distinguish insider from outsider. Consequently, Shylock enters the play caught not only in the stage conventions associated with Jews but also in those associated with Moors.

The play further promotes this association of Jew and Moor by linking the way they themselves manipulate the discourse of insider/outsider. Morocco claims his right as a suitor by questioning the criterion chosen by Portia—"complexion of a devil"—and offering his own: "let us make incision for your love / To prove whose blood is reddest" (2.1.6–7). As with the caskets, Morocco's new criterion also takes the form of a contest, a contest in which Portia would be compelled to distinguish one thing from another. The shift from "complexion" to "blood," from outer surface to inner substance, links Morocco's claim with the other gestures in the play (caskets, bonds, rings) that require one to go beneath a deceptive surface. More specifically, however, Morocco's contest prepares for Shylock's challenge to Salerio: "If you prick us, do we not bleed?" (3.1.58). Significantly, both Moor and Jew claim that what seems different on the surface can be better judged by what is beneath it; that the less favorable exterior they present can be neutralized by reference to an interior dimension: the blood that flows in all people's veins.

By rejecting surface and privileging depth, Moor and Jew attempt to use the operative discourse of the play—outside/inside—to redefine their relation to other characters. This discourse works generally to make clear who is the resident and who the intruder. In the case of Morocco, his skin color excludes him from Portia (and the Elizabethan audience's) favor. His ornamental language and choice of the golden casket allegedly betray a concern with surfaces that reinforces his rightful exclusion. In the case of Shylock, his literalism highlights concern with the letter rather than the spirit, with the outer form rather than the inner meaning. In this attempt to challenge their marginalization, then, Morocco and Shylock mobilize the very discourse that enforces the distinction between insider and outsider and that confers on them, Moor and Jew, the status of Other.

But this attempt to turn the discourse of exclusion back on itself fails. For both Morocco and Shylock use images of violence—"incision" and "pricking," acts committed with a sharp, invasive instrument—to exhibit their solidarity with the rest of humankind. The two intruders, moreover, are the ones who brandish weapons in the play, a detail that enforces the association of alien and violence. Even as Moor and Jew try to undermine and overcome the terms which set them apart from the Christian characters, these images of violence continue to dramatize the danger they pose, justifying their exclusion. The images of violence also enforce the fantasies of the audience, for the wounds that Morocco and Shylock envision are rhetorically inflicted upon themselves (Morocco will make an "incision" on himself; Shylock will be "pricked"), thereby substantiating the belief in an alien threat while simultaneously having the danger recoil upon those who are believed to threaten. Taken to its furthest point—as some critics have done—the recoil of the violence causes both Morocco and Shylock to undergo a symbolic castration (again scenically juxtaposed): the Moor, who has pledged not to marry, leaves Belmont uttering "farewell heat and welcome frost" (2.7.75); the Jew, whose fortune has been stolen, is reported to focus his grief on the loss of his "two stones, two rich and precious stones" (2.8.20).[35] The punishment, then, links the two intruders even as it renders them impotent.

This impotence no doubt underscores failure. Yet, through the eccentric discourse of its intruders, *The Merchant* sets forth alternative systems of meaning that challenge more conventional ones: Shylock's repetitions begin to erode the order articulated by semantic difference,[36] while the juxtaposition of Moor and Jew indicates the attempt to rewrite the categories of exclusion. Neither challenge meets with success. But the play must work hard to neutralize the threat posed by these outsiders. Indeed, one may speculate that the threat to conventional meaning tested here in *The Merchant* becomes more fully realized in the later tragedies, in which Shylock's repetitions modulate into Lear's maddened iterations and Morocco's eloquence informs Othello's captivating tales.

Notes

I first presented this essay as a paper for the 1993 Shakespeare Association of America seminar, "Race, Ethnicity and Power in Shakespeare and His Contemporaries." I would like to thank my colleagues in that seminar, and also Ruth Clements, Kinereth Meyer, and Murray Roston for their reading of and comments on earlier versions of this essay.

1. For a recent consideration of England and the Jews in the context of *The Merchant of Venice*, see James Shapiro, *Shakespeare and the Jews* (New York: Columbia University Press, 1996); and, in a more general context, including the arrest and trial of R. Lopez, see Cecil Roth, *History of the Jews in England* (Oxford: Oxford University Press, 1941). On England's relation to the Moors in the 1590s, including the developments leading up to the visit of a Moroccan ambassador to England at the end of the decade, see Jack D'Amico, *The Moor in English Renaissance Drama* (Tampa: University of South Florida Press, Florida, 1991).

2. See esp. B. I. Evans, *The Language of Shakespeare's Plays* (London: Chatto & Windus, 1964). Compare C. L. Barber, *Shakespeare's Festive Comedy* (Princeton: Princeton University Press, 1959); Thomas Fujimura, "Mode and Structure in *The Merchant of Venice*," PMLA 81 (1966); Jane Donawerth, *Shakespeare and the Sixteenth-Century Study of Language* (Urbana and Chicago: University of Illinois Press, 1984); Sigurd Burckhardt, *Shakespearean Meanings* (Princeton: Princeton University Press, 1968). On the equivocal claims of "plainness" and "plain-speaking," see Kenneth J. E. Graham,"'Without the form of justice': Plainness and the Performance of Love in *King Lear*," *Shakespeare Quarterly* 42.4 (1991), 438–61.

3. M. M. Mahood, ed., *The Merchant of Venice* (Cambridge: Cambridge University Press, 1987). All subsequent citations are from this edition.

4. "Well, thou shalt see, thy eyes shall be thy judge, / The difference of old Shylock and Bassanio—" (2.5.1–2). The elaborate form of Shylock's salutation to Lancelot reinforces the fact that the difference between Shylock and Bassanio, while discernable, is not to be taken for granted.

5. Sander Gilman, *Jewish Self-Hatred: Anti-Semitism and the Hidden Language of the Jews* (Baltimore: Johns Hopkins University Press, 1986).

6. Sigurd Burckhardt, *Shakespearean Meanings*; Marc Shell, "The Wether and the Ewe: Verbal Usury in *The Merchant of Venice*," *Kenyon Review* NS 1 (1979), 65–92.

7. James Bulman notes that in Komisarjevsky's iconoclastic production of *The Merchant of Venice* not only Lancelot but also Old Gobbo echos Shylock here, creating a "double echo." *The Merchant of Venice* (Manchester and New York: Manchester University Press, 1991): 60.

8. For a discussion of parody as repetition, see Linda Hutcheon, *A Theory of Parody: The Teachings of Twentieth-Century Art Forms* (New York: Metheun, 1985).

9. Lawrence Normand, "Reading the Body in *The Merchant of Venice*," *Textual Practice* 5.1 (1991), 57.

10. Burckhardt, 29; Marc Shell's attempt to analyse Shylock's "verbal usury" sees puns (rather than repetition) as his emblematic verbal gesture. "The Wether and the Ewe: Verbal Usury in *The Merchant of Venice*," 66–67.

11. Burckhardt, 30.

12. A. R. Braunmuller, "The Arts of the Dramatist," *The Cambridge Companion to English Renaissance Drama*, edited by A. R. Braunmuller and Michael Hathaway (Cambridge: Cambridge University Press, 1990), 63–67.

13. Ibid., 63.

14. Ibid., 67.

15. Normand, 66.

16. From a different perspective than the one I am pursuing here, Lawrence

Danson emphasizes the relation between courtroom and language in *The Harmonies of* The Merchant of Venice (New Haven: Yale University Press, 1978).

17. Interestingly, the two-faced Janus also hints at repetition. Sarah Korman has recently examined the Janus figure in relation to *The Merchant;* her analysis, however, does not consider repetition as such but emphasizes instead how doubleness is the real theme of the play. See "Conversions: *The Merchant of Venice* under the Sign of Saturn," *Literary Theory Today,* edited by Peter Collier and Helga Geyer-Ryan (Cambridge: Cambridge University Press, 1990), 142–66.

18. See my remarks, note 4 above. On the issue of eloquence, see James J. Murphy, ed., *Renaissance Eloquence: Studies in the Theory and Practice of Renaissance Rhetoric* (Berkeley and Los Angeles: University of California Press, 1983).

19. Burckhardt, 209.

20. While critics generally say little about Morocco, the little they say comments on the role of his eloquence. See, for example, Donawerth (see note 2); Frank Whigham, "Ideology and Class Conduct in *The Merchant of Venice*," *Renaissance Drama* 10 (1979); James Shapiro,"'Which is The Merchant here, and which The Jew?' Shakespeare and the Economics of Influence," *Shakespeare Studies* 20 (1987), 269–79. While Emily Bartels does not discuss Morocco, she notes the role of eloquence in relation to the Moor Aaron in *Titus Andronicus:* "What threatens to undermine Aaron's function as an absolute sign of the Other is his cultural literacy and . . . his eloquence. . . . [But] Aaron's speech simultaneously betrays his malign differentness" (445). Aaron's malign differentness is not, however, betrayed by exaggerated eloquence but by a "purposelessness that makes his villainy all the more insidious" (445). In contrast, most commentators insist that Morocco's otherness is represented not by motivation (or lack thereof) but by style (or excess thereof). In "Making More of the Moor: Aaron, Othello, and Renaissance Refashionings of Race," *Shakespeare Quarterly* 41.4 (1990).

21. A. D. Moody is the only commentator I have encountered who does not justify psychologically or morally Morocco's failure to choose the winning casket; on the contrary, Moody argues Morocco deserves to win Portia. *Shakespeare: The Merchant of Venice* (Woodbury, NY: Barron's Educational Series, 1964), 34–35.

22. M. C. Bradbook, *Shakespeare and Elizabethan Poetry* (London: Chatto & Windus, 1951), 175–76; and "Shakespeare's Recollections of Marlowe," *Shakespeare's Styles,* eds. Philip Edwards, Inga-Stina Ewbank, and G. K. Hunter (Cambridge: Cambridge University Press, 1980), 191.

23. Whigham, 98–99.

24. James Shapiro focuses on the contention between Marlowe and Shakespeare in "Which is the The Merchant here, and which The Jew?"

25. Sigmund Freud, "The Theme of the Three Caskets," (1913) in *The Standard Edition of the Complete Psychological Works of Sigmund Freud,* ed. James Strachey (London: Hogarth Pres, 1955), 12:289–301.

26. Freud, 299.

27. Renaissance views of Hercules, including the association with Tamburlaine, are documented in Eugene M. Waith, *The Herculean Hero in Marlowe, Chapman, Shakespeare and Dryden* (London: Chatto & Windus, 1962).

28. Raymond Waddington draws attention to the association of Hercules with Morocco and Bassanio, only to argue ingeniously that the shared attribution is meant not to link but to distinguish the two suitors and their contrasting views of fortune. In "Blind Gods: Fortune, Justice and Cupid in *The Merchant of Venice,*" *ELH* 44 (1977).

29. In her study of Shakespeare's Moors (see note 20), Bartels argues that, in

Titus Andronicus, the early Shakespeare unironically demonizes Aaron but, in *Othello,* the late Shakespeare exposes the process of demonization. In a footnote, Bartels indicates that she does not consider the Prince of Morocco because he is a minor character (435).

30. Eldred Jones, *Othello's Countrymen: The African in English Renaissance Drama* (London: Oxford University Press, 1965); Mahood, *The Merchant of Venice.*

31. G. K. Hunter, "Elizabethans and Foreigners," *Shakespeare Survey* 17 (1964); Anthony Barthelemy, *Black Face, Maligned Race: The Representation of Blacks in English Drama from Shakespeare to Southerne* (Baton Rouge: Louisiana State University Press, 1987).

32. Michael Ferber, "The Ideology of *The Merchant of Venice,*" *ELR* 20.3 (1990), 448.

33. Barthelemy, 147.

34. Barthelemy emphasizes that even though Morocco is not a villain, he continues to present "an obvious and unwelcome sexual threat to Portia," a threat directly associated with Moors (149–50).

35. Zvi Jagendorf links Morocco's departing words to castration in "Innocent Arrows and Sexy Sticks: The Rival Economies of Male Friendship and Heterosexual Love in *The Merchant of Venice,*" *Hebrew University Studies in Literature and the Arts* (1991), 37; more graphically, Shell writes of Shylock's castration: "the two sealed bags and stones . . . are confused with his two testicles. . . . Shylock lost his *Geld* when Jessica 'gilded herself with ducats' (II.vi.49–50) and has also been 'gelded'" (77). Additionally, in *Shakespeare and the Jews,* James Shapiro argues that castration plays a central role in the *The Merchant* and, more generally, in the image of the Jew in early modern England.

"The Poor Sequestered Stag": St. Augustine Metaphor in *As You Like It*

Ahuva Belkin

The movement from the banal, corrupt experience of life in the palace to the supposedly ideal world of the Forest of Arden, at the opening of act 2 of *As You Like It*, lends itself to more than one interpretation, in the two descriptions of the forest that follow. First, the Duke Senior presents his views on the ideal life in the Forest, alluding to the unnaturalness of the situation. This is immediately followed by the second, more concrete description, delivered by the First Lord:

> Under an oak whose antick root peeps out
> Upon the brook that brawls along this wood
> To the which place a poor sequestered stag
> That from the hunter's aim had ta'en a hurt
> Did come to languish; . . .
>
> (*As You Like it*, 2.1.)

This poetic description of the Forest of Arden had been the object of much attention from critics and scholars. Jan Kott has called it "the most English of all Shakespeare forests."[1] Further on, the description of the forest, with its exotic fauna and flora, removes it from the English country scene and Ernst Robert Curtius believes it to be imported from ancient and biblical poetry and from the rhetoric tradition of the Middle Ages.[2] Other critics have maintained that Arden is an imaginary forest, or a Chaucerian wood, or one borrowed from the pastoral convention.

Scholars, however, do not regard the scene as being of major importance. Georg Von Greyerz thinks it matters little in the general scheme of the play.[3] It takes the form of a reported description simply in the interest of dramatic economy or, possibly, because the hunted stag could not be presented on stage. Greyerz claims that the technique of report was the easiest way to convey the significance of the event: to characterize Jaques while avoiding

The Peterborough Psalter. Fol. 14. Psalm I. Historiated initial B.

the pitfall of a comic portrayal, and to create an ambiance of melancholy.[4] At the same time, however, this specially evoked atmosphere also sets this pleasant and enchanted forest as a background for the refugees' adventures.

J. Wilcox, in his article "Putting Jaques into *As You Like it,*" sets out to show that were we to eliminate the five scenes in which Jaques either appears or is mentioned (including the one under discussion), there would be no need for any alteration in the play, and its logic and continuity wold still be maintained, because Jaques was added to the play as an afterthought.[5]

We suggest here that together with the topicality of the background and with Shakespeare's reference to the pastoral convention, the origin of the recounted scene is also a common Christian image—the wounded stag running to the spring, often mentioned in sermons and featured in the illuminations of many Psalters as part of a scheme of visual images. *As You Like It* is a secular play dealing with the temporal order. It is certainly no Christian sermon.[6] And yet, Shakespeare eloquently and poetically uses the images spread by the Fathers of the Church for his own dramatic and thematic purpose. The theological interpretation of the hunted stag corresponds with other associations and images which Shakespeare employs in order to deal in depth with the romantic and pastoral conventions. The scene thus serves as an important crossroads of dramatic activity. The description of the hunted stag evokes literary and philosophical images related to both plot and characterization, and being placed at our first introduction to the Forest of Arden suggests the central motifs to be developed: the conversion of nature and love.

The verse in Psalms "Quem ad modum desiderat cervus ad fontes aquarum: ita desiderat anima mea ad te Deum" (41:2) was part of the baptismal liturgy and the concept of the stag as a symbol of purification and regeneration became extremely popular.[7] We find the stag as a symbol of baptism in the Physiologus tales, in which the traditional antagonism between the deer and the serpent reinforces the patristic interpretation. In one of these tales the stag swims in a pool of putrid water and swallows a snake. Being thus poisoned, the stag loses its horns, symbol of light; they grow anew when it is led to the fountain and drinks of its pure water.

This interpretation of Ps. 41:2 established the commentary for all reference to the stag in the Bible. Although it does not actually state that the stag is running to the fountain for his life, the tripartite connection between the battle against evil, escape, and purification can be often found in allegory.[8] The deer fleeing the hunter was seen as man escaping the Devil, or fighting evil. The analogy between the stag and the saintly, pure penitent Christian also influenced the attitude toward deer-hunting: although a popular pastime, it was nonetheless perceived as negative. Howard Helsinger, who studied deer-hunting scenes in illuminated Psalters, found in one of the earliest manuscripts, the Utrecht Psalter, a running stag pursued by two dogs. In later versions the hunt scene was given greater prominence and moved to the Beatus page, which opens the Psalms. Although hunting scenes commonly feature in the margins of illuminated manuscripts, Helsinger maintains that in the Psalter they take on special meaning and, in the context of the fight against evil, express, allegorically, man's struggle to escape Satan and his desire to find salvation.[9] Noteworthy in this respect are the English Psalters from the mid-13th century, in particular those from the eastern counties, the diocesan boundaries of which included Stratford,

Shakespeare's birthplace. Along the margins are prominently placed hunting scenes.[10] Not only can the idea underlying the iconography be related to the themes of the play, but the pictures, too, resemble Shakespeare's description. We find the most striking instance in the celebrated Peterborough Psalter (ca. 1300).[11] At the *bas-de-page* of the Beatus, among oak trees, a deer is pursued by two dogs and two hunters—one blowing his horn and the other aiming a bow at the running deer, the arrow already lodged in its flesh.

Likewise it seems that act 2, scene 1, of Shakespeare's play goes beyond a mere description of the place where the plot is now to unfold. The two opening monologues are meant, to use Northrop Frye's terms, to transport us to the "green world" and to introduce the ideal world of innocence and romance.[12] Some hints given in act 1 already suggest a "golden world" and "liberty" as opposed to the "banishment" imposed upon the exiles. The play, however, is not a straightforward representation of the pastoral genre. Shakespeare's pastoral is equivocal, a fact that has led several scholars to regard the play as a satire on the bucolic genre.[13] When the transformation to the forest scene occurs, our hopes are not fulfilled. Instead of Ovid's golden world we find a paradise which is imperfect, and only the Duke Senior " . . . translate[s] the stubbornness of fortune into so quiet and so sweet a style." Critics point to the change in tone and agree that this is no pure pastoral. They differ, however, in their interpretation of the change. John MacQueen shows us that the forest—"nature," is the place of truth, of refuge from "fortune" that is no more than an illusion.[14] The Duke's address to his brothers in exile emphasizes his sober view of the situation. The inhabitants of Arden are not free of the destiny of man. The seasons change, the weather is most definitely earthly, and manna does not fall from Heaven. Food is obtained by the force of arms.

The pastoral world does not prove to be any more comfortable than the corrupt court.[15] The comparison is immediately made by the First Lord. There is a flaw in the idyll of the forest. The convention of idyllic nature is violated when nature's creatures are slaughtered. The wood is the stag's natural habitat and it is man who invades its domain and menaces it. Claus Uhlig sees in the opening of act 2 an emblematic triptych structure in which the dialogue of the Duke Senior and the First Lord forms the motto: "the unreasonability of hunting" and "hunting as usurpation." To his mind, the scene is bound to an historical context: Shakespeare amplifies the humanistic topos of Criticism of Hunting borrowed from Sidney's *Arcadia* into a reported emblematic scene.[16] Arden, therefore, is not the imaginary Arcady but rather, as Jan Kott calls it, "Bitter Arcadia." The Kingdom of Nature, says Kott, is as selfish and ferocious as the civilized world. There is no primeval harmony. Here, too, the dispossessed dispossess and those who run for their lives kill in their turn.[17]

With the sequestered stag scene in the first introduction to the forest, the exile of the Duke and his men, brought about by an act of political usurpation assumes a metaphoric meaning. Christian writers refer to the boundaries of exile in order to define humankind's place in the world.[18] Augustine, as Tertulian before him, uses the term *exile* to refer to Adam's expulsion from paradise. St. Bernard modifies Augustine's notion and claims that exile is where man's sins result from the diminution in his resemblance to the divine and in his greater earthliness. Arden is thus not a domain of the golden age but part of the territory where the original sin is punished. However, the alien world is not a place where one only suffers separation and loss; exile is also a way to salvation and rediscovery.

St. Augustine likens the stag's course to the water to a pilgrimage.[19] Thus, the running deer provides a link between the treacherous, destructive court and the forest. The stag belongs to the forest, a presumed Eden, but it is chased and pursued and thus completes the exposition of the broken pastoral concept. It is not just the literary convention of the forest but also its ethos which is questioned here. The mortally wounded deer darting off in the pursuit of fresh water not only exposes the flaw in the pastoral idyll but prophesizes the conversion. Where paradise no longer exists, a process of atonement and redemption is required.

The transition from the "red world" to the "green world" generally involved a process of self-knowledge—the touchstone of the pastoral genre. All the characters are in need of learning, conversion, and atonement. As D. J. Palmer puts it: "Arden is a meeting place of Art and Nature, a world whose inhabitants may recognize themselves more truly in the reflections that are cast upon them. . . ."[20] Life in the forest means adventure and discovery and the stag provides the movement of their conversion through learning, by the characters wandering the woods.

Act 1 portrays the disruption of order within the kingdom and within the family through an unnatural relationship between brothers. Thomas McFarland observes that the usurpation and banishment produce a gloomy atmosphere more appropriate for the opening of a tragedy.[21] Jan Kott claims that the atmosphere of *As You Like It* recalls that of the Histories, where the only hope of salvation lies in escape.[22] The shift to Arden interrupts the tragic beginning, and the family intrigue which separates the good characters from the bad ceases to develop and, as act 1 ends, a process of learning and redemption begins. Michael Taylor mentions that nothing really happens after act 1 except the conversion of nature.[23]

The wounded stag dashing to the fountain particularly creates the trope of conversion. All the characters undergo a healing process in the wood and pass from one state of consciousness to another. The negative characters undergo conversion. The good ones go through a process of learning and purification. Interestingly enough the progress of the good from one state of mind to another is concretized on the stage in great detail while the conversion of the bad is merely reported. Not only does the change from hatred to love take place offstage, but it happens abruptly and miraculously.[24] Oliver describes his own conversion:

> 'Twas I, but 'tis not I: I do not shame
> To tell you what I was, since my conversion
> So sweetly tastes, being the thing I am.
> (*As You Like It*, 4.3)

and De Boys summarizes that of Duke Frederick:

> And to the skirts of this wild wood he came,
> Where, meeting an old religious man,
> After some questions with him, was converted. . . .
> (5.4.156–58)

The suffering characters at the beginning of the play are pure and innocent, made through their very virtues a target of evil schemes.[25] The varied designations of the stag as pure may well apply to the virtuous characters in the play who must suffer and flee although they are guiltless. The groaning stag whose " . . . big round tears Coursed with one another down his innocent nose" brings pain to Arden. Even if what we have here is not a theological concern, nor a straightforward adaptation of topoi usually applied to Christ, the weeping deer evokes an endless succession of portraits of Christ agonizing on the Cross and accepting his torment with love. In the same way, the Duke Senior willingly endures life in the forest and Orlando resigns himself gladly to the pangs of love. The deer's innocence and the injustice of the hunt are a dramatic illustration of the usurpers on the one hand and the exiles on the other. The languishing stag accentuates human sin. Despite their innocence, the good characters, too, must undergo purification. But in their case, the process of learning and trial is described at greater length, especially in matters of the heart. Love and Loyalty characterizes Adam, Celia, and even the Fool who join the princesses in their flight.

Purification through the deer running to the water is also associated with Jaques and with similar types. Helen Gardner notes that Jaques, who likes himself the way he is, does not want to immerse himself in the water (is Gardner consciously using a term borrowed from the ritual of baptism?) and prefers to remain on the riverbank, is really a penitent who chooses the hermetic life.[26] Indeed, he is eager to study the experience of conversion from Duke Frederick:

> To him I: out of these convertities
> There is much matter to be heard and learned.
> *(As You Like It,* 5.4.181–82)

The "big round tears" stir up in Jaques a strong sense of identification which have led some critics to propose that the stag characterizes Jaques. The deer as a symbol of melancholy has a long tradition in literature and Shakespeare uses it in its variations in other plays, as for example "Why let the strocken Deere goe weepe" (*Hamlet,* 3.2) and " . . . and then to sigh, as 'twere the mort o' th' deer'" (*The Winter's Tale,* 1.2).[27]

Flood typology provides the most common means of interpreting baptism. As Luther said, the old Adam is drowned—and the baptized person belongs henceforth to the new creation, is a member of the new covenant.[28] Small wonder, then, that after Rosalind arranges the four marriages, Jaques exclaims:

> There is sure another flood toward, and these
> couples are coming to the ark.
> *(As You Like It,* 5.4.35–36)

Of course, in his cynicism he is also saying that they are "strange beasts." We might agree with Uhlig that Jaques does not weep out of unfulfilled love; however, love, grace, and piety flourish in baptism, as the play strongly spells out.

The interweaving of theology and literature has influenced the symbolic concept of the hunted stag and places the first scene of act 2 as an introduction to the subject of love. The stag serves as an allegorical-figurative means of weaving together the themes of love.[29] There has been some controversy as to the romanticism of the play. However, the pastoral theme of four variations of love and courtship, the discussion of what love should be like, the hymeneal ending of the play, with the quadruple wedding—all point to love as a central theme of *As You Like It*.[30] Literature reinforces the theological image of the deer as a blessed animal. Since the classical period the deer had been invested with miraculous powers, a tradition that remained alive down to the Renaissance. In medieval writings we find the wounded deer as an allusion to a saint. D. C. Allen mentions that salvation is often attained through the intervention of the white deer—possibly symbolizing Christ, the good Christian, or a repenting sinner. An interesting story in this context is that of Guigemar who had wounded a white doe, was hurt himself, and was told by the dying doe that his injuries would not be healed until he had known suffering caused by a woman.[31] In *As You Like It* the sequestered stag, alluding to the process of learning and cleansing which most strongly associate it with the woes of love—is itself a metaphor of love and calls forth the time-honored equation: love-hunt. Allen cites several instances of the deer portrayed as a *sureogatus amoris*—hence, an "emblem of passion." The sixteenth- and seventeenth-century literature both in England and France used the deer hunt metaphor to tell of the quest for love.

La Chasse and l'Amore were inseparable. Allen reminds us that the same image dominates act 2 of Shakespeare's *Titus Andronicus* as well as his *Venus and Adonis*. The dying stag also alludes to the woes of love due to its frequent connection with death in the pastoral genre. Should Rosalind not take him, Orlando declares that he will die. Rosalind disguised as Ganymede in the familiar pastoral theme of transvestism makes light of this coinage, advising Orlando to "die by attorney," though Amore's arrow is already well lodged in her heart, as it is in the stag's flesh. She discounts the convention of courtly love and its school of poetry, and teaches Orlando, Silvius, and Phebe the nature of true love, and in the process, enables Orlando to "hunt" her.

The love-struck Orlando, who is intended to be cured of love through illusion, wins her heart at the end of the learning process. His long road toward true love receives a dramatic concretization on stage—unlike Oliver's penance, which we do not experience, but who nevertheless wins the second princess by way of "I came, saw and overcame" with sudden wooing and "sudden consenting." Jenkins points out that Oliver wins Celia because he has changed his ways and is thus rewarded for his new positive image.³²

Thus, we see that the account of the pursued stag is not merely a matter of verbal decor or poetic ornament. Shakespeare includes the story as an expositive scene, closely related to the main ideas of the play. This is possible since the wounded stag is a theological metaphor as well as a secular one, open to any number of interpretations woven throughout the play.

Northrop Frye writes that romantic comedy "may well be named the comedy of the green world because the plot is assimilated with the ritual theme of the triumph of life and love over the waste land."³³ Baptism is regarded as death and rebirth into Christ. He who is baptized, is freed from sin in advance to participate in life. The stag, which conjures up the concept of baptism as rebirth, unifies the themes of the play, emphasizing, in *As You Like It*, the triumph of life and love.

Notes

1. Jan Kott, "Shakespeare's Bitter Arcadia," in *Shakespeare Our Contemporary*, trans. B. Taborski (London: Methuen), 223.

2. Ernst Robert Curtius, *European Literature and the Latin Middle Ages*, trans. W. R. Trask (1948; reprint; New York: Pantheon, 1953), 184. Comparing *As You Like It* with Lodge's *Rosalynde*, Shakespeare's source for the play, Homer Smith concluded that Shakespeare subordinated the pastoral element as far as possible and restored the true forest atmosphere in order to make a better play. Thus Lodge's Forest of Ardenne is Arcadia. Shakespeare's is Sherwood. Smith, "Pastoral Influence in the English Drama," *PMLA* 12 (1897): 355–460. John Dover Wilson sees here a Warwickshire scenery—a landscape as Shakespeare's birthplace. See Wilson, *Shakespeare's Happy Comedies* (London, 1962). L. G. Clubb argues that Shakespeare's green world belongs entirely to the English countryside. See Clubb, "The Making of the Pastoral Plays: Italian Experiments between 1573 and 1590," in *Petrarch to Pirandello*, ed. J. A. Molinaro (Toronto: University of Toronto Press, 1973).

3. Georg Von Greyerz, *The Reported Scenes in Shakespeare's Plays* (Bern, 1965).

4. The report technique does not add to Jaques's characterization: hearing of the wounded stag, the Duke merely mocks Jaques's sentimentality. About this see Robert B. Pierce, "The Moral Language of Rosalinde and *As You Like It*," *Studies in Philology* 68 (1971): 167–76. P. J. Frankis believes Shakespeare here may be following the literary convention that has likened the stag to a dying man, and that what we have here is the testament of the stag. Frankis, "The Testament of the Deer in Shakespeare," *Neuphilologische Mitteilungen* 59 (1958): 65–68.

5. J. Wilcox, "Putting Jaques into *As You Like It*," *The Modern Language Review* 36 (1941): 388–94.

6. We shall not here concern ourselves with the continual debate over the Christian doctrine in the Shakespearean plays. For this see, for example, R. M.

Frye, *Shakespeare and Christian Doctrine* (Princeton, 1963); and Sylvan Barnet, "Some Limitations of a Christian Approach to Shakespeare," *Journal of English Literary History*, no. 2 (June 1955): 81 ff. Even those who reject the religious interpretation will admit that Shakespeare was familiar with the doctrine and made use of Christian emblems and terminology. With regard to *As You Like It*, see, for example, Adam: " . . . He that doth the ravens feed / Yea, providently caters for the sparrow. . . ." (*As You Like It*, 2.3.43–44); Orlando. "If ever you have looked on better days; / If ever been where bells have knolled to church; / If ever sat at any good man's feast; / If ever from your eyelids wiped a tear; / And know what 'tis to pity and be pitied (2.7.114–18).

7. The course of the stag to the fountain as a symbol of purification have caused the Fathers of the Church to compare it to a saint and even to Christ himself. To quote Bede: "Imo Cervi Cervorum id est Christi." See Gertrud Schiller, *Iconography of Christian Art* (Greenwich, Conn.: New York Graphic Society, 1971).

8. As, for example, the deer flight to the water is an analogue to the temptation of Christ who was baptized before he went to the Wilderness. *Glossa Ordinaria* PL 114 181 in Howard Helsinger, "Images on the Beatus Page of Some Medieval Psalters," *Art Bulletin* 53 (1971): 161–76.

9. Ibid, 165.

10. As, for example, Gorleston Psalter, ca. 1310 (London, B. L. Add. Mss 49622, fol. 8^v; Ramsey Psalter, fol. 107^v.

11. Today in Brussels, Bibliotheque Royale, Mss 9961-2, fol 14^r, fig. 1. See L. Freeman-Sandler, *The Peterborough Psalter in Brussels and Other Fenland Mss* (London: Harvey Miller, 1974).

12. Northrop Frye, *Anatomy of Criticism* (1932); reprint; (New York: Atheneum).

13. Young disagrees with the idea of the satire. In his opinion the Forest is stylized and artificial and reflects the human moods as in the pastoral romances. By foregoing a pastoral escapist setting Shakespeare turns the Forest into a microcosmos of possibilities and presents the pastoral convention as such: See David Young, *The Heart's Forest, A Study of Shakespeare's Pastoral Play* (New Haven: Yale University Press, 1978), 50, 64. The same opinion is presented by Mary Lascelles who denies altogether the claim that *As You Like It* is a satire on the pastoral convention. See Lascelles, "Shakespeare Pastoral Comedy," in *More Talking of Shakespeare*, ed. J. Garrett (New York: Theatre Art Books, 1959), 70–86.

14. John MacQueen, "*As You Like It* and Medieval Literary Tradition," *FMLS* 1 (1965): 216–29.

15. Shakespeare returns to this again and again, each time the refugees enter the forest. When Rosalind, Celia, and the fool enter they are tired and show no enthusiasm. The fool states: "Ay, now am I in Arden, the more fool I. When I was at home I was in a better place. . . ." (2.4.13–13; Rosalind describes the forest "desert," as does Orlando later on (2.7.16).

16. Claus Uhlig, "The Sobbing Deer": As You Like It, 2.1.21–66 and the Historical Context." *Renaissance Drama* New Series 3 (1970): 79–1109.

17. Kott, "Shakespeare's Bitter Arcadia," 224.

18. Robert Edwards, "Exile, Self and Society," in *Exile in Literature*, ed. M. I. Lagos-Pope (Lewisburg: Bucknell University Press, 1988), 19.

19. St. Augustine, "Ennarrationes in Psalmos 41," *Corpus Christianarum Series Latina*, 38 (1956): 463.

20. D. J. Palmer, "Art and Nature in *As You Like It*," *P.Q.* 49 (1970): 30–40.

21. Thomas McFarland, *Shakespeare's Pastoral Comedy* (University of North Carolina Press), 98 ff.

22. Kott, "Shakespeare's Bitter Arcadia," 286–342.

23. Michael Taylor, "*As You Like It:* The Penalty of Adam," *Critical Quarterly* 15 (1973): 76 ff.

24. John Shaw agrees that the protagonists in *As You Like It* clearly manifest an interest in self-knowledge. He finds that there is a basic philosophical discord between fortune and nature in the play, and the speedy conversions of Frederick and Oliver occur since they were not inherently evil but, rather, lacking self-knowledge they allied themselves with the goddess of Fortune. Shaw, "Fortune and Nature in *As You Like It*," *Shakespeare Quarterly* 6 (1955): 45–50. John MacQueen maintains that the forest is nature's domain and a refuge from its opposite—the outside world: fortune. According to MacQueen, the conversion of Oliver and the Duke Frederick takes place upon their very entry into the forest, because this is when their illusions vanish. See MacQueen, "*As You Like It* and the Medieval Literary Transition," *Forum for Medieval Language Studies* 1 (1965): 216–28.

25. For this see Taylor, "*As You Like It*," 76.

26. Helen Gardner, "As You Like It," in *More Talking of Shakespeare*, ed. John Garrett (New York: Theatre Art Books, 1959), 17 ff.

27. Lawrence Babb, quotes more examples. See Babb, *The Elizabethan on Malady* (East Lansing, Mich., 1951), 73–101.

28. Schiller, *Iconography of Christian Art*, 129.

29. Henry Green might be inaccurate in referring to a specific emblem (from Gavriele Symeoni, *Imprese heroiche et mordali*). However, to our mind the idea that the reported scene evokes the love emblem is still valid. See Uhlig, "Sobbing Deer," 84.

30. James Smith, for example, thinks that the play is unromantic. See Smith, "*As You Like It*," *Scrutiny* 9, no. 1 (June 1940): 9–32. Caesar L. Barber proposes that the play is romantic and pastoral. See Barber, "The Use of Comedy in *As You Like It*," *P.Q.* 21, no. 4 (October 1942): 353–67.

31. See D. C. Allen, "Marvell's Nymph," *Journal of English Literary History* 23, no. 2 (1956): 102.

32. Harold Jenkins, "As You Like It," *Shakespeare Studies* 8 (1955): 40–51.

33. Frye, *Anatomy*, 182.

"I See a Voice": The Desire for Representation and the Rape of Voice

Elizabeth Freund

I

A trope of Voice recurs in our discursive practices with remarkable persistence. The trope is as old as poetry or as the arts of language and as new as the latest postdeconstructionist endeavors to recover and represent the absent voices of the living as well as the dead. That the trope is foundational to essentialist notions of presence, identity, origin and intention, selfhood, and self-possession, and much else, is by now a familiar complaint. Yet its unremitting durability testifies to a steadfast desire if not for presence then for adequate representation of the thing itself; adequate enough to make us feel—like Leontes, overwhelmed by the bitterness of verisimilitude in the presence of Hermione's "statue"—that "we are mock'd with art" (*The Winter's Tale*, 5.3.68).[1] It is the onlooker Camillo who risks a Pygmalion fantasy, transgressing the boundary between art and life and calling for the crowning lifelike touch, a voice: "If she pertain to life, let her speak too" (5.3.1.113).

"Let her speak too." This is the desire that gives birth both to literary representation and to certain modes of its reception. It constitutes the grounds, for instance, of the "Philomela Project,"[2] Geoffrey Hartman's apt name for the restitutive and largely feminist scholarship devoted to the recovery and representation of muted, marginalized, ventriloquized, appropriated, suppressed, and silenced voices. But this "let," whose liberating fiat restores history or intelligibility, hinges on the treacherous rhetoricity of language (to say nothing of the waywardness of desire) and can all too easily turn (trope) into yet another violent silencing or distortion. The archaic (call it repressed) meaning of the word *let*—a hindrance or prohibition—always threatens to return.

The desire for voice is frequently enmeshed in a tropological system with its uncanny twin, a trope of sight. Mimetic poetry and the poetics which grow out of it have traditionally resorted to the operations of two basic organs of perception, the eye of the mind and the inner ear, which generate the "speaking pictures" of verbal art. Sir Philip Sidney's *Apologie,* for example, articulates a typically Renaissance desire for representation. It believes that the philosopher's "infallible grounds of wisdom . . . lye darke before the imaginatiue and iudging powre, if they bee not illuminated or figured foorth by the speaking picture of Poesie,"[3] and acknowledges the mediatedness of vision by voice. Even divinely inspired eyes see, so to speak, linguistically and tropologically, as in David's Psalms whose prophetic song is "meerely poetical":

> For what els is the awaking his musicall instruments; the often and free changing of persons; his notable *Prosopopeias,* when he maketh you, as it were, see God comming in his Maiestie; his telling of the Beastes ioyfulnes, and hills leaping, but a heauenlie poesie, wherein almost hee sheweth himselfe a passionate louer of that vnspeakable and euerlasting beauties to be seene by the eyes of the minde, onely cleered by fayth?[4]

Poetic voice makes it possible to see and hear, by imitation or representation, the otherwise invisible or inaudible. Its *verba* reveals the *res;* the signifier unveils the signified.

But the signified is not necessarily a ground of wisdom or a feature of nature. According to Sidney it is also the poet's particular distinction, his superiority over philosophers and historians, to figure forth something he never saw. The difference between them

> is such a kinde of difference as betwixt the meaner sort of Painters (who counterfet onely such faces as are sette before them) and the more excellent, who, hauing no law but wit, bestow that in cullours vpon you which is fittest for the eye to see: as the constant though lamenting looke of *Lucrecia,* when she punished in her selfe as others fault; wherein he painteth not *Lucrecia* whom he neuer sawe, but painteth the outwarde beauty of such a vertue.[5]

Cullours, of course, is a term that technically refers to the rhetorician's palette too, in its widest sense denoting the figures of a discourse. The more excellent painter or poet, following no law but the zodiac of his wit, will represent a surface whose signified is a fiction. Sidney's text is haunted by a subtle and unstable difference between "bringing forth" (which may be understood as the poetic function of revealing a hidden truth, "the infallible grounds of wisdom") and "counterfeiting" (which might release the poet from the platonic shadow of responsibility for truth and lies)—both of course tropes that fail to maintain a stable binary opposition between voice and sight. In his conceptualization of the poetic imagination, Sidney disconcertingly shifts ground on the question of this difference in a fruitful and dialectical instability that, according to Murray Krieger, allows him to enact in his own poetry a "desire for representation, or, rather, presentation."[6]

The Shakespearean representation is also acutely aware of this tension. Bottom in *A Midsummer Night's Dream* represents a sophisticated burlesque of the visionary Sidneyan legacy of representation:

> ... I have had a most rare vision. I have had a dream, past the wit of man to say what dream it was. Man is but an ass, if he go about [t'] expound this dream. ... The eye of man hath not heard, the ear of man hath not seen, man's hand is not able to taste, his tongue to conceive, nor his heart to report, what my dream was. I will get Peter Quince to write a ballet of this dream. It shall be called "Bottom's Dream," because it hath no bottom; and I will sing it in the latter end of a play. ...
>
> (*MND*, 4.1.206–16)

Bottom's dream, his desire for representation, is dramatized in the struggle to find a voice of his own with which to expound the dream, and an art form with which to figure forth or counterfeit a dark oneiric experience whose immediacy, however, defies his powers of representation and rapidly fades into a ridiculous disordering of sensory information. Mocked by art, his "most rare vision" is soon displaced by the "tedious brief scene" and "very tragical mirth" of "Pyramus and Thisby." The self-reflexive interlude is usually read as Shakespeare's parodic and self-congratulating foil to his own successful feats of representation in the framing comedy—he succeeds where Bottom fails. What is usually overlooked is the way in which Shakespeare's witty glance at the slippage between figuring and disfiguring (3.1.60–61) that besets Bottom's desire for representation is also a wry metacritical and self-mocking meditation on all desire for representation and for its idealizing poetics of presence.

The poet, according to Sidney, can make us see God ("as it were") coming in his majesty by invoking or inventing a prosopopoeia; Bottom, no poet and engulfed in rhetorical confusion, fails to summon up a credible impersonation, let alone a Fairy Queen, although his desire for representation is no doubt as strong as Sidney or the Psalmist's (especially in the theater where he is a natural in more than one sense). Yet he intuits the instrumentality of trope, even as he fails to get a grip on it. "The eye of man hath not heard, the ear of man hath not seen. . . ." points rather complexly, if only he knew it, to the interface of voice and gaze discovered in prosopopoeia, "a figure by which an imaginary or absent person is represented as speaking or acting" *(OED)*, and the rhetorical vehicle on which the desire for representation can comfortably ride. "The Counterfait in personation" (Puttenham), a rhetorical strategy by means of which we "attribute any humane quality, as reason or speech to dombe creatures or other insensible things,"[7] is a figure that patently meshes the work of eye and ear and answers to Bottom's intuitions. Etymologically the term derives from the Greek meaning to make a mask or face (the visible), but its rhetorical sense focuses on conferring voice (the audible) upon the face. In his well-known essay on autobiography, Paul de Man demonstrated its centrality to a topos dealing with the "giving and taking away of faces, with face and deface, *figure*, figuration and disfiguration."[8]

Bottom, impersonating Pyramus, makes manifest this strategic interfacing when he greets his Thisby thus: "I see a voice! Now will I to the chink, / To spy and I can hear my Thisby's face" (*MND*, 5.1.192–93). Rhetorically speaking, to "see a voice" is a catachresis, Anglicized by Puttenham as a figure of Abuse, "neither naturall nor proper"[9]; and yet, in a very literal sense, it is the legal fiction on which theatrical representation of absent presences is constructed. And it is precisely the literalization of that which refuses the literal that Shakespeare dramatizes in the hilarious blunders of the Athenian artisans. The clownish malapropisms of Bottom and his crew are at once "the silliest stuff that ever I heard" (5.1.210), and the sly trace of Shakespeare's metacritical voice, so to speak, or what Margaret W. Ferguson, in a different context, calls his "letter to the audience."[10]

What does it mean to "see a voice"? To hear with eyes (*Sonnet* 23) and look with ears (*King Lear*, 4.6.151) are what Theseus calls "tricks" of imagination, the aberrant visions and voices produced by the seething brains of "the lunatic, the lover and the poet" (*MND*, 5.1.7,18), or by a clown such as Bottom. But readers too, in their reception of these productions, in their attribution of meaning to the spectacle or to the text they subject to their scrutiny, are driven by an acute and strangely compounded lust of the eyes and of the ears. Criticism's scene of interpretation repeats the desire for representation.

Critical interpretation is, arguably, a practice that invents itself (to paraphrase Michel de Certeau) by poaching on the property of others.[11] We scrutinize minutely on the assumption that "more is meant than meets the ear" (Milton) in order to be able to represent what we see and hear of the dark or hidden "more." That so much detective effort or interpretive labor on behalf of lost or muted voices structurally *requires* their silence or dispossession in order to constitute itself is a piece of irony that contributes to the conception of this essay.

The following pages will stage a minor allegory of these observations by examining, in a heuristic spirit, two Shakespearean scenes of interpretation—Shakespeare's ekphrastic inset in "The Rape of Lucrece," and Shakespeare's (or Shakespeare's Ulysses') representation of Cressida as a speaking body—each of which appeals to the eye of mind and to the inner ear in a performance that exhibits some version of the peculiarly catachresical or abusive intersection of ocular and auricular desires in the voices both of critics and fictional characters. I propose to read these scenes in relation to a controversial Madonna video clip and to its readings in order to highlight by means of this triptych arrangement a characteristic release of prosopopoeic impulses. In each of these scenes the performative "let her speak too" engenders a profusion of contending voices, the circulation of whose rhetorical violence enables and at the same time puts in doubt the very possibility of faithfully representing the immanent by way of a viable voice or image. Not accidentally each constellates itself in some relation to a question of rape.

II

In "Lucrece" Shakespeare represents a remarkable scene in which his heroine lingers, for the space of some two hundred lines, over the details of a "skillful painting, made for Priam's Troy" ("Lucrece," 1.1366). In this masterpiece the ravished and unhappy Lucrece can see "A thousand lamentable objects" to which, "in scorn of nature, art gave liveless life" (1.1373–74). It is a crowded scene, swarming with familiar heroes and villains as well as nameless men and women, in which the Trojan legend (*legenda*: "what is read"), the narrative of rape, destruction, and grief, is rendered with magnificent craftsmanship. All the carefully deployed elements of the portrayal—blood, tears, gleaming or dying eyes, facial expressions, postures of trembling cowardice, or graceful courage—arouse the sympathetic imagination, and contribute to the production of an effect of the real, of the fullness or plenitude of nature, history, and living experience.

But Shakespeare goes out of his way to alert us to the fact that the same scene of "*liveless* life" (italics mine) also "show[s] the painter's strife" (1.1377) to achieve this effect of presence.

> For much imaginary work was there,
> Conceit deceitful, so compact, so kind,
> That for Achilles' image stood his spear,
> Grip'd in an armed hand, himself behind
> Was left unseen, save to the eye of mind:
>   A hand, a foot, a face, a leg, a head
> Stood for the whole to be imagined.
>
> (1.1422–28)

The painting reveals its own mediating representational strategies, the tricks and distortions by whose means the artist stages his desire for representation. It thus invites, put very roughly and schematically, two kinds of responses. On the one hand, it is a mimetic triumph. Every "conceit deceitful" of its artistic economy (each gap, absence, synecdoche, dismembered part, icon, and perspectival foreshortening) figures forth a phantasmal wholeness "left unseen, save to the eye of mind": it is the labor of the viewer's eye that guarantees the success of the artist's labor. But on the other hand the very reflection, bestowed by the eye's scrutinizing gaze, upon these artistic and deceitful conceits, and upon the crafted and crafty nature of the representation, threatens to undo the desired effect of presence by laying bare the design of its "life." Both these responsive roles converge neatly in the figure of Lucrece (appreciative art lover and wretched rape victim at once) whose voice and gaze mediate the scene for us.

If it is the case that the ekphrastic poem[12] is always a reflection on acts of representation and perception, a mediating role such as Lucrece's will inevitably perform a self-reflexive turn as well. Shakespeare's elaborate ekphrastic scene thus works in several and oppositional ways. It deepens and thickens the mimetic illusion on the level of fable and character. On a metadiegetic level, it links the arts of poet and painter in the usual and almost trivial sense. The trope of *ut pictura poesis* implies a kinship or similarity which their skills and techniques share, and which generates a mutually enriching collaboration. In this particular case the linkage also stakes out Shakespeare's claim to a superb mastery of his own craft, equal to the master-painter whose work he re-creates through Lucrece's eyes. But beyond this implied brotherhood of master-craftsmen we can detect a subtle dissonance and asymmetry that eventually become explicit. Shakespeare's ekphrastic scene fills in the blanks (thoughts and feelings, e.g., which painting cannot represent) but it does so by *narrativizing* the act of perception as a violent intervention and appropriation. When he represents Lucrece as speaking for Hecuba he presumes (through her agency) to supply precisely that which is missing from the iconic, namely a redemptive and restitutive voice for inwardness. And when finally he depicts the enraged Lucrece physically tearing at the senseless portrait of Sinon with her nails, he concludes the sequence of appropriation with an extremely ambivalent act of destruction. The apparent harmony and symmetry of the sister arts thus becomes a kind of deadly rivalry. Let me retrace the outlines of this narrative as it is played out in the ekphrastic meditation.

It is not accidental that the thirty-odd stanzas describing Lucrece's interactive perusal of the painting interrupt and arrest her story at the very juncture at which she is herself driven by a desire for representation or voice.[13] The sequence of events leading up to this pause in her tale is also relevant. After the rape, Lucrece rails and complains through the night like a "lamenting Philomele" ("Lucrece," 1.1079), racked by the "deep torture" (1.1287) experienced "when more is felt than one hath power to tell" (1.1288). She then determines to "utter all" (1.1076). Calling for paper, ink, and pen, she prepares to write her husband but finds herself beset by an anxiety of representation, and by the rhetorical decisions and indecisions characteristic of Shakespeare's own artistic strife. (This same strife is frequently enacted in the struggles of his dramatis personae—Richard II comes to mind—to invent an authentic language of interiority in which heart and tongue will coincide in voicing "the unseen grief / That swells with silence in the tortured soul" (*Richard II*, 4.1.294–95). Lucrece's quill hovers ("Lucrece," 1.1297) as she considers the (in)adequacy of her rhetorical or representational options:

> Conceit and grief an eager combat fight,
> What wit sets down is blotted straight with will:
> This is too curious-good, this blunt and ill:
>   Much like a press of people at a door,
>   Throng her inventions, which shall go before.
>
>   (1.1298–1302)

In the end she manages no more than a "brief" account of her "tedious" woes (1.1309), and—"her certain sorrow writ uncertainly" (1.1311)—finds herself "pausing for means to mourn some newer way" (1.1365). It is now that she goes off to stare at the painting of the Trojan legend. Her rhetorical ordeal has mirrored the poet's, and her present pause to seek for more representation coincides exactly with Shakespeare's ekphrastic digression. The invitation to compare Shakespeare's art with the painter's is overlaid with the invitation to compare the Shakespearean desire for representation with his creature's.

As Lucrece scans the painted throng (as crowded with figures as was her mind with rhetorical inventions a moment earlier), her eyes come to rest on the image of "despairing Hecuba," a portrayal in which "all distress is stell'd" (1.1444). The painter's exquisite anatomy of ravage and destruction elicits Lucrece's acute empathy; but she also feels he has done her wrong

> "To give her so much grief, and not a tongue":
> "Poor instrument," quoth she, "without a sound,
> I'll tune thy woes with my lamenting tongue"
> (1.1463–65)

What's Hecuba to her or she to Hecuba? Aside from her natural identification with the scene of "woe" and the spectacle of female victimage, the desire for a redeeming voice, for a possibly healing speech of woe, animates Lucrece, just as it animates Shakespeare's invention of her, an invention largely organized around the genre of lament.

Hecuba is to Lucrece as Lucrece is to Shakespeare: a motive for prosopopoeia and representation. She determines to give a voice to the ruined Hecuba just as Shakespeare has given a voice to his lamenting Philomele. Indeed, Shakespeare's insistence on the analogy verges on bathos when he risks the collapse of his doleful heroine into an industrious artist of lament:

> So Lucrece, set a-work, sad tales doth tell
> To pencill'd pensiveness and color'd sorrow:
> She lends them words, and she their looks doth borrow.
> (1.1496–98)

His staging of Lucrece's staging of the "means to mourn some newer way" (the representation of more desire for more representation) threatens to turn into a race for artistic emulation. Lucrece's prosopopoeic provision of a lamenting tongue for Hecuba's ravaged but mute face ("let her speak too"!) dissolves into the lamenting tongue Shakespeare has given his "counterfait in personation" who is, in any case, already an appropriation and reinvention from some master-precursor's representation (say Ovid's) of the legend.

What is highlighted by Lucrece's labor and, beyond that, by the ekphrastic encounter as a whole, is a multifaceted and agonistic economy of exchanges—all the numerous lendings and borrowings between painter and poet, looks and words, telling and coloring, between narrative frames, between Lucrece and Hecuba, Shakespeare and Lucrece, reader and text, life and art—exchanges that feed, articulate, and perpetuate the desire for representation. This set of complex entanglements of gaze and voice, painter and writer, creature and creator circulating in Shakespeare's staging of the desire for representation is given a further unsettling and astonishingly violent prominence as the scene moves to its ambivalent conclusion. "Set a-work," Lucrece's roving gaze comes to rest on a "wretched image" (1.1501) who "entertain'd a show so seeming just" (1.1514) that "jealousy itself could not mistrust / False creeping craft and perjury" (1.1516–17). It is the image of the treacherous Sinon, but the name is suspended for the duration of three stanzas while we hear how perfectly invisible his deceit remains. His face, "though full of cares, yet show'd *content*" (1.1503, italics mine)—the pun registers a savage mockery on the part of art not because the villain appears to be gloating but because the "show" is entirely unreadable, empty of any true content (and thus empty even of the punning contents that language seems to confer on it).

I would like to suggest that what the painted image of Sinon exhibits is not an index to his state of mind, which remains utterly inscrutable, but a case of quintessential representation. By that I mean the paradoxical case of a representation both *outdoing* itself mimetically—by depicting such perfectly camouflaged deceit (and the impenetrability of deceitful camouflage, we should recall, was the ruin of Troy), yet at the same time also *undoing* itself—by failing to show anything at all except the act of showing. One even wonders by what markers (there are none) Lucrece recognizes this figure to be Sinon. All this raises the question of what a mimetic representation might be when it deceives the viewer so thoroughly, when indeed it reveals nothing (or the nothingness) of the thing represented. The glory of the painter's iconic craftsmanship, as we saw earlier, was to suggest the real by leaving most of it unseen or unheard, not without, however, providing some helpful clues to ground reading and interpretation. But in the case of Sinon there are no such clues; and when, spying "such signs of truth in his plain face . . . she concludes the picture was belied" (1.1532–33), the entire mimetic system of the painting threatens to unravel. Only the violent desire for representation continues to circulate.

With nothing else to ground her reading of the "show" except her own experience of rape and treachery and her unquenchable desire for representation Lucrece now identifies not with a female figure but with Troy. Sinon is to Troy what Tarquin was to Lucrece before the rape: an utterly impenetrable camouflage of innocence.

> For even as subtile Sinon here is painted,
> So sober sad, so weary and so mild
> (As if with grief or travail he had fainted)
> To me came Tarquin. . . .
>
> (1.1541–44)

Instead of simply rehearsing one more time the scene of her rape, what she enacts is a twofold movement toward a possibly cathartic release from her torment: first an imagined return to a time before the rape, and then an astounding reversal of the roles of victim and victimizer as she metaphorically rapes Tarquin in the image of the painted figure, "tear[ing] the senseless Sinon with her nails, / Comparing him to that unhappy guest / Whose deed hath made herself detest" (1.1564–66).

The hallucinatory enactment of desire for representation is a resounding cathartic failure. The act yields neither the sweetness of revenge nor a redemptive fulfillment of desire for representation. Lucrece's transformation into rapist is an overdetermined outcome, to say the least, of her desire, since wounding the painting will not heal her wound or wipe out the stain. It only compounds the elusiveness and ambivalence of desire: for in this last impulse to master the experience of rape and thus control its horror, it is hardly possible to distinguish between her loathing for Sinon/Tarquin and her self-hatred, between her reactive revulsion from representation and her greedy and violent appropriation of it, between Shakespeare's rather cheap victory over the rival artist (by an act of iconoclasm through the agency of his creature Lucrece) and the acknowledgemtn of this act's hollowness. In the very next line of the poem Lucrece is already smiling bitterly at the futility of it all; and in the line after that she turns away from the painting back to the "ebb and flow" of the "current of her sorrow," and to her last desperate enactment of the desire for representation in her artfully staged suicide.

Ultimately we too, like Lucrece, remain "mock'd with art." All that remains with any certainty is the ebb and flow of representation, its continuing circulation in violent acts of appropriation. Her mode of suicide ("she sheathed in her harmless breast / A harmful knife, that thence her soul unsheathed" (1.1723–24]), meticulously mirrors the rape ("And then against my heart he set his sword" [1.1640]), but Shakespeare's rather clumsy chiasmus suggests the unredemptive weariness of repetition in all these crossings of the desire for representation. Voiceless in death and beyond desire for representation, she is transformed into the icon of a battleground:[14] her blood, "bubbling from her breast . . . circles her body . . . like a late-sack'd island" (1.1737–40). The bleeding body her iconic self-destruction bequeaths does not empower her; like the sacked Troy it is immediately appropriated for more representational circulation, in the event for specific ideological and political gain by the male survivors who bear her away "To show . . . thorough Rome, / And so to publish Tarquin's foul offence" (1.1851–52) and thus secure his lasting political defeat. The "show" of Lucrece's body "speaks" the public indictment of Tarquin, a speech that, sadly and ironically, takes its force not from her proper voice but from the male-generated conceit of prosopopoeia, the fiction of conferring voice on a voiceless entity.

III

The literary traffic in women's voices and bodies is not an exclusively male market. Sometime in the fall of 1990 MTV banned the airing of a steamy new Madonna video entitled "Justify My Love." But early in December the video was screened in its entirety on the ABC news program "Nightline" in the context of an interview with the star. According to the *New York Times* (16 December 1990): "Overnight ratings were the second highest in the program's 10-year history, topped only by Tammy Bakker's crying jag." Almost immediately women's voices were raised across the nation in praise and condemnation of Madonna's provocative voice and image. What did they see and hear in this speaking picture to provoke the clamor? Predictably, the beholder's share, heavily ideological, predominated.

My intention here is to represent something like "The Rhetorical Rape of Madonna" in two favorable journalistic reports of the spectacle that, in their deployment of tropes of voice and sight, betray some of the same structures of rhetorical violence and appropriation to be found in "The Rape of Lucrece."

On 14 December 1990, Camille Paglia, the controversial author of *Sexual Personae: Art and Decadence from Nefertiti to Emily Dickinson*,[15] and something of an icon herself, published a short encomiastic piece in the *New York Times* in which she declares Madonna to be "the *true* feminist"[16]—as opposed to "the beaming Betty Crockers, hangdog dowdies and parochial prudes who call themselves feminists" and who "fear and despise the masculine." With characteristic panache Paglia informs us that "The video is pornographic. It's decadent. And it's fabulous," and goes on to praise it as "*truly* avant-garde," representing "a sophisticated European sexuality of a kind we have not seen since the great foreign films of the 1950's and 1960's . . . an eerie, sultry tableau of jaded androgynous creatures, trapped in a decadent sexual underground. Its hypnotic images are drawn from such sado-masochistic films as Lililana Cazani's 'The Night Porter' and Luchino Visconti's 'The Damned' . . . the perverse and knowing world of the photographers Helmut Newton and Robert Mapplethorpe."

The video clip Paglia admires was framed like a play-within-a-play by the interview. It is her perception of the entire Madonna spectacle, of the dissonant relationship between outer and inner play, between Madonna's awkward and unimpressive performance as interviewee and her professionally slick and polished video performance that elicits some of Paglia's more violent rhetorical moves. Her stylistic vigor, here as elsewhere, possesses the vividness of description that the ancient rhetoricians called *enargia*, a term that refers specifically to that liveliness of representation that "sets the scene before our eyes" and makes the hearers "see things."[17] Since Paglia describes a spectacle that most of her readers would presumably have seen and heard a few nights earlier, the rhetorical energies of the *New York Times* review are not deployed in the service of (re)creating an *imaginary* scene or conferring a voice on the voiceless, but precisely in making us see a voice.

Paglia's text begins with an ironic admonishment to the star to shut up and then 'fess up:

Madonna, don't preach.
Defending her controversial new video "Justify my love" on "Nightline" last week, Madonna stumbled, rambled and ended up seeming far less intelligent than she *really* is.
Madonna, 'fess up.

This coy opening effectively suppresses the empiric utterance or voice heard in the course of the interview, a move that then enables Paglia to call on the *image* to speak instead, as happens in the conventional *prosopopoeia*, where the addresser confers voice on the mute addressee. The apostrophe—"don't preach . . . 'fess up"—dismisses as inauthentic Madonna's apparent dumbness in the course of the interview, and proceeds to replace it with the smarter speech of her interpreter. (The fiction of a dialogue that apostrophe invites us to entertain only underlines its silencing thrust.) The confession Paglia solicits—and confessions are, by definition, supposed to be *true,* utterances made in one's *proper* or *authentic* voice—is spoken by Paglia. The apostrophe that invites the true voice to emerge is then nothing if not a rhetorically engineered appropriation of the empirical voice by way of its transposition into a *prosopopoeia*—a speaking image—speaking very distinctly in Paglia's voice.

Paglia as inquisitor and hermeneutic go-between[18] makes explicit and visible—always with great rhetorical resourcefulness—what Madonna appears unable or unwilling to say or reveal. Madonna, she tells us with the voice of one who has access to this person's heart and tongue, "loves *real* men" (unlike the "academic feminists" who "think their nerdy bookworm husbands are the ideal model of human manhood.") "She sees the beauty of masculinity, in all its rough vigor and sweaty athletic perfection." Indeed, she is to be hailed as "the future of feminism," exposing the puritanism and suffocating ideology of an American feminism stuck in a whining adolescent mode.

That Paglia's tropological ammunition is used for explicit ideological and polemical purposes is important but not my main concern; the validity of her rhetoric of persuasion can be judged independently of this analysis. My primary concern is to show how quickly the figure of prosopopoeia becomes an instrument of overt violence in Paglia's enactment of the struggle over voicing. The heart of the struggle is specifically thematized around the question of the voicing of a woman's "no"—"the new cliché of the date-rape furor" as she calls it. Ironically, her derisive targeting of women's specious "no's" is preceded by her own firm "no" to Madonna's voice:

> Mr. Sawyer asked for Madonna's reaction to feminist charges that, in the neck manacle and floor-crawling of an earlier video, "Express Yourself," she condoned the "degradation" and "humiliation" of women. Madonna waffled: "But I chained myself! I'm in charge."

Well, no. Madonna the producer may have chosen the chain, but Madonna the sexual persona in the video is alternately a cross-dressing dominatrix and a slave of male desire.

For more abrasive voice-erasure we move to the next paragraph: "But who cares what the feminists say anyhow? They have been outrageously negative" because they have failed to understand Freudian ambivalence properly. Hence the date-rape furor, introduced by Paglia's derisive "'No' always means 'no'":[19]

> "'No' always means 'no'." Will we ever graduate from the Girl Scouts? "No" has always been, and always will be, part of the dangerous, alluring courtship ritual of sex and seduction, observable even in the animal kingdom.

Her ostensibly anthropological point, bolstered by the apparent authority of the natural sciences, that in courtship "no" is always a masked, ritual mode of "yes" determined by nature, is a gendered construction overwhelmingly rejected by today's feminists, as Paglia no doubt knows; hence its deliberate and grating provocativeness.

Paglia's message is single, but her rhetoricity produces two contradictory effects: on the one hand, in saying a silencing "no" both to the Madonna she admires and feminists she despises, it invites us to discredit women's "no's" (along with their empirical voices) in a mode of they-know-not-what-they-say, a mode which reaffirms traditional patriarchal strategies of suppression and appropriation for the control of female voice and desire. (At the end of Madonna's video, if I remember correctly, a legend appears on the screen: "Poor is the man whose pleasures depend on the permission of another.") But on the other hand, the subversive underside of this same resourceful rhetoric is that *no one* can control the truth-claims of her assertions or denials; no speaker can be in possession of her speech or of herself when her words can be so easily represented, that is, appropriated, reversed, antithetically manipulated. *Is* Madonna an artist in control of her art? Or Paglia (or Freund) a critic in control of her discourse? Whose voice is it anyway when it is a construction or trope emanating from a "speaking picture" or from a "verbal icon" or from a (mis)-reading of the icon?

Let me sharpen the question by adding the testimony of another, less aggressively polemical viewer of the same speaking-picture event who nevertheless also freely manipulates the relationship of voices and icons. Caryn James ("Pop View" *New York*

Times [16 December 1990]) paid tribute to Madonna's "honesty about using sexuality to gain control and power," and took the feminist message to be "that Madonna can control a career as shrewdly as any man." Madonna, she wrote, "is redefining feminism itself," not through "her intellectual grasp of the subject" (she was in fact "shockingly inarticulate") but through "the impact of her image." And what does that image say? (Madonna's actual words were: "I may be dressing like the traditional bimbo, whatever, but I'm in charge.") James reports that she "*spoke* forcefully to feminist issues, even if they were delivered by a bimbo in control of her own bimboness." Given James's impatience throughout with Madonna's shocking inarticulacy, this forceful "speaking" can refer only to the eloquence of the icon rather than to the utterance.

James, like Paglia, has a problem with the intrusion of Madonna's own utterances, and she too performs the structurally identical gestures of appropriation and erasure of voice.

> The video, in fact, was less intriguing than the incarnation that appeared in the course of the interview: Madonna as talking head. It was not a convincing role. She rambled about censorship and conservative opposition to the arts, cluttered her answers with "you know" and "I mean," and seemed ill at ease with predictable questions. Didn't she rehearse?
>
> But scattered throughout this floundering performance were sound bites that were pure Madonna. . . .

If Madonna cannot *properly* speak for herself, James is implying, others can undertake to do so, rehearsing and editing her voice to extract the "pure" (Cf. Paglia's "true") Madonna. James reports that when asked about an earlier video, "Express Yourself," in which she appears chained up, Madonna replied: "I have chained *myself*. There wasn't a man that put that chain on me," and then added this astonishingly dense rider: "I was chained to my desires"—a wonderfully overdetermined sound bite (sexual desires or artistic desires? captive or captor? master or slave of the desire for representation?) in which the disturbing ambivalence of the visual images is uncannily replicated in the verbal ambivalence of the commentary. For James, who rushes past this complicating loop because she is busy denying Madonna her voice, this "loopy bit of symbolism" cannot be an instance of "pure" Madonna:

> "I have chained *myself*," she said. "There wasn't a man that put that chain on me." You don't have to buy Madonna's next loopy bit of

symbolism—"I was chained to my desires"—to believe the feminist subtext she finds in the video. "I do everything by my own volition. I'm in charge, O.K."

James will entertain the subtext but not the voice which she will silence by *visualizing*, and thereby translating into a more manageable unit of meaning, an icon of Madonna purified of her loopy language. Madonna as sensual, singing body speaks forcefully; Madonna as talking head is a grotesque. One or the other must be suppressed in order to iron out the contradictions and to retain a coherent and unitary image. It is as though an unresolvable perceptual predicament (such as Troilus experiences when he watches Cressida's betrayal: this is and is not Madonna) is felt to be unsustainable, intolerable, even psychotic. Yet it is precisely such predicaments or puzzles that the reading of literary texts has traditionally invited us (trained us) to tolerate. In my concluding section I will examine the case of the representation of Cressida as a raging desire for coherence.

IV

"Tell me. . . . What Cressid is, what Pandar, and what we," wails the lovesick Troilus (*Troilus and Cressida*, 1.1.98–99), and the Petrarchan in him replies:[20]

> Her bed is India; there she lies, a pearl.
> . . . .
> Ourself the merchant, and this sailing Pandar
> Our doubtful hope, our convoy and our bark.
> (1.1.100–104)

This courtly rhetoric in praise of women, in which gaze and voice perform the patriarchal traffic in women,[21] is one more aspect of the exchanges and circulations in the economy of what I have been calling the desire for representation, a desire in which author, fictional persona, and reader are inescapably implicated.

No reader or viewer of this play, to my knowledge, perceives Shakespeare's Cressida as a "pearl," but the question whether she is or isn't a bimbo continues to exercise the minds and representational desires of readers, especially since bimbos are apparently recognizable chiefly by their appearance: they speak to the gaze. To Ulysses' gaze the spectacle of Cressida speaks with perfect clarity and consonance:

> *Ulysses.* Fie, fie upon her!
> There's language in her eye, her cheek, her lip—
> Nay, her foot speaks; her wanton spirits look out
> At every joint and motive of her body.
> O, these encounterers,[22] so glib of tongue,
> That give accosting welcome ere it comes.
> And wide unclasp the tables of their thoughts
> To every ticklish reader: set them down
> For sluttish spoils of opportunity,
> And daughters of the game.
> (*Troilus and Cressida*, 4.5.54–63)

And even though we know better than to trust the negotiation of meanings performed by this pandar of politicians, himself no doubt a "ticklish reader," it is striking that Shakespeare does not deny or countermand Ulysses' reading in the remainder of the play. Instead, he abandons Cressida to the male gaze and to the fortunes of interpretation.

Cressida has just entered the Greek camp to be displayed, literally, as the spoils of war and opportunity. She is "kissed in general" (4.5.21) in a symbolic gang rape, after which her voice is appropriated by Ulysses in a savage antiblazon which ironically renders her "speechless" by conferring voice on her defamed body. For the remainder of the play Shakespeare does not undo this silencing. A shadowy Philomela figure lurks behind this representation, the "tables of [her] thoughts" a blank.

What I perceive as a dark and silent Philomela is, to Ulysses, an opportunistic slut, glib of tongue, whose association with the generals of both camps links her with the morally ambivalent casus belli, the "ravished Helen." Moreover, his devastating portrayal is "generally" acknowledged in the Greek camp when the stage direction (the sound of a trumpet blazing the arrival of the Trojans) is also vocalized in a damning pun spoken in unison by *All* [the Greek generals]: "The Trojan's trumpet" (1.64), a unanimous vote (vox) affirming the Ulyssean construction of "the Trojan strumpet."[23] And although we think we know that "this is and is not Cressida," his reading of Cressida's body, and its strategic placement in the economy of the narrative, nevertheless performs a staggering feat of alienation from the complexity and ambivalence of the character that we have become acquainted with. From this point on in the play we perceive Cressida only from a deeply mediated, male-oriented distance. Her erstwhile voice (already compromised by her ambivalent prevarications and by the recurrent allusions to a legendary falsehood) is muted by the loud speech issuing from the icon of her body on display to men. Although she will still literally speak (also to observe—against herself—that "Minds sway'd by eyes are full of turpitude" [*Troilus and Cressida*, 5.2.112]), the play does not allow her to recover from this alienating mutation. Her "encounter" with Diomed in act 5, scene 2 is watched and overheard by Troilus and Ulysses, watched and overheard by Thersites, watched and overheard by us. This is the kind of framing device that Shakespeare liked to use in comedy, especially for the "unmasking" of a character. Does it here unmask the true Cressida?

What Shakespeare stages, I suggest, is not a revelation of the "true" Cressida but an agonistic scene of interpretation at which "th'attest of eyes and ears" (5.2.121) is confronted with an antithetical blazoning. The poetic tradition of the blazon ("her bed is India; there she lies, a pearl"), which is an epideictic performance of the male voice celebrating female beauty, presupposes the woman's silence. Her body is a voiceless icon whose eloquence is rendered in the male voice. The consequences of this particular intersection of the tropes of voice and sight can be construed in many ways. Nancy Vickers has brilliantly demonstrated the strategic function of the blazon in the intertwining of rhetoric and narrative in Shakespeare's *Lucrece* to inscribe "a battle between men that is first figuratively and then literally fought on the fields of woman's 'celebrated' body."[24] The term *blazon*, Vickers reminds us, derives both from the French *blasonner* and from the English "to blaze" ("to proclaim as with a trumpet, to publish, and by extension, to defame or celebrate"), but its primary meaning was "a conventional heraldic description on a shield" from which came the secondary meaning, "a conventional poetic description of an object praised or blamed by a rhetorician-poet."[25] Martial object and sexual object put on display converge in the blazon.

In *Troilus and Cressida* (which has also been read as the wholesale mockery of an entire epideictic tradition[26]) the troping of "war" and "lechery"—the constant burden of Thersites' raillery—converges on the blazon. The Petrarchan Troilus exemplifies the conventional secondary meaning of poetic praise, but he also construes his Petrarchan stance as "womanish" (*Troilus and Cressida*, 1.1.107) because it keeps him from a display of martial prowess on the field of battle. Ulysses' description of Cressida's speaking body performs a contrasting blazon of defamation. A little further in the same scene comes an anatomy of carnage in the blazon mode performed in the swaggering dialogue between Hector and Achilles.

Achilles. . . . .

Achilles.
Now, Hector, I have fed mine eyes on thee;
I have with exact view perus'd thee, Hector,
And quoted joint by joint.

Hector. Is this Achilles?

Achilles. I am Achilles.

Hector. Stand fair, I pray thee; let me look on thee.

Achilles. Behold thy fill.

Hector. Nay, I have done already.

Achilles. Thou art too brief: I will the second time,
As I would buy thee, view thee limb by limb.

Hector. O, like a book of sport thou'lt read me o'er;
But there's more in me than thou understand'st.
Why dost thou so oppress me with thine eye?

Achilles. Tell me, you heavens, in which part of his body
Shall I destroy him—whether there, or there, or there
That I may give the local wound a name,
And make distinct the very breach whereout
Hector's great spirit flew?

(4.5.230-45)

Hector and Achilles appropriate the strategy of the blazon to dismember and slaughter each other rhetorically. The male gaze directed at the male body conjoins the sexual motives of "ticklish" readers and the martial motives of bloodthirsty readers, also suggesting a profound anxiety about gender. The flip side of the gaze is a speech act that simultaneously reads and violates the body. Hector's and Achilles' gaze at each other's celebrated bodies enacts the eroticizing of war. The dialogue is itself embedded in the bizarre context of an encounter of warriors that includes deadly jousting (between Hector and Ajax) followed by cordial embracing and fraternizing (they remember they are cousins) and then by emulous goading and verbal wounding.[27] Dismembering and remembering, wounding and embracing, insult and praise circulate in a whirligig of displacements.

It is within this resonant context that Ulysses' inventory of Cressida's eye, her cheek, her lip, her foot, occurs, employing the rhetorical strategy of celebration for purposes of degradation by treating the fragments of her body as spoils of war. These fragments are themselves represented as part of a rhetorical performance: there's language in every joint and "motive of her body."

We tend to associate motive with mind and purpose but the unusual phrase (according to the *OED* "motive" in the sense of "moving part" occurs only in Shakespeare) collapses the suggestion of involuntary movement of limbs (like a puppet's body) into the inward motivation (spirit, thought) that looks out at every joint and invites or moves the reader to respond. But whose puppet and whose motive? Ulysses' identification of Cressida with "encounterers, so glib of tongue" combines the reference to a class of brazen or "forward" women not only with the reference to an antithetical rhetoric ("that glib and oily art to speak and purpose not" [*King Lear*, 1.1.224–25]) whose duplicitous motives are perspicuous to "every ticklish reader," but also with a reference to encounterers on the battlefield.

But where is Cressida in relation to these tropes? Unlike Hector and Achilles, who hurl antiblazons at each other in each other's presence, Cressida is absent from the scene of mock-praise, is denied the privilege of speaking for herself, and is not allowed to recover from this rigidifying silence for the rest of the play. This is the Pygmalion fantasy reversed: the living woman is frozen into an object whose inwardness is superseded by the speech that the male gaze confers.

Throughout the earlier scenes of Troy, as Janet Adelman has precisely and painstakingly shown, Shakespeare establishes in us a keen sense both of Cressida's inwardness, and of our own privileged glimpses into this inwardness.[28] The voice animating the persona, to be sure, is puzzling from the start, not only because of its insistent reference to a divided self and to a legendary betrayal always already inscribing the character's duplicity, but also because of its defensive refusal to reveal its full or "true" nature. Nonetheless, in the earlier acts we are invited to share in the mimetic illusion of her personhood to whose complicated interiority we are made privy. Her witty and secretive strategies of defense, ironically revealed in bantering dialogue with Pandarus or in soliloquy (*Troilus and Cressida*, 1.1.); the particular mixture of hardness and softness that betrays the vulnerability of her desires and fears; her brittle language of selfhood and her fragile intimacy with Troilus (3.2.); above all the vehemence of her grief at the separation from Troy and Troilus (4.2)—all are constitutive of a consciousness, a voice whose embodied coherence we believe we might learn to read and understand. Yet all the representational strategies that contribute to the realization of the character's "reality" are abandoned, even denied, when she is turned over to the Greeks. From this point on, Adelman observes, "she recedes from us. As Troilus and Diomed quarrel over her, she stands silent, as though she has become merely the object of their competitive desire, as though she has no voice of her own."[29]

The shift so ironically articulated by Ulysses' violent appropriation of "the motive of her body" opens up a puzzling disjunction. The "sudden move into opacity"[30] performed at this point of the play is all the more striking because immediately preceding this move we have had Cressida's last voicing of her desire. In contrast to her specious and calculating resistance to Troilus' wooing (not "stubborn-chaste against all suit" [*Troilus and Cressida*, 1.1.97] as he thinks, but "hard to seem won" [3.2.116] as she confesses), her poignantly uninhibited refusal to leave Troy is unusually compelling. When she learns that she "must to thy father and be gone from Troilus" (4.2.94) she says "no" to the law of fathers, of history, and of legends with such passionate vehemence that we are invited briefly to contemplate the possibility that Shakespeare too might be risking a vehement "no" to literary consanguinity, and to her legendary inscription in a tale of falsehood.

> *Cressida.* O you immortal gods! I will not go.
> *Pandarus.* Thou must.
> *Cressida.* I will not, uncle, I have forgot my father;
> I know no touch of consanguinity,
> No kin, no love, no blood, no soul so near me
> As the sweet Troilus! O you gods divine,
> Make Cressid's name the very crown of falsehood
> If ever she leave Troilus! Time, force, and death,
> Do to this body what extremes you can;
> But the strong base and building of my love
> Is as the very center of the earth,
> Drawing all things to it. I'll go in and weep—
> *Pandarus.* Do, do.
> *Cressida.* —Tear my bright hair, and scratch my praised cheeks,
> Crack my clear voice with sobs, and break my heart
> With sounding "Troilus". I will not go from Troy.
> (4.2.97–112)

Can Cressida say "no" to consanguinity, forget the father, and extricate herself from the role of "daughter of the game"? Has she found her true voice in this "no"? And can Shakespeare say "no" to the literary fathers and to the legend that has named her by rewriting her wretched destiny otherwise, or is he toying with vain desires? He certainly tantalizes us with these possibilities by enlisting us so strongly on the side of what appears to be an authentic "motive of her body"—the willingness to sacrifice this praised body to the titanic struggle between "no" and "must" in order to become the other who might be her "true" self. But the dream of restitution is conjured only to be dashed. Neither she nor we are allowed to represent her body as a strong base and building. It is a body she cannot repossess or prize away from the grip of male ownership (blood, kin, and consanguinity) or from the "divine" copyright (the gods' will that she be made the very crown of falsehood) that Ulysses authenticates by silencing this last echoing wail of her desire.

Much commentary on the play reads like a campaign of rehabilitation, correcting the misogynistic image to reflect our changing sensibilities. This seems to me to miss the point as much as did the now despised phallocentric criticism. In the haste to confer on her the dignity of victimhood and collateral damage, Cressida is perceived to be a casualty of her circumstances and society. From the perspective which emphasizes her subjection to a treacherous father, a lecherous uncle-pimp, a falsely idealistic lover, and an unscrupulous politician, it is indeed small wonder that her image of herself shatters, and that she reneges on her vows. And it makes perfect sense to adopt the view that her downfall, her tragic, if unheroic, failure to sustain a continuous and coherent selfhood in a male-dominated and value-deficient world at war reflects less on her moral character than on her environment.[31] The extenuating circumstances are undoubtedly valid, and their affective pathos is considerable.

Yet Cressida's intolerable social situation and her psychic vulnerability notwithstanding, this still is and is not Cressida. Her arbitrary violation of promises sticks, and the abruptness of the change of voice or character in the passage from one camp to the other continues to vex the interpreting mind, above all the mind in pursuit of psychological and charactero-logical sense. Such logic refuses to tolerate the blockage of our privileged access to the inwardness we associate with a fully articulated "character" and to persist in filling or explaining away the aporias and discontinuities, as though our sensibilities cannot rest until we choose between the tart and the victim.

This felt need is a result of what Barthes called the "effect of the real" and what I have been presenting here as an effect of voice. Generally speaking, any semiotic notion of character as a cipher, an inscription (which is the root meaning of the word character), cancels out this effect. But deconstructing Shakespeare does not make the question of voice disappear; it only reiterates its return in a counterplot.[32] In the mimetic narrative Cressida is the subject available to us through the medium of voice, consciously participating in transactions of political, military, and erotic exchange over which she has almost no control, left with little choice but to experience the full humiliation and self-destruction of her own desire. In the counterplot she is literally a figure of speech, an inanimate creature of ecriture, textual rather than sexual object circulating in male-stream Western culture from Homer through Chaucer, Lydgate, Caxton, and so forth. In the first plot, "voice" is the distinctive marker or carrier of personality, of human agency and desire. (This is palpably the case, of course, in the theater where voice is firmly embodied in the player.) In the counterplot, which occurs mainly in the theater of the mind, "voice," if it is anything at all, is a disembodied blank or trope, the trace of the poet's desire for representation, his claim to a certain space or status within a literary tradition. It is also the space for which critical commentary competes.

To tilt the balance strongly in the direction of the rhetorical counterplot (as I did in my earlier essay on this play[33]) strikes me today as not wrong but "blind" in de Man's sense of the blindness necessary to generate an insight; also "somdel deaf," like our protofeminist, the Wife of Bath. Both plots are of paramount concern to the responsible reader. One would not wish to sacrifice either the cool detachments of rhetorical analysis or the hot engagements of the sympathetic imagination. I am inclined to hypothesize that what I call plot and counterplot reflect and shadow each other just as our desire to acknowledge the other reflects and shades into our desire to appropriate the other. At all events, the problem of voice will not go away easily; its figurings and disfigurings return as surely as the repressed. And for a critical agenda that wishes to include the literary representation of voices—and women's voices in particular—it will simply not do to try to marginalize or leave unheard, by "rhetoricizing," the mimetic or affective pathos of any character.

Notes

I am very grateful, as always, to Ruth Nevo for many hours of stimulating conversation, and for assistance in controlling what threatened to become an interminably meandering essay. Thanks also to John Landau and Nita Schochet for vigilant reading. An early version of sections 3 and 4 of the essay was included in a talk given at the University of Connecticut, Storrs, in March 1991. I would like to thank William and Barbara Rosen for their kind reception and hospitality on that occasion.

1. All quotations, with the exception of *Troilus and Cressida,* are from *The Riverside Shakespeare,* ed. G. Blakemore Evans (Boston: Houghton, 1974).

2. Geoffrey Hartman, *Minor Prophecies: The Literary Essay in the Culture Wars* (Cambridge: Harvard University Press, 1991). Chap. 9 is entitled "The Philomela Project."

3. Sir Philip Sidney, *An Apologie for Poetrie* in *Elizabethan Critical Essays,* vol 1, ed. G. Gregory Smith (London: Oxford University Press, 1904), 165.

4. Ibid., 155.

5. Ibid., 159.

6. Murray Krieger, "Poetic Presence and Illusion: Renaissance Theory and the Duplicity of Metaphor," *Critical Inquiry* 5, no. 4 (summer 1979): 597–620, esp. 599.

7. *The Arte of English Poesie,* Facsimile Reproduction, ed. Baxter Hathaway (Kent, Ohio: Kent University Press, 1988), 246.

8. Paul de Man, "Autobiography as De-Facement," in *The Rhetoric of Romanticism* (New York: Columbia University Press, 1984), 76.

9. Puttenham, 190.

10. Margaret W. Ferguson, "*Hamlet:* Letters and Spirits," in *Shakespeare and the Question of Theory,* eds. Particia Parker and Geoffrey Hartman (New York and London: Methuen, 1985), 300. Ferguson's point is that Shakespeare asks us to see that "the desire to *interpret* literally, to find one single sense . . . leads to murder." My own point here is that Shakespeare asks us not only to ponder the way in which comic literalizing can "murder" a dramatic performance but also invites reflection on the uses and abuses of dramatic and rhetorical inventions.

11. Michel de Certeau, *The Practice of Everyday Life,* trans. Steven Rendall (Berkeley: University of California Press, 1984). "Everyday life," writes de Certeau in his introduction, "invents itself by *poaching* in countless ways on the property of others" (de Certeau, xii).

12. I have learned much about the paradoxical relationship between painting and poetry from Shimon Sandbank's essay "Poetic Speech and the Silence of Art" (*Comparative Literature* [forthcoming]). Sandbank discusses the relation between poems and paintings in terms of "absence and supersession" and his argument is that ekphrastic poets "exploit the lacunae of the visual medium to assert the power of their own." See also S. Clark Hulse, "'A Piece of Skilful Painting' in Shakespeare's 'Lucrece,'" *Shakespeare Survey* 31 (1978): 13–22, for useful reflections on the iconic.

13. Cf. Richard Lanham's reading of Lucrece in *The Motives of Eloquence: Literary Rhetoric in the Renaissance* (New Haven: Yale University Press, 1976), 94–110. Reading the poem as a study in dramatic motive, Lanham represents Lucrece as indulging in an obsessively histrionic drive that is the opposite of the critical detachment Lanham construes as being Shakespeare's ideal poetic paideia.

14. Nancy Vickers, "'The Blazon of Sweet Beauty's Best': Shakespeare's *Lucrece* (in *Shakespeare and the Question of Theory,* eds. Parker and Hartman, 95–115) has demonstrated brilliantly the complicity of rhetoric and narrative in appropriating Lucrece's body.

15. New Haven: Yale University Press, 1990.

16. All italics are mine.

17. Aristotle's *Rhetoric,* trans. W. Rhys Roberts (New York: Modern Library, 1954), 187, 190. See also Sidney's *Apologie,* 201.

18. On Hermes as a cunning and occasionally violent patron of interpreters (as well as thieves, merchants, and travelers) see Frank Kermode, *The Genesis of Secrecy: On the Interpretation of Narrative* (Cambridge: Harvard University Press, 1979), 1.

19. And, no, this citational awkwardness of layered and embedded quotation-within-quotation marks is *not* a typographical error, but necessitated by, and representative of, the drama of voice-appropriation that I am staging: Freund quoting Paglia quoting a feminist "Girl Scouts" quoting some anonymous or generic female "no."

20. All quotations from *Troilus and Cressida* are from the Arden edition, ed. Kenneth Palmer (London: Methuen, 1982).

21. See Vickers, 95–97 passim.

22. Which "encounterers"? The fleeting ambiguity is, I believe, revealing and resonant; it takes the rest of the sentence to clarify that by "these encounterers" (glossed by Palmer [247 n.] as "those who meet one halfway"). Ulysses does *not* mean the Greek generals who gave an "accosting welcome" to Cressida, but a class of brazen women like Cressida (or the fragments of body which represent her). The noun "encounter" may also refer to a fragment of language: it is a term in rhetoric for "antithesis" *(OED).*

23. The pun was noted by A. P. Rossiter, *Angel with Horns,* 1961; quoted by Palmer, 247–48 n.

24. Vickers, 96.

25. Ibid., 95.

26. See Rosalie Colie, *Shakespeare's Living Art* (Princeton, N.J.: Princeton University Press, 1974), 317–49.

27. Cf. Thersites' proleptic use of this strategy to perform a rhetorical evisceration of the inflated Ajax: "I will begin at thy heel, and tell what thou art by inches, thou thing of no bowels, thou!" (2.1.50–52).

28. Janet Adelman, *Suffocating Mothers: Fantasies of Maternal Origin in Shakespeare's Plays, Hamlet to The Tempest* (New York and London: Routledge, 1992), 46–50.

29. Ibid., 50.

30. Ibid.

31. See, for example, Gayle Greene, "Shakespeare's Cressida: 'A Kind of Self,'" in *The Woman's Part: Feminist Criticism of Shakespeare,* eds. Carolyn Ruth Swift Lenz, Gayle Greene, and Carol Thomas Neely (Urbana: University of Illinois Press, 1980), 133–49; Rene Girard, "The Politics of Desire in *Troilus and Cressida,*" in *Shakespeare and the Question of Theory,* eds. Partricia Parker and Geoffrey Hartman (New York and London: Methuen, 1985), 188–209; and Jan Kott, *Shakespeare Our Contemporary* (Garden City, N.Y.: Doubleday, 1966). 75–83. Incidentally, an august precursor of Cressida's "rehabilitation" was Dryden who transformed Cressida's victimization into an act of heroism. In the last act of his version of the play Cressida, on her father's advice, *pretends* to accept Diomed's addresses in order to find an opportunity of escaping from the Greek camp. Troilus believes her to be unfaithful, and she commits suicide—on the battlefield!

32. See Elizabeth Freund, "'Ariachne's Broken Woof': The Rhetoric of Citation in *Troilus and Cressida,*" in *Shakespeare and the Question of Theory,* eds. Parker and Hartman, pp. 19–36, esp. 24.

33. Ibid.

"War and Lechery Confound All": Identity and Agency in Shakespeare's *Troilus and Cressida*

Michael Yogev

SHAKESPEARE'S *Troilus and Cressida* has occasioned a number of critical discussions of the psychodynamics of identity formation as well as poststructuralist accounts of how its powerfully ambiguous and enigmatic language subverts identity.[1] To my knowledge, however, these two approaches have not been combined to analyze the way in which language and "heroic" activity at once constitute and subvert the identities of the protagonists in Shakespeare's bitter drama. Like Chaucer and Boccaccio before him, Shakespeare juxtaposes the martial plot of the Trojan War with the amorous tale of Troilus and Cressida. But in sharp contrast to his sources, Shakespeare lends neither Troilus or Cressida any tragic depth of character nor even the very qualified comic closure we may find in such figures as Angelo and Isabella from *Measure for Measure*. Instead, Shakespeare reduces this medieval love story to a sordid mirror of the Trojan War itself. As Thersites succinctly puts it, "War and lechery confound all" (*Troilus and Cressida*, 2.3.77).[2] This caustic characterization of the world of the play recognizes the connection between the psychodynamics of love and war at the same time as it lays bare a fundamental instability in the codes of courtly love and chivalric honor that underlie this central legend of Western literature. Thersites' remark highlights the sexual desire and aggression that "con-found," coconstitute the individual and collective identities in the play—even as they erode and threaten to annihilate those identities. In its dramatic presentation of the erotic disintegration of Troilus, and its biting critique of the heroic ethos of the Trojan War, Shakespeare's text at once anticipates and offers a useful critique of contemporary psychoanalytic explanations of the development of male subjectivity. The stark discrepancy between the heroic ideals and the ultimate lack of chivalric integrity in heroes like Achilles and Hector suggests that this Shakespearean text also leaves room for a more extensive examination into the psychological roots of chivalry and courtly love.

Valerie Traub has argued persuasively that a central element in the sexual dynamics of Shakespeare's plays is the erotic vulnerability of men in a society preoccupied with female chastity as a linchpin of patriarchal, patrilineal culture.[3] Discussing the act of sexual intercourse as the familiar Elizabethan pun on death, she points out that

> in the act of orgasm, male experience of the female body is not so much that of an object to be penetrated and possessed, but of an enclosure into which the male subject merges, dissolves, and in the early modern pun, dies. (Traub 1992, 27)

This analysis, together with her reference to the famous Sonnet 129, "The Expense of Spirit," leads her to conclude that male orgasm in fact underlines the "myth of the unity and self-identity of the masculine subject," and thereby leads to an intense male anxiety about female erotic mobility, which "threatens the process by which male subjectivity is secured" (Ibid., 27).

While Traub's analysis helps us understand the tyrannical fathers and pervasive male suspicion of apparently chaste female characters in Shakespeare's plays, her description of the male experience of orgasm closely resembles the Freudian pre-Oedipal narcissistic union between male infant and mother. This "myth" of male unity and self-identity may therefore be based (as many myths are) on a related psychological phenomenon—the primary narcissistic phase of a self undifferentiated from the body of the mother, which in turn gives way to the crucial transition from the mother/infant dyad into a discrete male identity and (m)other. It is precisely this phase of male psychological development that appears to me to offer a useful paradigm for an analysis of the grim dynamics of love and war in *Troilus and Cressida*.

In his essay, *Beyond the Pleasure Principle,* Freud relates an anecdote that he claims has caused him to ponder a psychic economy that may exceed his view of the dominance of the pleasure principle in the process of identity formation. Observing a young boy at play in what Freud calls a *fort/da* game, the child throws away and retrieves a small wooden spool, repeating this action numerous times in connection with its verbal signs, *fort* (gone) and *da* (there); the child's articulations are in fact only the vowels *o* and *a*, but Freud provides the terms.[4] Freud speculates that this game is a means for the boy to achieve agency (and hence a first stage of identity formation) despite—indeed precisely *through*—the fact that his mother has begun to leave home:

> The interpretation of the game then became obvious. It was related to the child's great cultural achievement—the instinctual renunciation (that is, the renunciation of instinctual satisfaction) which he had made in allowing his mother to go away without protesting. He compensated himself for this, as it were, by himself staging the disappearance and return of the objects within his reach. It is of course a matter of indifference from the point of view of judging the effective nature of the game whether the child invented it himself or took it over on some outside suggestion.[5]

Freud's language, as always, is as suggestive as the observed phenomenon itself. While the "effective" outcome of a nascent male subjectivity may not be altered by the game's origins, the affective character of the game itself is very intriguing. By viewing this as a "great cultural achievement" Freud hints at a broader dimension to this phase of the male infant's abdication of the primary narcissistic connection to his mother. But Freud leaves ambiguous the question of whether this game is autogenetic or culturally defined and inherited, a lingering ambiguity that marks the affective nexus of individual psychology and culture. In this discussion of the *fort/da* game, then, it is my impression that Freud not only outlines a paradigm of male subjectivity acquisition, but also begins to reveal the entangled roots of the codes of chivalry and courtly love that continue to inform modern culture. Hence, we should examine a bit more carefully that discussion.

This *fort/da* game may also be, Freud admits, an enactment of revenge on the mother for violating the primary narcissistic unity her child has hitherto felt with her:

> Throwing away the object so that it was "gone" might satisfy an impulse of the child's, which was suppressed in his actual life, to revenge himself on his mother for going away from him. In that case it would have a defiant meaning: "All right, then, go away! I don't need you. I"m sending you away myself."
>
> (Freud 1961, 9)

This aggression is likewise remarked by Lacan in what he terms the "Imaginary register," when the child remains caught in a realm of visual experience before moving into the "Symbolic" register of language.[6] Lacan's Imaginary register is the phase in which the child enters the "mirror stage" and

> sees an image of himself as something "other." . . . an ideal image, not only in the sense of the root connotation "visibility," but because it is in fact the image of someone perfectly formed. . . . Hence his earliest "image" of himself is not only alienated, but ideal. (Kopper 1988, 155)

Such an ideal image can cause a sense of inadequacy due to the discrepancy between the male child's experienced self and its ideal image. Shakespeare's Troilus evidences something akin to this sense of inferiority in the opening scene of *Troilus and Cressida*:

> Call here my varlet; I'll unarm again:
> Why should I war without the walls of Troy,
> That find such cruel battle here within?
> Each Trojan that is master of his heart,
> Let him to field; Troilus, alas! hath none.
> . . . .
> The Greeks are strong and skilful to their strength,
> Fierce to their skill and to their fierceness valiant;
> But I am weaker than a woman's tear,
> Tamer than sleep, fonder than ignorance,
> Less valiant than the virgin in the night
> And skilless as unpractis'd infancy.
> (*Troilus and Cressida*, 1.1.1–5, 7–12)

The "cruel battle within" and lack of mastery over his "heart" indicate that Troilus is caught in the Lacanian visual stage where he measures himself against an image of the ideal warrior and comes up wanting. Troilus' alienation from this ideal image is also connected to the phase of primary narcissism by his self-comparisons with abstract qualities cast in feminine terms ("weaker than a woman's tear," "Less valiant than the virgin in the night") rather than with specific male warriors or ideal role models. Troilus' "unpracticed infancy" is not, however, so much linguistic as chivalric; rather than suffering from an inability to attain the Symbolic register of language (in a play whose language is so pervasively deconstructive),[7] Troilus instead dramatizes the cultural as well as individual affect of a pre-Oedipal drive to deal with a disrupted self-image.

Elizabeth Bronfen indicates indirectly how the *fort/da* game appears to articulate a different dynamic of identity formation than that Lacan would tie to the achievement of the Symbolic register.[8] Remarking that Freud's child has learned "to obey laws before it has learned the language of those laws," Bronfen continues:

> What Freud sets up in this preliminary description, then, is a different scene in the developmental stages of a child from the one governed by an Oedipal complex, another narrative for the way in which language acquisition and subjectivity are grounded on an acknowledged experience of loss. For the negation that serves both as catalyst for the game and as object or reference of its articulation marks a site independent of the father's castrative "no." The anxiety-engendering symbolization and self-consciousness in this narrative is of another kind. Initially, there is not father in this game at all, not even an absent one. Though the child plays in an intermediary zone connecting the imaginary register of the mother/infant dyad (governed exclusively by unrestrained drives) and the symbolic register (governed by forbiddances), the anxiety at stake does not involve the father as the disrupting third element. (Bronfen 1989, 969)

This distinction of the *fort/da* game from the mirror stage is denied by Lacan; he laughs off the notion that the *objet à* or spool of Freud's game is anything but a part of the alienated subject which helps lead him into the symbolic phase.[9] But Freud himself is genuinely puzzled by one aspect of the *fort/da* game:

> The child cannot possibly have felt his mother's departure as something agreeable or even indifferent. How then does his repetition of this distressing experience as a game fit in with the pleasure principle? It may perhaps be said in reply that her departure had to be enacted as a necessary preliminary to her joyful return, and that it was in the latter that lay the true purpose of the game. But against this must be counted the observed fact that *the first act, that of departure, was staged as a game in itself and far more frequently than the episode in its entirety, with its pleasurable ending.* . . . (Freud, 9; my emphasis)

Precisely at this point in his essay, Freud makes his own observations on what Lacan extensively develops as the "mirror stage":

> A further observation subsequently confirmed this interpretation fully. One day the child's mother had been away for several hours and on her return was met with the words "Baby o-o-o-o!" which was at first incomprehensible. It soon turned out, however, that during this long period of solitude the child had found a method of making

himself disappear. He had discovered his reflection in a full-length mirror which did not quite reach to the ground, so that by crouching down he could make his mirror-image "gone". (Freud, n. 9)

What needs clarification here is precisely *which* "interpretation" of the *fort/da* game Freud's reading of this mirror stage fully confirms. There appears to be some deeper psychological compensation in the child's repetition of the first act itself, in the making "gone" of the spool/mother, and later of his causing his own image to vanish from the mirror. Lacan asserts that the repetition compulsion here simply confirms his sense of the *fort/da* game as equivalent to the mirror stage. As Barbara Freedman explains it,

> Even if the child associates his mother's absence with his playing at his own absence, the association itself doesn't imply an effort to master maternal loss. Rather, it suggests a discovery of his own presence as predicated upon absence, and so a splitting that alone makes self-reference possible.[10]

Lacan himself is insistent that the distinction between the *fort/da* game and the mirror stage is a moot one, as far as the constitution of subjectivity is concerned:

> If the young subject can practice this game of *fort/da*, it is precisely because he does not practice it at all, for no subject can grasp this radical articulation. He practices it with the help of a small bobbin, that is to say, with the *objet à*. The function of the exercise with this object [like the function of the mirror stage] refers to an alienation, and not to some supposed mastery, which is difficult to imagine being increased in an endless repetition, whereas the endless repetition that is in question reveals the radical vacillation of the subject.[11]

Shakespeare's text, however, *dramatizes* the "radical vacillation" of a number of male subjects, most prominently Troilus and Achilles. And *Troilus and Cressida* also presents the disturbing affective corollary of male subjectivity acquisition in an ethos of chivalry: erosion or erasure of female identity, particularly in the cases of Helen and Cressida. Precisely the same dynamic is involved in the transition of Freud's young boy from the *fort/da* game to the mirror stage, and in the remainder of this essay I will outline why poststructuralist and Lacanian analyses of Shakespeare's texts slight two very significant aspects of the play: its representation of the affect of desire, and the dramatic and psychological outcomes of that desire for male and female identity.

Shakespeare's Ulysses articulates the limits of the "mirror stage" in affective terms which suggest those I find so interesting from Freud's essay. Ulysses turns to mirrors—and language—to highlight the slippage of Achilles' stature and the subversion of his very identity among the Greeks:

> ... A strange fellow here
> Writes me: "That man, how dearly ever parted,
> How much in having, or without or in,
> Cannot make boast to have that which he hath,
> Nor feels not what he owes, but by reflection;
> As when his virtues shining upon others
> Heat them and they retort that heat again
> To the first giver."
>
> (*Troilus and Cressida*, 3.3.95–102)

We should note, however, that the "reflection" here is achieved only through the agency of the "others," not with a mirror that allows absenting and re-presenting of the self. The mirrors *are* others, and the "heat" is that generated by action, not by self-regard. Achilles, stung by the deliberate and exaggerated disregard of his fellow Greeks that has just been staged by Ulysses, acknowledges that the mirror is not sufficient to maintain the identity of the "man" he feels himself to be:

> The beauty that is borne here in the face
> The bearer knows not, but commends itself
> To others' eyes; nor doth the eye itself,
> That most pure spirit of sense, behold itself,
> Not going from itself; but eye to eye oppos'd
> Salutes each other with each other's form;
> For speculation turns not to itself,
> Till it hath travell'd and is mirror'd there
> Where it may see itself.
>
> (3.3.103–11)

The aural pun of "eye-I" is relevant here, for if we are speaking about the self-construction of identity, Achilles acknowledges that it must involve another "eye-I." In fact, "eye to eye opposed" and its punning variations constitute a matrix of identity strategies that are dramatically portrayed in the play: self-reflection ("I to I"), reflection via another ("I to eye"), reflection on/by an ideal image ("eye to I"), and reflection or identity via active combat ("eye to eye opposed"); that each of the terms of this punning matrix are open to alternative and slipping interpretations strengthens my contention that the basis of identity in such characters as Troilus and Achilles is far from stable, and that it requires an *active*, ongoing reinforcement.

Ulysses' investment in this discussion is not merely theoretical, but instrumental. He brings up the subject of mirrors to suggest the vanity of the greatest Greek warrior resting on his mere image, and by contrast he presents the image of the foolish Ajax as the "I" to whom Achilles is now opposed. To Achilles" irritated query, "what, are my deeds forgot?" Ulysses responds:

> . . . to have done is to hang
> Quite out of fashion, like a rusty mail
> In monumental mockery.
> . . . .
> The present eye praises the present object.
> Then marvel not, thou great and complete man,
> That all the Greeks begin to worship Ajax,
> Since things in motion sooner catch the eye
> Than what stirs not.
> (3.3.151–53, 180–84)

Shakespeare's text thus suggests, in Freudian terms, that the significance of the mirror stage lies in the male subject's active manipulation (and hence ongoing constitution) of his image. The affective dimension of this liminal phase of identity appears in the male characters" compulsion to continually measure themselves, in combat, "eye to eye opposed." While Kopper and other poststructuralists have focused on how language subverts the characters of the play, I propose to concentrate on how Troilus' jealous formulation of the Greeks as "Fierce to their skill and to their fierceness valiant" articulates an affective frustration. Shakespeare's play indeed seems to me to depict a both unconscious and explicit desire on the part of the male protagonists to continuously re-present themselves in the "mirror" of battle. Moreover, *Troilus and Cressida* painfully represents the reliance of chivalry and courtly love on a return to the reiterated first term of the *fort/ da* game, a compulsion to make the (m)other *fort* or absent as a vain (in both its senses) attempt to constitute male identity. By deliberately maintaining as *fort* or "gone" the (female) object of their desire, the male protagonists inaugurate the potentially interminable "game" of martial combat, the only means through which their honor and distinction can be maintained.

Elizabeth Bronfen's summary of the work of Melanie Klein and

D. W. Winnicott may provide insights into the complex dynamics of Shakespeare's knights' relationship to their "ladies." Recognizing the narcissistic wound that separation from the mother represents for the male infant, both Klein and Winnicott suggest that this wound engenders a latent violence and is countered by the construction of an idealized "internal mother" who neither threatens to engulf or to completely abandon the child. This "internal mother" then allows the male child to make the transition from an undifferentiated world centered in his union with the mother's body to the cultured external world of objects and signs. What Bronfen usefully highlights, however, is the paradox that the stability and effectiveness of Klein's "internal mother" is "contingent on the fact that the material maternal body is already fading before the child's ego":

> Thus a stable relation to the external cultured world not only doubles an internal stability, but in both instances stability is gained through a moment of destruction and loss. I wish to emphasize that Klein sees this emotional trajectory—from destructive impulse, through idealization and denial, to the ambivalent sense of guilty yet triumphant omnipotence in respect to a potentially wounding other—as "the central position in the child's development," a step in the process of organization and integration that is parallel to but different from and other than sexual development. (Bronfen 1989, 974)

Winnicott, for his part, addresses the Freudian *fort/da* game directly, seeing in the spool of the game a "transitional object,"

> representing the child's transition from a state of being merged with the mother to a state of being in relation to the mother as something outside and separate, representing, that is, a wounding of the purely narcissistic type of object relating. (Ibid., 974)

Bronfen's analysis of Winnicott then elaborates how this wounding is overcome by the stability of the returned object now invested as an loving, dependable, and amenable "internal mother." For Winnicott, then, the ultimate significance of the *fort/da* game is that "the child gains reassurance about the fate of his internal mother,"

> that is, that this internal representation will not fade, will not become meaningless. . . . Winnicott significantly shifts his interest from body to image—not the maternal body to be secured from fading, but rather the child's internal image. I would add that, if what is secured

as "reliable" in the process of this game is the internal image created of the mother, then what is also secured is the child's ability to create. Thus the substitution from real, external maternal body to internal representation and external symbol (transitional object) is one that includes the move from disappearing/reappearing mother to revenging/representing child. (Ibid., 975)

What emerges from Bronfen's able summary of the work of these two analysts is a paradigm of normal male subjectivity development. But the world of *Troilus and Cressida* is, as Pandarus continually points out, one of disease. Indeed, what we witness in *Troilus and Cressida* may be seen as a process of personal and cultural infantilization, in which the male protagonists cannot achieve a stable sense of identity due to the discrepancy between the women in their lives and the "internal image" of Woman they hold as a chivalric culture. Shakespeare's male characters, with the single exception of Pandarus (whose very name embodies the principle of constant transition and "trans-action") are fixated in the first phases of *fort/da* and mirror games, suggesting perhaps a summary judgment of the ethos of chivalry and courtly love that Shakespeare so often questions in his work.

What sets off Homer's account of the Trojan War from that of Shakespeare is precisely their different "internal image" of the most significant (m)other of the legend, Helen. While both sides to the conflict in *Troilus and Cressida* see Helen as the effective cause of the nine years' siege of Troy, they have nevertheless all but abandoned her as the basis of their justifications for this ongoing battle. This indeed makes her the sort of transitional object just described, but the problem is that Helen herself, in Shakespeare's version, if far from inspiring the sort of noble internal image of beauty that she represents in Homer. Shakespeare's Greek Diomedes describes Helen as he delivers a caustic formulation of the dynamic that has perpetuated the war. To Paris' question of who most deserves Helen, he or Meneleus, Diomedes replies in very unidealized terms:

> Both alike:
> He merits well to have her that doth seek her,
> Not making any scruple of her soilure,
> With such a hell of pain and world of charge;
> And you as well to keep her that defend her,
> Not palating the taste of her dishonour,
> With such a costly loss of wealth and friends.
> He, like a puling cuckold, would drink up

> The lees and dregs of a flat tamed piece;
> You, like a lecher, out of whorish loins
> Are pleased to breed out your inheritors.
> Both merits pois"d, each weighs nor less nor more;
> But he as thee, each heavier for a whore.
> *(Troilus and Cressida,* 4.1.55–67)

Shakespeare's text depicts a Helen vain to the point of being insipid, in contrast with Homer's portrayal of her as noble and inspiringly beautiful. In either case, however, the function of Helen is more significant than her identity, for Shakespeare and Homer alike the tale of Troy is one of the achievement and exercise of male agency, not of the redress of promiscuity. Shakespeare's Hector bluntly expresses the opinion that Helen herself is a "thing" not worth the cost of keeping:

> . . . Let Helen go.
> Since the first sword was drawn about this question
> Every tithe soul "mongst many thousand dismes,
> Hath been as dear as Helen—I mean, of ours.
> If we have lost so many tenths of ours
> To guard a thing not ours nor worth to us. . . .
> (2.2.17–22)

For his part, however, Troilus immediately translates the loss of Helen into the loss of his father's and, by extension, of all Troy's honor (an ambiguity of identity instituted by a combination of Elizabethan political theory and the chivalric ethos):

> Fie, fie, my brother!
> Weigh you the worth and honour of a king
> So great as our dread father's in a scale
> Of common ounces? Will you with counters sum
> The past-proportion of his infinite,
> And buckle in a waist most fathomless
> With spans and inches so diminutive
> As fears and reasons? Fie, for godly shame!
> (2.2.25–32)

Hector's reply is one that indicates, similar to Freud, the psychological logic of completing the *fort/da* game. He recognizes the legitimacy of Menelaus' desire to regain Helen:

> . . . Nature craves
> All dues be render"d to their owners: now,

> What nearer debt in all humanity
> Than wife is to the husband? If this law
> Of nature be corrupted through affection,
> And that great minds, of partial indulgence
> To their benumbed wills, resist the same,
> There is a law in each well-order"d nation
> To curb those raging appetites that are
> Most disobedient and refractory.
> If Helen then be wife to Sparta's king,
> As it is known she is, these moral laws
> Of nature and of nations speak aloud
> To have her back return'd: thus to persist
> In doing wrong extenuates not wrong,
> But makes it much more heavy.
>
> (2.2.174–89)

Yet while this is "Hector's opinion . . . in way of truth" (2.2.189–90), he nonetheless acquiesces in Troilus's appeal to their collective and personal honor as sufficient justification for keeping Helen as one of the "counters," in effect perpetuating her as *fort* in the chivalric game. She is *fort* for the Trojans as an "theme," and literally *fort* for the Greeks; on both sides her status as a cathected object of the game induces them to continue the war and thereby burnish their identities:

> My spritely brethren, I propend to you
> In resolution to keep Helen still,
> For 'tis a cause that hath no mean dependance
> Upon our joint and several dignities.
>
> (2.2.191–94)

Troilus seconds Hector's chivalric resolve to *not* end the conflict over Helen in terms that suggest an answer to Freud's question about the more numerous repetitions of the "departure" phase of the *fort/da* game:

> Why, there you touch'd the life of our design:
> Were it not glory that we more affected
> Than the performance of our heaving spleens,
> I would not wish a drop of Trojan blood
> Spent more in her defence. But, worthy Hector,
> She is a theme of honour and renown,
> A spur to valiant and magnanimous deeds,
> Whose present courage may beat down our foes,
> And fame in time to come canonize us
>
> (2.2.195–203)

The slight syntactic ambiguity of "Whose" here is symptomatic; it cannot refer to Helen, so it must refer to the "deeds" that become then the only way to constitute an enduring fame, to "canonize" their identity.

Hector not only endorses this cathexis of Helen as a "theme of honour and renown," but personally demonstrates its affective dynamic in his earlier challenge of the Greeks to single combat, delivered by Aeneas to the Greek camp:

> If there be one among the fair'st of Greece
> That holds his honour higher than his ease,
> That feeds his praise more than he fears his peril,
> That knows his valour and knows not his fear,
> That loves his mistress more than in confession
> With truant vows to her own lips he loves,
> And dare avow her beauty and her worth
> In other arms than hers—to him this challenge:
> Hector, in view of Trojans and of Greeks,
> Shall make it good, or do his best to do it,
> He hath a lady, wiser, fairer, truer,
> Than ever Greek did compass in his arms,
> And will tomorrow with his trumpet call
> Midway between your tents and walls of Troy,
> To rouse a Grecian that is true in love.
> If any come, Hector shall honour him:
> If none, he'll say in Troy, when he retires,
> The Grecian dames are sunburnt and not worth
> The splinter of a lance. Even so much.
> (1.3.264–82)

The terms of address and challenge here collapse the courtly love ethos with the chivalry that idealizes Woman—but often demonizes actual women. Shakespeare's text continually presents the masculine heroes with the troubling discrepancy of their ideal Woman contrasted with those very real women in their lives. Hector's reaction to his own wife, Andromache (so chivalrically evoked in the above passage), who begs him not to fight due to her foreboding dreams, is dismissive to the point of being rude: "You train me to offend you; get you in" (5.3.4). Their ideal of Woman is what convinces the Trojans to continue to hold Helen, and the terms of Hector's challenge clearly reflect how such idealizations provide the psychosocial groundwork for chivalric action. Helen is the lover of Paris and the kidnapped wife of Menelaus, but she has become a "theme of honour and renown," due only to her status as "A spur to valiant and magnanimous *deeds*." Neither

Hector nor his brothers will heed the dire warnings of Cassandra, their prophetic sister, for they are all, as Hector aptly puts it, "in the vein of chivalry" (5.3.32)—the pun on "vain" is psychologically telling.

Among the Greeks, the issue has almost stopped being Helen; the stalemated battle is the pressing problem. Achilles has been insulted by Agamemnon, and therefore refuses to take the field. In *The Iliad*, the insult to Achilles is Agamemnon's arbitrary decision to take the maiden, Briseis, from him after Agamemnon has been compelled to return one Chryseis, the daughter of a priest of Apollo, to her father. These two women are cousins, and they have in fact been tied to the emergence of Cressida in medieval legend, for there is no mention of her in the classic myths; she is in fact invented as eponymous of female treachery. Cressida's identity is hence even more ambiguous than Helen's, but her function will be much the same. Both Helen and Cressida become, in Shakespeare's text, a form of "anti–ideal image," so we should not be surprised that the male characters who base their identity to some degree on these women, even as objects, suffer from varying degrees of "dis-ease." In its representation of the medieval tale from Chaucer and Boccaccio, Shakespeare's text suggests a critique of the objectification of these women as part of the "gear" essential for the ongoing constitution of male identity in the chivalric world.

Our first glimpse of the Greeks (*Troilus and Cressida*, 1.3) opens with Agamemnon outlining the progress of the long and costly war and Ulysses continuing with the famous speech on the decay of degree as the chief explanation for the stalemate. Agamemnon, the king of the Greeks, discusses at length the need for "persistive constancy in men" (1.3.21) a solidity of character the martial dimensions of which he constructs in a metaphor:

> . . . in the wind and tempest of her frown,
> Distinction, with a broad and powerful fan
> Puffing at all, winnows the light away,
> And what hath mass or matter by itself
> Lies rich in virtue and unmingled.
>
> (1.3.26–30)

The metaphor's physical lack of substance (mass and matter) and feminine gender are significant here, for Agamemnon's wind of distinction is to reveal male identity; "mass and matter" accrue only to male warriors who (as we have already seen in Ulysses' discussion with Achilles) persist in their combat.

For his part, Troilus is also anxious about "distinction." Imagining his first meeting with Cressida, Troilus' fear that "I shall lose distinction in my joys" (*Troilus and Cressida*, 3.2.25) voices a concern for self-presence that is threatened in the "death" of sexual intercourse. But the distinction between these two "distinctions" collapses in Cressida's most candid moment of the play, which Shakespeare masterfully places just prior to the political and philosophical discussions of Agamemnon and Achilles:

> Things won are done; joy's soul lies in the doing.
> That she beloved knows nought that knows not this:
> Men prize the thing ungain'd more than it is. . . .
> (1.2.282–84)

Cressida here formulates the role women as objects of desire play in the constitution of male identity, and hence in the establishment of the "distinction" essential to any assessment of degree. Cressida recognizes the insubstantial or "thing" status of women in both the martial and marital plots, and the necessity for these things to be "ungain'd" in order to provoke and perpetuate male agency and desire. Joy (like its obverse, grief) is an intense experience of self-presence. Cressida outlines here the psychological roots of the idealization of Woman in the ethos of chivalry and courtly love, where she is at once desired and (at least initially) elevated above any actual possession or "en-joy-ment." Indeed, the desire of the beloved is "lust in action" until that beloved is in fact achieved, at which point the male lover may recoil from the experience that constitutes a death of that intenser self founded on desire:

> Enjoy'd no sooner but despised straight;
> Past reason hunted; and no sooner had,
> Past reason hated, as a swallowed bait,
> On purpose laid to make the taker mad:
> Mad in pursuit, and in possession so;
> Had, having, and in quest to have, extreme;
> A bliss in proof, and proved, a very woe.
> (Sonnet 129, l.4–10)

As we have seen, Troilus sounds the most strident note of "joint and several honour," so we are not surprised to see from the opening scene of the play that his individual sense of honor—

hence identity—is unstable. His deeds have not matched his heroic aspirations early in the play, a fact underscored by the debunking comments of Cressida in response to Pandarus' panegyrics in praise of Troilus (*Troilus and Cressida*, 1.1.256–276). Troilus is fixated in the Lacanian Imaginary register, where he must face both his ideal figure (and the figures of heroes like Hector and Achilles) and the real figure he has cut to this point. The discrepancy is painful, so he seeks a different mirror, or rather another object through which to attempt to constitute his identity. In effect, he has regressed in Freudian terms, moving back from the mirror stage to that of the *fort/da* game. Now the object against/through which he will establish his identity is Cressida, the amorous "counter" to his martial desire for honor. The terms in which he imagines their first "en-counter" are fraught with anxiety:

> I am giddy; expectation whirls me round.
> Th'imaginary relish is so sweet
> That it enchants my sense: what will it be
> When that the wat'ry palate tastes indeed
> Love's thrice repured nectar? Death, I fear me,
> Sounding destruction, or some joy too fine,
> Too subtle-potent, tuned too sharp in sweetness
> For the capacity of my ruder powers.
> I fear it much; and I do fear besides
> That I shall lose distinction in my joys,
> As doth a battle, when they charge on heaps
> The enemy flying.
>
> (3.2.16–27)

In effect, Troilus here is the little boy contemplating the joy of the again present (*da*) (m)other, of a completely restored primary narcissism through total union with the maternal body (the metaphors of "wat'ry palate" and "sounding destruction" are only a few of the liquid, dissolving images associated with the female body in this play). Particularly in Chaucer but also in Shakespeare's text, Cressida emerges as a sexually experienced and worldly wise woman, a point Pandarus highlights in exasperation when he exclaims at her witty debunking of his fulgent descriptions of Troilus, "You are such another" (1.2.266). Cressida represents for Troilus not so much an other sexual conquest as "sounding destruction" and "some joy too fine," the paradoxical experience of psychic dissolution and intense joy in union with the (m)other. Troilus explicitly conflates Cressida with the figure of the mother in his shocked exchange with Ulysses after she has gone over to the Greek camp:

Ulysses. . . . Cressid was here but now.
Troilus. Let it not be believ'd for womanhood!
Think, we had mothers; do not give advantage
To stubborn critics, apt, without a theme
For depravation, to square the general sex
By Cressid's rule: rather, think this not Cressid.
(5.2.127–32)

The battlefield simile he has chosen to express this loss of distinction further indicates the interrelated character of courtly love and chivalric action. Both of these codes of male honor and distinction are, paradoxically, threatened by the prospect of Troilus actually *achieving* Cressida, or of Helen being returned to the Greeks by force of arms.[12]

When he finally does meet with Cressida, Troilus' imagined possession of her robs him of any symbolic distinction from her, leading him back to a preverbal phase of primary narcissism: "You have bereft me of all words, lady" (3.2.54). Again Shakespeare seems to have intuitively anticipated Freud and his interpreters, for now Troilus attempts to constitute a ideal image of himself prior to the physical union with Cressida, speaking of his "integrity and truth" as "true as truth's simplicity / And simpler than the infancy of truth" (3.2.163,167–68); his metaphor of childhood represents a return to the presexual phase of Freud's *fort/da* game, a desire for narcissistic union and not sexual conquest. Cressida, for her part, is allowed only negative formulations of her fidelity: ". . . let them say, to stick the heart of falsehood, / "As false as Cressid" (3.2.193–94).

Pandarus reinforces the dynamic tension of the courtly lover's simultaneous desire to have the woman of his idealized vision and the urge to "hold I off" (Cressida's turn of phrase is equally true of the male protagonists in the play), thereby maintaining the distinction that is threatened by their union. Pandarus, true to his name, recognizes and attempts to break the courtly stalemate Troilus and Cressida seem to have entered, even as he ironically voices the theme of deeds over words that I view as so central to the play, a critique of too close a focus on language at the expense of the dramatic plot:

Words pay no debts, give her deeds: but she'll bereave you o' the deeds too, if she call your activity in question.
(3.2.55–57)

The activity she will call into question is in effect Troilus' own imagined version of the *fort/da* game, for he will soon become the victim of the inevitable narcissistic wound, the unavoidable loss of the (m)other.

After Cressida rather falteringly admits her love for Troilus, the courtly love tradition of the lady remaining aloof and untouchable begins to break down, and yet both Cressida and Troilus appear to "hold I off" yet a bit longer. One of Cressida's remarks that has become a favorite of those who would attack her touches upon this stasis and destabilization at the same time as it reinscribes the *fort/da* paradigm I have been discussing—but this time from the (m)other's perspective:

> I have a kind of self resides with you,
> But an unkind self, that itself will leave
> To be another's fool. I would be gone:
>
> (3.2.146–49)

Kind as kinship or relation in human terms is a common Shakespearean pun, but here we find an ironic depth in Cressida's use of the term to describe her imminent connection with, and yet ultimate distinction from, Troilus. Deborah Hooker, discussing at length the nuances of the term *kind,* remarks usefully that in speaking of her "unkind self" Cressida is asserting "that part of herself, that region not specularized, not mirror-imaged, not resident in man, her "un-man-kind self"—the feminine."[13] It is as if the cathected object of the *fort/da* game, the (m)other made into a spool, now articulates the fundamental ambivalence of many Shakespearean heroines toward their comic or tragic situation as the means whereby male identity and agency are constituted.[14] The fragmented subjectivity she articulates here is one of Shakespeare's most keen anticipations of the bind of being an object of cathexis (an "un-kind self"), a lover and/or mother ("a kind of self resides with you") and a counter in the games men play to assert their identity ("I would be gone"). Hooker states succinctly the psychology of the chivalric world and the role Cressida and other women play in it:

> Though the men of Greece and Troy, Troilus chief among them, fight in the name of women, what truly motivates them is a compulsion toward transcendence, to finally out-appetite appetite. This compulsion, ironically, invokes Irigaray's definition of hysteria.... Male hysteria manifests as an inescapable fixity, a paralysis-through-action,

an inability to respond to any given situation outside the parameters prescribed by the male/warrior status quo. (Hooker 1989, 923)

Ulysses himself describes the self-perpetuating aspect of chivalric appetite in terms that are, ironically, intended to reestablish a proper sense of "degree" and identity as inherent in noble characters and paternal hierarchy, rather than being based merely in the brute achievements of "power:"

> Power into will, will into appetite,
> And appetite, an universal wolf,
> So doubly seconded with will and power,
> Must make perforce an universal prey,
> And last eat up himself.
>
> (1.3.120–24)

Ulysses has in fact been addressing what Hooker calls "paralysis-through-action," the stalemated war for Troy that neither side can appear to win. But winning is not the point, in fact; the alternative to the unbridled ambition/appetite he describes and the perpetual warfare it institutes is to find "a theme of honour and renown" through which to legitimate the ongoing warfare and somehow ennoble it. As we have seen, this involves a reinscription of the woman as an object that, paradoxically, must never in fact be won—"joy's soul lies in the doing."

On the morning after Troilus has finally "won" Cressida, the decision to send Cressida over to her father in the Greek camp has already been made. Thus, while the psychocultural machinations are at work to make Cressida a pawn in the male games of war, on the individual level we also see an affect of separation in Troilus himself. Standing outside the room in which their union occurred, when he is approached by Cressida, Troilus attempts to convince her to leave him and go back inside. Speaking in high, courtly terms, he nonetheless betrays a certain violence in his invocation to her to let "Sleep kill those pretty eyes" (again, a pun on "eye-I"?), and in a concise formulation of the narcissistic state of total union/oblivion: "As infants empty of all thought" (4.2.4–6). She, however, will not be put off so facilely:

> *Cressida:* Are you a-weary of me?
> *Troilus:* O Cressida! but that the busy day,
>   Waked by the lark, hath roused the ribald crows,

> And dreaming night will hide our joys no longer,
> I would not from thee.
>
> (4.2.8–11)

Beneath his "I would not from thee" and his adjective "ribald"[15] we may read a desire to push her away from him, and Cressida reacts to what is clearly a sense of postcoital distance in his tone, remarking almost bitterly:

> Prithee, tarry:
> You men will never tarry.
> O foolish Cressid! I might have still held off,
> And then you would have tarried.
>
> (4.2.15–18)

More telling yet, however, is the flat tone of Troilus's response to the news that Cressida must go over to the Greek camp that very morning: "Is it so concluded?" is all he asks, and he then muses, "How my achievements mock me!" (4.2.68,71). The latter comment is indeed the heart of the matter, in psychological terms: Shakespearean men must look to "achievements" to constitute masculine identity, and while achievements may constitute them, in themselves they are as "rusty mail" for an idle Achilles, paradoxically inadequate and even subversive of identity. Hence, the love and war games must go on. Endless repetition is the only answer to a self-subversive mockery, and the spool/other must be sent *fort* again.

Troilus's rage is now directed toward the masculine figures who make Cressida their own object of desire. He does not evidence the extreme lover's grief that Cressida so movingly expresses (4.2.99–112). Instead, he questions her fidelity in a painfully repetitive insistence, "Be thou true" (4.4.61,64,65,73); we may see here precisely the process of Klein's ideal or internal (m)other being established. She must be true *for* him, not to him, and her anguished cry "O heavens, you love me not!" (4.2.81) is one of the deep truths of the play. Troilus sounds a chivalric warrior's challenge to Diomedes, and the latter's response to Cressida is only a function of the intensity and degree of Troilus' threat; the men have now established their identities as warriors, and Cressida will become no more significant than the glove Troilus gives to her—and that she ultimately gives to Diomedes.

Once she is in the Greek camp, Troilus' idealized and internalized image of her is radically undermined by her behavior. In this new dramatic context, we no longer have any view of her interior self, but can only uneasily calculate her exchange value as an object sent off and retrieved, lost and won. The scene in which she is welcomed by being kissed in common by all those present in the Greek camp would seem to totally undo any "kind" interpretation of her character. But Shakespeare's genius here is to recognize that her function in the psychocultural drama I have been describing has now changed. Cressida has become as little a "character" as his thinly depicted Helen. Both are merely "daughters of the game" (4.5.63) as Ulysses disgustedly puts it.

Indeed, immediately following the scene that begins the process of Cressida's denigration, we witness Hector arriving in a formal challenge, and hear Aeneas' inflated chivalric rhetoric underlining the two sides' view of themselves as noble "knights" (4.5.65–86). The same Ulysses who only moments before has described Cressida and other "daughters of the game" with undisguised loathing now waxes Homeric to set forth the chivalric warriors from Troy, including Troilus himself:

> The youngest son of Priam, a true knight;
> Not yet mature, yet matchless; firm of word,
> Speaking in deeds, and deedless in his tongue;
> Not soon provok'd, nor, being provok'd, soon calm'd;
> His heart and hand both open and both free;
> For what he has he gives, what thinks he shows;
> Yet gives he not till judgment guide his bounty,
> Nor dignifies an impare thought with breath;
> Manly as Hector, but more dangerous;
> For Hector in his blaze of wrath subscribes
> To tender objects, but he in heat of action
> Is more vindicative than jealous love.
>
> (4.5.96–107)

All the terms of the praise here are active, even those of an internal character ("Speaking in deeds," "what thinks he shows"), and in his loss of Cressida, then, Troilus has gained the chief distinction he holds in the eyes of his enemies, "dangerous." Because he has suffered his final disillusionment in the ideal, internal (m)other, his cry "This is and is not Cressid" (5.3.145) indeed indicates how dangerous he will become as a male stuck in the hysteria of chivalric honor and action. In his discussion with Hector in act 5, scene 3 about whether he will fight, Troilus confirms his sense of masculine identity and agency; both the brothers are "in the vein of chivalry" (5.3.32), and their vanity will not brook the misgivings or even the mention of the women with whom they have shared a constitutive bond. Shakespeare's Ulysses is the most callous example of this disregard of women, for he undercuts any sense of Cressida (or Helen) as particular, whole characters; they are simply "daughters of the game." Troilus' real pain over the loss of Cressida sets the stage for him to seek other "achievements" that will not "mock him," just as the male child in Freud's *fort/da* game overcomes his grief at his mother's departure by first playing the game, then moving into a mirror stage that effectively substitutes self-presence for the absence of the (m)other.

More poignantly, however, Troilus here may also serve as a resonant figure for Freud himself. As Bronfen points out, Freud represses the fact that the mother and child of his essay, *Beyond the Pleasure Principle,* are in fact his own daughter, Sophie, and his grandson, Ernst. Sophie died at the age of twenty-six of influenzal pneumonia, "snatched away," in Freud's own words, "from glowing health, from her busy life as a capable mother and loving wife, in four or five days, as if she had never been" (Freud, 961). For Freud this event is a true crisis, for his grief threatens to paralyze him. He writes to Ernest Jones in a letter from 8 February 1920 that

> You know of the misfortune that has befallen me. It is depressing indeed, a loss to be forgotten. . . . Now I may be declining in power of thought and expression, why not? Everyone is liable to decay in the course of time." (Freud, 962)

Bronfen sees this as Freud's "rhetorical move from the Other to the self," a personalizing of the loss as a sign of his own vulnerability and mortality. But, she continues, this movement from the Other to the self also inaugurates a new phase and strategy of identity. Linking this moment to Lacan's analysis of the "destability" of the subject in the mirror stage, Bronfen points out that

> what is also contained in this second version of the [*fort/da*] game, not usually noted by critics, is the notion of imaging as a moment of erasure of the Other when this Other is substituted for an image of the self. (Bronfen, 976)

This accords well with Freud's own reaction to this terrible event, for rather than sink into a paralysis of grief, he plunges into his work—ironically enough, work on the essay that deals with his daughter and grandson, *Beyond the Pleasure Principle.* Like Troilus, Freud fears losing his distinction as the eminent psychologist and therapist in his terrible grief over Sophie's death, so again like Troilus (and Ernst), he engages in activity that simultaneously constitutes him as agent or actor while depersonalizing and finally erasing one of the women most close to his heart. Sophie is consigned to the status of an anonymous mother in a footnote, the same note in which Freud points out that what he earlier called the young boy's successful "cultural achievement" in accepting his mother's departure, has now become the fact that he evidences no grief over the real death of his mother (Freud, 10).[16]

The repressed always returns, however, for in his immersion into the writing of this little essay, Freud writes the story of his own struggle to gain and maintain his intellectual distinction and fame—over the dead body of his daughter, the "scar" in the footnote (Bronfen, 983). Indeed, the most significant parallel between Freud and Troilus is that the impending or actual removal of a beloved woman catalyzes their identity strategies at that same time as it erodes the subjectivity and individuality of the woman on whom those identities are at least initially and partially contingent. This is, and is not Cressid; even the elimination of the last vowel participates in her erasure as a fully human being in the male world of Shakespeare's play, and Freud more authoritatively yet expunges all reference to the identity of his daughter, focusing instead on little Ernst who has achieved a rather pathetic place in the symbolic order, the world of the Father and its chivalric laws of male self-constitution. Sophie Freud is one of the literal "daughters of the game," and Cressida is her invented and demonized literary sister.

The Trojan War, as a reiterated *fort/da* game played with the women whose presence/absence and erasure perpetuated it, emerges and reemerges throughout the culture of patrimony. The endurance of its chivalric renunciation/aggression complex in Western culture is remarkable,[17] enacted by Shakespeare's Troilus (heir to the medieval invention and demonization of Cressida, by Freud in his erasure of a daughter in service of his prestige and identity, and by any of the many variations of pre- and post-Rambos via the bodies of often anonymous, objectified, and/or dead women. This *fort/da* complex reflects a fundamental insecurity at the core of the male identity, which leads to compulsive attempts at reaffirmation through, on the one hand, the agency achieved in the patriarchal exchange of women, and on the other hand, through the competitive emulations of the mirror stage—in which the woman is simply erased. Neither strategy is wholly successful, however, in a world of "war and lechery," and Shakespeare's particular genius is to allow Pandarus the role of chorus at the close of his play. Eponymous of the uneasy traffic in desire that both determines and subverts male identity, Pandarus indeed can only promise one thing to a culture unwilling to acknowledge the voice of the "unkind" (m)other: an unbroken legacy of "dis-eases."

Notes

1. Most notable among the psychoanalytic approaches that also address the dramatic function of the characters' (particularly Cressida's) strategies of identity in the play are James O'Rourke, "'Rule in Unity' and Otherwise: Love and Sex in *Troilus and Cressida*," *Shakespeare Quarterly* 43, no. 2 (summer 1992); and Janet Adelman, "'This Is and Is Not Cressid': The Characterization of Cressida," in *The (M)other Tongue*, eds. Shirley Nelson Garner, Claire Kahane, and Madelaine Sprengnether (Ithaca: Cornell University Press, 1985), 119–41; a revised and expanded version of this essay appears in her *Suffocating Mothers: Fantasies of Maternal Origin in Shakespeare's Plays*, Hamlet to The Tempest (London: Routledge, 1992). See also Carol Cook, "Unbodied Figures of Desire," in *Performing Feminisms: Feminist Critical Theory and Theatre*, ed. Sue Ellen Case (Baltimore: Johns Hopkins University Press, 1990); Linda Charnes, "'So Unsecret to Ourselves': Notorious Identity and the Material Subject in Shakespeare's *Troilus and Cressida*," *Shakespeare Quarterly* 40 (1989); and Douglas B. Wilson, "The Commerce of Desire: Freudian Narcissism in Chaucer's *Troilus and Criseyde* and Shakespeare's *Troilus and Cressida*", *ELN*, Sept. 1983. More specifically deconstructive accounts of *Troilus and Cressida* are Gayle Greene's "Language and Value in Shakespeare's *Troilus and Cressida*," *SEL* 21 (1981); and Elizabeth Freund, "'Ariachne's Broken Woof': The Rhetoric of Citation in *Troilus and Cressida*," in *Shakespeare and the Question of Theory*, eds. Patricia Parker and Geoffrey Hartman (New York and London: Methuen, Inc. 1985) other deconstructive accounts of the play appear in the following notes. Coppélia Kahn's valuable study, *Man's Estate: Masculine Identity in Shakespeare* (Berkeley: University of California Press, 1981), while not discussing *Troilus and Cressida* at any length, provides an essential background to my more specific focus on the psychodynamics of chivalry.
2. All quotations from *Troilus and Cressida* are from the Arden Shakespeare edition, ed. Kenneth Palmer (1982; reprint, London: Routeledge, 1989).
3. Valerie Traub, *Desire and Anxiety: Circulations of Sexuality in Shakespearean Drama* (London: Routledge, 1992). The discussion of these fundamental sexual characteristics of late Elizabethan England occurs in chap. 1, esp. 27–28.
4. Derrida discusses this eruption of the paternal into the prelingual world of the child at length in his early essay on *Beyond the Pleasure Principle*, "Coming Into One's Own," trans. James Hulbert, in *Psychoanalysis and the Question of the Text*, ed. Geoffrey Hartman (Baltimore: Johns Hopkins University Press, 1978), 127–28.
5. All quotations from Freud are from *Beyond the Pleasure Principle*, trans. James Strachey (New York: Norton, 1961).
6. This discussion of Lacan is drawn in part from John M. Kopper, "Troilus at Pluto's Gates: Subjectivity and the Duplicity of Discourse in Shakespeare's *Troilus and Cressida*," in *Shakespeare and Deconstruction*, eds. G. Douglas Atkins

and David M. Bergeron (New York: Peter Lang Publishing, 1988), 149–71. My basic contention, however, is that Kopper and others who read *Troilus and Cressida* as a play whose subversion of identity and values is to be found in language miss the psychologically cogent aspect of the actual drama, the action of the play, which is primarily that of the amorous encounter between Troilus and Cressida, her exchange for Antenor, and all the chivalric posturing and vengeful activity around the Trojan and Greek camps than accompany them. In a sense, I am using the words of the play to attempt to approach a preverbal analysis of the roots of the ethos of chivalry, an ethos of which *Troilus and Cressida* constitutes a devastating critique.

7. Kopper's essay finally takes essentially this position, arguing that the dissolution of order in the play is the result of a lack of the Lacanian "Law of the Father," an erosion of authority systems. But his remark that "*Troilus and Cressida* enacts the moment of transition from comedy to tragedy, the fence on which confused editors have abandoned the play" (Kopper, 163) posits a sort of generic ambiguity to Shakespeare's dramatic examinations of chivalry and courtly love that coincides with the psychological oscillation and liminality I will suggest. Kopper usefully connects this play to the "problem plays" of 1602-4; I would add that it should be compared with the thoroughly sceptical, Jacobean treatment of chivalry that appears in *The Two Noble Kinsmen*, on which Shakespeare collaborated with John Fletcher.

8. Elizabeth Bronfen, "The Lady Vanishes: Sophie Freud and *Beyond the Pleasure Principle*," *The South Atlantic Quarterly*, 88, no. 4 (fall 1989): 961–91. Bronfen's essay has been extremely useful to me as a source of various interpretations of the *fort/da* game, as well as suggesting parameters for a feminist critique of chivalry that Shakespeare's play may offer.

9. For his discussion of the spool's significance in the *fort/da* game, see Lacan in "Tuche and Automaton," in *Ecrits: A Selection*, trans. Alan Sheridan (New York: Norton, 1977), 62.

10. Barbara Freedman, *Staging the Gaze: Postmodernism, Psychoanalysis, and Shakespearean Comedy* (Ithaca: Cornell University Press, 1991), 210. In this essay I have drawn extensively on Freedman's incisive analysis of Lacan's view of the *fort/da* game, though my ultimate focus is more cultural and affective than hers.

11. Lacan, "Of the Subject Who Is Supposed to Know," in *Ecrits*, 239.

12. As William O. Scott points out, Helen's own story has a variant in classical literature, one source of which is Plato's *Phaedrus*. This variant legend "keeps Helen faithful to Menelaus though separated from him, somewhat as Troilus had hoped for himself (in the case of Cressida)." Scott, "Self-Difference in *Troilus and Cressida*," in *Shakespeare and Deconstruction*, 130–31.

13. Deborah Hooker, "Coming to Cressida Through Irigaray," *The South Atlantic Quarterly* 88, no. 4 (fall 1989): 922.

14. Many heroines come to mind here, but especially Portia, Hero, and Isabella. Portia, in particular, appears to enact a qualified vengeance on the male world that has imprisoned her through the casket test. By setting up the test of Bassanio through an inversion of the marriage ritual, giving him a ring which he is never to lose, she sets the stage for the weighing of Bassanio's love for her with his bond and love for Antonio. But she can only achieve her small measure of vengeance on the Law of the Father by posing as a man, and the outcome of her test clearly indicates Shakespeare's awareness of the essentially male homosocial character of the chivalric world.

15. The *OED* lists one variant of "ribald" as *ribaude*, "a woman of loose charac-

ter, a wanton." Although a rare and obsolete usage (*OED* cites two occurrences from the sixteenth century) it nonetheless adds metaphorical depth to the sort of postcoital distance we see in Troilus' affect here.

16. Derrida has discussed at length the significance of this footnote, and of *Beyond the Pleasure Principle* itself. See his "Coming Into One's Own," trans. James Hulbert, in *Psychoanalysis and the Question of the Text*, ed. Geoffrey Hartman (Baltimore: Johns Hopkins University Press, 1978), 139–42.

17. Julia Kristeva discusses this renunciation/aggression complex in her chapter on male sexuality through Plato's dual sublime and manic *eros* and in her examination of narcissism; see her *Tales of Love* (New York: Columbia University Press, 1987), 61–136.

Motive and Meaning in *All's Well That Ends Well*

Ruth Nevo

All's Well That Ends Well has been classified among the problem comedies, perhaps mainly because Bertram has failed to captivate; he has been found even more devoid of charm than Angelo in *Measure for Measure*, the companion "problem" comedy. Bertram is, as my students invariably inform me, a creep. And in this they have the critics on their side: that he is "a thoroughly disagreeable, peevish and vicious person" (Lawrence 1931, 61) seems to be the consensus. One is hard put to it, indeed, to think of a fictional character less popular than the young Count of Rossillion. Yet Helena has come in for her share of criticism too. She is forward, obstinate, manipulative, opportunistic. She does not heal the King out of patriotic fervor but because she has an eye for the main chance. And so on. To rebellious, feminist Katherine Mansfield,

> Helena is a terrifying female. Her virtue, her persistence, her pegging away after the odious Bertram (and disguised as a pilgrim—so typical!) and then telling the whole story to that good widow-woman! And that tame fish Diana. As to lying in Diana's bed and enjoying the embraces meant for Diana—well, I know nothing more sickening. It would take a respectable woman to do such a thing. The worst of it is I can so well imagine . . . acting in precisely that way, and giving Diana a present afterwards. . . . But to forgive such a woman! Yet Bertram would. There's an espece of mothers-boyisme in him which makes him stupid enough for anything. (Mansfield 1927, 274)

Critics who, on the other hand, fall in love with Helena—Coleridge, it will be recalled, found her "Shakespeare's loveliest character" (Raysor 1970, 2:113)—attempt desperately, for her sake, to exculpate Bertram of at least the worst of his lies and infidelities. Those who scold her for being a shameless hussy forcing himself (twice!) upon an unwilling partner feel that a thoroughly unattractive couple, evidently conceived by Shakespeare "in a time of illness or mental disturbance" (Nicoll 1952, 116) get, in each other, no more than they deserve.

On the face of it, and considered in terms of the modular properties it shares with the festive comedies and their New Comedy paradigms, *All's Well* would not seem to be in line for presenting a problem at all. It possesses, conspicuously, many of the features of its distinguished predecessors. It has a resourceful heroine; an autocratic father-figure to be eluded or outwitted; true love which doesn't run smooth; a comic device involving mistaken identities which through its deception reveals a truth; a wonderful fop who is resoundingly exposed; and a fool whose ribaldries provide a low-life counterpoint to the concerns of his betters. And there is a final matchmaking that puts the recalcitrant young man firmly in his place in the scheme of things by making an honest father of him. To make of it a problem because its male protagonist is a callow youth and its female protagonist determinedly in pursuit of her man (which of the comic heroines, save Beatrice, is not?) is surely nonsense as criticism, reducing our expectation of a Shakespearean play to the level of a tabloid magazine.

Yet generic uneasiness, a sense of generic impropriety, remains. The paradigm ground plan outlines as many problems as it sets out to skirt. For the play seems to break as many rules as it keeps. It starts, not with young men and women in search of a mate but with the death of a father, two fathers indeed, and with mourning. A foster-father is at once provided, but instead of constituting the obstacle to a match desired by the young he positively forces a marriage upon his resistant foster-son. Instead of the canonical *senex* of the Terentian New Comedy formula, whose law or writ or interference with young lovers must be overcome or evaded, we have a blocking son. This too is a clash between a father, or father figure, and a son, but upside down, as it were. Similarly topsy-turvy, the young woman, enterprising and triumphant trickster-heroine of the earlier comedies, is a victim-bride (like her single precursor, Hero) who must be done to death before resolutions can be found, and she plays the role of therapeutic, even thaumaturgic, quasi daughter to the King which becomes canonical for daughters only in the later romances.

Then again, though it looks like a courtship comedy, it is one which is constrained to get along without courtship, since the young man takes flight to the Italian wars, and the young woman follows him to Italy, but not, as previous comedies might have led one to anticipate, in page disguise. One has only to imagine

Helena in pursuit of her Bertram in page disguise, with the opportunities thus offered for masked witty courtship, for a playful battle of the sexes in which a balance, for both sexes, between pursuit and defense, winning and losing, is articulated, to see that this device might well have transformed *All's Well* into the supreme successor to *Two Gentlemen of Verona, As You Like It,* and *Twelfth Night.* I make the point not because one would expect or wish a dramatist simply to go on repeating his inventions, but to throw into prominence the peculiar distribution of differences with which we are presented in *All's Well.* For what we have instead of the page disguise is the pilgrim disguise and the bed trick, a mock death and a trick consummation. And the bed trick notoriously pleases no one. On the contrary, it crystallizes the general sense of impropriety, and throws into relief the split in critical opinion concerning Helena: saint or strumpet, and the near-unanimous critical repudiation of Bertram, tricker tricked, but not, it is felt, thereby improved.

For all these reasons the festive end is felt to be a flop, or a merely mechanical or superficial closure. And it lacks the grand harmonic completion the festive comedies have accustomed us to. The King, cured of his wasting disease in act 1, and "of as able body as when he number'd thirty" (*All's Well*, 4.5.77–78), remains unmatched, though the widowed Countess, it would seem, is an available and ideally suitable partner for her. "You shall find of the king a husband," says Lafew, incorrigible matchmaker, already in line 6 of act 1, but that carefully planted option is not taken up. Nor is a mate found for the virtuous and goodhearted Diana. There is even another unmarried young woman, possibly jilted, in the wings at the play's end. The play provides all the constituents for a grand celebratory wedding closure in which "individual fulfillment, marital intimacy and communal renewal are celebrated" (Wheeler 1981, 3), but it is felt to be a question whether there are any truly festive marriages at all, or rather quite the contrary: a disillusioned rendering (for good or ill—some will praise the absence of illusion) of a cynical and sterile world. *All's Well,* it is generally agreed, has no commanding center, does not integrate its realism (which is usually admitted to be of a power and veracity equal to Shakespeare's peak period) either with its folklore motifs—the Healing of the King, the Clever Wench, the Fulfillment of the Tasks[1]—or with conventional expectations, and produces an effect of unease and confusion.[2] *All's Well* is unable, it seems to make up its generic mind. It is neither fish, flesh, nor good red herring; neither comedy, tragedy, nor romance.

I would like to submit that *All's Well*, so far from having to be apologized for, can be seen as a particularly interesting successor to the festive or, as it might be better to call them, the maturation comedies; that the critics' problems are often reflections of their own unaware masculine or feminine identifications, embodying defenses and resistances which themselves repeat the conflicts dramatized in the play; and that therefore, the better to understand both critics and play, we must attempt to read, as we say, between the lines, and to hear with a third ear. The space between the lines is the psychic space of evocation and resonance shared by both audience and dramatis personae. It is the space of precipitation by the text into consciousness of the normally unconscious. It is there that we can find what Peter Brooks calls the "complex history of unconscious desire, unavailable to the conscious subject but at work in the text" (Brooks 1980, 516). This, "the self's other story," is what we must set out to discover if we wish to do justice to the drama enacted in *All's Well* and to see as significant the anomalies just mentioned. The complaint, for example, of the Arden editor that the play lacks a "central, acceptable, and unified viewpoint" to define its values, and to integrate its incompatibilities (p. xxxv), acquires a different kind of truth when we perceive that *All's Well* places itself at a node where three dreams cross: the dream of the elders, reliving their lives through their children; the dream of the young man escaping parental domination; and the dream of the young woman desiring a child and a father. And these dreams neither coincide nor harmonize.

In *All's Well*, still in outline and plan a courtship comedy, parents have become, if not central as in the romances, at least not completely instrumental. The point of view is predominantly of the young, but since the parents, with their own problems of aging, of holding on, and letting go, are not mere obstacle figures, their point of view is operative too. They exist within the play both in their own right, and as their wills, desires, fantasies, and memories intermesh with those of the younger generation. This intermesh is a feature neither of the festive comedies nor of the romances, and it is what gives to *All's Well* its peculiar richness and density.

If there is a problem in this text, it is to be found in the unfinished business—unresolved tensions or repressed fears and desires that every play, every text, leaves in its wake to motivate the writing of the works to follow. But so far as its comic project is concerned, it quite triumphantly contains, while it also reveals, its potentially explosive and painful material.

* * *

Comedy, Chaplin once said, "is at its best when it flirts with death, plays with it, mocks it, pokes its nose into it." If there is validity in the view that comedy is the mode of drama which defers, denies, evades, or overcomes death, then one can see the play's opening not as an abrogation of comic conditions, but as a foregrounding of them. The deaths of the two fathers are undone by the adoption of Bertram and of Helena by the King and Countess respectively. The initial mourning, already past as the play begins, suggests precisely such a denial, renewal, or overcoming. But if death is thus vigorously defended against at the very start, its shadow remains to haunt the play. If we listen, as perhaps we always should, with half-closed eyes to the verbal texture of the opening scenes, we become aware of major themes that are the older generation's: nostalgia, the vulnerable body, the dereliction of time, impotence. "In delivering my son from me," says the Countess, "I bury a second husband" (*All's Well*, 1.1.1). The King's disease—that mysterious fistula—is immediately introduced, together with the wishful fantasy of his restoration to youthful fitness. A strangely skeletal image—"virtue's steely bones / Looks bleak i' th' cold wind' (1.1.101–2)—appears in Helena's defense of Parolles; the consequences she envisages should her gamble for Bertram fail are vividly imagined: "Let the white death sit on thy cheek for ever" (2.3.71). Parolles' adjurations on the subject of virginity not unexpectedly turn the age-old carpe diem theme into a very explicit memento mori: "Your date is better in your pie and your porridge than in your cheek; and your virginity, your old virginity, is like one of our French wither'd pears: it looks ill, it eats drily; marry, 'tis a wither'd pear" (1.1.154–59).

The peculiar anxiety the play's body language expresses lies in a vacillation between images of desire and of decrepitude. The passionate Helena, who has loved (though it was "a plague" to do so) "To see him every hour; to sit and draw / His arched brows, his hawking eye, his curls" (1.1.91–92), who longs to "feed [her] eye . . . / To join like likes, and kiss like native things" (1.1.217, 219) grieves that "wishing well had not a body in't / Which might be felt" (1.1.177–78). This vehemence is curiously echoed by Bertram, newly wed and in flight, as he parts from one of his new companions: "I grow to you, and our parting is a tortur'd body"

(2.1.36). We have the unvarnished plain speaking of Lavatch (of Touchstone's ilk) to drive the point home, as he seeks permission to marry his Isbel: "My poor body, madam, requires it; I am driven on by the flesh, and he must needs go that the devil drives"; "Service is no heritage, and I think I shall never have the blessing of God till I have issue a' my body; for they say barnes are blessings" (1.3.26–28, 21–24). "Issue of the body" is the leitmotiv of the King's elegy for his own, and for his old friend's, youth:

> But on us both did haggish age steal on,
> And wore us out of act. . . .
>
> (1.2.29–30)

> Would I were with him! . . .
>   "Let me not live", quoth he,
> "After my flame lacks oil, to be the snuff
> Of younger spirits, whose apprehensive senses
> All but new things disdain; whose judgments are
> Mere fathers of their garments. . . ."
>   This he wish'd.
> I, after him, do after him wish too,
> Since I nor wax nor honey can bring home.
>
> (1.2.52, 58–65)

"Oil" for his flame, "wax" or "honey" for the hive, suggest that the loss of sexual potency underlies the melancholy of this Fisher King. We note his resigned reply to the courtier's "You're loved, sir": "I fill a place, I know't" (1.2.67, 69). The lewd Lafew leaves no room for doubt about the nature of the King's disease, or at least of its symptomatic manifestation. He himself refers to his task—the bringing of the physician's daughter to her royal patient—as a pandar's role: "I am Cressid's uncle / That dare leave two together" (2.1.96–97); describes what "Doctor she" will achieve in language which barely cloaks its sexuality; and takes a salacious pleasure in persuading the melancholy King to attempt the cure:

> O, will you eat
> No grapes, my royal fox? Yes, but you will
> My noble grapes, and if my royal fox
> Could reach them. I have seen a medicine
> That's able to breathe life into a stone,
> Quicken a rock, and make you dance canary
> With spritely fire and motion; whose simple touch

Is powerful to araise King Pippen, nay,
To give great Charlemain a pen in hand
And write to her a love-line.

(2.1.68–77)[3]

It is precisely the King's virility that Helena restores. After his recovery, he is "lustique" enough to lead his "preserver" in a coranto (2.3.41). "Your dolphin is not lustier," Lafew informs us (2.3.26). This restoration by the daughter of his old friend is the magic fulfillment of a wishful fantasy; but it also provides the King with—what? a surrogate daughter as well as a surrogate son? An Avishag for his declining years? A greater warmth, perhaps, than one would feel for one's physician is to be caught in the King's resolve to become her patient: "more to know could not be more to trust" (2.1.205). His violent repudiation of the recalcitrant Bertram, the transformation of "My son's no dearer" (1.2.76) into

                    Check thy contempt;
Obey our will. . . .
Or I will throw thee from my care for ever
Into the staggers and the careless lapse
Of youth and ignorance; both my revenge and hate
Loosing upon thee in the name of justice.
Without all terms of pity

(2.3.157–66)

is the provision of the tyrannical *senex* of New Comedy with a vengeance. But if he is, as we intuit, more than half in love, not any longer with easeful death, but with a young woman who promises rejuvenation, it is not difficult to understand the intensity, and the ambivalence, of his emotional investment in this match.

By the same token we recall the words of the widowed Countess, as the play opens with the dispatching of Bertram to Paris: "In delivering my son from me," says the Countess, "I bury a second husband." On the face of it, this is the patrician gesture of a dignified and courtly lady distancing with art a double sorrow. This second "birth" is a second death, she says. But in the rhetorical condensation may we not descry a telltale parapraxis? The Countess is in mourning for her husband; she is also, we perceive, rather more than half in love with her son.[4]

The Countess's second exchange with her fool, which follows Helena's confession and her departure for Paris, is similarly revealing. She is sending him off in Helena's wake to the King's court and is prepared, with good-natured irony, to indulge his scapegrace effrontery. On the whole she treats his scurrilities with much the same matronly indulgence as Olivia does Feste's, but the open sexuality of his bawdry this time, it seems, is provocative of more than cool irony. His "answer," he says, fits all questions "like a barber's chair that fits all buttocks" (2.2.16); is as fit

> as ten groats is for the hand of an attorney, as your French crown for your taffety punk, as Tib's rush for Tom's forefinger, as a pancake for Shrove Tuesday, a morris for Mayday, as the nail to his hole, the cuckold to his horn, as a scolding quean to a wrangling knave, as the nun's lip to the friar's mouth; nay, as the pudding to his skin. . . . From below your duke to beneath your constable it will fit any question.
>
> (2.2.20–30)

"It must be an answer of most monstrous size that must fit all demands," is the Countess's reply; and then suddenly, in the midst of the thrust of parry and repartee, comes a striking non sequitur: "To be young again, if we could" (2.2.37).

They are mourning their youth, this autumnal pair, it seems. And in consequence they are projecting upon their children (or their adopted children) their longing to relive their lives. It is no wonder that currents of ambivalence will crisscross this inverted family romance.

Read in this light the testing scene between the Countess and Helena becomes as iridescent as Helena's tears. The Countess receives the steward's confirmation of Helena's love for Bertram with an immediate, motherly empathy, shadowed, however, in its reference to "faults," by the hint of a jealous reservation:

> Even so it was with me when I was young; . . .
> this thorn
> Doth to our rose of youth rightly belong. . . .
> Such were our faults, or then we thought them none.
> (1.3.123–25, 130)

The scene that follows is masterly in its representation of ambivalence, of simulation and dissimulation, between the two women, both contenders for Bertram's love. "You know, Helen, / I am a mother to you" (1.3.132–33) is the Countess's opening ploy, and it serves her purpose of eliciting response and testing intention excellently when Helena replies, with modestly disavowing emphasis, "Mine honourable *mistress*" (*my italics*):

> Nay, a mother.
> Why not a mother? When I said a "mother",
> Methought you saw a serpent. What's in "mother"
> That you start at it? I say I am your mother,
> And put you in a catalogue of those
> That were enwombed mine. . . .
> You ne'er oppress'd me with a mother's groan,
> Yet I express to you a mother's care.
> God's mercy, maiden! does it curd thy blood
> To say I am thy mother? what's the matter,
> That this distempered messenger of wet,
> The many colour'd Iris, rounds thine eye?
> —Why, that you are my daughter?
> (1.3.134–48)

The Countess exploits Helena's embarrassed feint—"The Count Rossillion cannot be my brother . . . must not be my brother" (1.3.150, 155) to point out that Helena as her daughter-in-law would solve the semantic problem, and she drives home her advantage:

> God shield you mean it not! daughter and mother
> So strive upon your pulse. What! pale again?
> My fear hath catch'd your fondness; now I see
> The myst'ry of your loneliness, and find
> Your salt tears' head. . . .
>   Speak, is't so?
> If it be so, you have wound a goodly clew.
> (1.3.163–67, 176–77)

She is playing the role of indignant matron that she has set herself. But in doing so, she is playing it out. The ambiguous irony of "you have wound a goodly clew" allows us to register simultaneously the angry resentment she is professing, and the compensatory acceptance she is working her way toward. Since she cannot have a husband in her son, she will identify with the girl who would be his wife, and so transform her love for Bertram into a double maternal solicitude. This is an admirable solution: it is indeed the way of women in Shakespearean comedy to resolve their inner conflicts more successfully, more benignly, than do the men.

At the end of the scene, Helena has the Countess's leave and love and approval for her project. But in order to understand Helena in the testing scene we must retrace our steps.

The predicament that is developed in act 1 of *All's Well* offers a powerful exemplification of Freud's observation upon family quadrangles. "I am accustoming myself," he wrote in a letter to Fleiss in 1899, "to regarding every sexual act as an event between four individuals." "Every sexual thought" perhaps he should have said. Much of interest emerges when we turn our attention to the Countess's foster daughter, also, like Bertram, in mourning for a father: "The remembrance of her father never approaches her heart but the tyranny of her sorrows takes all livelihood from her cheek" (1.1.45–47), we are told. We are immediately alerted by a scene curiously reminiscent of the opening scenes of *Hamlet* but with the sexes reversed. "I do affect a sorrow indeed, but I have it too" (1.2.50) is Helena's reply to the Countess's chiding: 'No more of this, Helena; go to, no more; lest it be rather thought you affect a sorrow than to have—" (1.2.47–49). Helena, it seems, like Hamlet, has something to hide, something that presses for utterance and chafes at the need for dissimulation. Helena, like Hamlet, as we speedily learn, is "too much in the *son*":

> I think not on my father,
> And these great tears grace his remembrance more
> Than those I shed for him. What was he like?
> I have forgot him; my imagination
> Carries no favour in't but Bertram's.
>
> (1.1.77–81)

The lines are obscure, but possibly uncannily shrewd. To make sense of the antithesis we must read "remembrance" as a metonymy for "remains"—all that remains of her father is her memory of him. So: the great tears grace his memory more than those she shed at his funeral, tears shed "for *him*," (*my italics*) still, so to speak, present in the flesh. This is very condensed, more particularly since "grace" carries with it its subliminal contrary—"disgrace." Surely a considerable tinge of guilt colors Helena's acknowledgment of the displacement, in her passionate affection, of father by beloved. The denials, like most denials, are self-betraying. What the speech tells us is that she is very far from having forgotten her father; but that her love for Bertram has, quite literally, and not without guilt, taken the place of her love for her father, the one image overlaying the other. If so, it is no wonder that her love is perceived by her as unattainable, out of reach, never to be consummated. Yes, he is socially above her, and this provides the ostensible reason for her despair. But since nothing, we are told, is fortuitous in the world of the mind, Helena's choice of the object of her affections could be in accordance with a deeply ambivalent inner need. If it is her father she loves, and therefore a father that she seeks in the mate she chooses, the latter will be, for that very reason, impossible, untouchable, a forbidden *prince lointain:* "twere all one / That I should love a bright particular star / And think to wed it" (1.1.83–85).

We are offered a great deal more data for the fathoming of Helena's complex motivation in the dialogue with Bertram's friend, Parolles, whom she loves "for his sake" though she knows him for the liar, fool, and coward that he is. With Parolles she enjoys a relationship of ironic equality despite her lowly birth and his complacent patronizing. "Save you, fair queen" is his greeting, and her reply, "And you, monarch!" (1.1.104–5), shows, as does the flyting that concludes their conversation (1.1.187–200), that she can give as good as she gets in this power game. Helena is shrewd and self-reliant as the scene makes very clear: it ends with her bold resolve to seek the remedies that "in ourselves do lie" (1.1.212):

> Who ever strove
> To show her merit that did miss her love?
> The king's disease—my project may deceive me,
> But my intents are fix'd, and will not leave me.
>
> (1.1.222–25)

She is also preoccupied, as the scene makes clear, with the very subject Parolles, with preternaturally cunning complicity, has chosen for their conversation.

Parolles is a mine of information on the subject of virginity, which is the topic he first provocatively launches. Helena parries his provocation to good effect, but in the process of inquiring of Parolles, who should know, how one may "barricado it" against man the enemy, Helena also inquiries, "How might one do, sir, to lose it to her own liking?" (1.1.147). Parolles' diatribe against withered pears concludes with the challenge "Will you anything with it?" (1.1.159–60), and is followed by an elliptical speech from Helena, perhaps half to herself, which has proved no less a challenge to interpreters:

> Not my virginity; yet. . . .[5]
> There shall your master have a thousand loves,
> A mother, and a mistress, and a friend,

> A phoenix, captain, and an enemy,
> A guide, a goddess, and a sovereign,
> A counsellor, a traitress, and a dear.
>
> (1.1.161–66)

The ellipsis, a characteristic of Helena's which suggests a reflective inwardness, is open to a number of interpretations. Are we to hear an emphasis upon "my" virginity? Is the implied other virginity, if any is implied, Bertram's? Is "yet" temporal or concessive? Whatever is unspoken crystallizes finally upon what is evidently the dominant preoccupation—"your master": "There shall your master have a thousand loves." But where shall this take place? In Paris? Or in "my virginity," the immediate antecedent for the anaphoric "there"? However we read what follows, whether as an envious and ironic catalog of sonneteering epithets (a denigration of the loves Bertram will find in Paris) or as an ardent outdoing even of the chivalric passions of the sonneteers (and so a valorization of the love that she can offer), immediately after "a thousand loves" there occurs an oddity we can surely only interpret as another astonishing slip of the text. What follows is "a mother, and a mistress, and a friend." For while one has encountered fantastic, hyperbolic, even outrageous, epithets in High Renaissance sonnets, even the most assiduous reader of these confections will be hard put to it to recall a mother among them. No occurrence, the Arden editor assures us, is on record.

Why has this "mother" entered Helena's mind? Has she perceived the bond between the Countess and Bertram? And, seeking herself a father surrogate in her love, does her wise unconscious fear a contrary quest in Bertram? Or, on the contrary, is it her wish too to "mother" Bertram? These are the questions which resonate further in the testing scene between the Countess and Helena, which we will consider now from Helena's point of view.

The Countess's outburst:

> does it curd thy blood
> To say I am thy mother? what's the matter,
> That this distempered messenger of wet,
> The many-colour'd Iris, rounds thine eye?
> —Why, that you are my daughter?
>
> (1.3.144–48)

receives the opaque reply, "That I am not." Helena, elliptical as ever, may mean by this "I am not *that*," by way of emphatic disavowal, or "Because I am not" by way of concession. How are we to read the elliptical Helena? Does she inadvertently reveal her true feelings, or cannily mask her feelings with a declarative equivocation? The reason she gives for her continued insistence is disingenuous: "Pardon, madam; / The Count Rossillion cannot be my brother":

> My master, my dear lord he is; and I
> His servant live, and will his vassal die.
> He must not be my brother.
> (1.3.153–55)

Embarrassed, Helena falls into confusion as she struggles between the Scylla of impoliteness or ingratitude and the hypothetical Charybdis of brother/sister incest:

> You are my mother, madam; would you were—
> So that my lord your son were not my brother—
> Indeed my mother! or were you both our mothers
> I care no more for than I do for heaven,
> So I were no this sister.
> (1.3.156–60)

It can surely escape no one that Helena's double bind here is factitious. The Countess can be her mother only metaphorically. Certainly the semantic absurdity does not escape the Countess, who, as we have seen, uses it to drive home her advantage.

Helena's agitation serves the Countess's testing purposes, and she is trapped into the confession the Countess wants to hear. But we must seek a deeper reason for her extreme discomposure. Her ostensible reason—the desire not to be Bertram's sister since she wishes to be his wife—since it is absurd, can only be a screen upon which we can read an inner conflict. That she is made so nervous by the idea of being Bertram's forbidden sister could well be symptomatic of the deeper taboo. Daughter and mother so strive upon her pulse in a sense truer than the Countess knows: shall she continue to be her father's docile daughter, submissive and self-effacing, or become her lover's active pursuer, challenger and replacer of his mother? That it is the father's daughter that at this point dominates her mind is to be inferred from the posture of helpless, hapless adoration from afar that she expresses, in excess, one feels, of what is required to pacify the Countess, but in keeping with the masochistic note we have already heard

("The hind that would be mated by the lion / Must die for love"[(1.1.89–90]):

> I know I love in vain, strive against hope;
> Yet in this captious and inteemable sieve
> I still pour in the waters of my love
> And lack not to lose still. Thus, Indian-like,
> Religious in mine error, I adore
> The sun that looks upon his worshipper
> But knows of him no more. . . .
>   O then, give pity
> To her whose state is such that cannot choose
> But lend and give where she is sure to lose;
> That seeks not to find that her search implies,
> But riddle-like lives sweetly where she dies!
>   (1.3.196–202, 208–12)

Richard P. Wheeler says that Helena's main task is to overcome a difficulty "that originates in Bertram's revulsion from her" (Wheeler 1981; 15). But this is surely not so. Helena's main task is to overcome a difficulty that originates in the Oedipal taboo. She is as passionate a woman as she is an affectionate daughter, but not yet able to break the father's spell. The phoenix image fantasizes a sublime self-immolation, but pursuit of Bertram to Paris is seductive, too. The will to pursue Bertram to Paris under the guise of healing the King, since it is also the will to heal the King under the guise of pursuing Bertram, is for her a wonderfully composite and legitimizing wish fulfillment. Using the craft of her own father, she will restore a proxy father figure to health, and receive, at his grateful hand, a husband.

Helena consciously conceives her problem as a conflict between boldness and self-effacement, or presumption and modesty, in terms both of the social hierarchies and the maidenly proprieties, but also in terms of chastity and sensuality. "Loving dearly," for Helena, is no matter for platonic abstractions and Diana, her much invoked goddess, was, it will be recalled, the goddess of childbirth as well as of virginity. But it is Diana, not of the Ephesians but of virgins, whom she invokes in order to formulate her plight at this point:

>   My dearest madam, . . . if yourself,
> Whose aged honour cites a virtuous youth,
> Did ever, in so true a flame of liking,

>   Wish chastely and love dearly, that your Diana
>   Was both herelf and love—
>
>   (1.3.202–8)

Only later, and, typically, when she steels herself for possible humiliation in the self-exposure of the choosing scene, does she see herself as deserting Diana for "imperial Love, that god most high" (2.3.75).

Helena's fantasied plot of success, in which she will choose her man and the King-father will sanction her choice, fails. It is at the French court, following the triumph of her cure of the King, that humiliation—the "Tax of impudence, / A strumpet's boldness, a divulged shame" (2.1.169–70) which, she told the King, she was ready to venture, in other words, had deeply feared, as the consequence instinctively associated for her with sexual love—becomes indeed her lot. In a way she has tempted Providence, for her replies to the reluctant courtiers are self-abasing: "Love make your fortunes twenty times above / Her that so wishes"; "I'll never do you wrong, for your own sake. / . . . in your bed / Find fairer fortune if you ever wed!"; "You are too young, too happy, and too good, / To make yourself a son out of my blood" (2.3.82–97). We conceive the drama that she has conceived, empowered by her father's power: the response she hoped for from Bertram would have reversed the situation, dignified her humility by triumphantly vindicating her intrinsic worth. But at her grand moment of choice, she is despised and rejected, punished, if you will, by a chauvinist text. The choice-of-a-suitor scene has understandably troubled critics, both on her behalf and on Bertram's. The latter indeed has troubles of his own, to which I now turn.

They interestingly mirror Helena's. For where Helena seeks, and struggles with, a father in her love, Bertram fears, and flees, a mother in his. Understanding this, we will understand the pathos of the crossed vectors of desire, the knot of conflicting needs which this comedy of maturation must untie.

Critics scold Bertram for being so unchivalrous about Helena, but we should surely register the authenticity of his resistance to a marriage forced upon him by a foster father, to the socially inferior, and domestically familiar, receiver of his mother's patronage. Even to a kind of sister—Helena's anxiety on this score can alert us to his. That he chafes is hardly to be wondered at. Bertram has emerged from beneath the maternal wing only to fall under the sway of a new paternal authority. It is surely incumbent upon us to see the matter from his point of view when he bursts out with

> My wife, my liege! I shall beseech your highness,
> In such a business give me leave to use
> The help of mine own eyes.
>
> (2.3.106–8)

And seeing it thus we may perceive the bind in which he is placed. It would hardly make things better for Helena if his repulsion were so great as to make him defy the King's threatened "revenge and hate." His surrender has been construed as abjectly, cynically opportunistic. But it could also be read as a bitter acceptance of force majeure:

> Pardon, my gracious lord; for I submit
> My fancy to your eyes. When I consider
> What great creation and what dole of honour
> Flies where you bid it, I find that she, which late
> Was in my nobler thoughts most base, is now
> The praised of the king; who, so ennobled,
> Is as 'twere born so.
>
> (2.3.167–73)

It depends where we locate the irony, whether we monopolize that commodity as a critical prerogative, or allow the dramatized persona access to the sarcasm that is the defense of the powerless. And Bertram *is* powerless. That he is "not yet old enough for a man, nor young enough for a boy" (as Malvolio says of Cesario in *Twelfth Night* [1.5.158–59]) is the play's generational starting point.

Already in act 2 Bertram's plight is presented as one of extreme frustration. He is

> commanded here, and kept a coil with
> "Too young", and "The next year" and "'Tis too early". . . .
> I shall stay here the forehorse to a smock,
> Creaking my shoes on the plain masonry,
> Till honour be bought up, and no sword worn
> But one to dance with.
>
> (2.1.27–33)

Seeking honor in battle, action, and manhood, he is kept childishly at home by a King who is as patronizing as he is paternal.

And this situation reaches a crisis when even freedom of marital choice is denied him.

But more is at stake for Bertram than freedom of marital choice. Lafew's comments throughout the scene of Helena's choice brand all the reluctant courtiers as beardless boys, objects of his macho contempt before their lackluster performance. "Do all they deny her? And they were sons of mine I'd have them whipp'd, or I would send them to th' Turk to make eunuchs of" (2.3.86–88). They are "boys of ice . . . bastards to the English; the French ne'er got 'em" (2.3.93–95). In particular he despises Bertram, and in terms which suggest the condescending arrogance of the grown man for the sexually immature youth. "There's one grape yet. I am sure thy father drunk wine; but if thou be'st not an ass, I am a youth of fourteen; I have known thee already" (2.3.99–101).

In the scene which follows, the mutual hostility between Lafew and Parolles also hinges specifically upon the question of manliness: Lafew excoriates Parolles for his effeminate clothes—he is a "good window of lattice" (2.3.212)—and for his foppish airs and affectations—"I must tell thee, sirrah, I write man; to which title age cannot bring thee" (2.3.197–98). And his insinuations go further than aspersions cast merely upon Parolles' sartorial foppishness: "Why dost thou garter up thy arms a' this fashion? Dost make hose of thy sleeves? . . . Thou were best set thy lower part where thy nose stands" (2.3.245–48). To Lafew, aggressively male, Parolles is "a hen." As far as Lafew is concerned, it seems, Parolles is nothing but a male punk and he cannot stand him. Parolles for his part throws Lafew's "antiquity" in his face, and, once Lafew is safely absent, swears "Well, thou hast a son shall take this disgrace off me; scurvy, old, filthy, scurvy lord! . . . I'll beat him, by my life, if I can meet him with any convenience" (2.3.231–35). It is to this braggart "sweetheart" that Bertram turns for sympathy when he enters, "Undone and forefeited to cares for ever!" (2.3.263). Parolles' bravado, characteristic defense of the sexually and personally insecure, presents the refuge of a homoerotic attachment as a valorization of the male camaraderie of warfare:

> To th' wars, my boy, to th' wars!
> He wears his honour in a box unseen
> That hugs his kicky-wicky here at home,
> Spending his manly marrow in her arms,
> Which should sustain the bound and high curvet
> Of Mars's fiery steed.
>
> (2.3.274–79)

And off to the wars go the bachelor companions in perfect agreement that "A young man married is a man that's marr'd" (2.3.294).

For Bertram, frustrated by his forced marriage, Mars is a welcome substitute for Venus. But that a fear of impotence lies just beneath the surface of his martial posture is suggested not only by the Parolles connection but by his own telltale envoi:

> I have writ my letters, casketed my treasure,
> Given order for our horses; and tonight,
> When I should take possession of the bride,
> End ere I do begin.
>
> (2.5.23–26)

Effeminate Parolles, "jackanapes with scarfs" (3.5.85), is Bertram's refuge from "the dark house [a displaced image of female enclosure?] and the detested wife" (2.3.288). The danger, bawdy Lavatch informs us, is in "standing to 't': in battle, "that's the loss of men"; elsewhere, "the getting of children" (3.2.40–41). Bertram, who runs away, the clown's irony seems to suggest, has double indemnity. Lavatch's caustic comment is important because it links the two masculine prerogatives, and puts them both in question vis-à-vis Bertram. But we must ask our own questions of the text that represents Bertram.

First of all, we note, the nearly universal critical prejudice against him leads to a cardinal misjudgment. Bertram does in fact exhibit prowess in battle. And he does not, at this stage at least, lie to Helena. He does not declare to her a love he does not feel. He will not kiss her even when they part, and she pleads for at least a formal embrace.

Moreover, the riddle with which he sets Helena her impossible task: "*When thou canst get the ring upon my finger, which never shall come off, and show me a child begotten of thy body that I am father to, then call me husband*" (3.2.56–58) is double-tongued, like all riddles. It states an apparent impossibility but represents an unacknowledged desire. To see this, one has only to suppose the conditional *form* changed, not the primary substance; to read instead of "When thou canst, . . ." "If only thou couldst. . . ."[6]

And when he dispatches her to his mother, it is with almost a plea on his part for her understanding:

> And rather muse than ask why I entreat you;
> For my respects are better than then seem,
> And my appointments have in them a need

Greate than shows itself at the first view
To you that know them not.
                                    (2.5.65–69)

The need "Greater than shows itself," as Richard P. Wheeler persuasively demonstrates, stems from the fact that Helena is ineluctably bound up in his mind with his mother: "A son's affection for a mother is directed by Bertram toward the countess; a son's fears of female domination and of his own Oedipal wishes are aroused in Bertram by Helena" (2.5.42). Hence "I cannot love her nor will strive to do't" (2.3.145). Wheeler concludes, however, that the play's "comic purpose, to free Bertram from anxieties that originate in family ties," is not achieved. "The action of *All's Well*," he says, "dramatizes neither a liberation from nor a transformation of obstacles that obstruct the marriage to Helena" (2.3.80).

It is at this point that my own reading of *All's Well* diverges from Wheeler's. He reads into the play the problems of the Sonnets, with Helena as a screen figure for the humiliated and self-humiliating lover and Bertram as the Sonnets' young man, presented now with a savage mockery the self-excoriating author of the Sonnets could not permit himself. My own reading is dramatically opposed. I see these two as chiastic doubles, mirrors of each other. Where Helena seeks a (forbidden) father in her love, Bertram fears a (forbidden) mother; but the text also inscribes their shared desire for sexual enfranchisement, for fatherhood and motherhood, and provides the means for its attainment.

The reversals, which will make possible the happy ending, occur in the play's middle act. Helena's great speech of renunciation is worth quoting at length for the subtlety with which it articulates a momentous transformation.

> Nothing in France, until he has no wife!
> Thou shalt have none, Rossillion, none in France;
> Then hast thou all again. Poor lord, is't I
> That chase thee from thy country, and expose
> Those tender limbs of thine to the event
> Of the none-sparing war? And is it I
> That drive thee from the sportive court, where thou
> Wast shot at with fair eyes, to be the mark
> Of smoky muskets? O you leaden messengers,
>   . . . do not touch my lord.
> Whoever shoots at him, I set him there;
>   . . . I am the cause

>   . . . No; come thou home, Rossillion,
>   . . . I will be gone;
>   My being here it is that holds thee hence.
>   Shall I stay here to do't? No, no, although
>   The air of paradise did fan the house
>   And angels offic'd all. I will be gone,
>   . . . Come, night; end, day;
>   For with the dark, poor thief, I'll steal away.
>   (3.2.100–129)

In the parting scene Helena begged for her kiss "like a timorous thief, [who] most fain would steal" (2.5.81) what is legally hers. Now she will herself steal away, so only she be no obstacle to Bertram's return. It is to be noted, too, that in thus renouncing him she refers to him in his own patronymic right, as Rossillion. It is a turnabout for the determined young woman who has outfaced a king and a court to gain her end, and gained it. But what the accents of the speech tell us is that this self-abrogation, which springs no doubt from the masochism of infantile taboo, has undergone a transformation. Her guilt here is reality-tested, objective, since she really is the cause of Bertram's escape into soldiering. The tenderly maternal solicitude that we hear in this speech is a transference wonderfully, and movingly, caught. Helena has broken the spell of the father in this fantasy of herself as a mothering, protective figure to the man she desires.

It is for this reason, I suggest, that there is no page disguise in *All's Well*. Helena's problem has not been the sorting out, balancing, and harmonizing of masculine and feminine components in her own personality as it was for her hermaphrodite sisters of the earlier comedies. They had to reconcile themselves to a woman's role without loss, if possible, of the adventurous, maverick male attributes they also possessed, and cherished. She has had to free her sexuality from the archaic bond of infancy, to undertake a pilgrimage into mature sexuality. It is beautifully in keeping with this trajectory of "the other plot" that we are following that disguise as a girl called Diana, women's camaraderie, and the bed trick mark her achievement of the passage from virgin chastity to marital sexuality.

The bed-trick represents enabling fantasy for both partners. For Helena it offers camouflage—anonymity, invisibility—under cover of which she can transcend the inhibitions of a threatening sexuality. For men, conversely, bed-trick fantasies represent fears of being tricked in bed. But for Bertram the bed-trick is his sexual conquest of the woman he believes to be Diana and so fulfills an analogous liberation. Helena is dead. We do not know the nature of the change that came over Bertram when he received the news of Helena's death, but "on the reading it he chang'd almost into another man" (4.3.3-4). Already in his wooing of Diana, he was liberated enough to be able to contemplate, and to exorcise by invoking, a primal scene: "now you should be as your mother was," he says, "When your sweet self was got" (4.2.9-10). Now, in bed with a light o'love—Fontybell!—and therefore unhampered by any honorable intentions whatsoever, "he fleshes his will" (4.3.15), confirming his potency. Thus Bertram outgrows Parolles. Or rather, he is in a position to outgrow Parolles. His repudiation of his erstwhile "sweetheart," however, is still to be brought about.

* * *

Parolles, often seen as a quasi vice figure in a morality play contest with virtuous Helena, and about whom Wheeler, oddly, has very little to say, is perhaps the most brilliant dramatic invention in *All's Well*. Bertram's virtual sibling, brother-at-arms, alter ego, he is our essential vehicle for an understanding of Bertram's rake's progress as an authentic reflection of masculine adolescence. Perhaps too much so for the comfort of spectators, male and female, who cannot free themselves from masculine idealizations of romantic protagonists.[7] But let us examine the exposure of the inimitable Parolles.

The exposure of Parolles in act 4 marks, together with the bed-trick, the remedial phase of the Shakespearean comic plot. Characteristically, folly, become hyperbolically excessive, extrudes itself, exposes itself, or is exposed, exhausts, and so eliminates itself.[8] The lords have a double remedial project in hand in the gulling scene. Parolles, "most notable coward, an infinite and endless liar, an hourly promise-breaker" (3.6.9-10), is to be openly and palpably disgraced, but Bertram, too, is due for chastisement for the brazen callousness with which he has received the news of Helena's death and for his seduction of "a young gentlewoman . . . of a most chaste renown" (4.3.13-14). The French lords will "gladly have him see his company anatomiz'd, that he might make a measure of his own judgments wherein so curiously he had set this counterfeit," and they economically set their trap so that each will be "the whip of the other" (4.3.30-35). The first stage of the trap exposes Parolles, in sham pursuit of his lost drum, as the fraud and coxcomb, the "counterfeit module" (4.3.96) and craven informer that he is. The second stage turns the tables upon the now indignant, and betrayed, Bertram. The latter appears, in extremely high spirits after his rendezvous with Diana, and that he deserves what he gets is underlined by his airy account of the "sixteen businesses" he has dispatched (4.3.82–89) since the news of Helena's death.

Parolles, having surrendered unconditionally at the first syllable of the Lords' "terrible language," is now beyond shame—"If ye pinch me like a pasty" (4.3.119–20), he says, he can betray no more military intelligence than he possesses, which, when it comes to a run-down on the French commanders, he is determined to embellish with details that will, he is confident, endear him to his interlocutors. Thus it comes about that the trickster Lords, including Bertram—"a foolish idle boy, but for all that very ruttish" (4.3.207)—hear no good of themselves. The blindfold removed, face-to-face with the objects of his "pestiferous" slanders, Parolles' exposure is complete.

The "cure" proves wonderfully effective; more so than Malvolio's even, perhaps because Parolles has had a measure of self-knowledge all along concerning at least his "foolhardy tongue": "Tongue, I must put you into a butter-woman's mouth, and buy myself another of Bajazeth's mule if you prattle me into these perils" (4.1.41–43). But he goes on paroling himself into perils, and that it is by the Lords' gobbledygook—"choughs' language" (4.1.19)—that a meanspirited braggart is undone is no more than poetic justice. Or homeopathy. Self-knowledge, self-acceptance can hardly go further than that of Parolles, shamed beyond words, disgraced, despised, but alive:

> Yet am I thankful. If my heart were great
> 'Twould burst at this. Captain I'll be no more,
> But I will eat and drink and sleep as soft
> As captain shall. Simply the thing I am
> Shall make me live. . . .
> Rust, sword; cool, blushes; and Parolles live
> Safest in shame. . . .
> There's place and means for every man alive.
>
> (4.3.319–28)

But what of Bertram vis-à-vis his ex-alter ego? He repudiates him of course. He is now, "A pox upon him! . . . a cat" (4.3.254–55)—whom he detests. But does he see anything of himself in this unmasking? "What a past-saving slave is this!" "Damnable both-sides rogue!" (4.3.135, 214), he says, failing to recall that the only afterthought he had about Diana was a fear of ever hearing of her again. We might adapt the courtier's rhetorical question regarding Parolles: "Is it possible he should know what he is, and be that he is? " (4.1.44–45). Is it possible that Bertram knows what Parolles is, and be as *he* is?

Bertram's own exposure, indeed, is still to come. At present he still "thinks himself made" (4.3.16–17) by his battle honors and bed victories. If the gulling of Parolles dramatizes the demise in Bertram of Parolles the effeminate tongue-man, Parolles the feather-man remains to be demolished. Parolles himself, though he smells, is still very much alive—on handouts from the contemptuous Lafew. He must still run the gauntlet of Lavatch's olfactory insults, just as Bertram will run the gauntlet of the women's unmasking. The foppish kinship between them is neatly brought out by Bertram's affectation of a velvet patch (we have not heard that he was wounded) upon which Lavatch lavishes his scurrilous witticisms.

The final scene has the curious effect of a replay, only this time with the young women firmly in charge of the act. The elders are once more engaged in matchmaking, Lafew's daughter and Bertram this time, an opportune circumstance Bertram seizes with alacrity. Once more paternal benevolence turns into ferocity when Diana's possession of Helena's ring, given her, we recall, by the King as a pledge of his gratitude, makes the King suspect foul play, even murder, on Bertram's part.

And Bertram, trapped between rings, the inherited, patrilinear ring that he gave, the virginal, betrothal ring that he took? Yes, he lies, and wriggles and prevaricates. His snobbery is distasteful; chivalry was never his strong point. Like Parolles, in his recognition scene he is disgraced, left with no face to save, his "champion Honour" exposed for the broken reed it is.

But what, after all, do his critics expect? He is trapped, as he was at the beginning; he has a face, a life, to try to save.

He too is restored by Helena, who, like Mariana in *Measure for Measure*, wants no other, nor no better, man. Her "O my good lord, when I was like this maid / I found you wondrous kind" (5.3.303–4)[9] is, for his wounded ego, the one most restorative thing she could say. The bed trick, it turns out, served his fantasy of virile masculinity, and trumped it. For he finds in the woman he seduced, the woman he fled—a nurturing, saving presence, a sexually compatible bride and the mother of his child. He is still bewildered when he says to the King, "If she, my liege, can make me know this clearly / I'll love her dearly, ever, ever dearly" (4.3.309–10). But I myself do not find his "Both, both. O pardon!"

(5.3.302) necessarily perfunctory. Certainly an actor need not make it so.

Are they a mismatch? More, or less, than anyone else in life or in literature?

Is *All's Well* a "problem" play, and as such deserving of relegation to second-class status? It has been my claim that no such special category is required for the elucidation of *All's Well*. It exhibits a firm structural family resemblance to the earlier maturation comedies, and if it anticipates in certain aspects a late romance like *Cymbeline*, it is no more problematic for that reason than any other play in the Shakespearean opus (or any other), each play being manifestly transitional between its precursors and its successors.

Certainly the vicissitudes of motive and meaning of fear and desire, which are caught and displayed in the web of its text engage our closest attention. Its complexities, its psychological depth and finesse, its brilliant mirroring of intra-psychic conflicts as these are acted out, and paralleled, in confrontations between characters might well admit it once more into the canon of Shakespeare's most admired plays. Where, to adapt once more Parolles' famous self-summation: simply the thing it is shall make it live.

Notes

1. See Lawrence, *Shakespeare's Problem Comedies*.
2. See, for example, Richard A. Levin, "*All's Well* and All Seems Well," *Shakespeare Studies* 13 (1980): 131–42.
3. Wheeler, 75, quotes Eric Partridge, *Shakespeare's Bawdy* (New York, 1955) on the sexual suggestiveness of "stone," "fire," "motion," "touch," "[a]raise," and "pen."
4. Otto Rank noted the Oedipal motif in the very first lines of the play as early as 1912, and found "the tabooed relationship of mother and son underlying a good deal of the play." See Holland, 154. Literary critics, on the other hand, have made surprisingly little of suggested unconscious motivations. Significantly, however, Bernard Shaw, in whose "deeper affections" the play was "rooted" found the Countess "the most beautiful old woman's part ever written": *Shaw on Shakespeare*, ed. Edwin Wilson (London, 1961), 10.
5. G. K. Hunter provides an account of the textual problem in his commentary on the lines in the New Arden edition.
6. Cf. Helena's "riddle" in 1.3.212: "But riddle-like lives sweetly where she dies," in which the wit masks a wish by way of the Elizabethan *double entendre* in "dies." Phyllis Gorfain, "Puzzle and Artifice: The Riddle as Metapoetry in *Pericles*," *Shakespeare Survey* 29 (1976), makes the interesting suggestion that the paradoxes and contradictions out of which riddles are contrived constitute a "schema of marriage"—children being born of male and female, and mediating

between past and future. See also Freud's account of the *aliquis* "riddle" in *The Psychopathology of Everyday Life,* (Pelican Freud Library 5, 46–49).

7. G. K. Hunter admits Parolles' stage success as a humor character but finds no way to "fit him into this play," or "to balance him against the different kind of reality" of Helena (xlviii). But see Rogers, *Psychoanalytic Study of the Double in Literature,* chap. 8 passim, for a very useful account of character "doubling," especially the latent, "secret sharer" kind, as "a fundamental mechanism" for the representation of psychic conflict.

8. I have attempted to develop a theory of exorcist Shakespearean comic form in *Comic Transformations in Shakespeare* (London, 1980).

9. "Sexually responsive" was one of the many nuances of the word in Elizabethan English, which included the archaic "natural" and the modern "well-intentioned" or "good-natured."

Bibliography

Brooks, Peter. "Repetition, Repression and Return: *Great Expectations* and the Study of Plot," *NLH* (1980).

Frye, Northrop. *Anatomy of Criticism* (Princeton, N.J.: Princeton University Press, 1957).

Holland, Norman. *Psychoanalysis and Shakespeare* (New York: Farrar, 1979).

Lawrence, W. W. *Shakespeare's Problem Comedies* (New York: Macmillan, 1931).

Mansfield, Katherine. *Journal,* ed. John Middleton Murray (1927, reprint; London: Constable, 1954).

Nicoll, Allardyce. *Shakespeare* (London, 1952).

Raysor, T. M., ed. *Coleridge'sShakespeare Criticism* (London: Dent, 1960).

Rogers, Robert. *A Psychoanalytic Study of the Double in Literature* (Detroit: Wayne State University Press, 1970).

Ure, Peter. *Shakespeare: The Problem Plays* (London: Longman, 1961).

Wheeler, Richard P. *Shakespeare's Development and the Problem Comedies* (Berkeley and Los Angeles: University of California Press, 1981).

The Isolation of the Tragic Protagonist: Tragedy and *Richard III*

Baruch Kurzweill

> This deficiency of all bind and attachment, for the personality is centered only on its own Self, is also what casts, over Universe and God, this special dimness in which the tragic hero moves.[1]

AMONG all of Shakespeare's protagonists, none is more engrossed in himself nor exacts—with a pride more obstinate and exceeding all that is human—only for his own self-hood than Richard III. His isolation is absolute. His ambition, his yearning for might and power, these are not the main motives behind his actions. The absolute isolation—for which there are deep emotional reasons—the feeling of having no bind or connection whatsoever with either the human or the divine spheres, these are what clear the path for Richard to gratify his uninhibited craving for power.

Unlike Iago, with whom he shares many emotional traits, no threats of Nothingness and Unworthiness ever reach Richard's awareness and attempt to rouse it. He is unable to feel emptiness or unworthiness within himself because, in the depths of his own self, he creates for himself some kind of complete cosmos. The material world does exist for Iago, but all its contents are painful objects that serve to remind him of his own nothingness and emptiness. Iago must destroy all that is of value, in order to transform the All into Nothing and thus to succeed in overcoming his own feelings of alienation and isolation. The absolute Nothing devours these feelings, as it devours him as well. This is not true for Richard, who finds his complete satisfaction within himself. Richard's personality is incomparably superior to Iago's. His actions, unlike Iago's triumphal cries of Nothingness, are the result of a consistent and extreme exaltation of the Ego until it reaches the level of One and Only, the all-important value.

One can say the rest of humankind does not exist at all, as far as Richard is concerned. All are merely demonic objects, to be used by him as needed. Due to his purely technical relation with others, with his peers—for he lacks all reservation or emotional restraint, essential in a relation to Man—Richard appears to be so "successful." Formally speaking, he has mastered all the rules of social etiquette required to interact with people. Assisted by a sharp and unusual intellect, Richard has perfected the practice of this perfunctory technique in human relations, and thanks to his absolute lack of human attachment, he succeeds in beguiling all creatures into complying with his designs. Shakespearean scholars who claim that Richard's actions are influenced by hypocrisy and deceptiveness are mistaken, in my opinion. Hypocrisy presumes some sort of minimal feeling for the universe, where something such as truth perhaps exists; however, such criteria have no hold in Richard's soul. In Shakespeare's entire world, he alone has no knowledge whatsoever of Love. Iago knows it as Passion. For its sake he is jealous of other men and, above all others, of Othello, who is Man with a capital *M*. Iago's jealousy, which is indeed of a lowly kind, is nevertheless a miserable manifestation of some perverse Love. Even jealousy is alien to Richard's spirit. By the love he professes for himself, Richard loves whatever is at all worthy of Love in his diabolic world. This singularity serves to measure the great distance between Macbeth—also a tragic victim of obsessive craving for power—and Richard. Macbeth loves his wife. Human emotion is not alien to him. He hesitates before murdering his king. Macbeth's isolation is not absolute because Love binds him to the human sphere. The same applies to King Claudius in *Hamlet*. Neither Macbeth nor Claudius belong to the absolutely unethical sphere. Macbeth's indecision and, to a greater extent, Claudius' prayer, testify to the existence of some contact between themselves and the Ethic sphere. Not even the slightest iota of ethical behavior can be detected in the isolation of Richard's selfhood. Elements of humanity that were restricted and suppressed, come forth only in his dreams; the horrid images that surface in Richard's nightmare are the only remnants of humanity left in him.

Lear's isolation—similar to that of Timon—is the result of Love hatched in heedlessness. What at first seems like excessive Love, an abundance of innocent trust in the goodness of man, is in fact a sin that stems from heedlessness and self-love. Timon's extreme misanthropy is merely the expression of a tremendous disappointment at his sudden and cruel awakening from the deceptions of Love. And if the faith of Lear and Timon, up until the outset of the tragic crisis, was also based on a misconception about the world and humanity, their consciousness, however, has experienced Love.

Richard's consciousness is utterly unable to feel Love. As far as his Ego is concerned it has never experienced Love. From his earliest existence Love has been alien to him. Thus, he is unaware that something is lacking in him. Indeed, one can further question whether Richard's rational-intellectual "awareness" of himself is the essential truth about his entire self and, surely, one can wonder whether his "awareness" of the world can possibly bring him any closer to his understanding of it.

On the other hand, I doubt whether one can possibly compare Richard with Mephistopheles, in Goethe's *Faust*: "Intellect devoid of Love, such as that of Goethe's Mephistopheles; for he, because of his lack of Love, was banished beyond the pale of human nature," according to L. C. Knights.[2] This evaluation is doubly erroneous. First, because—according to Goethe's testimony—Mephistopheles on his own is no tragic character for, among other things, there are no demonic elements in him: " . . . the demonic . . . is that which can not be deciphered, not by means of reason nor by means of wisdom alone. . . . Mephistopheles is too negative a creature; the demonic expresses itself by means of an active and, indeed, positive force." I believe it would be quite difficult to find a tragic character completely devoid of demonic elements. As for Richard, the existence of an active positive force within him is undeniable. Unlike Iago, he is no coward; he is a true hero on the battlefield, and Shakespeare, despite Richard's heinous crimes, knew how to bring him closer to the hearts of audience and reader alike.

Secondly, Richard owes his tragic character, precisely, to those vanquished and latent remnants of humanity—those last shreds of human emotion—which surface from time to time, and float around in his dreams or daydreams, far reminders of a long-lost identification with the sphere of humankind. All this is undetectable in Mephistopheles who embodies the flawless unity of all that is negative, and within him, of course, there is no possibility of differentiating between his state of conscious—intellectuality and a state of vague speculation on other emotional options. The absolute Evil and Negative that are stripped of the faintest traces of humanity, are unsuitable objects for the tragic plot. And despite the fact that in Richard's case, as just stated, his actions insinuate themes beyond those of Good and Evil, still, Shakespeare allows us to glimpse at the formative process of things as it takes place within Richard's soul, and whoever observes the protagonist's path, from the opening scenes of *King Henry VI*, part 3, will surely witness the not insignificant emotional fluctuations in Richard's development.

According to Greek tragedy, the tragic plot begins long before the curtain rises on the play. Tragedy itself does not deal with the development of the protagonist. By the beginning of the play, he is unable to change and all his characteristics are already embedded in his personality. But here and there, at certain moments in the course of tragedy, sudden flashes of light illuminate the "Now" of tragic events as they take place, until it is finally revealed in full depth. At such a time, the whole dramatic present seems saturated with elements of the past and, in any event, the present in dramatic art—and all dramatic art is an art of the present—acquires special meaning and weight. From the very beginning, *Antigone* echoes with the tragedy of the Labdacus family—the tragedy of the house of Oedipus—which serves as background to Antigone's own tragedy. Prometheus, in his opening words, refers to the tragic rebellion against the gods on Olympus.

Richard III opens with Gloucester's long monologue, which is not only the protagonist's personal testimony of his isolation and the psychological factors behind his actions.[3] Though he is unaware of it, Richard's words also convey suggestions of the past and open horizons—concealed before him—but only they can portray the entire truth and significance of the events.

> Now is the winter of our discontent
> Made glorious summer by this sun of York;
> And all the clouds that lour'd upon our House
> In the deep bosom of the ocean buried.
> (*Richard III*, 1.1. ll. 1–4)

Richard here reveals the true background of the play's entire plot: The civil war in England; the strife lasting for generations, between the Houses of York and Lancaster; and Richard himself who is, unwittingly, just some sort of personification of all the hatred, of the nonhuman, that has accumulated here through generations. Though all along, Richard has been aware that he is a fringe effect of the human species, in the opening scenes of *King Henry VI*, part 3 his connection with the human realm can still be felt: He is devoted to both his father and younger brother, Rutland. Furthermore, one is almost inclined to believe that all Richard does, is done for the express purpose of ingratiating himself with the father after whom he is named. It seems as if Richard, by his deeds, were trying to prove that no one among his brothers is worthier than himself to bear the title of Son of Richard the Elder. And great is his satisfaction upon hearing his father's words, "Richard hath best deserv'd of all my sons."[4] He, the hunchback, the one deprived by Nature, by means of heroism shows his predilection, and his name, Richard, is both commitment and evidence, all in one. In the identification with his father, are embedded the human and nonhuman elements that coexist in Richard's soul: The human—for here one can still detect signs of Love (in *King Henry VI*), which vanish entirely in the course of the play; and the nonhuman—for already here, some infirm force compels Richard to see himself as the only one worthy and suitable to carry on after his father—in other words, he alone, after his father, deserves the kingdom. For this reason, he alone is worthy of ousting Henry VI. Hence, just after his father's words of praise, Richard declares, "Thus do I hope to shake King Henry's head," (*Henry VI*, 3.1.1.l. 20).

It is clear from the outset that kings and princes of the House of Lancaster are considered, first and foremost, merely as obstacles that are to be eliminated. Yet, in the figure of Richard, all that is inhuman and immoral in this war between the two royal houses, turns against its self-essence, against its own family blood. The major importance of Richard's relationship with his father, in understanding Richard's own character, is revealed in *King Henry VI*, part 3, at the beginning of act 2, scene 1:

> I cannot joy until I be resolv'd
> Where our right valiant father is become.
> (2.1. ll. 9–10)

These words are sincere. Richard is still unaware of his father's death, which, when revealed, will put an end to his joy and extinguish the faint human flicker that still burns in him. With the tragic news, Richard spurns tears and chooses vengeance:

> I cannot weep, for all my body's moisture
> Scarce serves to quench my furnace-burning heart . . .
> To weep is to make less the depth of grief:
> Tears then for babes; blows and revenge for me!
> (3.2.1. ll, 79–80, 85–86)

And instantly, as if the father's soul had fused with his own, in the father's name, he recalls his own.

> Richard, I bear thy name; I'll venge thy death,
> Or die renowned by attempting it.
> (3.2.1. l. 87–88)

Step by step, Shakespeare proceeds to shape the protagonist's development. In Richard's long monologue, in act 3 of the same play, his words imply the final break with the human sphere. Now—after the death of his beloved father—for the first time, he confesses that Love is absent in his soul. This though, is only a partial truth. For, in fact, he loved his father and his younger brother. But, out of his infirm identification with the father—symbolized by the fact that they both bear the same name—and in a compulsive effort to redress the suffering brought on him by his deformity, he silences within himself the voices of humanity and denies the existence of Love in his soul. As far as intellectual awareness is concerned—in the emotional state he is in after learning of his father's death—there is no doubt that Richard's words reflect his inner truth about himself. But only now does he become fully aware that even the most minute trace of Love has disappeared from within himself. The world, to Richard, now seems drained of all meaning and joy. Thus, only the Ego exists. In his absolute isolation and infirm yearning for power, he admits:

> Well, say there is no kingdom for Richard;
> What other pleasure can the world afford?
> (3.3.2. ll, 146–47)

There is no place in Richard's world for Eros, even in the broadest sense. Life seems to have frozen and warmth seems to have evaporated. Human beings are merely objects, monsters, means, obstacles, speaking contraptions. All, his own relatives no less than the Lancasters. All are just hurdles in the path toward his only goal in life, in this immoral and loveless world. And we must again marvel at Shakespeare's brilliant insight, when he allows Richard, from the first words, to express the essential, the painful awareness concerning his frigid world, now despoiled of the last shreds of warmth of Eros:

> Why, Love forswore me in my mother's womb:
> And, for I should not deal in her soft laws,
> She did corrupt frail Nature with some bribe,

> To shrink mine arm up like a wither'd shrub;
> To make an envious mountain on my back,
> Where sits Deformity to mock my body.
>> (*Henry VI*, 3.3.2. ll. 153–58)

His brother Edward loves women and is loved by them; they are the most natural contact with all that is human, an area closed before Richard. The decision on the most heinous and despicable of all his acts—the murder of his brother's children, which so revolts us in *Richard III*—seems to have been taken by Richard, already at this stage. Clearly, in a frigid world inhabited only by demons and obstacles, which block the Ego's path in its pursuit of itself, the Ego must feverishly run from isolation to isolation and destroy everything that obstructs its way. It is no coincidence, however, that here, in this long monologue, Richard links the theme of his love-deprived soul to his physical impediments. In a passionate need for self-punishment, he continues to enumerate his deformities while attempting to discover why his universe is depleted of the charms of Eros,

> And am I then a man to be belov'd?
> O monstrous fault to harbour such a thought!
>> (3.3.2. ll. 163–64)

Thus, Richard feels he has no other choice:

> Then, since this earth affords no joy to me
> But to command, to check, to o'erbear such
> As are of better person than myself.
>> (3.3.2. ll. 165–67)

The deprived Ego elevates itself to the position of divine ideal and inverts the whole world, which reminds him of his absolute isolation, into Hell:

> I'll make my heaven to dream upon the crown;
> And, whiles I live, t'account this world but hell,
> Until my misshap'd trunk that bears this head
> Be round impaled with a glorious crown.
>> (3.3.2. ll. 168–71)

It is clear to Richard that in this arbitrary inversion of the world he is taking revenge for the complete isolation in which he finds himself. The path to his "heaven" is paved with torture. Yet, unable to submit to his fate, and with the Christian road to submissiveness closed before him—for he is "God's enemy," in Richmond's words (*Richard III*, 5.3.1. 153)—in order " . . . to find the open air" (*Henry VI*, 3.3.2. l. 177), Richard has no alternative but to ". . . hew my way out with a bloody axe" (3.3.2. l. 181). The searing experience of this tormented and inhuman path, and his awareness of the cruel compulsion his inhumanity imposes on him, are what elevate Richard to the position of tragic protagonist. But the same experience and awareness also reveal that somewhere, in the most secluded and obscure corners of Richard's soul, flickers of humanity had indeed once nested, sometime in the past:

> And I,—like one lost in a thorny wood,
> That rents the thorns and is rent with the thorns,
> Seeking a way, and straying from the way . . .
> Torment myself to catch the English crown:
> And from that torment I will free myself.
> (3.3.2. ll. 174–76, 179–80)

But, alas, all efforts are unable to save him from the torments of isolation, for even the most complete control over other human beings—one that succeeds to transform them into obedient objects—is no substitute for the most basic and humble contact between Man and his fellow, for a relation that begins in a warm spark of Love.

Richard though, rejects all feeling, and seeks shelter in his cold intellect. He seems to despise all but his head. How symbolic, then, this yearning for a crown, a wreath, to place on his head! The wreath, to emphasize his head, his intelligence, and to divert attention from a loathsome body. His crowned head will help him forget this body; his intellect will stifle any remnants of warm feeling.

For the second time, near the end of *King Henry VI*, part 3, Richard unveils in a monologue the nature of his subhuman existence, right after he murders King Henry. He again needs to stress the lack of Love in his soul and, typically, couples the confession of belonging to a sphere completely devoid of Eros, with the thought that Nature has deprived him by physically deforming his body:

> I that have neither pity, love, nor fear . . .
> Then, since the heavens have shap'd my body so,
> Let hell make crook'd my mind to answer it.

> I have no brother, I am like no brother;
> And this word "love", which greybeards call divine,
> Be resident in men like one another,
> And not in me: I am myself alone.
>
> (3.5.6. ll. 68, 78–83)

Just as his first monologue in act 3 is a disclosure in small-scale of the most hideous murder, that of his brother Edward's children, as just mentioned—the fate of his brother Clarence is actually sealed in the second monologue, where Richard stresses the extent of his isolation, to the point of obliterating all traces of brotherly feeling from his soul. The certainty of being singular, destined, and chosen, signifies the sign of denial for all other mortals, and does not represent an increase in positive attributes that, in any event, would single out and isolate no less than they elevate the destined individual. Being chosen, singular, and destined, in Richard's case, does not constitute any sorrowful addition to the human aspect but rather its absolute negation.

"I have no brother"—words of double meaning. On one level: I am isolated, on my own, and there is no one who resembles me. But also: Why not kill my brother Clarence and then, also slay my brother Edward? We are again astonished by Shakespeare's genius. Immediately after declaring, "I have no brother," Richard adds

> Clarence, beware; thou keep'st me from the light,
> But I will sort a pitchy day for thee. . . .
> Clarence, thy turn is next, and then the rest.
>
> (3.5.6. ll. 84–85, 90)

With the strength of intellectual persuasion, Richard convinces himself that he no longer belongs to the human sphere, and freezes within himself all remnants of emotion and conscience that, from now on, will only surface in the dreadful nightmares that are to plague his tormented nights.

By the end of *King Henry VI*, part 3 this development is final. Richard's third monologue, at the opening of *Richard III*, is a summary of the previous ones. The "glorious summer by this sun of York"[5] (*Richard III*, 1.1.1. 2), is in fact a desolate, frigid, and loveless world, populated only by demons, and the "sun of York" is actually Richard. But this sun of his shines exclusively for itself. If someone were foolish enough to seek its warmth, his end is to be scorched by it. And this sun, which denies its life—giving rays to the world, has grown to consume itself in the blaze of its own solitude. After the last sparks of Love vanish, the fact that Richard's negative and inhuman isolation is also the result of guilt and not only of fate, will at last become clear to the protagonist in his final monologue, when he is about to face his enemy, Richmond, at the battlefield near Bosworth. Only when Richard is in a state of mind beyond that of lucid intellectual awareness, will we again encounter a breach in his complete isolation:

> O coward conscience, how dost thou afflict me!
> (5.3.1. 180)

In fact, everyone shows up: Prince Edward, King Henry, his brother Clarence, all the noble people executed at Richard's orders, the ghosts of his brother's children, his wife Anne, and his aide, Buckingham. Man is not only cold intellect, and his deeds are not arranged according to the fiction which maintains that the most suitable sphere for man is the immoral. For then he will not only forfeit all true approach to the "You," but the path to himself will also elude him. This tragic and paradoxical situation is the final truth about Richard. He, who was pathologically committed only to himself and denied all others the right to actual existence, regarding them as mere objects, must ultimately stand before the enigma of the Ego, now a total stranger to him.

What depths of human soul are revealed to us by Shakespeare! No one is left for Richard to fear. Here, at this late hour of the night, no one is left but himself. Even now, as before, his Ego fills the entire universe, and no place or existence remain for others, just as in the past:

> The lights burn blue; it is now dead midnight.
> Cold fearful drops stand on my trembling flesh.
> What do I fear? Myself? There's none else by.
> (5.3.2. 181–83)

No reason to fear. Yet, nevertheless. . . . But, why? Clearly, the only one that counts, Richard, loves himself, is confident of himself. There is certainly ground for self-love:

> Richard loves Richard, that is, I and I.
> (5.3.1. 184)

Alas! This Love is just as suspicious. The Ego does not trust itself and, in fact, never did. It actually hated itself all along, and externalized its hate on others. His denial of the world and of his fellowmen was indeed an extension of his self—denial. Richard does not love Richard. This horrible Ego of his is a tragic, cruel-heroic, and satanic mask and, beneath it, the remnants of a human Ego belonging to someone who's name was also Richard, were stifled to death! But this Richard does not—and never did—love the other Richard, who was still linked, by a spark of Love, to Richard, the father. The "I" is not "I." If true, then the "I" must flee from the "I."

> Is there a murderer here? No. Yes, I am!
> Then fly. What, from myself? Great reason why,
> Lest I revenge? What, myself upon myself?
> Alack, I love myself. Wherefore? For any good
> That I myself have done unto myself?
> O no, alas, I rather hate myself
> For hateful deeds committed by myself.
> I am a villain—yet I lie, I am not!
> Fool, of thyself speak well! Fool, do not flatter.
> (5.3.2. 185–93)

Each word seems to surface from two different emotional levels. "Is there a murderer here?" In other words, someone to kill Richard. And the answer is, "No." Immediately after, the voice of the second "I": "Yes, I am!" There is a killer here and his name is Richard. Thus, Richard must flee from Richard. But, can a person flee from himself? Especially, if he loves himself?

"Alack, I love myself." What a tremendous mistake! The truth is otherwise: " . . . alas, I rather hate myself. . . ." This is the key to the enigma called Richard. Not only does Richard hate himself now; the quarrel between Richard and Richard has raged all along. And he continues to list his sins and accuse himself. "Guilty, guilty!" (l. 200). Then, in a sigh of deeply repressed pain—so unlike the previous monologues that soared from a recalcitrant pride—Richard articulates these poignantly simple words:

> I shall despair. There is no creature loves me,
> And if I die, no soul will pity me—
> And wherefore should they, since that I myself
> Find in myself no pity to myself?
> (5.3.2. 201–4)

In a desolate and bewildered world—the Ego, also desolate and bewildered, not being at peace with itself, must silence and engulf its self-hatred in a sea of blood. How miserable and senseless were all of Richard's deeds as he fled from Richard! How futile, those aspirations of glory and honor, what poor substitutes for a bit of Love! Vanity of vanities, all. This theme, so central to all of Shakespeare's works, originates in the spiritual world of the baroque and reaches a climax here: Self-hatred and lack of Love—these are the true motivating force behind Richard's actions: " . . . since that I myself / Find in myself no pity to myself." But, as is already clear, the voice of conscience emerges in Richard's soul only when he is in an altered state, between slumber and awakening or in his dreadful dreams.

Before his death, Richard again recovers, one last time. In his oration to the troops, before the final battle, the mask again overpowers Richard—who appeared to be at peace with himself—and silences the Richard who hates Richard. Before facing his soldiers, he reassures himself:

> Let not our babbling dreams affright our souls;
> Conscience is but a word that cowards use,
> Devis'd at first to keep the strong in awe.
> Our strong arms be our conscience, swords our law.
> (5.3. ll. 309–12)

The same sophistic argument has been voiced ever since by all tyrants who, like Richard, have sought to silence their conscience and the hum of their self-hatred, in the rivers of blood of all those who dared to disappoint their love. Their activities, like Richard's, are engendered in absolute isolation, in a posture at once immoral and devoid of Eros.

"Conscience," the notion which shortly before brought the protagonist so near to a true self-awareness, and revealed before him the Human-Ethic sphere, is now forcefully rejected by Richard. In this he remains true to himself. Hamlet also pondered on the position of conscience, on the conscious recognition of Good and Evil, and seemed occasionally attracted to the possibility of ridding himself of conscience, of the dependence on an awareness of Good and Evil:

> Thus conscience does make cowards of us all.[6]

Almost identical to Richard's words,

> Conscience is but a word that cowards use.
> (5.3. l. 310)

By eliminating Conscience from his soul, Richard destroys all binds and attachments, and remains engrossed in his own selfhood until death, in his own singular darkness, distanced from both the divine and the human sphere.

Notes

1. Rosenzweig, *Star of Redemption*, part 1.
2. Knights, *Some Shakespearean Themes*.
3. William Shakespeare, *Richard III, The Arden Shakespeare*, ed. Anthony Hammond (New York: Methuen & Co., 1981). The same edition is used for all further references which are included parenthetically in the text, preceded by *Richard III*.
4. Shakespeare, *King Henry VI*, part 3, 1.1. l. 17. The same edition is used for all further references, which are included parenthetically in the text, preceded by *Henry IV*. 3.
5. Although evidence seems to indicate that Shakespeare here used the word "son," "virtually all editors have followed . . . [the] emendation 'sun' to give point to the pun . . . [for] Edward IV assumed the device of a sun as his emblem . . ." See comment in Shakespeare, *Richard III*, 125 n. 2.
6. Shakespeare, *Hamlet, The Arden Shakespeare*, 3.1. l. 83.

Bibliography

Knights, L. C. *Some Shakespearean Themes, and an Approach to Hamlet*. Harmondsworth, Middlesex: Penguin Books, 1966.

Kurzweil, Baruch. *European Drama: Studies and Essays*, eds. Jacob Abramson and Chaim Shoham, trans. R. Pancer, 1933. First published, *Bamah, Theatrical Journal* 4 (57) January 1960, Ramat Gan, Israel: Bar-Ilan University Press, 1979.

Rosenzweig, F. *Star of Redemption*, part 1.

Shakespeare, William. *Hamlet*, ed. Harold Jenkins. *The Arden Shakespeare*. New York: Methuen & Co., 1982.

———. *King Henry VI*, part 3, ed. Andrew S. Cairncross. *The Arden Shakespeare*. London: Methuen & Co., 1964.

———. *Richard III*, ed. Anthony Hammond. *The Arden Shakespeare*. New York: Methuen & Co., 1981.

Prophecy as a Cultural Model: The Politics of *Tamburlaine* and *Julius Caesar*

AVRAHAM OZ

> *Touchstone.* For all your writers do consent that *ipse* is he.
> Now you are not *ipse,* for I am he.
> *William.*   Which he sir?
>
> (*As You Like It,* 5.1.42–44)

IN an angry book fiercely disposing with normal academic decorum, Christopher Norris attacks Baudrillard's prediction, made just a few days before the break of the Gulf War, that "la guerre du Golfe n'aura pas lieu."[1] Following Baudrillard's views concerning the bankruptcy of factual verification in the postmodern era, his prediction may still be regarded error-proof by him and by his disciples (and indeed, after the war Baudrillard did publish a defense, or rather vindication, of his theoretical stand relating the war to some level of "hyperreality").[2] Norris has many well-founded and well-argued points in his quarrel with Baudrillard's total subjection of reality to his radically postmodern delusions, or rather, theoretical configurations. And yet, as one who, from an arguably both tangential and detached stance, had witnessed the effects of the Gulf War simultaneously exposed to the shrieks of Scud-cum-Patriot missiles and the uninterruptedly interpretive narrative of CNN, I can testify from experience to the diabolic allure of relieving oneself from all fetters of cognition and epistemology in the face of an evidently broken vision of reality. My concern here is with a possibly similar, though otherwise motivated, strategic response adopted by early modern writers to cope with the ennui of an identity crisis leading to an evident shattering of recognized structures of reality. One should scarcely be encouraged to burden the plethora of recently circumscribed regions constituting the early modern world with postmodern fractured narratives or identities; and yet the absolute authority of the word of God gave way in that interim zone between medieval clericalism and seventeenth-century scientific revolution to other, diffused providences, whose authority relied on questionable, open-ended tropes. At the risk of confusing the latter with other, not entirely related cognitive phenomena, I will refer to them as prophetic tropes, by which I mean here the appropriation of a historical narrative from the suddenly incoherent or displaced diachronic continuum of reality and its reconstruction or codification within a virtual master narrative, controlled by human interpretation. At an age in which human cognition was confident enough already on its road to institutionalized rationalism to deride superstitious, charismatic, or "drunken" prophecies (*Richard III*, 1.1.33), but not ripe enough as yet for elaborate scientific predictions, the twilight zone in which that trope of prophetic riddles (whether inherent in language, rituals, or the body) captured conscientious unions of reason and imagination, was highly acute and significant.

Anyone addressing the issue of historical representation in the theater cannot help stumbling on the paradox ever investing the drama of history on- and offstage alike: designed primarily to represent a succession of events, historical drama becomes almost by definition a version of character study. There is a close proximity between the practice of modern media to conceive historical events in terms of individual motivations, represented by personal agencies, and the practice of historical drama to read political patterns and processes in terms of individual will. Rather than exploring the possibilities of developing a narrative, the factual enclosure by which historical theater is bound delegates a particular significance to the representation of psychological constitution, or, at best, the structures of identity, of historical characters. The real innovation left to the author, is to determine who are the goodies and baddies of history, we feel, and authors of historical drama would often go along with that kind of expectation. A predicament even an eminent anti-Arisotelian dramatist such as Brecht fails to avoid in his *Life of Galileo* gets the better of more Cartesian-minded playwrights professing to represent history without attempting to escape the illusory domination of the liberal humanist concept of unity of character. At best, one may subvert the dominating moral judgment qualifying a given character (as Büchner or Brecht are relatively successful in doing), thus undermining the Cartesian fallacy of the unified historical subject and leaving the play open-ended. Since our habits of passing moral or political judgment are still largely dominated by well-rounded hegemonic ideologies, open-endedness often tends to baffle us or seem wrong. We therefore require different sets of discursive parameters. Such open-ended practices, becoming more and more detectable recently within the bulky corpus of early modern historical drama, thus may be best construed, with due precaution, in the light of postmodern critical discourse.

Representation plays, of course, a major role within history itself even before we transform the latter into drama. The frequent parodylike uses of charisma in offstage history are profusely exemplified in the ever-increasingly mediated practice informing election campaigns throughout the democratic world, whereby the shape of current history is often determined by the commanding effect of a face posted on walls; a look, or body language on a TV screen. To skip the much-dwelled-upon cases of the United States, let me draw an example from home. The two opposing ideologies addressing the Israeli voters in the June 1992 election campaign, while a peace process seemed to gain momentum, never touched the revolution of the times more acutely. And yet the crucial return to power of the Labor party had rather to do with charisma than ideology. The almost parodic factor in that historic overturn of government was that the dynamic new authority who gained power to become Israel's new leader was no other than he who, fifteen years earlier, was the last prime minister of a worn-out Labor government that (although not in a campaign led by him personally) lost the elections to a right-wing coalition. Rabin's successor as prime minister in 1977 was the perplexingly charismatic Menahem Begin, master of rhetorical and theatrical gestures, who became a symbolic father figure for voters who yearned for such a figure since the retirement of Ben Gurion, Israel's first prime minister. In 1992 Begin's own tired, unimaginative, and ultraconservative successor became a liability for his party. At the expense of exposing him as a central focus of attention, the party made use of Begin's death, which happened to coincide with the very opening of the election campaign; turned his funeral into a civic pageant; promoted a mass pilgrimage to his fresh grave; used profusely his old portraits, recorded speeches, and video appearances, and even assigned a central role in the campaign to Begin's son, an inexperienced, uncharismatic politician whose pathetic attempts to imitate the gestures, intonations, and rhetoric of his late father aroused many satiric comments from friends and foes alike. His major properties whereby he claimed public support were his father's name and face. While the right-wing party used every trick in its book in attempting to undermine Rabin's personal credibility, the opposite party presented seventy-year old Rabin as a fresh, new hope. His face, both shy and confident, was widely posted and screened, a surrogate father figure for disillusioned right-wing voters. However, the real tour-de-force of manipulating this target constituency came at the last evening of the election campaign: in a secret operation, the Labor party released and replayed a sixteen-year-old TV film in which Menahem Begin, then still the leader of the right-wing opposition in Parliament, warmly congratulated the then prime minister Yitzhak Rabin for the successful Entebbe operation, stressing Rabin's personal role in planning and ordering the release of hostages held at the Ugandan airport. Many have argued that Begin's ghost appearance that evening brought to Labor the vital couple of seats that assured its return to power.[3] History provided yet another example of how its changing of course often travels through the center point of character representation. What holds for history itself proves even more acute regarding its theatrical representation.

Relating postmodern criteria to early modern forms of representation is problematic, since in the preindustrial phase of capitalism the fusion of institutional and personal identity had not yet been entirely eliminated. The institutionalized conception of man as the representation of the second figure in the Trinity has indeed lost its grip by the sixteen century, but no clear cognitive patterns rendered that heroic gesture, called by Stephen Greenblatt "Renaissance self-fashioning," a common practice among the general public. In the domain of "expressive culture,"[4] no major changes had occurred before the scientific revolution of the late seventeenth century. The collision between the early-modern urge to dispense with obsolete cognitive patterns and the still-coercive power of institutionalized self-images called, however, for liberation through artistic representation, which may partly account for the popularity of Elizabethan theater, in which self-fashioning became a prominent feature and theme.

Thus, a major sense in which both Marlowe and Shakespeare's dramatic practice yields itself to postmodern discourse lies in their frequent tendency to break patterns of subjectivity by interchanging, appropriating, and tampering with human identities. Rather than insisting on circumscribing holistic, complex psychological constructs, both contemporaries often regard their characters as transcending the boundaries of a totalized subject, making them constantly fashioned by themselves or others. Faces, looks, and bodies become prophetic tropes, mostly open-ended, riddling representations of multifaced, dialogic narratives. Since Elizabethan theater preceded the Cartesian discourse, which was to dominate centuries of liberal humanism, one cannot literally identify that practice with postmodern deconstruction proper, if such at all exists. And yet the free fashioning of identities that were represented in many of the plays of Marlowe and Shakespeare (whether as an impulse assigned to a given dramatic subject or as an overt or implicit dramaturgic strategy) may be construed as a prophetic resistance to a corrupting process of individualization that the sharp political sensors of both contemporaries detected, each after his own dramaturgic fashion, in the passage of Western culture into the phase later to be known as early-modern discourse. In the world of the comedies, the resistance against totalization often breeds prefigurations of postmodern parody, anticipating the deliberately disenchanting denouements of the later mature and problem comedies: such parodic patterns may be traced in the Beatrice-Benedick plot in *Much Ado,* in the Phebe-Ganymede affair in *As You Like It,* and possibly in the main plots of an early comedy like *The Taming of the Shrew* or a late one like *All's Well That Ends Well.* Disguise, impersonation, and bodily manipulation play a big part in this dramatic strategy. Nor did Shakespeare have to go too far in order to seek inspiration for such parodic representation, as a rather trivial record from court in 1597 may tell us:

> Lady Mary Howard is possessed with a rich border powdered with gold and pearl, and a velvet suit belonging thereto which has moved many to envy; nor has it pleased the Queen who thought it exceeded her own. Wherefore the Queen sent privately and got the lady's rich vesture, which she put on herself and came among the ladies. the kirtle and border were too short for her Majesty's height and she asked everyone how they liked her new fancied suit. At length she asked the Lady Mary herself if it was not made too short, and ill becoming; to which the poor lady did consent. 'Why then,' quoth the Queen, 'If it become not me as being too short, I am minded it shall never become thee as being too fine; so it fitteth neither well.' By this sharp rebuke the Lady Howard is abashed and had not adorned her herewith sithence.[5]

In Elizabethan tragedy, however, parody gives way to insoluble probing of a unified concept of character: playing a part is not anymore a dramatic strategy alone, but a sweeping epistemological and, as the case may be, political statement, in which, as

Emily Bartels says of Marlowe's *Tamburlaine*, "what is at risk is autonomy, agency, and individuation."[6]

In the realm of Marlowe's tragedies, as Greenblatt is not alone in arguing, the grotesquely comic constantly exists "as the mechanical imposed upon the living": Tamburlaine may be parodically conceived as "a machine, a desiring machine that produces violence and death."[7] Respectively, the mechanical transportation of the shepherd into an ever-mightier dominating position almost paradoxically simplifies a major parameter of theatrical characterization such as class distinction: while Tamburlaine himself is mythically accounted for (e.g., in Menaphon's description of him in 1 *Tamburlaine*, 2.1), and whereas a certain amount of crude individuation is still retained among the variety of kingly figures victimized by Tamburlaine and made to kneel at his feet throughout his picaresque voyage along the courses of victory, anyone ranking below their princely position is reduced to a digit within a mechanical enumeration of reified "humanoids." One distinctive feature of this dramatic strategy is Marlowe's representation of cavalry as an impersonal war machine, a compound military mechanism, whose human components are metonymically referred to, if at all, by the name of the beast they are riding. Accounting for the army at the outset as "a horse" ("Theridamas, / Charg'd with a thousand horse" [1 *Tamburlaine*, 1.1.46–47];[8] "To send my thousand horse incontinent / To apprehend that paltry Scythian" [Ibid., 52–53]), the horses then assume their expected natural shape at the expense of their potential masters, appropriating, and transforming after their own fashion, what should have been logically conceived as their riders' attitudes toward their foe:

> Thou shalt be leader of this thousand horse,
> Whose foaming gall with rage and high disdain
> Have sworn the death of wicked Tamburlaine
>
> (Ibid., 62–64)

The riders themselves, however, have by now vanished entirely from our view, as if melted into thin air:

> That I may view these milk-white steeds of mine
> All loaden with the heads of killed men,
> And from their knees even to their hoofs below
> Besmear'd with blood; that makes a dainty show.
>
> (Ibid., 77–80)

It is significant that when the cavalry is referred to by a lower ranked character, a nameless spy who accounts in his report for his fellow men, it is depicted as "An hundred horsemen of my company" (1 *Tamburlaine*, 2.2.39). "Common soldiers," indeed, may be addressed, when needed, as "noble soldiers" (Ibid., 63, 59) or even "my masters" (Ibid., 74); and they are capable of humanly "conceive more joy" (1 *Tamburlaine*, 1.1.152), which may amount even to reversing their reified status into appointing an Emperor who vows in return not only "to reign sole king" by their "desires of discipline in arms," but "Cause the soldiers that thus honor [him] / To triumph over many provinces" (Ibid., 172–75). However, once the shadow of war returns to haunt the discourse, human beings would be again referred to by the horses they ride ("there are in readiness / Ten thousand horse to carry you from hence / In spite of all suspected enemies" [Ibid., 184–86]). As soon as Tamburlaine appears on the scene, with whom the blind, stormy war machine is to take over and dominate representation, humans are regularly invested in beasts, or, by the same token, depicted by the instruments they operate in battle, their virginity, or, on a higher, yet not high enough level, by the crowns allocated to them for their loyalty to the victor:

> Two thousand horse shall forage up and down
> That no relief or succor come by land,
> And all the sea my galleys countermand.
> Then shall our footmen lie within the trench.
> (1 *Tamburlaine*, 3.1.61–64)

>   the great commander of the world
> Besides fifteen contributary kings,
> Hath now in arms ten thousand janissaries,
> Mounted on lusty Mauritanian steeds,
> Brought to the war by men of Tripoli;
> Two hundred thousand footmen that have serv'd
> In the two battles fought in Graecia;
> (Ibid., 3.3.13–19)

> Three hundred thousand men in armor clad
> Upon their prancing steeds, disdainfully
> With wanton paces trampling on the ground;
> Five hundred thousand footmen threat'ning shot,
> Shaking their swords, their spears, and iron bills.
> (Ibid., 4.1.21–25)

The members of an ethnic or national group are thus consistently conceived throughout both *Tamburlaine* plays as an extension of the power of their current leader. And if this practice may be partly ascribed to the alienated vision of the orient of a Christian author, given almost obsessively to the portrayal of the strangeness of others, it is equally applied here to Christian nations:

> Besides, King Sigismund hath brought from Christendom
> More than his camp of stout Hungarians:
> Slavonians, Almains, Rutters, Muffs, and Danes . . .
> Vast Gruntland, compass'd with the frozen sea,
> Inhabited with tall and sturdy men,
> Giants as big as hugy Polypheme,
> Millions of soldiers cut the arctic line.
> (2 *Tamburlaine*, 1.1.20–22, 26–29)

The only instance in which this pattern is broken is Zenocrate's words of compassion (1 *Tamburlaine*, 5.1.319ff), where suffering provides for some degree of individuality. It is she who encounters most clearly in the play the true experience of a tragic cleavage to be resolved solely by a decisive solution. It is she who has to learn to be "wounded in conceit" (Ibid., 415) and be content with her father's overthrow, "else should [she] much forget [her]self" (Ibid., 500). The real tragic hero of the plays, however, is Tamburlaine himself, who not fortuitously knows to compare her at that very moment of resolution to double-faced Juno (Ibid., 510). Significantly, it is only when he sees Zenocrate for the first time that Tamburlaine is made to discern the most distinctive mark of individuality, namely a face. Faces, eyes, and looks as mirrors of individuality and coded prophetic riddles are reserved in the *Tamburlaine* plays, as we are invited to see, solely for the very few figures whose desire soars above the flow of human fate on which the historical narrative runs. Like her closest soul and guide so far, Agydas, who attempts rather simplistically to read Zenocrate's "heart's sorrow" in her "heavenly face" (1 *Tamburlaine*, 3.2.4–5), does Tamburlaine prophetically, and hence with more complexity—bred by a conscientious union of passion and reason, peruse fate and her worth in her "fair face and heavenly hue;" though in his vision even this most intimate touch of gentle feeling toward the one woman, among all women bought with flattery, with whom he is in love; toward she whose "person is more worth to [him] / Than the possession of the Persian crown" significantly promised to him at his birth by a benevolent prophecy (1 *Tamburlaine*, 1.2.90–92), is phrased in a crude language of possession and intermingled with terror:

> this fair face and heavenly hue
> Must grace his bed that conquers Asia
> And means to be a terror to the world
>
> (Ibid., 1.2.36–38)

Later on, their love is sealed and symbolized by their children, more precious in his eyes than all the kingdoms he subdued, "Plac'd by her side, look on their mother's face" (2 *Tamburlaine*, 1.3.18–20). And yet their own looks, he feels, are not martian enough, which makes for another riddle of identity interpreted differently by him and Zenocrate. It is an old riddle in the play: Agydas, a rather flat reader of looks and faces, is not sophisticated enough to decipher Tamburlaine's marital bliss beyond the "martial stratagem" displayed by his "looks so fierce" (1 *Tamburlaine*, 3.1.40–41). The only channel of genuine human tenderness in the world of Tamburlaine, his love for Zenocrate, is indeed the sole outlet capable of producing human individuation for the victims of history. But this acknowledgment of their individuality will not bring any conciliation to the sufferers in Tamburlaine's world of undiscriminating iniquity. Zenocrate, constance in her alleged inconstancy; who, though changed from her "first conceiv'd disdain" for him, and, moved by that same complex desire born of the conscientious marriage of intellect and passion, can read in Tamburlaine's looks his more tender merits and true love for her, nevertheless prophetically senses that invincible iniquity, and propounds her helpless knowledge through her wan and pale face:

> since, a farther passion feeds my thoughts,
> With ceaseless and disconsolate conceits,
> Which dyes my looks so lifeless as they are
> And might, if my extremes had full events,
> Make me the ghastly counterfeit of death.
>
> (Ibid., 12–17)

Is Marlowe passing judgment on a world such presented? The critical debate regarding the play is well-known: some critics argue that he studies the world of a "Herculean hero," some will assign him didactic intentions, and some would regard Marlowe to be morally indifferent. Those later ones may regard his greatest daring as shown in translating history into epic by suggesting that this historical being has quasi-divine powers, and by equating that god-like capacity with a mythological interpretation of the nature of things which makes mind, nature and the idea of god reflections one of the other. At this juncture what Tamburlaine does is to justify himself in terms of a cosmology of which he is revelatory. As the play develops, Marlowe with extraordinary boldness goes further. The protagonist is changed, by the imagination and the power of art into a god. We see the apotheosis of the tyrant.[9]

Power is inextricably intertwined with knowledge in typical Foucauldian patterns: Tamburlaine prizes himself not just for overpowering human foes, but for holding "the Fates bound fast in iron chains, / And with [his] hand turn Fortune's wheel about" (1 *Tamburlaine*, 1.2.174–75). Oracular expressions are crucial to the structure and characterization of the two *Tamburlaine* plays, whose central figure runs throughout its epic narrative a course started by a prophecy given him by the stars at birth. Prophetic messages abound and are directly conveyed in both parts through the use of fully realized riddles. Sometimes the significance of their use scarcely transcends the level of dramatic effectiveness. Tamburlaine, for whom an utmost expression of contempt would be

> a knot of kings,
> Sitting as if they were a-telling riddles
> (2 *Tamburlaine*, 3.5.58–59)

is himself constantly fascinated by his ability to exert his power on human destinies by way of propounding prophetic riddles, bearing divine validity

> Nor are Apollo's oracles more true
> Than thou shall find my vaunts substantial.
> (1 *Tamburlaine*, 1.2.211–12)

For the initiate, it is his very individuality, expressed in his face, that "bears figures of renown and miracle" or, alternatively, "figure[s] death" (1 *Tamburlaine*, 2.1.4, 21). Unlike Bajazeth, invoking his supposedly awesome looks vainly but in vain (1 *Tamburlaine*, 3.1.49), Tamburlaine's looks, "the face and personage of a wondrous man," portayed in epic detail by Menaphon (1 *Tamburlaine*, 2.1.32), both challenges the universe and offers the ready answer for his prophetic riddle. Indeed, Theridamas, immediately taken by "his looks [which] menace heaven and dare the gods," instantly peruses the prophetic message challenging him to "judge the inward man" by his "outward habit," and admits to being "won with [his] words and conquered with [his] looks (1 *Tamburlaine*, 1.2. 157, 163, 228). Tamburlaine, by the same token, is capable of reading in Theridamas' "martial face and stout aspect" the folly of his emperor (Ibid., 165–70), whom he is soon to poke fun at in a comic riddling session ("a pretty jest," or "sport," as he lightly refers to his most presumptuous enterprises [2.5.90, 101]), which baffles Mycetes' poor wit entirely (2.4.22–41). To Cosroe, Theridamas' newly self-appointed emperor designate, who, more wisely than his grotesque brother, would take the Scythian's doom for satisfaction "even as from assured oracle" (a metaphor Tamburlaine often uses himself),[10] Tamburlaine replies with an oracular statement:

> For fates and oracles of heaven have sworn
> To royalize the deeds of Tamburlaine
> (1 *Tamburlaine*, 2.3.7–8)

—which Cosroe totally misconstrues. He learns his answer too late: to his complaint about Tamburlaine's depriving him of his crown and life, Tamburlaine could easily bring Cosroe's own case of usurping his brother's throne as a precedent, but, overtaking human enterprise, he invokes directly "What better precedent than mighty Jove?" (1 *Tamburlaine*, 2.7.17). Later on, however, Tamburlaine's art of riddling becomes more and more explicit. The murder of Agydas is designed and staged by him as the confirmation, by means of a visual riddle, of his victim's prophetic fears identifying the Tyrant's will and the inevitability of fate:

> (Enter Techelles with a naked dagger [and Ususmcasane].)
> Techelles. See you, Agydas, how the king salutes you.
> He bids you prophesy what it imports.
> Agydas. I prophesied before and now I prove
> The killing frowns of jealosy and love.
> He needed not with words confirm my fear,
> For words are vain where working tools present
> The naked action of my threat'ned end.
> It says, "Agydas, thou shalt surely die,
> And of extremities elect the least;
> More honour and less pain it may procure,

> To die by this resolved hand of thine
> Than stay the torments he and heaven have sworn".
> (1 *Tamburlaine*, 3.2.88–99)

and the very tension between the different uses of "prophesy" by Techelles and Agydas (the one meaning "expound," the other, "foretell") results here in a verbal riddle, complementary of the visual one. At the very moment when frowns are turned into action (Ibid., 92–94), foreknowledge is "proved" in the complex insight of true prophecy and its bearer ranked with the initiate. Having put into effect his interpretation of the Tyrant's prophetic riddle, the dead Agydas is hailed as a sage and as an honorable interpreter:

> Techelles.   Usumcasane, see how right the man
>   Hath hit the meaning of my lord the king.
> Usumcasane.   Faith, and Techelles, it was manly done;
>   And since he was so wise and honourable,
>   Let us afford him now the bearing hence,
>   And crave his triple-worthy burial.
>   (Ibid., 107–12)

The same identification of his will with fate, as exercised in the case of Agydas, is translated by Tamburlaine into a prophetic challenge when delegationg his own frowns and looks to his ready soldiers, still conceived as a collective identity, a silent extension of the tyrant's own power and knowledge:

> View well my camp and speak indifferently:
> Do not my captains and my soldiers look
> As if they meant to conquer Africa?
> (1 *Tamburlaine*, 3.3.8–10)

Which Basso misses, since, though appreciating the valor of Tamburlaine's soldiers, he reads them as a separate entity from their leader's prophetic sense of will and fate united, and tells them by their number (as will later the King of Arabia, turned fortune-teller following Capolin's quantitative report). That lack of commitment to looking before and after and peruse the moment prophetically is soon manifested in Basso's emperor, Bajazeth, and his wife, Zabina, who both will not acknowledge the complex, multilayered identity of Tamburlaine and Zenocrate, respectively, and unlike Tamburlaine, whose "words are oracles" (Ibid., 102), since he is capable of reading the complexity of the moment, judge them simplistically by prejudice. Having missed his time to be attentive to his conscience, Bajazeth will later make fool of himself when trying, after his defeat, still to command "dread god of hell" (1 *Tamburlaine*, 4.2.27) or the furies (4.4.17, 5.1.217). The same concept displayed in the death of Agydas' scene is once again conveyed and exercised by Tamburlaine in a dramatic riddle form when encountering the virgins of Damascus:

> Tamburlaine. Virgins, in vain ye Labor to prevent
> That which mine honour swears shall be perform'd.
> Behold my sword; what see you at the point?
> 1 Virgin. Nothing but fear and fatal steel, my lord.
> Tamburlaine. Your fearful minds are thick and misty, then,
> For there sits death; there sits imperious Death,
> Keeping his circuit by the slicing edge.
> (1 *Tamburlaine*, 5.1.106–12)

In 1 *Tamburlaine*, Tamburlaine's prophetic insight into fate matches the structure of the play's action. "What would have been even in the mouth of Achilles or Caesar the rant of overweening pride, has metaphysical justification for Tamburlaine."[11] It is only in 2 *Tamburlaine*, however, where many of the tensions of the first part are resolved, that the Tyrant's prophecy is proved false once his own fate is concerned. At the outset, Orcanes' insistence on separating Tamburlaine from "Fortune that hath made him great" (2 *Tamburlaine*, 1.1.60), as well as Sigismund's quantitative appraisal of his power (Ibid., 106*ff*), seem still to suggest the continued pattern of false prophecy as practiced by Tamburlaine's foes in the first play. However, the differentiation between Tamburlaine's and Zenocrate's opposite readings of their sons' faces marks the futility of Tamberlaine's sterilized militarist ideology, when not directed anymore to turning the world upside down but mercilessly to preserving his own power at all cost. Satisfied by flattering, shallow reiterations of the former emblem of his prophetic abilities:

> mighty Tamburlaine, our earthly god,
> Whose looks make this inferior world to quake
> (2 *Tamburlaine*, 1.3.138–39)

—now mobilized for the sake of unqualified fear and terror alone, he responds in kind by "surfeit[ing] in conceiving joy" just by their sycophantic sight (Ibid., 152–56), and then burst with them in an ecstatic fit of expansionist celebration, sanguinely banqueting on geography. Zenocrate's death, to which Tamburlaine responds by vowing to be "raving, impatient, desperate, and mad" (2 *Tamburlaine*, 2.4.112), drags him further into binding his prophetic practice to futile "fiery meteors . . . presag[ing] / Death and destruction" (Ibid., 3.2.4–5), interpreting the picture of Zenocrate wrongly, her living face no more in sight to qualify his will, after his own fashion, as "Bellona, goddess of the war" (Ibid., 40). From now on he is the rival of true prophecy. After Olympia foreshadows the peripeteia in reversing Tamburlaine's riddle, making Theridamas believe that Death does not sit at the point of the sword (Ibid., 4.2), Tamburlaine is himself deceived by his own riddle, when shaking his sword against heavenly majesty (ibid., 5.1.194) makes him yield his life to "his servant Death."

In spite of what seems a neatly woven master narrative, leading especially the second play along a route of rise and fall, does indeed Tamburlaine's failure to read properly the world's prophetic riddles necessarily bear on his former success to construe them? Or, in other words, should we necessarily read Tamburlaine's inevitable fall at the end of 2 *Tamburlaine* as a judgment passed by Marlowe on the character of Tamburlaine as a unified subject? Defending Paul de Man's attraction to the Nazi ideology at the early stage of the war, Shoshana Felman quotes a text of his uncle, Hendrik de Man, who must have been a great influence on his nephew's ideas:

> the [Nazi] system, despite everything in it that strikes our mentality as alien, had lessened class differences much more efficaciously than the self-styled democracies, where capital continued to lay down the law. Since then everyone has been able to see that the superior morale of the German army is due in large part to the greater social unity of the nation and to the resulting prestige of its authorities. In contrast, the plutocracies offer us the spectacle of authorities deserting their stations and the rich crossing the border by car without worrying about what happens to the masses.[12]

Is one's blindness to the catch in the flattening of social interdependency necessarily criminal? Bad it certainly is, but could it perhaps be interpreted sometimes in terms of tragic blindness? Does Marlowe demand of his hero to be totally and constantly alert to an absolute code of morality (as C. P. Taylor, for example, not unjustifiably demands of his main character in *Good*)? Or is there some political significance in Marlowe's ruthless tyrant's crude belief in shattering by force the iniquity of corrupt, existing hierarchies

> for all my birth,
> That virtue solely is the sum of glory,
> And fashions men with true nobility
>
> (1 *Tamburlaine*, 5.1.125–27)

Which he passes accordingly to his fellow rebels?

> Deserve these titles I endow you with
> By valour and by magnanimity
> Your births shall be no blemish to your fame,
> For virtue is the fount whence honour springs,
> And they are worthy she investeth kings.
>
> (Ibid., 4.4.188–90)

And is their crude attraction to his ideology necessarily corrupt? At best, Marlowe leaves these questions open.

In a Shakespearean historical tragedy such as *Julius Caesar*, however, the open-ended practice of subverting subjectivity and individuation takes a different, still-political but perhaps more mature turn. The analogy between the emblematic historical figures of Tamburlaine and Caesar is hardly fortuitous: it is already drawn by Marlowe himself:

> Tamburlaine. My camp is like to Julius Caesar's host,
> That never fought but had the victory;
>
> (Ibid., 3.3.152–53)

But whereas Tamburlaine's Caesar is significantly that of the battle of Pharsalia, in which he defeated Pompey, Shakespeare concentrates his drama on a later Caesar, about to undergo the problematic attainment of absolute ruling power by a democratic process. It is a complex political juncture in the political history of Rome, but Shakespeare toils to reflect its ambiguity most acutely in the characters of Caesar and Brutus. There is hardly an individual subject more flexible and enigmatic in Shakespeare than Caesar: obsessed with demarcating the boundaries of his own identity, the major concern of the action is to press his diffused subjectivity into a well-confined body, turning a crowning piece of work into a "bleeding piece of earth" (3.1.254), an act that is to be inverted in turn by Antony. It comes as no surprise that Brutus, whose major moral strife is marred by an intellectual limitation, his inability to transcend the confines of his cogito into the prophetic knowledge of Caesar's future behavior, will turn to the practice of fashioning: first by rationalizing an argument (2.1.30), and later by rearranging the constituents of his own self by disavowing Portia's part in him, adopting Cassius's conspiratory discourse in the illusory image of the noble sacrificer, and perpetrating his death through penetrating the surprised, just wakened (5.5.32) consiousness of Strato, his bondman. The practice of fashioning may be traced in the Shakespearean canon along a wide gamut of dramatic representations enacting energies of disguise or empathy, and ranging from the effacing of subjective confines of the body and bodily gestures to the breaking of subjectivity as a social flow, whether between the hard nucleus of the individual and the collective parameters of a group, or transcending gender and/or class barriers.

Occasionally, transcending the body serves as a vehicle for leaping over class barriers. The constant presence in most Shakespearean tragedies of that same class interdependence that is totally absent in Marlowe's *Tamburlaine* varies in degree—from its almost mute deployment behind the scenes in *Hamlet* to its cataclysmal dramatic enactment in *Coriolanus*. In *Julius Caesar* it provides for both prominent and subtle dramatic effects. Whereas the former are too obvious, the latter are too often overlooked. Seeking a necessary help in terminating his life, Brutus is turned down by his friends and officers, since, as Volumnius puts it, "That's not an office for a friend" (5.5.29). He finally turns to the one person in the company on whom he may impose that last service, Strato, who is apparently bonded to him as a servant: a variation on Cassius's Parthian slave, Pindarus, who rendered Brutus's fellow conspirator a similar service. We do not know for certain whether Strato is ethnically an alien, as is Pindarus, but class difference serves to alienate him enough for the present purpose. That which is not an office for a friend is obviously an appropriate *service* for a bondman, as testified by Messala's later recommendation to Octavius to take Strato to follow him, "That did the latest service to my master" (ibid., 5.5.66–67). In addition to the technical facet of the bondman's service, however, there is also an act of empathy here. Both Brutus and Cassius are practicing an act of self-fashioning in invading the identities of their helpers through the use of bodily gestures. The first motive Brutus had cited to his fellow conspirators as calling for Caesar's death was "the face of men" (2.1.114). Now, when rendering Brutus "the latest service" (5.3.67), Strato is required to "turn away

[his] face" (ibid., 5.5.47). This intriguing demand of the central piece of work of creation to hide its face is an inverted variation on Cassius's instruction to Pindarus: "And when my face is cover'd, as 'tis now, / Guide thou the sword" (5.3.44–45). Symbolically, both helpers are to mark the hierarchical difference between their masters' respective ideological standings by the end of the play. Cassius, who covers his face, is to immerse into his bondsman's interpretation of liberty as fleeing "where never Roman shall take note of him" (5.3.50), namely beyond the discourse of Western culture (a diabolic domain into which Cassius had already been banished in Marc Antony's ironic "honourable men"), into which Cassius is to "sink to night" like the setting sun (ibid., 5.3.59–61) and his body sent to Thasos:

> His funerals shall not be in our camp,
> Lest it discomfort us.
>
> (Ibid., 105–6)

Brutus, who instructs Strato to turn away his face but looks death in the eye, delegates his nobility to his bondsman's act. Strato is to merit absorption into the ranks of the dominant culture for rendering his service to "the noblest Roman of them all" (5.5.68): the same Marc Antony now rescues Brutus's name from his former ironic inversion (though disillusioned, Brutus himself had already preceded him in proclaiming that "dishonour shall be humour" (4.3.108). But there is more to it: Brutus's demand of Strato also marks the opposite gesture of Caesar's earlier command related to another low-classed vehicle of fate: "Set him before me; let me see his face" (1.2.20). Just as Caesar attempts in vain to learn more about his fate in ascribing it to an individual face—a traditional representation of subjectivity—so Brutus tries to efface the subjectivity of his accomplice in bringing about his own death. It is this evasion of subjectivity that is to earn him shortly the generalized description as "a man" (5.5.75), in whom the elements are "so mix'd" that he shuns any particular individuality. And it is telling that any crucial move in *Julius Caesar* cannot be performed or completed successfully by anyone without permeating the identity of others (either individual or collective), while breaking class barriers.

The negotiation of the social discourse and the aesthetic discourse may prove fruitful for both when, bearing in mind the crucial presence of the historical moment in one's discourse, the reading of a given text of fiction, in Louis Montrose's words, "reorients the axis of intertextuality, substituting for the diachronic text of an autonomous literary history the synchronic text of a cultural system."[13] A crucial token of such a cultural system, and one of the telling tenets of the Copernican revolution that Western perception of culture and humanity is undergoing in the later decades of the twentieth century, is Lacan's widely cited apothegm that "the unconscious of the subject is the discourse of the Other."[14] In the spasmodic rhythm of cultural integration that has shaken Western consciousness and identity since the early modern period, the process of inhabiting the external archetype of the monster (whether political, racial, or religious) within our own framework of culture forms a history of global crises. The locus of that discourse of the Other may often be internal, namely the figure formed within the complex structure of the divided self of the subject.[15] Edward Said, who has presented Western consciousness with one of its most significant discourses of Otherness to date, admitted to BBC interviewer Michael Ignatieff in the middle of the Gulf crisis (which presented the West with yet another mythical construct of Antichrist in the public image of Saddam Hussein) that two persons were holding a dialogue within his soul (the intellectual and the political), and he felt this dialogue rather enriching.[16] In many ways, such an inner discourse serves as the point of departure of the present argument. In the wake of Said's position of "secular criticism," it cannot dissociate itself from actualities.[17] But it takes one step forward, I believe, in regarding political theater an extension of the actual political existence, using Shakespeare's Roman parable as a synchronic text of a current cultural system of identity and otherness. In that respect, rather than uncovering the world picture of a given period through what a "new historicist" would call symptomatic readings, such a project may provide a modest assistance to make some sense, by far nonsystematic, of a cultural practice investing the Western world from the early modern period onward.

If the interchangeability of social and aesthetic discourse may be seen as embodied in the reciprocal fashioning of reality as simulation and representation as reality, then *Julius Caesar*, a play whose both tragic and political actions are triggered by the charged phrase "fashion it thus," is a case in point. Both action and characters in *Julius Caesar* are informed by a strong sense of self-reference from the very outset. In the opening lines of the play, the artisans are reproached by Flavius for not wearing their "Laboring" attire, and hence for redefining their present identity from without the boundaries of "Being mechanical" (1.1.2–5).[18] The recurring pattern of disguising identities and assuming borrowed characters (especially at times of revels) is hardly new in Shakespeare, but whereas the "All the world's a stage" metaphor, which in previous plays served to enrich argument and action, was so far confined within the boundaries of representation, here it transcends them in embracing fictional characters and audience alike. Indeed, we have seen a group of mechanicals transforming themselves on stage in *A Midsummer Night's Dream*, and, in spite of their ridiculous portrayal, still bearing similarity to some of London's groundlings. But at the opening scene of *Julius Caesar*, the collective body of the commoners of Rome, whose only marks of individual identity are their respective trades without even private names attached to their persons, are making a point of taking off the very signs of their trade, to become sheltered and defined in the collective anonymity of the crowd. Thus, a new dramatic entity is fashioned, faceless and all-embracing at once, which extends to the no-man's-land in which the pit and galleries of the theater are not securely separated from the representational arena. From this point onward, their very anonymity enforces on us our complicity with their collective experience: not that we share or condone their stupidity, but we cannot resist the feeling that both in their power and their powerlessness they represent us directly in a way that none of the other characters do. They have not become an institution, nor are they "the constitutional representatives of the people," a role that Nietzsche scornfully denied the Greek chorus.[19] Rather, their anonymity deeply engages our sensibilities and responses to the dramatic action. When Caesar is murdered, the responsibility for the deed falls on a well-defined group of characters within the confines of representation; when Cinna the poet is murdered by the nameless crowd, first and foremost for having a name, but also for not having taken off the sign of his profession, we feel we take the blame, for the deed was done in our name as well. It is the very anonymity that we share with the commoners of Rome that makes us take part in the series of well-staged manipulative acts in which we offer Caesar the crown, bless Brutus for having murdered him for desiring the crown (and offer it him for his doing), and then rush to chase him to Antony's rhetoric. It is in our no-name that writings are thrown by Cassius at Brutus's windows and both parties rush to the battlefield to have us killed for their politics.

In terms of reality-as-simulation, that level on which media-promoted symbolism pervades the behavior patterns of individuals and groups, self-effacing has become a universal token of identification with a collective body. In Jerusalem, an age-old locus of convergence of myth and reality, both Palestinians protesting against their occupation and repression by Israel and Israeli "commoners" retaliating were known to adopt the practice of covering their faces while in action. In late 1991, public opinion in Israel was divided over the disclosure of the existence of special army units working undercover as "veil-faced" Palestinians: in the following months it was reported that volunteering to those units became a fashion among new conscripts to the Israeli army. Veiled faces have acquired a particular value on the level of signification and ritual meaning, which far exceeds any security motivation involved. In a unique and controversial ruling, an Israeli judge convicted on March 1992 a Palestinian poet for having published a poem interpreted by the court as "incitement"; the poem[20] begins: "No one knows the virtues of this veiled-face person / But the crumbling survivors." But the process of appropriating aesthetic characterization works in the opposite direction as well, where reality and fiction are negotiating in the no-man's-land of ritual activity. On 20 May 1990 a young Israeli arrived early morning at a crossroad near his hometown, where Palestinian workers from the Israeli-occupied Gaza strip used to assemble daily for being hired by Israeli contractors. He wore military trousers and carried an automatic gun, as "the sign of his profession." Thus, looking like a regular soldier, he ordered the large group of Palestinians to hand him their IDs for inspection. There was no official routine requiring them to comply; there was only the paralyzing charisma of the trinity of military trousers, a gun, and military jargon. The workers having obeyed his orders, he suddenly started to shoot frantically, killing seven workers and wounding many more. One of the most striking features of this incident was its dependence on ritual and mimesis. In order for the deed to be done, both parties, killer and victims, had to assume borrowed identities. The Palestinians, for him, could not pass for individual human beings. In a long process of political effacement and reification promoted by manifold channels of nationalist propaganda, the signifier "Arabs" for many Israelis had been converted into an object or commodity. The killer, who apparently had been rejected by his girlfriend the night before the massacre, needed an outlet for his rage. Rather than directing his agony toward himself, the girl, or any other human being bearing face and name, he felt the need to retaliate against a nameless object. In order to perform his vengeance, he chose to don the identity of a soldier, namely, one "authorized" by profession to kill a faceless enemy. There was not any practical reason why he should do so: the workers who obeyed his orders so readily were most likely to obey any civilian who did not pretend to be a soldier. Ironically, the killer, dismissed from service some time earlier as a misfit, used his borrowed identity to conduct a ritual "identity check" of his victims. By assuming the simulacrum of the soldier, he attempted to turn murder into sacrifice.

In this he had some notable forerunners in *Othello*, who is made to call what he "intend[ed] to do / A murder, which [he] thought a sacrifice" (*Othello*, 5.2.64), or Brutus, who would have his conspirators "be sacrificers, but not butchers" (*Julius Caesar*, 2.1.166). Because of the assimilation of psychoanalytic clichés into the political mental disposition perpetrated by the media and nationalist propaganda, the rationalization of the modern murderer refers to a personal motive. He lacks the poetic self-reference of Cassius and Brutus, who entrust their supposed sacrifice to the realm of poetics (3.1.111–18).

The dramatic ritual of veiling or appropriating faces uses representation (or its articulate absence) as an antidote of "authentic" subjectivity. *Julius Caesar* is a tragedy of errors, all founded on misleading and futile beliefs in the totalization of the subject. Whereas Brutus and his fellow rebels are conspiring against an imaginary construct fashioned by themselves, Caesar for his part is heavily immersed in self-fashioning in the spirit of Lacanian narcissism. Caesar's fate, at the point of dismissing the Soothsayer as "a dreamer," is still dramatically open. This openness owes less to the hypothetical notion that Caesar might have saved his life by taking heed of the Soothsayer's warning than to the implicit level of self-knowledge offered to Caesar by the inspiringly enigmatic prophecy. Reading the Soothsayer's prophecy as" a simple warning of future fact, which is then arranged to occur"[21] betrays a linear, or "monologic," concept of history, where the only possible opposition is the one between the individual consciousness and "objective reality." It is never suggested in the play, however, that Caesar—or any other character, including the Soothsayer himself—could gain, through a supernatural agency, a literal foreknowledge of what would actually happen on the ides of March. The Soothsayer never predicts anything in the strict sense of the term. Neither do the natural prodigies reported by Casca and Calpurnia. However, the augurs' vision and Calpurnia's dream yield visual images that are as suggestive of Caesar's present position as they may be of his future prospects. Calpurnia's dream, whose central image is the statue of Caesar, may equally agree with two contradictory interpretations—the one suggested by the still-dreaming Calpurnia when crying in her sleep: "Help, ho! they murther Caesar!" (*Julius Caesar*, 2.2.3) and the other deceptively, yet none the less soundly, proposed by Decius Brutus. Likewise, Caesar's actual portrayal in the play comprises at least two simultaneous images, which can hardly be negotiated: his genuine nobility, extremely distorted by his inflated self-image, and his "shaking god" portrayed by Cassius (1.2.120). That Cassius's account may well be biased or false is immaterial in this context; the prophetic significance of Calpurnia's crying in her sleep owes much to its echoing Caesar's own cry for help in Cassius's story (1.2.111)—the only two occasions where the word *help* occurs in the play. What is important is the perspective this kind of scene provides on Caesar's multileveled existence.

The chief barrier standing between Caesar and the Soothsayer's prophecy is Caesar's illusory countervision of individual self-sufficiency. "I rather tell thee what is to be fear'd / Than what I fear," he tells Antony, having just confessed to him his personal fears concerning Cassius. It is Caesar's unnatural attempt to divorce himself from his own experience, which sheds an ironic light on his concluding statement: "for always I am Caesar" (1.2.208-9). The various prophetic agencies Caesar encounters in the play urge him to consider that part of his personal, human existence that is fragile and constantly threatened by the world, rather than ambitiously to identify his lot with the world's destiny:

> these predictions
> Are to the world in general as to Caesar.
> (2.2.28-29)

Truly and wholly known, man's own self may become his oracle, holding a mirror up to his own nature where he may

> like a prophet
> [Look] in a glass that shows what future evils
> Either now or by remissness new conceiv'd.
> (*Measure for Measure*, 2.2.95-97)

and directing him to fulfil his personal part as ordained by "the world." Richard of Gloucester, who knows this teaching well (though fatally fails to live consistently by it), tellingly addresses Buckingham at a moment of insight as

> My other self . . .
> My oracle, my prophet.
> (*Richard III*, 2.2.151–52)

Caesar would hardly allow anyone to be his other self—a mirror or an oracle giving form to what he actually is. Rather, Decius Brutus would pass for a true oracle only when his interpretation of the dream has disjoined "remorse from power" and made it fit Caesar's own image of his cosmic stature. Imposing his own meaning upon the augurs' observations, Caesar sees himself as the world's oracle, as holding the mirror up to nature: the gods' token "in shame of cowardice" is indeed directed at the world in general as at Caesar, to judge by Caesar's lecture immediately preceding its delivery. Ironically, however, his language subtly betrays the very tactics of cowardice he is attacking. Rather than genuinely encountering danger by accepting its challenge and embracing it as part of his complex self, Caesar, faithful to his habit of telling what is to be feared rather than what he fears, safely projects it outward as a rival, lesser lion, in front of which he may pose as "the elder and more terrible" (*Julius Caesar*, 2.2.47). Rather than seeking to know himself in terms of "the world," Caesar would set a new order to the universe with his imagined unassailable rank, namely his individuality, at its center. By failing to distinguish consciously between reality and imagination, Caesar fails to benefit from the major advantage of imagination, namely: conquering a newly defined, liberated future for himself.

For the Elizabethans, the function of wisdom is to rectify reason's opinions in the light of higher understanding. But Caesar's wisdom is "consum'd in confidence" (2.2.49). Caesar falsely pretends to prophetic knowledge of himself, a pretense that ironically drives him gradually to dissociate himself from his actual experience. Considered in terms of the dramatic process of his growing blind to the evidence of his own experience, Caesar's initial encounter with the Soothsayer transcends its predictive function to serve as a crucial dramatic image. "The things that threaten'd me," he would later boast to Calpurnia,

> Ne'er look'd but on my back; when they shall see
> The face of Caesar, they are vanished.
> (2.2.1–12)

It is a telling remark, for it throws light on the somewhat awkward ceremony with which he treats the Soothsayer in the former scene:

> Caesar. Set him before me; let me see his face.
> Cassius. Fellow, come from the throng; look upon Caesar.
> Caesar. What say'st thou to me now? Speak once again.
> Soothsayer. Beware the ides of March.
> Caesar. He is a dreamer. Let us leave him. Pass.
>
> (1.2.20–24)

The evident persistence of the Soothsayer's "threat" even upon seeing "the face of Caesar," compels Caesar to choose between his pride-ridden, individualistic self-image, and manifest, multivocal reality. He chooses the former, proclaiming the prophet to be a dreamer. It is significant that at a later stage, having reasserted his confidence and totally ignoring his experience with the Soothsayer, Caesar falls an easy prey to a deliberately falsified (and ironic) interpretation of a dream.

That Cassius is the one to urge the Soothsayer to "come from the throng" and to face Caesar is no mere coincidence; nor is it a coincidence that in doing so Cassius chooses to modify Caesar's command in turning the passive role assigned to the Soothsayer in Caesar's phrase into the more active assignment of "looking upon Caesar." It is Cassius who, a short while later, still haunted by Caesar's interest in "seeing faces," offers himself to Brutus as a mirror capable of showing Brutus his "shadow" (1.2.50, 55–57). Whereas Caesar, his wisdom "consum'd with confidence," believes that he can see his face, Cassius, at least in his Epicurean period, is a typical exponent of what Nietzsche will designate "the school of suspect." For him, a night that seems to turn the tables on the accepted image of natural order is "a very pleasing night to honest men," since by way of deconstruction it exposes the Earth as "full of faults." He knows, however, that these faults are "not in our stars but in ourselves," and thus the first lesson he gives to Brutus is that though we cannot see our faces, we can fashion the mirror. The "shadow" that Cassius's mirror fashions for Brutus is of course nothing but the tentative construct of the noble deliverer of Rome from Caesar's assumed tyranny, which Cassius sees fit to sell to the nameless crowd (which includes us) as our own "naming" of reality. A quick-learning student, Brutus is soon to proceed to "fashion" first his own convictions and then Caius Ligarius.

Edward Said's BBC interview mentioned earlier referred mainly to the cultural and political circumstances in the world of the Gulf crisis. A former ally of Western capitalism was being dubbed an Antichrist by his former supporters, since the current state of economic affairs would have it so. On the other side of the political gamut, nameless Palestinian crowds were naming that same self-styled northern star a noble deliverer, even though it was clear that in his doings he had hampered long years of political endeavors. In a postmodern world of broken vision dominated by an undiscerning flow of media images, one should subscribe to a protective strategy of cognitive discrimination in order to distinguish veridical values from propaganda, reality from "simulacrum." Upholding any unified images of the subject or clear-cut ideological constructions, including Baudrillard's total subjection of experience and information to "hyperreality," have too often led one to false prophecy. The more sophisticated response, given in various phrasings by Said, Ghassan Salame, and by many clear-sighted Palestinians who read the political texts and contexts of the Gulf crisis carefully, namely: "with the Iraquis against the corruption of Kuwaiti capitalism; with the Kuwaities against Saddam's military aggression," may be, among other things, a token that the "new historicist" and "poststructuralist" projects may still have a long way to go in holding the mirror up to our consciousness. It may be one lesson the would-be prophets of reality may learn from the strategies of political representation in the theater.

Notes

All quotations from Shakespeare are cited from the "New Arden" editions.

1. Christopher Norris, *Uncritical Theory: Postmodernism, Intellectuals, and the Gulf War* (London: Lawrence and Wishart, 1992).

2. Jean Baudrillard, *La guerre du Golfe n'a pas eu lieu* (Paris: Galilée, 1991).

3. This article was written over three years prior to the assassination of prime minister Yitzhak Rabin on 4 November 1995. About the 1996 election campaign in Israel, which followed his assassination, and bear in a big way upon the present argument, see the afterword to this volume.

4. Defined as the "personal and collective identity models and meanings, symbolic templates for shared social consciousness, and religious interpretations, evaluations, and rituals." See John H. Marx, "The Ideological Construction of Postmodern Identity Models in Contemporary Cultural Movements," in Roland Robertson and Burkart Holzner, eds., *Identity and Authority: Explorations in the Theory of Society* (Oxford: Basil Blackwell, 1980), 155.

5. Sir John Harington etc., *Nugae Antique: being a miscellaneous collection of*

original papers . . . ed. T. Park (London, 1804), 1: 361. See G. B. Harrison, *A Second Elizabethan Journal* (London & Boston: Routledge & Kegan Paul, 1974), 188–89.

6. Emily C. Bartels's seminal *Spectacles of Strangeness: Imperialism, Alienation, and Marlowe* (Philadelphia: University of Pennsylvania Press, 1993), from which this quotation (p. 54) is taken in this slightly revised version of the present article, was not yet published when this article was written.

7. Stephen Greenblatt, The Renaissance Self-Fashioning (Chicago: University of Chicago Press, 1980), 195. See also Clifford Leech, "Power and Suffering in Edward the Second," *Critical Quarterly* 1, 1(1959): 181–96.

8. All quotations from *Tamburlaine* are from the Regent edition, ed. John Jump (London: Edward Arnold, 1967).

9. Lawrence Kelsall, *Christopher Marlowe* (Leiden: Brill, 1981), 79.

10. See, e.g., *1 Tamburlaine*, 1.2.212–13, and 3.3.102.

11. Kelsall 1981, 73.

12. Shoshana Felman and Dori Laub, *Testimony: Crises of Witnessing in Literature, Psychoanalysis, and History* (New York and London: Routledge, 1992), 125-26.

13. Louis Montrose, "Professing the Renaissance: The Poetics and Politics of Culture," in (ed.), *The New Historicism*, ed. H. Aram Veeser (New York and London: Routledge, 1989), 17.

14. Jacques Lacan, *Écrits: a Selection,* trans. Alan Sheridan (London: Tavistock, 1977), 172.

15. I use the term "figure" here in its Genettian meaning; see Gérard Genette, *Figures II* (Paris: Seuil, 1969).

16. "Late Show," *BBC Two,* 6 September 1990.

17. See Edward Said, *The World, The Text and the Critic* (Cambridge, Mass.: Harvard University Press, 1983).

18. See G. K. Hunter, "Flatcaps and Bluecoats," *Essays and Studies* 33 (1980): 35–36.

19. Nietzsche, *The Birth of Tragedy from the Spirit of Music.*

20. "The Leading" by Shafiq Haviv.

21. Joseph T. Shipley, ed., *Dictionary of World Literary Terms* (London, 1955), 320.

Hamlet's Entrails

David Hillman

> *Misanthropy and love:*—One speaks of being sick of man only when one can no longer digest him and yet has one's stomach full of him. Misanthropy comes of an all too greedy love of man and "cannibalism"; but who asked you to swallow men like oysters, Prince Hamlet?
> —Friedrich Nietzsche, *The Gay Science*

From the opening moments of *Hamlet*, with Francisco's command to a muffled figure in the night, "Stand and unfold yourself" (*Hamlet*, 1.1.2), a persistent concern throughout the play is with what cannot be seen, or known—what is beyond a threshold or "bourn" (3.1.79).[1] The question of what lies within—within, for example, the armor of the Ghost, beneath the smiling exterior of a person, or, as this essay argues, within the very bodies of the different protagonists—occupies a number of the play's characters, not least among them Hamlet himself. For him, it seems to me, the problem of other minds, of the truth of other minds, is inseparably a problem of other bodies; these bodies have their own truth, and access to this truth is to a remarkable extent equated with access to the interior of the human body. What is anatomically and physiologically inside people—inside himself no less than inside others—is something Hamlet harps on repeatedly.

This preoccupation with corporeal innards ties together a number of the play's—and its protagonist's—obsessions. We might include among these the problem of death and mourning, and of what happens to the body after death, as well as the problem of birth and bodily origins; the difficulties of sexuality, and of Hamlet's distaste at the idea of the sexual act; a concept of gender which is based on the contents of the body; and a deep concern with truth and truthfulness, with the sorting out of appearance and reality. All these are associated, in this "incorps'd" (4.7.86) play, with what we might call visceral knowledge: a sense of one's own as well as others' entrails, understood as ineluctably connected to the core of one's being, one's innermost truth.

The materialist habits of early modern thought, so well documented in recent years, formed the foundation of this association of interiority with corporeal inwardness. "In vernacular sixteenth- and early seventeenth-century speech and writing," as Katharine Maus explains, "the whole interior of the body—heart, liver, womb, bowels, kidneys, gall, blood, lymph—quite often involves itself in the production of the mental interior, of the individual's private experience."[2] "Humoral physiology," writes Gail Kern Paster, "ascribes to the workings of the internal organs . . . aspect[s] of agency, purposiveness, and plenitude"; it can "locate a form of selfhood, analogous with agency, within."[3] For the men and women of early modern England, the idea of personhood, and personality, was never far from the question of the internal composition (or "complexion") of the body.

In taking the idea of viscerality in *Hamlet* to be central and complex, I am taking issue with an idea that has become practically a commonplace of *Hamlet* criticism: the idea that Hamlet feels "a disgust at the physical body of man,"[4] a "despairing contempt for the body"[5] as such. Hamlet's ubiquitous and somewhat grotesque oral fantasies, coupled with his apparent "sexual disgust,"[6] have led many critics of the play to think of him as having, as Francis Barker puts it, a "desire to refine away the insistent materiality of the body."[7] But distinctions need to be made between Hamlet's attitudes to bodies that are healthy or sick, open or closed, full or empty, paternal or maternal. Hamlet's aversion to the state of corporeality is far less absolute and more specific than such descriptions of his "hatred of the flesh"[8] might suggest; it is rather, we could say, the pervasive lies that people tell about their bodies, with their bodies, that he hates: the possibility of giving someone "the lie i'th' throat / As deep as to the lungs" (2.2.569–70).

* * *

The words of a dead man / Are modified in the guts of the living
—W. H. Auden, "In Memory of W. B. Yeats"

I take as my point of entry a comment made by Stanley Cavell in his piece on the play, in which he speaks of "the everyday, skeletal manner in which human beings present themselves to [Hamlet]." He adds: "I think of this in connection with Nietzsche's statement in his autobiography (I mean *Ecce Homo*) that one trait of his nature that causes difficulty in his contacts with others is the uncanny sensitivity of his instinct for cleanliness, or, say, truthfulness, so that the innermost parts, the entrails (we might perhaps say drives) of every soul are *smelled* by him."[9] I would like to attempt to stick with the idea, very specifically, of entrails, avoiding (at least for the moment) the movement manifested in Cavell's brackets ["(we might perhaps say drives)"]. Nietzsche, after all, speaks specifically of "entrails"—and of his sensitivity to them as "physiological."[10] "The inmost parts," those least accessible to epistemological inquiry, are used again and again by Nietzsche as his central metaphor for the undecipherability or opacity of human thoughts and actions: "However far a man may go in self-knowledge, nothing however can be more incomplete than his image of the totality of *drives* which constitute his being. He can scarcely name even the cruder ones: their number and strength, their ebb and flood, their play and counterplay among one another, and above all the laws of their *nutriment* remain wholly unknown to him . . . our moral judgements and evaluations too are only images and fantasies based on a physiological process unknown to us, a kind of acquired language for designating nervous stimuli."[11] Elsewhere, for instance in the fragment "On Truth and Lie in the Extra-Moral Sense," he points out the irony involved in the fact that "the urge for truth" is so often a product of "our proud, deceptive consciousness, far from the coils of the intestines, the quick current of the blood stream, and the involved tremors of the fibers. . . ."[12]

Nonetheless, any hermeneutical undertaking must, for Nietzsche, begin from the body—and, moreover, from its interior, which is why he speaks of the "hard, unwanted, inescapable task" of philosophy as a kind of vivisection; Socrates, for example, is "the old physician and plebeian who cut ruthlessly into his own flesh, as he did into the flesh and heart of the 'noble.'"[13] The body, though, for Nietzsche, is useful less as a physiological foundation than as a principle of interpretation: since "soul is only a word for something about the body," it is "essential: to start from the *body* and employ it as a guide. It is the much richer phenomenon, which allows of clearer observation. Belief in the body is better established than belief in the spirit."[14]

We might say that *Hamlet*, as it were, starts from the body; as Coleridge was perhaps the first to note, the opening scene is filled with "the language of *sensation* . . . the broken expressions of a man's compelled attention to bodily feelings." The entire play, Coleridge adds, is "a tragedy the interest of which is eminently *ad et apud intra* [toward and about the inside]."[15] Coleridge doesn't go on to explain this somewhat enigmatic comment any further, and the question of how to understand his remark echoes that of what we make of Hamlet's own rather opaque "I have that within which passes show" (1.2.85).[16] Both point to an internality the contents of which are unspecified; "*Hamlet*," as T. S. Eliot famously complained, "is full of some stuff that the writer could not drag to light, contemplate, or manipulate into art."[17] Certainly, Hamlet's statement involves an insistence upon the insufficiency of the merely external, though it has never to my knowledge been taken to imply a corporeal "inner world." But, as this essay argues, in the context of his preoccupation with bodily innards, his celebrated introspection includes an intensely corporeal self-consciousness; his "within" can be understood as referring to, among other things, a strong sense of "the pith and marrow" (1.4.22), the viscerality, of "the inward man" (2.2.6).

The play opens under the shadow of the felt absence of Hamlet's father. In the Ghost's return to the prehistory of the play, in his relation of his own murder, we can find a number of indications of Hamlet's bodily state. His account is vivid in its details:

> Sleeping within my orchard,
> My custom always of the afternoon,
> Upon my secure hour thy uncle stole
> With juice of cursed hebenon in a vial,
> And in the porches of my ears did pour
> The leperous distilment, whose effect
> Holds such an enmity with blood of man
> That swift as quicksilver it courses through
> The natural gates and alleys of the body,
> And with a sudden vigour it doth posset
> And curd, like eager droppings into milk,
> The thin and wholesome blood. So did it mine,
> And a most instant tetter bark'd about,
> Most lazar-like, with vile and loathsome crust
> All my smooth body.
> Thus was I, sleeping, by a brother's hand
> Of life, of crown, of queen at once dispatch'd,
> Cut off even in the blossoms of my sin,

> Unhousel'd, disappointed, unanel'd,
> No reck'ning made, but sent to my account
> With all my imperfections on my head.
> O horrible! O horrible! most horrible!
>
> (1.5.59–80)

The account strikingly depicts the effects of the poison upon the body of Old Hamlet: first, an internal thickening ("it doth posset / And curd . . . The thin and wholesome blood"), followed immediately by a hardening of the boundaries of the body. The formerly markedly open body of the King, the "porches" of whose ears and "gates and alleys" of whose body have easily received the poison, is now "bark'd about," "lazar-like," "All" enclosed in a "tetter," a "vile and loathsome crust." The speediness of the whole process is heavily underlined ("swift as quicksilver," "with a sudden vigour," "most instant," "at once"). The swiftness of the action and the absoluteness of the closure combine to give the effect of a trapping within—as if something which should have been allowed to issue forth has been stopped up inside the instantly mummified body. And the Ghost himself stresses not so much the loss "Of life, of crown, of queen" as his own unpreparedness, the "Cut off" or obstructed nature of his death; this is what seems so "horrible!"

What has not taken place here is the preparation that is thought of as crucial to the passage into death. Hamlet later returns to this aborted process when he refuses to kill Claudius during just such an attempt at purgation: "[He] took my father grossly, full of bread, / With all his crimes broad blown, as flush as May. . . . And am I then reveng'd, / To take him in the purging of his soul, / When he is fit and season'd for his passage?" (3.3.80–86). The fullness ("full of bread"—perhaps recalling the Ghost's use of the phrase "loathsome crust") is what is galling to Hamlet, as it is contrasted to a "purging" that would prepare Claudius for the "passage" to the other world. Perhaps there is a clue here as to why Hamlet forces the already-dying Claudius to drink the poisoned cup of wine. The apparently excessive act ("objection has been made to Hamlet's forcing the liquor on the King," as the Arden editor notes) may be understood as a final act of vengeance, filling the very body of Claudius with his own sin-tainted liquid, and thus not allowing the emptying-out prior to death that Claudius has denied Old Hamlet. (As Hamlet says to Horatio early on in the play: "We'll teach you to drink deep ere you depart" (1.2.175): does the "deep" here refer to the emptying of the cup or to the filling of the body?) When told later that Claudius is "marvellous distempered . . . with choler," Hamlet "takes choler in the sense of the physiological 'humour,' i.e., bile"[18] and replies: "for me to put him to his purgation would perhaps plunge him into more choler" (3.2.293–98). Old Hamlet, asleep during the moments preceding his death, is unable to "season" himself prior to it; he is thus consigned to purgatory, where he is "confin'd to fast in fires, / Till [his] foul crimes . . . Are burnt and purg'd away" (1.5.11–13).

Fasting, purging, and burning away are purification rituals that have been connected with death in almost all cultures. Such last rites are at least partially an emptying-out, originally of the body, later (in confession, e.g.) of the soul, a discharge seemingly entailed by the process of dying.[19] This fantasied emptying-out seems to be Janus-faced in its uses: it is meant to allow both the passage of the deceased into the next world, and a form of continued existence of the dead person in this world. Death is symbolically overcome by a continuity in the very bodies of the survivors, and the latter are able to retain a contact with the one they have lost, to almost literally fill the gap created by the loss, by taking what is emptied-out symbolically into their own bodies; hence the widespread existence of funeral feasts.[20] It is the emptying-out of the deceased which makes possible the taking-in, the incorporation, by the survivors. Perhaps, too, what is being imagined in this purging is an opening, at least at the last moment before death, of one's innermost being, an acknowledgment, as Nietzsche might put it, of the truth of one's innards—an enabling of the "cleanliness" of one's death.

Freud's interpretation of the "work of mourning" parallels in some ways this description of funeral rituals. In "Mourning and Melancholia,"[21] he describes the process of overcoming the loss of a loved object as an installing of the lost object within ourselves followed by a "bit by bit" disengagement of the libido from the object. The slow and gradual nature of the process permits the "hallucinatory" prolongation of "the existence of the lost object" (Freud 1917, 166) until new libido-attachments can replace the lost one. The melancholiac, he says, refuses this displacement of the libido onto a new love-object; he rather withdraws it into his own ego, establishing "an identification of the ego with the abandoned object. Thus," he adds, "the shadow of the object fell upon the ego" (p. 170). Freud comes close to equating internalization with the "bodily ego" when he terms this process "incorporation" (ibid.), and characterizes it as a regression to an "oral or cannibalistic stage" which entails a "devouring" of the object (ibid.).

Death, then, involves a ritual emptying-out of the body of the deceased; mourning a symbolic incorporation of the corpse into the bodies of the survivors. In his reading of *Hamlet*, Jacques Lacan points out both the predominance of the theme of mourning in the play and the fact that this theme is characterized by an "insufficiency": "in all the instances of mourning in *Hamlet*, one element is always present: the rites have been cut short and performed in secret."[22] These "maimed rites" (5.1.219) are epitomized in Hamlet's description of the proximity of his father's funeral and of his mother's wedding: "Thrift, thrift, Horatio. The funeral bak'd meats / Did coldly furnish forth the marriage tables" (1.2.180–81). We may wonder at the exact nature of the relation between the "bak'd meats" and the body of Old Hamlet, remembering that a "coffin" meant, at the time, both a burial-chest and the crust of a pie or meat casserole.[23] Hamlet will later refer to a "fat king" and a "lean beggar" as "variable service [food]—two dishes, but to one table" (4.3.23–24), and here too there is (not, as we shall see, for the last time in the play) an idea of a king's body as food. A common practice in Elizabethan England involved the paying of poor people, called "sin-eaters," to take upon themselves the deceased's sins: "The manner was that when the Corps was brought out of the house and layd on the Biere; a Loafe of bread was brought out, and delivered to the Sinne-eater over the corps, as also a Mazar-bowle of maple (Gossips bowle) full of beer, which he was to drinke up, and sixpence in money, in consideration whereof he tooke upon him (ipso facto) all the Sinnes of the Defunct, and freed him (or her) from walking after they were dead."[24] Apart from the obvious relevance of this to the "Thrift, thrift" of reusing the funeral meats at the subsequent wedding, Hamlet's bitterness about the drinking habits of the Danes takes on another layer: just about the only "dram of evil" (1.4.36) that has *not* been drunk is the one containing his father's sins. The implication of Hamlet's "funeral bak'd meats" comment is not only that there has been an overhasty transition from "dole" to "delight" (1.2.13); the fact that the same meats furnished both the funeral and the wedding implies that they were *not* consumed at the earlier occasion. Neither end of the "bargain" of dying has been allowed: both the opening and purging of Old Hamlet's body, and the symbolic "incorporation" demanded by mourning, have been aborted. There is thus no sense of there having been any real grieving—it is both the meat and the mourners that are cold.

Old Hamlet's flesh, however, is eventually symbolically eaten—at his widow's wedding.[25] And Gertrude's coldness toward her former husband is repeatedly and specifically portrayed as a transference of her feeding from the body of Old Hamlet to that of Claudius: "Could you on this fair mountain leave to feed / And batten [grow fat] on this moor?" (3.4.66–67) exclaims Hamlet, pointing to the portraits of his father and his uncle; a little later in the same scene he inveighs against "that monster, custom, who all sense doth eat / Of habits evil" (3.4.163–64). Hamlet seems to be thinking of his mother as unable, or unwilling, to retain her connection with Old Hamlet through the symbolic "incorporation" of his body; she has replaced this kind of gratification, all-too-quickly, with the more immediate and sensual satisfaction of Claudius' body. The upbraiding of Gertrude in terms of who she is ingesting picks up on the Ghost's lament that, in marrying Claudius, his former Queen is revealing her "lust," which "though to a radiant angel link'd, / Will sate itself [gratify its appetite] in a celestial bed / And prey on garbage [offal]" (1.5.55–57).[26] Hamlet has earlier depicted Gertrude's original love for her first husband in similar terms: "Why, she would hang on him / As if increase of appetite had grown / By what it fed on; and yet within a month— / Let me not think on't—" (1.2.143–46).

Yet "think on't" he does, and, in trying not to dwell on it, his fantasies take on a compulsive quality. The comment about the "funeral bak'd meats" not only perfectly encapsulates the problematic status of mourning in the play but also marks the beginning of Hamlet's angry preoccupation with the idea of male innards as food, from his avowal to feed "all the region kites" with Claudius' "offal" (2.2.575–76) to his disquisitions upon the "worm that hath eat of a king" and the progress of an emperor "through the guts of a beggar" (4.3.27–31).[27] Nietzsche picks up on just this preoccupation (in the remark quoted in my epigraph) when he speaks of Hamlet's "swallow[ing] men like oysters," and of his "misanthropy" as coming "of an all too greedy love of man and 'cannibalism.'"[28]

We will return to Hamlet's knotting of "misanthropy and love," but for the moment we should note that the association of human innards with food in *Hamlet* is almost exclusively limited to male bodies. Janet Adelman has written of "the play's fusion of eating and death and sex,"[29] but differentiations need to be made in this context between male and female bodies, between who is being consumed and who is doing the eating. For while the maternal body may indeed, as Adelman argues, be "always already sexual" and the *source* of death in the world, it is the paternal body which is consistently fantasized as being at the other terminus of death—as being posthumously eaten[30]: the "matter" formed in the womb ends up in the worm. Maternal and paternal bodies are associated, respectively, with the bodily origins and ends of death—the two poles, as it were, of the process of dying.[31] Hamlet is habitually interested in this way-of-all-flesh. His apparent pleasure in bringing up the idea of the decay and putrefaction of dead bodies (e.g., "How long will a man lie i'th'earth ere he rot?" [5.1.15]; "if the sun breed maggots in a dead dog . . ." [2.2.181–82]; "we fat ourselves for maggots . . ." [4.3.22]) may be connected to the fact that through decomposition, and the idea of the generativity of decomposing matter, the two ends of the process are brought together:[32] as Georges Bataille writes, in archaic societies "decay summed up the world we spring from and return to, and horror and shame were attached both to our birth and to our death."[33] Immediately following his harangue on the subject of Polonius's guts, Hamlet's taunt to Claudius ("Father and mother is man and wife, man and wife is one flesh"—4.3.54–55) may be taken to refer to, among other things, his sense that maternal and paternal bodies are united not only in intercourse but also in death.

The play as a whole, and Hamlet in particular, repeatedly stress the beginnings of this process of decay in the body's afflictions; and, with some consistency, the metaphor is one of *internal* sickness[34]: "Something is rotten *in* the state of Denmark" (1.4.90). This "something" remains slightly vague, hidden within the body; thus Hamlet's explanation of Fortinbras' Polish expedition:

> This is th'impostume [=abscess] of much wealth and peace,
> That inward breaks, and shows no cause without
> Why the man dies.
>
> (4.4.27–29)

Like Hamlet's "that within which passes show," this too "shows no cause without." Again, Hamlet warns his mother that her avoidance of the truth

> will but skin and film the ulcerous place,
> Whiles rank corruption, mining all within,
> Infects unseen.
>
> (3.4.149–51)

There is presumably in these perceptions a recollection of the manner of Old Hamlet's death—the poison working first within, then shutting off the body's boundaries.

But "to the quick of th'ulcer" (4.7.123): Hamlet's cannibalistic fantasies are in part an attempt on his behalf to grieve for his father; in the absence of any community of mourners, they are also his insistent, angry rejoinder to the symbolic nonincorporation of his father's body by its survivors; to these he defiantly opposes the image of a grotesquely open and edible paternal corpus. The closure of his father's body, and the foreclosure of the grieving, leave Hamlet alone in a world of surfaces, surrounded by figures whom he sees as rejecting not only emotional but also corporeal openness to himself. It is not that he imagines these figures to be closed in any absolute way—he depicts his mother, for example, as feeding on Claudius' body, the two of them as "one flesh" (4.3.55)—but that he thinks of them as closed or inaccessible *to him*. Even Ophelia, who at one stage has been open to his love, "did repel his letters and denied / His access" (2.1.109–10); Hamlet has thought of these love letters as metaphorically "in her excellent white bosom" (2.2.112). The literal meaning of the phrase (in the bosom of her dress, "where a love-letter would be kept" [Arden]) does not abrogate the underlying sense that Ophelia's "repelling" (cf. 2.2.146) of the letters is akin to a closing-off of her body—her bosom—to his love.

This lack of any open bodies to turn to or identify with leaves Hamlet with a sense of bodily as well as spiritual isolation; his "doubts about the mother and the holding environment," as the psychoanalyst Adam Phillips has written in a different context, "are transferred onto the body, turned against it, as it begins to represent a new kind of internal environment, a more solitary one"; he is left "in the solitary confinement of his body."[35] Nor is his in any sense "a benign solitude, reliably alone in the presence of the body and its thoughts"[36]: his environment is described by Hamlet as a kind of "prison"; the whole world, indeed, is, for him, nothing but a prison, "in which there are many confines, wards, and dungeons" (2.2.243–46). In this perception he seemingly matches the pent-up condition of his father, his blood thickened and body "bark'd about" by the poison, "confin'd" in his posthumous "prison-house" (1.5.11–14).

During his encounter with the ghost in Act One, Hamlet signals a kind of internal stiffening: "My fate cries out / And makes each petty artire [artery] in this body / As hardy as the Nemean lion's serve" (1.4.81–83); "Hold, hold, my heart, / And you, my sinews, grow not instant old, / But bear me stiffly up" (1.5.93–95).[37] There is here, as elsewhere in the play, a forced rigidifying of his own body, a countermovement to the urge to "burst in ignorance" (1.4.45). This corporeal hardening literally embodies a state of skepticism, a doubting of the environment, of its capacity to acknowledge him, or him it. So, as Elaine Scarry has shown in relation to the Hebraic scriptures, "disbelief or doubt . . . is habitually described as a witholding of the body, which in its resistance to an external referent is perceived as covered, or hard, or stiff."[38] This stiffening is inevitably accompanied by an impulse on Hamlet's behalf to "burst in ignorance," "to shatter all his bulk [=trunk] / And end his being" (2.1.95–96). This is one way of understanding Hamlet's use of the phrase "this mortal coil" (3.1.67): the constriction implied by it is, among other things, specifically corporeal. His "too too solid flesh"[39] (1.2.129) may be taken in a similar fashion: the wish to "have shuffled off" the coil, like the one to "melt, / Thaw, and resolve" the flesh, expresses his anguish over his solitary imprisonment within what he calls "this machine" (2.2.123), his body: he is indeed too much *in* the son.

There is a striking congruence between the kind of corporeal confinement and hardening described here and standard early modern views of melancholy. Timothy Bright, for instance, whose *A Treatise of Melancholy* (1586)[40] was the most widely available Elizabethan text on the subject, speaks of the "hardness whereof the flesh of melancholy persons is" (Bright, 128): "the nature of the humor . . . closeth up the poores, or straightneth the passages" (Ibid., 127). Melancholiacs "shut up the hart as it were in a dungeon of obscurity . . . and locketh up the gates of the hart, whereout the spirits should break forth upon just occasion, to the comfort of all the family of their fellow members" (Ibid., 100). And, he adds, "The house . . . seemeth unto the melancholicke a prison or dungeon" (Ibid., 263).

These notions recall certain psychoanalytic descriptions such as those of Wilhelm Reich, who has postulated an "armouring" of the body (as well as of the ego) on the part of neurotic individuals. Reich compares such psychophysiological rigidity to the donning of a protective suit of armor, depicting the "stiffness" of "melancholic or depressive patients" and the "contactlessness" that such patients feel.[41] This concept of armoring has been echoed by Lacan. In the context of the mirror stage and of "the succession of phantasies that extends from a fragmented body-image to a form of its totality that I shall call orthopaedic," Lacan describes "the assumption of the armour of an alienating identity, which will mark with its rigid structure the subject's entire mental development." "This fragmented body," he continues, "usually manifests itself in dreams. . . . It then appears in the form of disjointed limbs, or of those limbs represented in exoscopy, growing wings and taking up arms for intestinal persecutions—the very same that the visionary Hieronymus Bosch has fixed, for all time, in painting."[42]

It is illuminating to juxtapose these formulations to a statement such as Hamlet's "O God, I could be bounded in a nutshell and count myself a king of infinite space—were it not that I have bad dreams" (2.2.254–56). The image of a nutshell perfectly encapsulates the ambivalence Hamlet feels about the "armouring" of the self: alongside the defensive need for a protective shell there is a concomitant wish to be cracked open; portraying himself as "bounded in a nutshell," while allowing a matching of his closed-off father ("and count myself a king"), is surely also a plea of this kind. (Nuts, unlike nutshells or "loathsome crusts," can be eaten.) We never learn the exact nature of Hamlet's "bad dreams"; we can conjecture a connection, however, with something inside the body—inside the "nutshell," or beyond the constrictions of the "mortal coil" ("For in that sleep of death what dreams may come, / When we have shuffled off this mortal coil"—3.1.66–67); we can thus perhaps tentatively relate them, through Hamlet's grotesque fantasies about innards, to Lacan's "intestinal persecutions"—to a form of disintegration anxiety. (In humoral physiology, as Benjamin succinctly puts it, "bad dreams come from the spleen."[43]) In any event, the unspecified nature of the content of the dreams recalls Hamlet's statement, early in the play, about having "that within which passes show" (1.2.85)—a statement that combines defiance and challenge. Its vagueness derives in part from a self-protective impulse not to reveal himself too fully in the alien world of "seeming" and unyielding surfaces in Claudius' court—a refusal to open "my heart's core, ay . . . my heart of heart" (3.2.73), "the heart of my mystery" (3.2.357), to the closed figures surrounding him. At the same time, it is an angry dare, a gauntlet thrown to these figures: what Hamlet has within, he says, passes show, not understanding.

Through much of the play, Hamlet displays a profound doubt about what is "within" not only himself, his own body, but also within the various figures around him, paternal and maternal. His early plea—"Let me not burst in ignorance" (1.4.45)—expresses a relation between *not* knowing and a need to be open—a need for "the hatch and the discharge" (3.1.168) of whatever lies within. For the closure, the corporeal refusal, of the figures surrounding him exacerbates his own uncertainty as to the accuracy of his sensitivity to others' entrails—frustrates what Nietzsche calls his "sense of smell." ("It is not easily possible," as Nietzsche writes, "to understand the blood of another."[44]) Hence (in part) Hamlet's famous idleness. Hence also an urge to penetration, which he exhibits repeatedly throughout the play—an urge that finds its sources both in the frustrating environment and in his own uncertainty. Perhaps the withholding—the refusal of access to the interior of another's body—is in itself sufficient cause for the urge to break open. (Even the God of the Old Testament, as Scarry implies, cannot abide bodily refusal: "the witholding of the body—the stiffening of the neck, the turning of the shoulder, the closing of the ears, the hardening of the heart, the making of the face like stone—*necessitates* God's forceful shattering of the reluctant human surface and repossession of the interior."[45]) Hamlet's epistemophilic impulse, as we shall see in a moment, is persistently imagined in both violent and bodily terms.

Ever since Freud's footnote on *Hamlet* in *The Interpretation of Dreams*, there have been numerous interpretations of Hamlet's sexuality—of his incestuous impulses, of his disgust at the corporeal aspects of sex, of his possible homosexuality: these have become practically commonplaces of *Hamlet* criticism. Such interpretations often place a wide range of "bodily" material under the category of the sexual. Here, I take the sexual in *Hamlet* as one aspect of what I have called visceral knowledge, understanding the urge to penetration as an urge to open up the other, to know or connect with another: *Carnal* knowledge in the fullest sense of the term. "Lady, shall I lie in your lap?" (3.2.110): the pun here, undeniably sexual, may equally betray a desire to *be inside* the other; and Hamlet's rather vicious turn to "country matters" (l. 115) would then be a vengeful cheapening of full knowledge to mere sexuality.

Freud, followed by many later critics, portrayed Hamlet's desires as Oedipal—indeed, as prototypically Oedipal.[46] If we try to imagine what the Oedipus complex would look like from the perspective of visceral knowledge—or, more accurately, from that of frustrated visceral knowledge—we might come up with something like this: the desire to know one's mother and one's father can manifest itself as a desire to inhabit, or to find a way into, their bodies; this may have a tendency to be sexual in the former case (though, as R. D. Laing has written, even incest fantasies may be merely defences against the dread of being alone[47]), and violent in the latter (though this is certainly no more than a tendency, and in any case the distinction is not, of course, so simple as this). Biblically, at least, the taboos against incest and violence antecede a more primary taboo against knowing.

In any event, in turning to the play for evidence of Hamlet's Oedipus complex, we find not so much an incestuous impulse as what we might call a Nero complex: a desire to open the parental body—to know one's parent's entrails—a desire inseparable from a wish to have one's own entrails known. (Less, perhaps, a sexual complex than a "Nerosis.") Here is Hamlet, on his way to his mother's chambers:

> Now could I drink hot blood,
> And do such bitter business as the day
> Would quake to look on. Soft, now to my mother.
> O heart, lose not thy nature. Let not ever
> The soul of Nero enter this firm bosom;
> Let me be cruel, not unnatural.
> I will speak daggers to her, but use none.
>
> (3.2.381–87)

First of all, there is here no hint of a sexual desire. What Hamlet expresses in this prayer is a violent impulse, suppressed only with difficulty, to use daggers on his mother: on her body. We can call the daggers phallic, the Neronian impulse an incestuous attempt to reach the mother's womb; but neither the immediate nor the wider context requires such a reading. In *King John*, as the Oxford editor tells us, "Shakespeare refers to the legend that Nero committed the murder [of his mother] himself and ripped open [her] womb in order to see the place whence he came": the Bastard brands the rebels as "You bloody Neroes, ripping up the womb / Of your dear mother England" (5.2.152–53).[48] Elsewhere in Shakespeare, Nero appears simply as the type of cruelty, without reference to incest. In addition, there is here again a striking relation between Hamlet's bodily self-image and that of a parent, an implicit need for corporeal matching. In his determination to be more a Dane than an antic Roman, Hamlet forces a shutting-off and hardening of his own body ("O heart, lose not thy nature. Let not ever / The soul of Nero enter this firm bosom") in order that he not have to open up his mother's (with daggers): the prohibition, in either case, reveals the desire for aperture.

When we turn to the closet scene (*not* "the bedroom scene," as many critics have referred to it since John Dover Wilson's *What*

Happens in Hamlet[49]), we see, for the first time, a Hamlet unable to suppress his violent impulses. Here again we can find no evidence of direct sexual intent; on the contrary, as Adelman points out, Hamlet attempts in this scene to *separate* his mother from her sexuality. His penetrative wish is here coupled with an attempt at closing his mother's body, primarily (though not only) sexually, to Claudius: "Not this, by no means, that I bid you do: / Let the bloat King tempt you again to bed" (ll. 183–84). This may be simply a matter of shutting out Claudius in order to open his mother to himself; but it involves two different kinds of aperture—the sexual, which for Hamlet is "rank" (l. 150), "enseamed, . . . / Stew'd in corruption" (ll. 92–93), and the kind of carnal knowledge just described. Thus, his desexualization of Gertrude is by no means incompatible with an imagined opening of her body:

> Peace, sit you down,
> And let me wring your heart; for so I shall
> If it be made of penetrable stuff,
> If damned custom have not braz'd it so,
> That it be proof and bulwark against sense.
>
> (3.4.34–38)

This expresses a desire, more than anything, for ingression, without any sense of the transgression which would accompany a sexual desire. And Hamlet is insistent about this wish to fashion a mother whose heart consists of "penetrable stuff": "You go not till I set you up a glass / Where you may see the inmost part of you" (ll. 18–19). (Hamlet's rather convoluted syntax here—"I set you up a glass"—leaves open the possibility that he is positioning *himself* as the mirror for his mother's "inmost part.") What this "inmost part" is precisely we never learn; Hamlet's language, though, throughout this scene, is relentlessly body-bound. He speaks of his mother's sexuality in specifically inner-bodily terms ("the heyday in the blood," "a matron's bones"—ll. 69, 83)—"his version," as Adelman writes, "of her soiled inner body" (p. 34). Her deed is "such . . . / As from the body of contraction plucks / The very soul" (ll. 45–47), one at which "but the sickly part of one true sense" would have blushed (ll. 80–81). Hamlet counterpoints his desire for a healthful internal matching—"My pulse as yours doth temperately keep time" (l. 142)—with the fear of the alternative, a crustlike covering of a diseased "within": "It will but skin and film the ulcerous place, / Whiles rank corruption, mining all within, / Infects unseen" (ll. 149–51). And his imagery harps on the idea of internally sick bodies: "Sense sure you have, / Else could you not have motion; but sure that sense / Is apoplex'd" (ll. 71–73). The intense corporeality of Hamlet's words clashes with Gertrude's reaction to the arrival of the Ghost: "you do bend your eye on vacancy, / And with th'incorporal air do hold discourse" (ll. 117–18), she tells her son; "This is the very coinage of your brain. / This bodiless creation ecstasy / Is very cunning in" (ll. 139–41). There is a relation between the denial of the body of Old Hamlet here and Gertrude's earlier refusal symbolically to ingest this body at its death; this may be imagined as a causal relation (i.e., the symbolic nonincorporation of the deceased incapacitates any relation with his ghost). In spite of this, and though his mother never explicitly confesses to any sin, nor makes a single promise about keeping Claudius from her bed, by the end of the scene Hamlet seems satisfied. His attempt has been successful, at least insofar as Gertrude sees within herself "such black and grained spots / As will not leave their tinct" (l. 90–91) and speaks of herself as "penetrable": "These words like daggers enter in my ears" (l. 95); "O Hamlet, thou hast cleft my heart in twain" (l. 158).

The closet scene, of course, contains not only this metaphorical penetration of Gertrude, but also the killing—the physical penetration—of Polonius. As Gertrude describes it, Hamlet

> In his lawless fit,
> Behind the arras hearing something stir,
> Whips out his rapier, cries "A rat, a rat,"
> And in this brainish apprehension kills
> The unseen good old man.
>
> (4.1.8–12)

Hamlet turns from an agonizing confrontation with his mother, at the moment when he comes closest to doing violence to her physical person ("What wilt thou do? Thou wilt not murder me? / Help, ho!"—3.4.20–21), and thrusts his rapier through the arras. The surge of penetrative anger is turned away from his mother and toward a symbolically obstructive object. Rather than attacking "the mobbled [muffled or veiled] queen" (2.2.498), he attacks another "mobbled" body. The action strikingly brings together two associated strands of the play's imagery: a separating integument (the arras), and a penetrative instrument (the rapier). Several critics have commented upon the play's stress on skin and its relation to the multiple images of seals and sealing.[50] These images, along with a number of others evoking obstructive membranes,[51] can be understood to symbolize for Hamlet the sense of other people's veiled or closed-off bodies. Their concomitant is a plethora of piercing weapons and tools—"the pass and fell incensed points / Of mighty opposites" (5.2.61–62)—a plethora which bespeaks the violence born of the frustration of inaccessibility.[52] Many of these objects appear as actual props on stage, making not only metaphorically but physically present the sharpness, the "edge" (3.2.244), of Hamlet's desire ("You are keen, my lord, you are keen"—3.2.243). Benjamin speaks of "the precision with which the passions themselves take on the nature of stage-properties" in baroque drama[53]—if this is so, the play's passions are nothing if not penetrative. Unlike in the cinema, it was, one assumes, virtually impossible to represent human innards convincingly on the early-modern stage. The difficulty could be partially overcome through the use of stage-properties such as penetrative weapons; these could, so to speak, externalize the idea of the insides of the body—the ubiquitous presence of these weapons works to ensure the audience's remembering of these hidden parts. As Scarry writes: "As an actual physical fact, a weapon is an object that goes into the body and produces pain; as a perceptual fact, it can lift pain and its attributes out of the body and make them visible."[54]

Alternatively, of course, the body's insides can be foregrounded through linguistic representation. When Hamlet thinks of catching the conscience of the king he thinks in terms of penetrating to the very center of his body: "I'll tent him to the quick" (2.2.593),[55] he says, as he plans the staging of "The Murder of Gonzago." But, as the earlier part of this soliloquy reveals, access to Claudius' "offal" seems inseparably linked to access to Hamlet's own entrails, "As deep as to the lungs":

> Am I a coward?
> Who calls me villain, breaks my pate across,
> Plucks off my beard and blows it in my face,
> Tweaks me by the nose, gives me the lie i'th' throat
> As deep as to the lungs—who does me this?
> Ha!
> Swounds, I should take it: for it cannot be
> But I am pigeon-liver'd and lack gall
> To make oppression bitter, or ere this

I should ha' fatted all the region kites
With this slave's offal.

(2.2.566–76)

Here again there is a kind of visceral matching. Coming as it does at the end of this self-castigating tirade (which began with Hamlet calling himself a "slave"—l. 544), and after the repeated mention of his own viscera (lungs, liver, gall), "this slave's offal" may sound for a moment like a reference to himself—almost as if there is some confusion between killing the king and killing himself. Indeed, Hamlet's suicidal impulses may be thought of as partially a desire to reveal his own innards. His imagined method of suicide—"a bare bodkin" (3.1.76)—entails the opening up of the body (we might say: the baring of the body, noting that a "bodkin" meant not only a dagger but also a "body"[56]). Shuffling off the constrictive "mortal coil" through suicide would thus be not only, as Freudian psychoanalysis would say, an aggressive act misdirected inward instead of outward,[57] but also a vengeful injunction to look (analogous to his verbal foregrounding of putrefaction)—the embodiment of a wish to be known.

In his "O what a rogue and peasant slave" soliloquy, however, Hamlet's self-accusation takes the form of seeing himself as *lacking*, quite literally, guts: "for it cannot be / But I am pigeon-liver'd and lack gall / To make oppression bitter." He is "A dull and muddy-mettled rascal . . . unpregnant of [his] cause" (2.2.562–63). Both the self-castigation and the images of internal emptiness accurately reflect "the self-torments of melancholiacs" described by Freud in "Mourning and Melancholia": "In grief the world becomes poor and empty; in melancholia it is the ego itself" (p. 167). As Melanie Klein puts it, "the poignancy of the actual loss of a loved person is . . . greatly increased by the mourner's unconscious phantasies of having lost his *internal* 'good' objects as well."[58]

But this sense of visceral poverty alternates, in Hamlet's fantasy, with a contrary sense of visceral plenitude. Freud, in his interpretation of the "complex of melancholia," describes an "alternation of melancholic and manic phases" (p. 174). Hamlet, of course, displays just such a vacillation, between suicidal despair and an "antic disposition" (1.5.180). (Heinz Kohut, in his brief discussion of the play, depicts Hamlet's "traumatic state" as "characterized (a) by discharge phenomena, ranging from sarcastic punning to reckless, aggressive, outbursts (the killing of Polonius); and (b) by retreat phenomena, ranging from philosophical brooding to deeply melancholiac preoccupations."[59]) What we are now in a position to see is the bodily correlatives of these two phases.

We can call the depressive pole of this dialectic Hamlet's "Stoic" disposition, noting Nietzsche's definition of the Stoic as one who "wants his stomach to become ultimately indifferent to whatever the accidents of existence might pour into it."[60] Associated with this attitude are what we have described as the closure and hardening of the body and the concomitant sense of internal corruption or emptiness. It is when in this state that Hamlet feels the world to be a prison, his own body a constriction; and it is this mood that his self-castigations spring from. In "Mourning and Melancholia," Freud briefly mentions Hamlet as an example of the depressive's tendency to be "devoured by remorse and self-reproach" emanating from a "critical institution in the mind which is here split off from the ego"; this self-criticizing institution is "the mental faculty commonly called conscience" (pp. 168–69). In *Hamlet*, of course, it is "conscience" that "does make cowards of us all":

> And thus the native hue of resolution
> Is sicklied o'er with the pale cast of thought,
> And enterprises of great pith and moment
> With this regard their currents turn awry.
>
> (3.1.83–87)[61]

The split within the ego can be seen as involving a thoroughly Stoic separation of mind ("thought") and body ("pith"), and an idealization on the part of Hamlet of reason (as it is embodied in Horatio[62]). Walter Benjamin, describing the paradigmatic baroque attitude of acedia, speaks of "the desolation with which the practice of stoicism confronts man. The deadening of the emotions, and the ebbing away of the waves of life which are the source of these emotions in the body, can increase the distance between the self and the surrounding world to the point of alienation from the body."[63]

The manic pole of the dialectic, Hamlet's "antic disposition," is accompanied by a sense of visceral plenitude. This is manifested from his early "I have that within which passes show" to his "though I am not splenative and rash, / Yet have I in me something dangerous / Which let thy wiseness fear" (5.1.254–56). The "discharge phenomena" (as Kohut calls them) associated with this attitude may stem from Hamlet's need to "discharge" some of this fullness. [Hamlet's model here is not Horatio but Fortinbras, who is described as "hot and full," and as having "Shark'd up a list of lawless resolutes / For food and diet to some enterprise / That hath a stomach in't" (1.1.99–103). It is after witnessing Fortinbras and his army on their way to Poland that Hamlet acknowledges, and vows to mend, the split between his mind and body, noting the "Excitements of my reason and my blood" (4.4.58): "O, from this time forth, / My thoughts be bloody or be nothing worth" (ll. 65–66).[64]] In this humor the penetrative urge is inescapable, and the violence barely under control.

But this mood at last meets its maker in the graveyard scene. Here the ultimate "truth of entrails" is finally 'smelled out' by Hamlet, and his very viscera react with revulsion to the fragments of bodies in the graveyard. Wherever he has broken through a surface he has encountered death—beneath the earth in which his father was buried, behind Polonius' arras, beneath the seal of his own death warrant; now he finds death inside the body itself, and he realizes that the body hidden beneath its skin is not altogether desirable. What Hamlet eventually finds is that the only truth hidden within the body, his fantasies and desires notwithstanding, is the truth of mortality—that there is no access to thought, emotion, or living knowledge through access to the interior of the human frame. What had begun, for Hamlet, as an insistence on the insufficiency of the external, has turned by the end of the play into an understanding of the insufficiency of the internal. His own bodily interior reacts less than favorably to Yorick's skull and to the other human remains: his "bones . . . ache to think on't" (5.1.90–91)—on, that is, corpsehood, the living body's terminus; his "gorge rises at it" (l. 181); and, he finds, mortality stinks:

Hamlet.	Dost thou think Alexander looked o' this fashion i'th'earth?
Horatio.	E'en so.
Hamlet.	And smelt so? Pah!

(ll. 191–94)

"But who asked you to swallow men like oysters, Prince Hamlet?"—Nietzsche's own sense of smell seems to be informing his gnomic comment on the play. Perhaps what he means when he speaks of Hamlet's "misanthropy and love" is something akin to the alternation between the two dispositions just depicted—the Stoic and the antic, the Senecan (at least, the Senecan of the moral essays), and the Neronian (the Senecan of the revenge tragedies). Nor are the two as different, or as separable, as they may seem at first glance: like misanthropy and "an all too greedy love of man," there is here too an all-too-human dialectic of isolation and fusion.[65] Hamlet's "cannibalism" is an expression of his overwhelming desire to inhabit, and to be inhabited by, his parents. We can describe him, as Nietzsche described Socrates, as one "who cut ruthlessly into his own flesh, as he did into the flesh and heart of the 'noble,' with a look that said clearly enough: 'Don't dissemble in front of me! Here—we are equal.'"[66] "Don't dissemble": the stakes of acknowledgment are, for Hamlet, screwed to their highest pitch, reaching into his "inmost part," his "heart's core." "The death of our capacity to acknowledge as such," as Cavell has written, is "the turning of our hearts to stone or their bursting."[67] This is Hamlet's heartbreaking choice: to shut himself off within his "too too solid flesh"—or to "burst in ignorance." Neither alternative holds the promise of satisfying his desire to know, and to be known by, the other—hence the impasse at which Hamlet finds himself for most of the play. "We are all," in Emerson's words, "discontented pendulums"; Hamlet's pendulum swings not so much between killing the king and not killing him as between the two Hamlets these would entail being. Caught between hard-hearted "misanthropy" and heart-shattering "greedy love," he can only adopt, while simultaneously rejecting, alternating strategies of self-protection—Stoic isolation and antic aggression—until, we could say, he breaks apart—internally, where else?—"Now cracks a noble heart" (5.2.364).

Notes

I would like to thank Stanley Cavell, Marjorie Garber, Nick Halpern, Jeff Masten, Carla Mazzio, Curtis Perry, and Scott Stevens for their valuable comments at various stages of this essay. Above all, I am (as always) deeply grateful to Ruth Nevo for her ever-generous help and support.

1. All quotations from *Hamlet* are from the Arden edition, ed. Harold Jenkins (London: Routledge, 1982).

2. Katharine Eisaman Maus, *Inwardness and Theater in the English Renaissance* (Chicago: University of Chicago Press, 1995), 195.

3. Gail Kern Paster, *The Body Embarrassed: Drama and the Disciplines of Shame in Early Modern England* (Ithaca: Cornell University Press, 1993), 10, 12.

4. G. Wilson Knight, "The Embassy of Death: An Essay on *Hamlet*," in *The Wheel of Fire: Interpretations of Shakespearean Tragedy* (London: Methuen, 1949), 23.

5. John Hunt, "A Thing of Nothing: The Catastrophic Body in *Hamlet*," *Shakespeare Quarterly* 39 (1988): 27–44; esp. 27. Though Hunt does see an eventual

redemption for bodily experience in the play, in his view Hamlet's overwhelming attitude is one of "disdainful, alienated contempt" for the "corrupt and corrupting" flesh (Hunt, 37).

6. Janet Adelman, "Man and Wife Is One Flesh: *Hamlet* and the Confrontation with the Maternal Body," in *Suffocating Mothers: Fantasies of Maternal Origin in Shakespeare's Plays, "Hamlet" to "The Tempest"* (New York: Routledge, 1992), 250 n. 14.

7. Francis Barker, *The Tremulous Private Body: Essays on Subjection* (London: Methuen, 1984), 40. Cf. Hunt's characterization of Hamlet as wishing "to remove himself from the compromising infection of corporeality" (Hunt, 38).

8. Adelman, "Man and Wife Is One Flesh," 250n.14.

9. "Hamlet's Burden of Proof," in *Disowning Knowledge: In Six Plays of Shakespeare* (Cambridge: Cambridge University Press, 1987), 179–91; esp. 186 (emphasis in the original). My reading of *Hamlet* is indebted to Cavell's *The Claim of Reason: Wittgenstein, Skepticism, Morality, and Tragedy* (Oxford: Oxford University Press, 1979), where tragedy is understood as "a kind of epistemological problem," and where "the problem of knowledge" is inextricable from the embodied condition of humanity (482).

10. Friedrich Nietzsche, *On the Genealogy of Morals and Ecce Homo*, trans. Walter Kaufmann (New York: Vintage Books, 1989), 233: "My instinct for cleanliness is characterized by a perfectly uncanny sensitivity so that the proximity or—what am I saying?—the inmost parts, the 'entrails' of every soul are physiologically perceived by me—*smelled.*" On Nietzsche's repeated use of a "gastroenterological metaphor," see Eric Blondel, *Nietzsche: The Body and Culture. Philosophy as a Philological Genealogy*, trans. Seán Hand (Stanford: Stanford University Press, 1991), chap. 9 ("The Body and Metaphors"), 201–38; esp. 219–20.

11. Nietzsche, *Daybreak: Thoughts on the Prejudices of Morality*, trans. R. J. Hollingdale (Cambridge: Cambridge University Press, 1982), 74–76 (§ 119).

12. Nietzsche, "On Truth and Lie in the Extra-Moral Sense," in *The Portable Nietzsche*, ed. and trans. Walter Kaufmann (New York: Penguin Books, 1954), 44. The idea of an inherent connection between truth and entrails is at least as old as the practice of haruspices (or, in the case of human entrails, anthropomancy). See, for instance, Walter Burkert, *Homo Necans: The Anthropology of Ancient Greek Sacrificial Ritual and Myth*, trans. Peter Bing (Berkeley: University of California Press, 1983), 5–6; and Jean-Louis Durand, "Greek Animals: Towards a Topology of Edible Bodies," in *The Cuisine of Sacrifice Among the Greeks*, ed. Marcel Detienne and Jean-Pierre Vernant, trans. Paula Wissing (Chicago: University of Chicago Press, 1989), 87–118. In both the Old and New Testaments, as Elaine Scarry has shown, "the interior of the body carries the force of confirmation [of belief]." (*The Body in Pain: The Making and Unmaking of the World* [New York: Oxford University Press, 1985], 215.) Elsewhere she speaks of "the mining of the ultimate substance, the ultimate source of substantiation, the extraction of the physical basis of reality from its dark hiding place in the body out into the light of day, the making available of the precious ore of confirmation, the interior content of human bodies, lungs, arteries, blood, brains." (137). Cf. Diego Rivera's comment on Frida Kahlo: "Frida is the only example in the history of art of an artist who tore open her chest and heart to reveal the biological truth of her feelings." (Rivera, "Frida Kahlo y el Arte Mexicano," *Bolitín del Seminario de Cultura Mexicana*, no. 2 [October 1943]: 101; cited in Hayden Herrera, *Frida Kahlo: The Paintings* (New York: HarperPerennial, 1991), 4.

13. Nietzsche, *Beyond Good and Evil: Prelude to a Philosophy of the Future*, trans.

Walter Kaufmann (New York: Vintage Books, 1989), 137–39 (§ 212): "By applying the knife vivisectionally to the chest of the very *virtues of their time,* they [philosophers] betrayed what was their own secret: to know of a *new* greatness of man."

14. Nietzsche, *Thus Spoke Zarathustra,* in *The Portable Nietzsche,* 146; *The Will to Power,* trans. Kaufmann and R. J. Hollingdale, ed. Kaufmann (New York: Vintage Books, 1968), 289; emphasis in the original.

15. *Coleridge's Writings on Shakespeare,* ed. Terence Hawkes (New York: Capricorn Books, 1959), 140; emphasis in the original.

16. "Within," rather oddly, is capitalized in the Folio; the opacity here extends to the grammar—the context allows the word to be taken as either an adverb or a preposition.

17. "Hamlet," in *The Selected Prose of T. S. Eliot,* ed. Frank Kermode (New York: Harcourt, 1975), 48.

18. Jenkins's footnote.

19. See R. B. Onians, *The Origins of European Thought: About the Body, the Mind, the Soul, the World, Time, and Fate* (Cambridge: Cambridge University Press, 1951), 254–91, esp. 279 and 283–85.

20. See Burkert, 48–58; esp. 50: "The most widespread element in funerals—so obvious it may seem hardly worth mentioning—is the role played by eating, i.e., the funerary meal. . . . The ritualization of hunting made possible a twofold transferral: the dead could take the place of the quarry . . . but in the subsequent feast, his place could in turn be taken by the sacrificial animal." Georges Bataille discusses the cannibalistic impulse underlying the taboo regarding the touching of corpses: "The taboo protected the corpse from other people's desire to eat it. This is a desire no longer active in us, one we never feel now. Archaic societies, however, do show the taboo as alternately in force and suspended. Man is never looked upon as butcher's meat, but he is frequently eaten ritually." In Bataille, *Erotism: Death and Sensuality,* trans. Mary Dalwood (San Francisco: City Lights Books, 1986), 71. W. Arens's *The Man-Eating Myth: Anthropology and Anthropophagy* (New York: Oxford University Press, 1979) supports this, showing that while actual instances of cannibalism are (and apparently always have been) rare, the idea of cannibalism—whether used as a marker of otherness or rendered permissible through symbolization in a ritual setting (as in the Eucharist)—is ubiquitous. (See esp. 131–35 and 159–61.)

21. Sigmund Freud, "Mourning and Melancholia," trans. Joan Riviere, in *General Psychological Theory: Papers on Metapsychology,* ed. Philip Rieff (1917; reprint, New York: Macmillan, 1963), 164–79. Paul Ricoeur's comments on "Mourning and Melancholia" are useful; see, for example, *Freud and Philosophy: An Essay on Interpretation,* trans. Denis Savage (New Haven: Yale University Press, 1970), 129–34 and 216–17. Steven Mullaney has recently juxtaposed Freud's essay with *Hamlet* in "Mourning and Misogyny: *Hamlet, The Revenger's Tragedy,* and the Final Progress of Elizabeth I, 1600–1607," *Shakespeare Quarterly* 45, no. 2 (summer 1994): 139–62.

22. Jacques Lacan, "Desire and the Interpretation of Desire in *Hamlet,*" trans. James Hulbert, in *Literature and Psychoanalysis: The Question of Reading: Otherwise,* ed. Shoshana Felman (Baltimore: Johns Hopkins University Press, 1982), 11–52, 39–40.

23. The word has both meanings in *Titus Andronicus* (1.1.35 and 5.2.188); see Alexander Schmidt, *Shakespeare Lexicon and Quotation Dictionary,* 3rd ed. (New York: Dover Publications, 1971), 1:212. On "the slight *frisson* of horror" accompanying Hamlet's "bak'd meats" comment, see Adelman, 27.

24. John Aubrey, *Remaines of Gentilisme and Judaisme* (London, 1686–87), ed. James Britten (Nendeln: Kraus Reprint, 1967), 35; see also 19, 23–24, 36, 99.

25. The poet Erich Fried, who translated *Hamlet* into German, claims that in his "funeral bak'd meats" comment, "Hamlet is suggesting that his father's flesh was eaten at his mother's wedding." See *Is Shakespeare Still Our Contemporary?* ed. John Elsom (London and New York: Routledge, 1989), 31.

26. The glosses in this paragraph are from, respectively, Schmidt, 1:80; the Arden edition (219); and Schmidt, 1:466.

27. We have seen Hamlet speaking about Claudius being "fit and season'd for his passage" (3.3.86). "Season'd" usually in Shakespeare means "to spice, to give relish to" when used as a transitive verb: see Schmidt, 2:1017. Hamlet may thus punningly refer to Claudius as being readied to be eaten. Indeed, there seems to be a fairly specific culinary fantasy in Hamlet's mind, of a dead body being prepared for eating by first being "season'd," as well as, perhaps, stuffed ("full of bread"), then "bak'd" till a crust has formed around it. Cf. the "blood of fathers, mothers, daughters, sons, / Bak'd and impasted [= made into a crust].... Roasted with wrath"—in Hamlet's part of the Pyrrhus speech (2.2.455–57), and his later "Now could I drink hot blood" (3.2.381) soliloquy.

28. Nietzsche, *The Gay Science*, trans. Walter Kaufmann (New York: Vintage Books, 1974), 200 (§ 167).

29. Adelman, 28; the following quotation is from 27.

30. The play's imagery of the insides of the body (as opposed to its surfaces) not surprisingly focuses on the torso; here too we can sense a tenuous distinction between male and female insides: images of the maternal inner-body tend to point to the upper half of the torso ("those thorns that in her bosom lodge" (1.5.87); "in her excellent white bosom" (2.2.112); "such love must needs be treason in my breast" (3.2.173); "let me wring your heart . . . if it be made of penetrable stuff" (3.4.35–36) or to the womb (1.1.140, and, implicitly, 3.2.385); images of the paternal inner-body are most often gastro-enteric ("guts" (3.4.214, 4.3.31), "offal" (2.2.576), "garbage [entrails]" (1.5.57), "stomach" (1.1.103), etc. (I exclude from this list most of the play's many references to "heart" and its derivatives.) It may also be worth mentioning the "incipient pun on matter and *mater*" (Adelman, 255, n. 36) in some of the twenty-six uses of the former word in the play; on *mater* as specifically "the trunk of the reproducing female body," see Elaine Scarry, Introduction to *Literature and the Body: Essays on Populations and Persons, Selected Papers from the English Institute, 1986* (Baltimore: Johns Hopkins University Press, 1988), xxii.

31. Cavell sees "Hamlet's question whether to be or not, as asking first of all not why he stays alive, but first of all how he or anyone lets himself be born as the one he is" (Cavell, "Hamlet's Burden of Proof," 187). Both he and Adelman (in her concern with the "devouring maternal womb" and with the "fantasy of spoiling at the site of origin"—23) are primarily interested in the question of the origin of the individual. The distinction between the problem of death and the problem of being born is, I think, important in the play, though it is hardly a simple binary: as Adelman says, in *Hamlet* "birth itself . . . immerses the body in death" (27).

32. Note the cyclical structure of many of Hamlet's comments about decomposition: "Not where he eats, but where he is eaten . . . we fat all creatures else to fat us, and we fat ourselves for maggots. . . . A man may fish with the worm that hath eat of a king, and eat of the fish that hath fed of that worm" (4.3.19–28).

33. Bataille, *Erotism*, 56. The body's decomposition is intimately connected to

the idea of the contagiousness of death, an idea whch recurs in Hamlet's imagery. (See ibid., 46–47; and cf. the uses of "pestilence" and "contagion" in the play: "a foul and pestilent congregation of vapours" (2.2.302); "pestilent speeches of his father's death" (4.5.91; cf. 5.1.173); "hell itself breathes out / Contagion to this world" (3.2.380–81); "I'll touch my point / With this contagion, that if I gall him slightly, / It may be death" (4.6.145–47; cf. 1.3.42).

34. Among the most prominent critics who have noted this strand of imagery are Caroline Spurgeon [*Shakespeare's Imagery and What It Tells Us* (Cambridge: Cambridge University Press, 1935), 133–34, 316–19] and Wolfgang Clemen [*The Development of Shakespeare's Imagery* (London: Methuen, 1977), 112–18].

35. Adam Phillips, "On Risk and Solitude," in *On Kissing, Tickling, and Being Bored: Psychoanalytic Essays on the Unexamined Life* (Cambridge, Mass.: Harvard University Press, 1993), 31, 28.

36. Phillips, "On Risk and Solitude," 32.

37. The Ghost has already signalled a kind of internal matching with his son, when characterizing his tale as one that should "freeze thy young blood" (1.5.16; cf. the similar effects of the poison on Old Hamlet's own blood: 1.5.65–70). His "Remember me" (1.91) may thus be taken literally as an injunction to his son to "re-member"—i.e., bodily reproduce—himself.

38. Scarry, *The Body in Pain*, 202. Scarry's examples are plentiful, but see especially Exod. 32:9; Zech. 7:11, 12; Neh. 9:29; Isa. 48:4.

39. I here adopt the Folio reading (rather than the Second Quarto's "sullied").

40. Timothy Bright, *A Treatise on Melancholy*, Reprinted Facsimile Text Society (New York: Columbia University Press, 1940; orig. London: Thomas Vautrollier, 1586).

41. Wilhelm Reich, *Character Analysis*, trans. Vincent R. Carfango (New York: Touchstone, 1945), esp. 337–54. The quotes are from 346 and 350, respectively.

42. Lacan, "Mirror Stage," 4.

43. Walter Benjamin, *The Origin of German Tragic Drama*, trans. John Osborne (London: Verso, 1977), 152. Cf. Freud, *The Interpretation of Dreams*, trans. James Strachey (New York: Basic, 1959), 35–36:

> If it is established that the interior of the body when it is in a diseased state becomes a source of stimuli for dreams, and if we admit that during sleep the mind, being diverted from the external world, is able to pay more attention to the interior of the body, then it seems plausible to suppose that the internal organs do not need to be diseased before they can cause excitations to reach the sleeping mind—excitations which are somehow turned into dream-images. . . . The obscurity in which the centre of our being . . . is veiled from our knowledge and the obscurity surrounding the origin of dreams tally too well not to be brought into relation to each other.

44. Nietzsche, *Thus Spoke Zarathustra*, 152.

45. Scarry, 203–4; italics mine.

46. Freud, *The Interpretation of Dreams*, 263–66; Cf. Ernest Jones, *Hamlet and Oedipus* (New York: Doubleday, 1954).

47. R. D. Laing, *The Divided Self: An Existential Study in Sanity and Madness* (London: Tavistock Press, 1960), 57.

48. The quotation is from *The Riverside Shakespeare*, ed. G Blakemore Evans (Boston: Houghton, 1974). Chaucer portrays Nero's relation with his mother, similarly, not in incestuous but in violent, epistemophilic terms: "His mooder made he in pitous array, / For he hire wombe slitte to biholde / Where he conceyved was—so weilaway / That he so litel of his mooder tolde [=es-

teemed]!" "The Monk's Tale," ll. 2483-86, in *The Riverside Chaucer*, ed. Larry D. Benson (Boston: Houghton, 1987). Marc Shell, however, in his recent piece on the play (Shell, "Hoodman Blind, or *Hamlet* and the End of Siblinghood," in *Children of the Earth: Literature, Politics, and Nationhood* [New York: Oxford University Press, 1993]) finds in this passage a refusal on Hamlet's part "to knowingly commit maternal incest and matricide" (Shell, 112), and cites Lydgate's *Falls of Princes* (1494) and Marsten's *Scourge of Villanie* (1599) as evidence of the connection between the incest theme and Nero in the English Renaissance (247, n. 56).

49. The Queen's closet was, as the Oxford editor remarks, "her own private apartment. A closet was not, it seems worth emphasizing, a bedroom" (276). Wilson's influential book was, I think, the first to call this "The Bedroom Scene" (246, chapter heading). Twentieth-century interpretations have more often than not gone along with this and used a bed as a central prop, following (perhaps) Freud's reading of the scene as portraying Hamlet's incestuous impulses.

50. For example, Maurice Charney, "The Imagery of Skin Disease and Sealing," in *Hamlet's Fictions* (New York: Routledge, 1988), 120-30.

51. To take some salient examples, apart from the many images of skin and sealing: the arras behind which Claudius and Polonius hide together (2.2.263), the one behind which Polonius hides, the "inky cloak" (1.2.77) of seeming, the multiple layers enclosing the body of Old Hamlet (armour, "crust," "cerements," coffin, "sepulchre"), and the "mobbled queen" of the Pyrrhus speech (a phrase over which Hamlet muses, interrupting the performance).

52. Penetrative instruments are ubiquitous in *Hamlet*, from Marcellus' "partisan [a long-handled spear]" (1.1.143), through Pyrrhus' "antique sword" (2.2.465), Hamlet's "slings and arrows" and "bare bodkin" (3.1.58; 76; cf. 4.7.21; 5.2.239), Laertes' poisoned "knife" (4.7.141) and "sword unbated" (4.7.137; the play's other references to swords are: 1.5.154, 156, 162, 166, 167, 169; 2.2.469, 473, 487, 510; 3.1.153; 3.3.88; 4.3.64; 4.5.211; 4.7.139), Gertrude's "words like daggers" (3.4.95; cf. 3.2.387), and Claudius' "great axe" (4.5.215; cf. 5.2.24), to the final trial by "rapier and dagger" (5.2.142) or "foils" (4.7.135; 5.2.250) the play is full of sharp weapons; there are, too, images of pins (1.4.65), thorns (1.3.48; 1.5.88), a "tent [an instrument for examining or cleansing a wound]" (2.2.593), a "worthy pioner [a foot soldier who preceded the main army with spade or pickaxe]" (1.5.171), and "a sexton's spade" (5.1.88). Compare Nietzsche's description of himself as "a subterranean man . . . one who tunnels and mines and undermines . . . a solitary mole" (*Daybreak*, 1), as well as his "I am no man, I am dynamite" (*Ecce Homo*, 326) with Hamlet's excitement about his own (and his father's) underground activity: "'t shall go hard / But I will delve one yard below their mines / And blow them at the moon" (3.4.209-11).

53. Benjamin, 133.

54. Scarry, 16.

55. "Tent" [probe]. "A *tent* was an instrument for examining or cleansing a wound" (Arden). "The quick" is "the tender or sensitive flesh in any part of the body . . . the tender part of a sore or wound" (*OED*). Claudius has spoken of himself as "the owner of a foul disease, [who,] / To keep it from divulging, let it feed / Even on the pith of life" (4.1.21-23) and of the raging of "the hectic [fever] in my blood" (4.3.69); Hamlet calls his uncle "this canker of our nature" (5.2.69). In Claudius' case at least, Hamlet's assumption of internal corruption seems to be an accurate assessment of the truth.

56. As it does 150 lines earlier, at 2.2.524.

57. Cf. Freud, "Mourning and Melancholia," 173: "No neurotic harbours

thoughts of suicide which are not murderous impulses against others redirected upon himself."

58. Klein, "Mourning and its Relation to Manic-Depressive States," 156 (emphasis in the original). Hamlet's sense of internal emptiness is also experienced by him in economic terms: "Beggar that I am, I am even poor in thanks . . . my thanks are too dear a halfpenny" (2.2.272–74). Fortinbras' imagined bodily plenitude is portrayed by Hamlet in terms of his willingness to spend "twenty thousand ducats" to "debate the question of this straw" (4.4.25–26). Perhaps Hamlet's anger over the "thrift, thrift" (1.2.180) of reusing the "funeral bak'd meats" at the subsequent wedding partakes of this monetary structure of feeling.

59. Heinz Kohut, *The Analysis of the Self,* (New York: International Universities Press, 1971), 236–37.

60. Letter to Franz Overbeck, 31 March 1885; cited in Blondel, 221.

61. I quote the Folio's "pith" rather than the Second Quarto's "pitch": this is supported by the Players' Quartos of 1676, 1683, 1695, and 1703; see G. R. Hibbard's note in the Oxford edition.

62. See, for example, 3.2.54–74. Hamlet's characterization of Horatio as "not a pipe for Fortune's finger / To sound what stop she please" can be taken as an image of bodily closure, made more explicit later in the same scene: "You would play upon me, you would seem to know my stops, you would pluck out the heart of my mystery. . . . 'Sblood, do you think I am easier to be played on than a pipe?" (ll. 355–61).

63. Benjamin, 140.

64. I take "bloody" here to imply not only the metaphoric sense of "taking revenge" but also the corporeal sense of actual blood—"My thoughts be bloody" thus links a unity of psyche-soma with the urge to violent aperture.

65. Cf. Gordon Braden, *Renaissance Tragedy and the Senecan Tradition: Anger's Privilege* (New Haven: Yale Univerity Press, 1985), 219: "Hamlet's case in effect shows that the unsuccessful avenger is also going to be . . . the unsuccessful Stoic. Stoicism is the natural alternative to revenge because it is a twin endeavor, a complementary strategy for establishing the self's belief in its own dignity and power."

66. See n. 13.

67. Cavell, *Claim of Reason,* 493.

Othello and Woyzeck as Tragic Heroes According to Aristotle and Hegel

Yedidia Itzhaki

I. Introduction

THE comparison we intend to make between Shakespeare's *Othello* and Büchner's *Woyzeck* is based on an interesting similarity found in the plots of these two plays. In both the protagonist is a soldier, who discovers about his wife's unfaithfulness; at this, his world comes to an end, for to him the woman signifies the entire world. After great suffering, in a fit of jealous madness, he finally kills the woman and takes his own life. Given the universal character of the story itself, this affinity could be completely unintentional, but due to the influence Shakespeare's work is known to have had on Büchner's it may just not be a coincidence. Yet, beyond this general line of likeness in the plot, both plays differ substantially. Most obvious is the oppositional difference between the protagonists—Othello and Woyzeck—which is so great that it nearly disguises the similarities between both plots. At first the only apparent affinity in these figures is the fact that both are soldiers, yet precisely in this one and only line of similarity, the major element of contrast is most clearly evident: Whereas Othello is the supreme commander of the army, Woyzeck belongs to the lowest military echelon, an impoverished and miserable batman of a minor army officer.

The assumption in Aristotle's theory is that the tragic hero must be *good*, and "of the number of those in the enjoyment of great reputation and property" (Aristotle, chap. 13, 1453a).[1] Thus, according to Aristotle, the tragic hero as an elevated person is in the very essence of Tragedy, and the quality of the hero—be it *good* or *bad, high* or *low*—is what determines how a literary work should be classified. Comedy "would make its personages worse, and the other [Tragedy] better, than the men of the present day" (Ibid., chap. 2, 1448a). Northrop Frye (1970, 33–34), in line with the Aristotelian approach, proposes that literary protagonists be classified into five categories, whereby Aristotle's *good* and *bad* are taken to relate to the hero's might and power of action: Mythological Hero, Hero of Romance, Hero of the high mimetic mode (*a leader*), Hero of the low mimetic mode, and Hero of the ironic mode.

A preliminary classification of Othello and Woyzeck according to Frye's method will clearly show that Othello is a *leader*:

> If superior in degree to other men but not to his natural environment, the hero is a leader. He has authority, passions, and powers of expression far greater than ours, but what he does is subject both to social criticism and to the order of nature. This is the hero of the *high mimetic* mode, of most epic and tragedy, and is primarily the kind of hero that Aristotle had in mind.

Woyzeck, on the other hand, is not even a hero of the *low mimetic mode*, who is supposed to be someone "superior neither to other men nor to his environment . . . one of us." Woyzeck, with his weak mind and limited intelligence, is at the lowest end of the social sphere and can only be classified as a hero of the *ironic mode*:

> If inferior in power or intelligence to ourselves, so that we have the sense of looking down on a scene of bondage, frustration or absurdity, the hero belongs to the *ironic* mode. This is still true when the reader feels that he is or might be in the same situation, as the situation is being judged by the norms of greater freedom.

For Frye, then, Othello is the paradigm of the tragic hero—the very kind Aristotle had in mind—and he exemplifies the tragic hero of the *high mimetic* mode (Frye, 38), whereas Woyzeck's dramatic figure is not fit to be more than a comedy hero who, according to Aristotle, mimics the "acts of the ignoble." Yet, no matter how one may define it, *Woyzeck* is far from being a comedy. In fact, it is closer to Tragedy than to any other genre. Indeed, due to the difference between the figure of Woyzeck and the Aristotelian definition of the tragic hero, some critics have seen in *Woyzeck* a new kind of tragedy, one that anticipates a change of approach toward the nature of Tragedy and of the tragic hero.

The question of changing criteria in the definition of Tragedy has been amply discussed and has provoked much argument. *Woyzeck* is often mentioned in connection with the subject: Although the play is considered a turning point in the approach to Tragedy, there are also those who have claimed that the play should not be considered a tragedy at all.[2] At any rate, the problems in classifying *Woyzeck* as a tragic play center on the question of whether the protagonist, Woyzeck, can be identified as a tragic hero; for the plot of the play is Tragedy at its best, and the fact that it is so similar to the plot in *Othello*—recognized as a paradigm of the tragic play—is evidence in favor of this argument. Indeed, the classification of a literary work as established by Aristotle, is related to the degree of *goodness* in the hero. According to this criteria, the problem in classifying *Woyzeck* is greater: How can so similar a tragic plot be possible, in two plays where the protagonists are so very different from each other? If we claim that Woyzeck is not a tragic hero, we imply that the play is not a tragedy, and we must explain the similarity of its plot with that of *Othello*, or indicate an essential difference in both plots—which may exclude *Woyzeck* from being a tragedy. On the other hand, if we classify Woyzeck as a tragic hero, we must explain how such an inferior and insignificant figure can possibly be the hero of a tragedy. To argue that this is due to changes in the traditional standards which have long been used for understanding the tragic form will, on its own, not exonerate us from this need, for we shall then have to adopt a new understanding for Tragedy and for the tragic hero. Like Walter Kaufmann, we may claim that the tragic hero is not necessarily the essence of Tragedy:

> Aristotle himself stressed the importance of the action and the plot above that of character. . . . Hegel realized that at the center of the greatest tragedies of Aeschylus and Sophocles we find not a tragic hero but a tragic collision.
> (Kaufmann 1969, 235–36)

Hence, the essence of Tragedy does not necessarily depend on the qualities of the tragic hero, but on the tragic situation he finds himself in, and this is what ultimately decides the characteristics of the tragic heroes, who may therefore be entirely different from each other. Indeed, for Aristotle, "Tragedy is essentially an imitation, not of persons but of action and life" (Aristotle, chap. 6, 1450a); but he also clearly defined the actions of which specific individuals are to be imitated in Tragedy. In other words, notwithstanding the fact that Aristotle did not see the tragic hero as the center and purpose of Tragedy, he did establish the hero's qualities and limits, so that "we ascribe certain qualities to their actions" (Ibid), depending on the attributes of the characters. Herein also lies the universality of a literary work: "By a universal statement I mean one as to what such or such a kind of man will probably or necessarily say or do" (Ibid., chap. 9, 1451b). Thus, as far as Aristotle is concerned, the plot and quality of the tragic hero depend on each other.

Hegel, for whom the importance of Tragedy is not necessarily in the fate and suffering of the hero, but rather in the tragic conflict in which the hero finds himself, also discusses at length the character of the tragic hero, and its relation to the conflict in which he is involved (Hegel 1962, 47, 85–89, 112–29). Whatever the case may be, we must clarify how and whether such an abysmal difference in character between these two heroes—Othello and Woyzeck—is sufficient reason to alter the dramatic situation in the plays, and to present the tragic conflict in either plot with an entirely different meaning.

In comparing *Othello* and *Woyzeck*, we will analyze the two protagonists according to the Aristotelian criteria for the tragic hero, and use Hegel's approach for appraising the dramatic situation depicted in both plays.

II. *Othello* According to Aristotle

Othello has been described as a play with a superior dramatic structure in the *classic* sense, according to the criteria established by Aristotle and Hegel for Tragedy. The course of *Othello's* story fits Aristotle's criteria for a tragic plot, and the protagonist seems to be exemplary as a tragic hero.[3]

The unfolding of the tragedy in *Othello* documents the hero's "passing from happiness to misery" (Aristotle, chap. 13, 1452b). Othello is "of the numbers of those in the enjoyment of great reputation and property" (Ibid., chap. 13, 1453a). He is of noble origin, the son of a king, and despite being captured and enslaved far from his native land, he manages to overcome these impediments, and soars to the heights of happiness and success in the city that hosts him. First, he is named commander in chief of the army of Venice, and later, governor of Cyprus. His qualifications and talents have earned Othello the right to these positions, and even Iago agrees: "For their souls, / Another of his fathom they have not / To lead their business" (Othello, 1.1.151–53).[4] Success and happiness reach a peak with Othello's marriage to Desdemona—daughter of Brabantio, a Venetian nobleman and member of the city's Senate. Such a union is bound to give Othello a firm basis for establishing himself and for continuing his achievements in Venice, and Iago remarks: "He tonight hath boarded a land carrack: / If it prove lawful prize, he's made for ever" (1.2.50–51). Othello is certainly not *a bad man,* and everyone praises his merits; for example, the Duke says to Brabantio, "If virtue no delighted beauty lack, / Your son-in-law is far more fair than black" (1.3.289–90); and Lodovico, at the end of the play: "O thou Othello, that wert once so good" (5.2.292). Even Iago celebrates Othello's virtues: "The Moor a free and open nature too" (1.3.397), and more.

Yet, which is the great error that makes Othello stumble and is responsible for peripety—the passing in the hero's fortune from happiness to misfortune—and which is the Discovery that leads to this peripety? Before his suicide, Othello says about himself:

> . . . then must you speak
> Of one that lov'd not wisely, but too well:
> Of one not easily jealous, but being wrought,
> Perplex'd in the extreme . . .
>
> (5.2.344–47)

According to this, Othello's great error lies in the extremism within him, in a love that is too intense and a jealousy that knows no boundaries.

Jealousy in its many and diverse facets is indeed the main subject and interest in *Othello,* and the driving force behind the play's plot. However, jealousy and the extreme emotions that trouble Othello do not account for the error, which according to the Aristotelian criteria, must be within the scope of a deed and should belong to the tragic action, whereas the character and feelings of the hero are not considered to be deeds. In this context, it is irrelevant whether Othello's jealousy stems from his love for Desdemona, who has become an unreal figure to him—as claimed by Bradley (Bradley 1965, 151–61) and many others—or whether it originates in self-love—as suggested by T. S. Eliot (Eliot, 1969, 130–31). Whether Othello was free of jealousy until Iago instilled it in him, or whether the seeds of jealousy were already rooted in his soul from before, makes no real difference to us.

But the blind trust with which Othello goes along with Iago, and his readiness for suspecting Desdemona when presented with such flimsy evidence, may be seen as Othello's tragic error. Which have nothing to do with Othello's innocent character and his faith in others—used by Iago to advance his designs: "The Moor [has] a free and open nature too" (Othello, 2.3.397)—for these, being character traits and not deeds, are therefore not in the range of a tragic error. Moreover, it is difficult to assume that innocence and trust in others are in the scope of guilt or error. On the other hand, *believing* in Iago and *allowing* himself to be trapped in the villain's intrigues may indeed be considered an Aristotelian tragic error.

Believing Iago's lies and suspecting Desdemona are in fact part of the play's action, and among the factors that bring about peripety, in the inevitable development of the plot. The swiftness with which suspicion and jealousy take hold of Othello, deserves notice. He speaks as if jealousy were completely alien to him, when he says to Iago, "Think'st thou I'ld make a life of jealousy?" (3.3.181), and affirms his wife's faithfulness with full conviction: "I do not think but Desdemona's honest" (3.3.229); yet, just moments later, he is overcome by suspicion and jealousy. Othello comes to believe Iago more and more and, convinced that Iago knows more than he says, he moans: "Why did I marry? This honest creature doubtless / Sees and knows more, much more, than he unfolds" (3.3.246–47).

If this is Othello's tragic error, peripety is when he discovers Iago's wickedness, Desdemona's devotion, and his own folly, which are revealed to him by Emilia's testimony, Cassio's disclosures and Roderigo's letters. The Discovery, arising from the play's action, is of the finest form: Desdemona's murder leads to Othello's need for confessing his suspicions and the evidence of Desdemona's betrayal; Emilia then recounts what she knows, exposing Iago's intrigues and his own foolishness.

If Othello's admission of his recent mistake and of his subsequent suicide, out of grief for having senselessly destroyed Desdemona, constitute the tragic peripety, it is brought about by the Discovery and, according to Aristotle, "The finest form of Discovery is one attended by Peripeties" (Aristotle, chap. 11, 1452a). For Othello, change occurs while he is chief commander of the army of Venice and still at the height of success, and his tragic fall follows instantly: Desdemona, whose love and loyalty become clear to him at the end, is spent, he is divested of authority and command, and nothing remains for him but suicide. Such developments arouse in us pity and fear, the tragic emotions which, as far as Aristotle is concerned, are the very object of Tragedy. So indeed, Othello does seem to conform to most of the Aristotelian requirements for the tragic protagonist, and the play follows the criteria established by the philosopher for defining Tragedy.

Yet this solution presents some difficulties with respect to the unity, wholeness, and consistency of the tragedy. If we understand Aristotle correctly, the spark that sets off the finest form of tragic action, that which combines the play's wholeness and artistic unity, is the tragic error. This error, which justifies the fall of the hero and stirs in the audience emotions of pity and fear, is what determines the peripety that follows Discovery. In other words, this error is the driving force behind the development of the tragic action. As just mentioned, although Othello's error—believing Iago with no reservations—is indeed what fuels the inevitable developments leading to peripety in the protagonist's fate, it is not the point of departure for such developments. For Othello is only ensnared in Iago's stratagem by the middle of act 3, at the climax of the play.

According to Aristotle, "a beginning is that which is not itself necessarily after anything else" (Aristotle, chap. 7, 1450b), and all that precedes Othello's tragic error is not directly related to the tragic action. Thus, Johnson was correct in affirming that for *Othello* to be a perfectly structured tragedy, the play's action should have opened in Cyprus. It is also possible that for *Othello* to conform precisely to the Aristotelian definition of tragedy, the Cassio affair—the main episode in act 2—should have been presented as background material, to introduce the action itself.

In this scheme, the drama's outcome presents another difficulty, related to the play's tragic approach. Othello's end and that of Emilia—who inadvertently supports Iago by stealing Desdemona's handkerchief—indeed arouse in us, as the tragic error should, strong emotions of pity and fear. But Desdemona, whom we are accustomed to see as innocent, virtuous and pure, is bound to arouse in us not pity and fear but rejection, for according to Aristotle this "situation is not fear-inspiring or piteous, but simply odious to us" (Aristotle, chap. 13, 1452b).

However, a different tragic arrangement that conforms with Aristotle's criteria can also be found. The play opens immediately after Desdemona's secret marriage to Othello. This union offends accepted conventions because it undermines paternal authority, due to the fact that Brabantio intensely objects to it. Yet it is not in the range of a crime or sin. Their love *softens* the sin, as well as the assumption that Brabantio's animosity to his daughter marrying the Moor, is based on prejudice and xenophobia if not outright racism. Thus, let us examine the possibility that the secret marriage is Othello and Desdemona's tragic error. It takes place before the beginning of the play, which opens with Iago's first intrigues, based on the antagonism expected from Brabantio at the news of his daughter's marriage to Othello. Hence, this error not only launches the tragedy, but also manipulates and establishes its course of action. And indeed, toward the end of act 1 Brabantio warns, "Look to her, Moor, have a quick eye to see: / She has deceiv'd her father, may do thee" (Othello, 1.3.292–293).

Deceiving her father establishes a tragic potential in Desdemona for her betrayal of Othello. It undermines the entire play and serves as the foundation for Iago's intrigues. Othello initially rejects the idea, saying to Iago, "I do not think but Desdemona's honest" (3.3.229); but this very statement—towards the middle of act 3—allows the Discovery to take place, and the spark that apparently triggers it is Iago's revelation to Othello that Desdemona has been unfaithful to him. Peripety is precipitated by this ominous discovery—Othello's bliss is lost forever—leading him inevitably on to the tragic denouement, when he murders Desdemona and takes his own life.

The problem with this solution is that the Discovery is false, merely set off by Iago's subterfuges: If only Iago's lies had been exposed earlier Othello's bliss may have been restored. Such a Discovery, coupled with the peripety it entails, is thus the result of chance and does not unfold in the probable or necessary sequence. However, if we recall Othello's emphatic declarations concerning his certainty of Desdemona's faithfulness, first to Brabantio in act 1, and then to Iago in act 3, when the scoundrel tries to arouse his jealousy, we can understand that what Othello discovers is not his wife's imaginary infidelity, but rather the *possibility* of her betrayal. Thus, his bliss—based on the certainty of Desdemona's love and fidelity—is by necessity destroyed. Even if Iago's deception had been exposed and it had become clear to Othello that his wife did not betray him with Cassio on this occasion, the prospect of her betraying him in the future continues to exist. Othello only becomes aware of this *possibility* when the tragic error—their lies to Brabantio—is brought into his consciousness by Iago's words:

> She did deceive her father, marrying you;
> And when she seem'd to shake and fear your looks,
> She lov'd them most.
> (3.3.210–12)

Indeed, Othello is convinced that Desdemona is faithful, until Iago reminds him that she has betrayed her father. Doubts and jealousy assail him simultaneously, but only when he comes to realize that the betrayal is *possible*, based on the error mentioned by Iago.

The tragic error of Desdemona's marriage to Othello against her father's will, is also specifically referred to near the end of the tragedy, after the murder of Desdemona and before Othello's suicide, at the height of the catastrophe:

> Poor Desdemona, I am glad thy father's dead;
> Thy match was mortal to him, and pure grief'
> Shore his old thread atwain: did he live now,
> This sight would make him do a desperate turn,
> Yea, curse his better angel from his side,
> And fall to reprobation.
>
> (5.2. 205–10)

Thus, the tragic denouement is directly related to the opening of the tragedy and comes as the result of the tragic error. Desdemona's tragic death as well as Othello's, stir up in the audience feelings of pity and fear, for Desdemona can no longer be considered the pure and virtuous angel depicted in the play. "Deceit and falsehood, whatever conveniences they may for a time promise or produce are, in the sum of life, obstacle to happiness" (Johnson 1915, 198).

According to the Aristotelian definition of Tragedy, this scheme of tragic structure in *Othello* is a model of wholeness and unity. Crafted to perfection, with no superfluous parts to it, *Othello* has a beginning, a middle, and an end, that are all causally and necessarily related to each other, and the development of the plot follows a necessary sequence.

III. *Othello* According to Hegel

For Hegel, *Othello* is the ideal example of a specific kind of tragic conflict, that which takes place between man and his environment:

> The third and last class of that type of collision which is based on purely natural conditions is that which is due to personal passion caused by natural peculiarities of temperament and character. The jealousy of Othello is a supreme example of this . . . Collision of this kind is only properly referred to such passions in so far as individuals, seized and dominated exclusively by the power of such emotions, are thereby forced into antagonism with the truly ethical constitution and

inherently justifiable course of human existence, and consequently are plunged into a still more serious conflict.

(Hegel 1962, 123)

According to Hegel, the conflict in *Othello* is one of character, as is frequently found in the *romantic* tragedy. It is not the typical conflict found in *classic* tragedy, where the hero-figures personify a collision between two values, which in turn are the expression of eternal and essential spiritual forces. Othello personifies no spiritual values. If anything at all is abstractly represented by him, it is the emotional trait of jealousy, which can certainly not be considered a positive value, one that is worth guiding a person's actions. Hegel compares the emotions that seize Othello to the negative feelings that dominate the nature and govern the actions of Macbeth and of Richard III (Hegel, 207). It is also difficult to see Othello personifying the trait of Loyalty—a positive value— since the play does not deal at all with the issue of his loyalty. His demand for loyalty from his wife is part of the jealousy that overcomes him and not a value on its own. As for Iago, he can certainly not be seen as a figure personifying any value; at best, he embodies Evil for the sake of Evil, Evil in abstract terms, but then, "abstract evil neither possesses truth in itself, nor does it arouse interest" (Hegel, 67). The relationship between Iago and Othello can not be considered a tragic conflict, for there is no collision between them except at the end of the play. Othello is Iago's victim: He is enticed by the villain and no collision whatsoever takes place between them.

A classic collision between Othello and Desdemona is also difficult to visualize. As discussed above, Othello embodies no positive value whatsoever, and it is quite difficult to see Desdemona as the embodiment of any value, the personification of fidelity or modesty, since her loyalty is never put to test throughout the play, and it is thus never challenged by any other value. In addition to this, as already mentioned, because of having betrayed her father, she has the potential for betrayal in her, and this is stated explicitly in the play.

Obviously, *Othello* is not a Hegelian tragedy in the *classic* sense. But also the conflict that arises between Othello and his environment as a result of the jealous turmoil within him, as described by Hegel, only surfaces at the beginning of Act IV, during Lodovico's visit to Cyprus on a Senate mission. Until the middle of act 3, Othello tries to adjust to his environment by serving it as best he can and by living harmoniously within it. By proposing to accept the judgement of Venice, he even averts the argument with Brabantio, after his marriage to Desdemona. In fact, the environment accepts Othello, thanks to the services he renders the city, and because of his character, honesty, integrity and courage. Lodovico recalls this as he observes with dismay that Othello, now in a fit of jealous rage, is a changed man:

> Is this the noble Moor, whom our full senate
> Call all in all sufficient? This the noble nature,
> Whom passion could not shake? whose solid virtue
> The shot of accident, nor dart of chance,
> Could neither graze, nor pierce?
>
> (4.1.260–64)

It is worth noticing that among the many positive traits Lodovico attributes to Othello, he also mentions the hero's immunity to being hurt by emotions. It is only in this scene, when overcome by jealousy, that Othello transgresses the accepted customs and norms, mainly by behaving aggressively toward Desdemona and offending Lodovico, the distinguished guest from Venice. The conflict intensifies and reaches a climax after Othello kills Desdemona, when he is dismissed from his position, when his weapons are seized, and when finally he commits suicide.

As Hegel suggests, the conflict between Othello—now crazed by jealousy—and his moderate and stable surroundings, does indeed exist in the play, but whether it can be seen as the tragic essence of the play must be put in doubt. The difficulties in accepting this solution are twofold. First, as just discussed, the conflict only emerges toward the end of the tragedy—acts 4 and 5— and does not motivate the play from the beginning. And second, the conflict between Othello and his environment is so acute, because Desdemona's betrayal was *imaginary* and therefore false, and Othello's acts were so rash.

There is place to assume that if Desdemona had actually been unfaithful to him, Othello's acts as well as his jealousy would have met with understanding. From the conversation between Desdemona and Emilia, at the end of act 4, we can infer that adultery in Venice, though not unusual, was not considered within the range of the acceptable or conventional. The great emphasis everyone places on Desdemona's virtue and complete fidelity is also an indication that, had she been otherwise, she would have deserved—at least to some extent—the horrible fate that befell her. Thus, the conflict between Othello and Venice does not stem from his insane jealousy, but from the false suspicion he casts on Desdemona. Furthermore, it is not quite clear whether the Venetian society and authorities with which Othello collides, are the "truly ethical constitution" or the "inherently justifiable course of human existence" that Hegel had in mind. The Senate settles the quarrel between Brabantio and Othello to suit its own interests—the urgent need to dispatch Othello to Cyprus—above any other consideration. Prejudiced Brabantio, foolish Roderigo, and corrupt, evil, and frustrated Iago are among the outstanding representatives of Venetian society. Iago depicts the women of Venice as frivolous and prone to love affairs:

> I know our country disposition well;
> In Venice they do let God see the pranks
> They dare not show their husbands; their best conscience
> Is not to leave undone, but keep unknown.
> (3.3.205–08)

Even Cassio, the Florentine, noblest among the play's heroes, reveals a degree of levity in his relations with Bianca.

The conflict between Othello and his environment is indeed very problematic, and perceiving in it the tragic quality of the play is quite difficult. In contrast, we can discover a genuinely tragic conflict, if we see "the truly ethical constitution" and "inherently justifiable course of human existence" with which Othello in his jealousy collides—not in his Venetian environment but in Desdemona.

We have already indicated how hard it is to see in Desdemona the embodiment of any value, as described by Hegel in relation to classic tragedy, mainly because in the play her loyalty is not challenged by any other value. But according to Hegel, figures in *modern* drama are not created to personify values, as was customary in *classic* tragedy. Desdemona is indeed depicted as a lively and vital creature, with contradictions and inconsistencies, and not as the embodiment of any value. Therefore, despite her error and the potential for deception within her, Desdemona bears the "truly ethical constitution," as defined by Hegel, and the course of her existence is "inherently justifiable." The path of existence within her asserts itself. In her own way, she feels that she is right in the conflict with her father, and states her case in no uncertain terms:

> I do perceive here a divided duty:
> To you I am bound for life and education . . .
> I am hitherto your daughter; but here's my husband;
> And so much duty as my mother show'd
> To you, preferring you before her father,
> So much I challenge, that I may profess,
> Due to the Moor my lord.
>
> (1.3.181–89)

The "ethical constitution" that guides Desdemona, is also evident in the obligations she takes upon herself for the sake of friendship with Cassio: "If I do vow a friendship, I'll perform it / To the last article" (3.3.21–22). In a conversation with Emilia on the possibility of unfaithfulness, Desdemona firmly rejects the idea—and not only for herself: "I do not think there is any such woman" (4.3.83). Finally, just before her death, she forgives Othello his terrible deed and adds, "Commend me to my kind lord, O, farewell!" (5.2.126).

The force that motivates and guides Desdemona in her relation with Othello is *Love*. Despite her father's objections, she marries the Moor because she loves him: "I did love the Moor, to live with him" (1.3.248), and anticipates her life with Othello as one of everlasting and increasing love: "The heavens forbid / But that our loves and comforts should increase, / Even as our days do grow" (2.1.193–95). In act 4, when Othello's jealousy and strange behavior toward her expose him, she still maintains, "My love doth so approve him, / That even his stubbornness, his checks and frowns, / . . . Have grace and favour in them" (4.3.19–21). And even when about to die, as mentioned, Desdemona forgives Othello and asks him to remember her kindly.

What is being tested in *Othello* is not Loyalty but *Love*. Desdemona chooses Love over the obligation toward her father, and this is the first test. Iago has little faith in such a love and forecasts its end: "It can not be / That Desdemona should long continue her love / Unto the Moor" (1.3.342–43). Nevertheless, Love outlasts even the grievous test of Othello's jealousy, until the tragic end. Thus, Desdemona's love stands in tragic conflict against Othello's jealousy. Although they do not personify such feelings, both figures are motivated and manipulated by them toward the dreadful confrontation, the tragic conflict.

In terms of the Hegelian tragedy, the problem with this solution is that the conflict depicted in *Othello* is imaginary, based on false information. And according to Hegel, such material is more appropriate for comedy, since events could have led to a happy ending if the truth had been discovered before the disaster. The problem here can also be settled if we ascribe Othello's jealousy, not to Desdemona's imaginary infidelity, but to the *possibility* of infidelity within Othello's consciousness; seen thus, the conflict between Othello's jealousy and Desdemona's love becomes much more tangible. Desdemona's faithfulness is the product of her love for Othello. Othello is suddenly seized by jealousy the moment Iago questions the likelihood of such love, before any evidence of Desdemona's unfaithfulness has been submitted, and even before Iago explicitly claims that it occurred. Hence, the awareness of a *possibility* of infidelity is enough to awaken Othello's jealousy. On the other hand, in order for Love and Jealousy to collide, Desdemona must love Othello and therefore be faithful to him. Hence, Othello's suspicion *must* be unfounded, and here in fact lies the tragic essence of the conflict. Jealousy and Love as a dialectic opposition reach their tragic collision, not only in the confrontation between Othello and Desdemona, but also within Othello's soul. The Moor, according to Iago, "Is of a constant, noble, loving nature" (2.1.284), and has repeatedly expressed his love for Desdemona. When Iago bares his "suspicions," Othello is confident of overcoming them: "When I doubt, prove, / And on the proof, there is no bore but this: / Away at once with love or jealousy!" (3.3.194–96). Thus, for Othello, jealousy and love are joined together, and since he is unable to stop loving—even after the imaginary infidelity is established—his jealousy intensifies. As he kills Desdemona he cries out: "I will kill thee, / And love thee after" (5.2.18–19). So he kills her because he loves her. Love and Jealousy struggle and collide within him, finally destroying each other. By Hegelian criteria, Othello is a torn hero with a tragic conflict raging within his soul, until it leads him to ultimate destruction.

Other conflicts can also be discerned in *Othello*, as well as a different resolution of the tragedy based on other sets of conflicting values or on conflicts of a different type. We could focus for instance on the conflict that arises between Othello as a representative of a primitive people who is activated by values of honor, moderation, chivalry, and love, as opposed to a society grown bourgeois that is dominated by greed, ambition and intrigue. Or we could highlight the conflict that stems from the protagonist's foreignness. All in all, not only do they not seem to exclude one another but the very opposite: they strengthen and supplement each other in the tragic action of the play. Nevertheless, the essence of universality in the tragedy has to do with Jealousy, which is illustrated from many angles throughout the play.

Although *Othello* cannot be considered a Hegelian tragedy in the *classic* sense, it does fit Hegel's description of a *modern* or *romantic* tragedy. The play's major significance is in the depiction of its characters, their personalities, and the emotions that motivate them. Othello is a torn hero and can easily be explained as such, whatever the case may be. Indeed, the play is built around a tragic conflict, or even around a system of multiple conflicts and subconflicts.

The essence of Othello as a tragic hero is in the Aristotelian passing of his fate from happiness to misery, as well as in the Hegelian conflict between Jealousy and Love, in which he is trapped. But in *Othello* the source of these can be found in a fuller and deeper tragic essence—namely the gap between *Being* and *Seeming*, to use the language of Shakespeare. This gap, long known to be a pivotal subject in the work of Shakespeare, becomes the central motif in *Othello*.

Tragic protagonists never seem to be what they really are. In Tragedy Evil Parades as Good and Good is presented as Evil. Friendship is portrayed as Betrayal and Betrayal is disguised as genuine Brotherhood. Desdemona, depicted as sincere and honest, says of herself, ". . . I do beguile / The thing I am, by seeming otherwise" (2.1.122–23). Whereas Iago, chief scoundrel and prevaricator, declares that "Men should be that they seem, / Or those that be not, would they might seem none!" (3.3.130–31). And the tragic hero is expected to work his way out of this mire of deception. Not only is he expected to distinguish between betrayal and loyalty, but to choose Good over Evil. To his great misfortune, Othello is unable to do this: "The Moor a free and open nature too, / That thinks men honest that but seems to be so" (1.3.397–98).

Thus, the tragedy of Othello is the tragedy of a nearsighted man who is misled by his senses. He must choose between Good and Evil although he is unable to see them as they really are, and to distinguish one from the other. Hence the tragic reversal of his fate and the tragic conflict that engulfs him.

IV. *Woyzeck* According to Aristotle

Woyzeck was never edited by its author, and no information has been found on how exactly he intended to do this. Even the ending of the play is in doubt. With this in mind, we have chosen the Fritz Bergemann edition (1965),[5] as an acceptable option for the play's final version, and will use it to base our analysis, according to the aesthetic criteria of Aristotle and Hegel, and comparing it all along to *Othello*.

Except for the protagonist's figure, the plot in *Woyzeck* is amazingly similar to the scheme for the development of Tragedy that was established by Aristotle. The play opens with the protagonist's tragic error: he lives in sin with a woman and has fathered a child out of wedlock. Discovery comes at the climax of the play—he finds out that the woman with whom he lives is unfaithful to him, and this brings about the peripety in his fate and leads him to murder and suicide. The only deviation from the Aristotelian scheme is in the depiction of the tragic hero, who not only is not "in the enjoyment of great reputation and property," but on the contrary, is from the lowest end of the social and economic spheres. Thus, it is difficult to perceive that the action constitutes the passing from happiness to misfortune, as Aristotle demands, since *happiness* is so remote from the hero, even as the curtain opens on the play.

Woyzeck's tragic error is explicitly and emphatically disclosed by the Captain in the opening scene of the play:[6]

> Woyzeck, you've got no sense of decency. Decency is when a chap acts decently, do you follow? It's a good word. You've got a child without benefit of clergy, as our right reverend padre puts it—without benefit of clergy. (Woyzeck, 107)

Just as with Othello, Woyzeck's tragic error has to do with his marriage. Othello weds Desdemona without her father's blessing, and Woyzeck lives in sin with Marie and has fathered her child without the blessing of the church. The Captain confronts Woyzeck with his error, and after, also brings about the Discovery, when he tells Woyzeck of Marie's infidelity, just as Iago is the one to tell Othello of Brabantio's stern opposition to his marriage to Desdemona, and later of her infidelity. Like Iago, who pretends to have nothing against Othello marrying Desdemona and pins the blame on Brabantio's antagonism, the Captain pins the blame for Woyzeck's error on the regiment priest and on the church. Like Othello, who rejects his guilt by relying on the Venetian Senate, a power greater than that of Brabantio, so Woyzeck also rejects his own guilt, and banks on God and Jesus, powers greater than those of the regiment's priest and the church: "God in heaven's not going to worry about the poor brat just because nobody said Amen before his making. Our Lord said: Suffer the little children to come unto me" (108). Othello's error is related to his being a foreigner, for had he not been one, Brabantio would not have objected to his marriage to Desdemona; Woyzeck's error is related to poverty:

> When you're poor like us, sir . . . It's the money, the money! If you haven't got the money . . . I mean you can't bring the likes of us into the world on decency. We're flesh and blood too. (108)

Othello's foreignness intensifies first his love and then his jealousy, for being a foreigner gives special importance to his marriage—a hold on his environment—and with his wife's unfaithfulness his whole world is destroyed. So, because of Woyzeck's poverty, Marie and the child are all he has in the world, and with her betrayal his world caves in on him: "I'm a poor man, Captain. She's all I've got in the world" (118).

Woyzeck's tragic error brings about the peripety in his fate. The fact that he lives in sin with Marie, without proper marriage, makes it easier for her to betray him, and he says so: "He's got her, like I had her once" (122). In other words, the Drum Major did not do to Marie but what Woyzeck himself had done before him, or "One thing after another," as the Captain states at the opening of the play (107); "one after the other," Marie also says, when Woyzeck questions her about her relations with the Drum Major (119); and after he is beaten up in the tavern, Woyzeck himself cries out, "One damned thing after another" (125). Woyzeck's discovery of Marie's unfaithfulness is clear and detailed, when the Captain tells him bluntly:

> Woyzeck, haven't you noticed a hair in your soup lately? Do you follow? A hair from somebody else's beard—an engineer's, a sergeant's, or—a drum major's? Eh, Woyzeck? But then your wife's a decent girl. Not like the others. (118)

Whereas Iago arouses Othello's jealousy out of evil intent, moved by frustration and wickedness, the Captain informs Woyzeck of Marie's infidelity out of sheer boredom, as implied by the way he jokes with the Doctor and with Woyzeck. Both Iago and the Captain conceal their real intentions: Iago feigns friendship and concern for Othello's well-being, and the Captain, when questioned, categorically denies he is teasing Woyzeck: "Joking? I joke with you?" (Ibid). Albeit in different degrees, both Iago and the Captain are colleagues of Othello and Woyzeck. All are soldiers; Iago is Othello's ancient and Woyzeck is the Captain's batman. The difference in rank between Othello and Iago is one of the factors that motivate Iago to hurt him, out of envy. The inverted gap in rank between himself and his batman, entitles and encourages the Captain to mock Woyzeck and to lead him on to discover Marie's unfaithfulness. But, whereas Iago is well aware of the evil he is inflicting, the Captain is convinced he is doing Woyzeck a favor: "It's all for your own good. You're a decent chap, Woyzeck, a decent chap" (Ibid). As with Othello, Woyzeck is instantly seized by a fit of jealousy and, as seen before with Othello, the first thing he ponders is the likelihood of Marie's betrayal. His immediate reaction to the Captain's words are, "I'd bet on that. It can't be true" (Ibid). He was unaware of the possibility of betrayal, and earlier, when he noticed Marie's gold earrings, he refrained from seeing their connection to her unfaithfulness. But now the realization sets in:

> A lot of things can be true. The bitch! Anything can be true. . . . Makes you want to knock a nail in and hang yourself. All because of one little train of thought. One that goes from Yes to Yes again, and then to No. (119)

The torments begin with the doubt that arises when he realizes the possibility exists, and only later does Woyzeck turn to look for evidence: "But can I know for sure? Can anyone?" (120).

This then is the Discovery. But where is the peripety in Woyzeck's fate, and how is the passing from happiness to misfortune possible, when even as the play opens, the hero is so far removed from *happiness*? Woyzeck's outlook of the world does undergo a clear change. From the very beginning he can see no harm in his relation with Marie "without benefit of clergy," and even expects God and Jesus to accept it understandingly: "God in heaven's not going to worry about the poor brat just because nobody said Amen before his making" (108). However, when he discovers Marie's infidelity, he is suddenly seized by a religious and moral fervor, and his beliefs shift to the opposite extreme: "A sin like that . . . It stinks fit to smoke the angels out of heaven" (119), and "Why don't you blow the sun out, God? Let them fall on each other in their lewdness. Male and female, man and beast" (122). The change leads Woyzeck, initially described as a *good man*, to become a murderer. Yet, in itself, this is surely not the passing from happiness to misfortune which, according to Aristotle, is responsible for arousing pity and fear. However, if we do not take Aristotle's theory literally—whereby the tragic hero must be someone who "enjoys great reputation and property"—we may agree that indeed Woyzeck's fortune also suffers a change from happiness to misfortune.

Although Woyzeck is certainly not someone who lives in great repute, in a way, it is possible to say that he has experienced some happiness in his life. He has a small family that constitutes his entire world and his woman, Marie, is beautiful and desirable, as the Drum Major notices: "I call that a woman!" (113). Although light-headed in her relations with men, as can be seen in her conversation with Margret (110), and by Andres referring to her as *das Mensch* (bitch, tart, 121), Marie is loyal to Woyzeck, who in turn sees her as an honest woman. The Captain ironically mentions this to Woyzeck, following his disclosure of her betrayal: "But then your wife's a decent girl" (118). They love each other and, as far as Woyzeck is concerned, "She's all I've got in the world" (Ibid); when Marie chastens herself after her betrayal, her own love for Woyzeck is also apparent. They have a child whom they both love and who is expected to bring them happiness; Woyzeck manifests this love when he says, "Hold his arm up, the chair's pinching him" (114), and also Marie: "Come on, boy. Let them talk. You're only a whore's brat but I love your bastard's face" (110). Woyzeck's delight in his family is the *happiness* that Aristotle believes should be the tragic hero's lot at the beginning of the play.

Happiness is both related to, and the result of, the tragic error. For Woyzeck, bliss comes from living with Marie "without the benefit of clergy." As suggested previously, Othello's *happiness* is also the result of his marrying Desdemona, and his bliss in the union is similarly related to his tragic error, marriage without the blessing of the bride's father. Woyzeck's happiness is shattered when he discovers Marie's unfaithfulness, and this in fact constitutes the Aristotelian passing from happiness to misfortune. He murders Marie, their child drowns, and he commits suicide—or is caught and brought to trial.[7] However, if Woyzeck does not fit Aristotle's model of the tragic hero as "enjoying great reputation and property," he does seem to conform to the spirit of this model, and thus his fall succeeds to arouse in us the tragic emotions of pity and fear.

There are those who see in *Woyzeck* a shift in the understanding of Tragedy, for—apparently for the first time—it deals with a tragic hero from the lower social sphere, as mentioned before. We have attempted to demonstrate that this does not necessarily contradict the spirit of the Aristotelian approach to Tragedy. Moreover, Woyzeck is not depicted as a figure "worse than the man of the present day," who in Aristotelian terms is suitable more to Comedy than to Tragedy. In fact, Woyzeck and his family clearly suggest the Holy Family: He himself cuts wood (108), like Joseph the Carpenter; Marie is the name of the woman with whom he lives in sin, and when she first appears in the play, she is "sitting at a window with her child on her arm" (109), as in famous portraits of the Madonna and Child; the child's name, a "bastard and a whore's brat," is Christian (Bergemann 1960, 135). Thus, Woyzeck's suffering is that of humanity and parallels the Passion of Christ.

Hence, Woyzeck is a representative figure who is endowed with universality, and his suffering reflects the sanctity of human suffering, to his great enhancement. Despite his being "inferior in power or intelligence to ourselves," we do not "have the sense of looking down," as we follow him in the play (Frye 1970, 34). Although several of the play's characters mock and ridicule him, he is not a grotesque figure; on the contrary, those who deride him seem grotesque themselves, precisely because they look down at Woyzeck. Thus, although Woyzeck does not literally fit the criteria set down by Aristotle for the tragic figure, he seems not so distant from the Aristotelian tragic spirit, regardless of the play's revolutionary innovativeness.

V. *Woyzeck* According to Hegel

In the opening scene of the play, according to Bergemann's version, the conflict between man's natural needs—the "call of Nature"—and morality—namely the *virtues*[8] of decency and self-control—is clearly depicted:

> Woyzeck, you have no self-control. You are not a decent man. Flesh and Blood? Why, when I'm lying by my window after a rain-shower and I see all those pretty white stockings twinkling across the street . . . damn it, Woyzeck, I feel love! I'm flesh and blood too. That's where self-control comes in, Woyzeck. The things I could waste my time on! But I say to myself: You are a decent chap, a good chap, a good chap. (108)

The Captain, who declaims this monologue, conquers his natural inclinations and desires, in favor of *virtue*. He values the "good man," as he tells both Woyzeck (Ibid) and the Doctor (118). For his part, Woyzeck rejects the Captain's call for virtue and morality; being so poor he can simply not afford them:

> Oh, self-control. I'm not very strong at that, sir. You see, the likes of us just don't have any self-control. I mean, we obey nature's call. But if I were a gentleman and had a hat and a watch and a topcoat and could talk proper, then I'd have self-control all right. Must be a fine thing, self-control. But I'm a poor man. (Ibid)

Nature's demands conflict not only with morality but with science as well, for the Doctor also orders Woyzeck to curb his natural inclinations:

> Haven't I proved that the *musculus constrictor vesicae* is subject to the will? Nature indeed. Man is free. Man is the transfiguration of the individual urge to freedom. Can't hold his water. (115)

Morals, science, and even art, as follows from the scene of the monkey dressed in military attire (111–12), are human values that deviate and stand in opposition to Nature and its values, and the person who lives according to them, must by necessity reach a point of collision.

Unlike *Othello*, where the human emotions of love and jealousy escalate to a dangerous level and collide with each other, the tragic conflict in *Woyzeck* is due to a collision of life values: natural needs on one hand, and on the other the human pattern of social existence, which deviates from the framework of Nature. In *Woyzeck*, the most outstanding human value which collides with the values of Nature, is the virtue of decency. And since according to Hegel the play's tragic conflict is a classic one, the question which at this point demands an answer is, who are the agents personifying these colliding values.

A similar conflict between identical values is presented in *Danton's Death*, also by Büchner, where Robespierre is the standard-bearer of *virtues*, whereas Danton, in the name of Nature, repudiates both the *virtues* and the *vices*. Danton and Robespierre do indeed reach a tragic collision, and both are destroyed in its course. Seen on their own, the values they personify are positive life values, but in the clash they are distorted and corrupted. The *virtues* are the expression of frustration and sexual inhibitions, which entail terror and murder, whereas the "call of Nature" leads to immorality and licentiousness. *Danton's Death* is therefore very near Hegel's description of a *classic* tragedy; in *Woyzeck* it is different, despite the similarity in the conflict.

In the play's opening scene, Woyzeck indeed represents natural instincts, whereas the Captain advocates the demands of the virtues. But in the entire play the Captain only appears in two scenes, and he never reaches any confrontation or collision with Woyzeck, except for a minor argument between them, during the shaving scene, and this is not necessarily a *collision*. Two other minor and rather grotesque incidents of collision take place between Woyzeck and the Doctor: First, when Woyzeck refuses to urinate for the benefit of the Doctor's "scientific research" (115), and then, when Woyzeck ruins the Doctor's "scientific presentation" before his students (124). However, the Doctor does not represent *virtues* but *science*, which is also a factor in the estrangement of Man from Nature. But if all these small *collisions* are viewed together, including the confrontation between Marie and her neighbor Margret (110), the outcome is that—due to acute poverty—Woyzeck and Marie behave according to their natural inclinations, and as a result are in conflict with their environment. This is indeed one of the types of conflict which Hegel describes as tragic (Hegel, 1962, 69, 123). The environment—meaning the Captain, the neighbor (116) and, in a different way, the Doctor—demands that Woyzeck and Marie master their natural inclinations, and behave according to the *virtues* or forgo their natural needs—food, drink, sexual relations, even bodily discharge—all in the name of morality or for the sake of science, and replace them with values conceived by human beings, which are beyond, and in opposition to, the values of Nature. The play's tragic consequences are the direct result of this conflict for, in the name of *Virtue* and for the sake of *Goodness*, the Captain informs Woyzeck of Marie's unfaithfulness, and adds, "It's all for your own good. You're a decent chap, Woyzeck" (118).

But the conflict that Marie and Woyzeck have with their environment does not explain the collision within themselves, which in fact constitutes the essence of the tragedy. Moreover, throughout the entire play—unlike Danton—Woyzeck and Marie do not act as personifications of the demands of natural values. The conflict between natural inclinations and virtues finds expression in Marie's soul. She indeed "behaves according to Nature," and then chastises herself for her "sins," when she says, "I'm a bad bitch. I could kill myself" (114). She sees herself as Mary Magdalene, the "adulterous woman" in the New Testament (John 8, Luke 7), and like her, asks God for forgiveness and for *virtues*, and begs, "Almighty God, at least give me strength to pray" (126). Whereas Woyzeck undergoes a complete inversion in outlook after he becomes aware of Marie's betrayal. Her infidelity, undoubtedly within the limits of "behavior according to Nature," is not only unacceptable to Woyzeck but, as a result of it, he is overcome by religious and moral zeal, and sets out to kill her in the name of supernatural forces which command him to do it:

> What's that you say? Louder, louder. Stab the she-wolf dead. Stab. The. She-Wolf. Dead. Must I? Do I hear it up there too? Is that the wind saying it? I keep on hearing it, on and on. Stab her dead. Dead. (122)

The tragic conflict in *Woyzeck* between Man's natural behavior and the behavior demanded from him for *virtue*'s sake, takes on diverse dramatic appearances. In Scene I it is personified by the figures of Woyzeck and the Captain. It is also evident in the first part of the play, in the collision of Marie and Woyzeck with their environment. Although it surfaces in Marie's soul as well, its main manifestation is in the change that occurs in Woyzeck, he himself embodying both sides of the conflict, not by means of a collision of values within his soul—as is customary in Hegel's torn hero—but by reversal. This is not the Aristotelian peripety, where the hero passes from happiness to misfortune, but a complete reversal in the hero's life values. Due to extreme poverty, Woyzeck initially chooses to follow the ways of Nature, for *virtue* is beyond his reach, as he explains, "You see, the likes of us just don't have any self-control. I mean, we obey nature's call . . . Must be a fine thing, self-control. But I'm a poor man" (108). But when he himself is hurt by the ways of Nature, for Marie betrays him by following her own natural inclinations, Woyzeck turns to *virtue*, in the name of religion and God. The ways of Nature are no longer suitable for him. And thus, swinging back and forth between the two extremes of the tragic conflict in which he is trapped, Woyzeck is driven to self-destruction.

Such a singular way for presenting the tragic conflict demands a tragic hero who is entirely different from the classic protagonist described by Hegel. Woyzeck possesses no great power, self-assurance, free will, or scope of action. Unlike the protagonists of classic tragedy, or the depiction of Danton and Robespierre in *Danton's Death*, he is not the uncompromising representation of the value he embodies. Nor is he a torn hero, for his is not the tragedy of being rent by two opposing forces of value or spirit which battle for his soul, while he himself is powerless to determine the outcome of the strife—as is usual for Hegel's protagonists of *modern* tragedy. The tragedy is that the very experience responsible for Woyzeck's happiness—life according to Nature—is also accountable for his disaster. Attempting to return to Nature, from a society ruled by moral and human values that supersede Nature, is a belated return which is doomed by necessity to failure. Accordingly, and also by necessity, Woyzeck is an *inferior* protagonist, who lacks power and greatness—a poor devil, devoid of the strength he would need for coping with the tragic conflict in which he is entangled—and who is thus tossed back and forth between two conflicting forces, and is inevitably impelled toward destruction. Nevertheless, the magnitude of tragic emotion aroused in us by the protagonist's fate, is related to the universality in him, which enhances his image without undermining his humble and inferior experience.

It is important to add that Woyzeck is trapped in a conflict that is not—as many assume—a collision between morality and poverty. Poverty is neither a value nor a trait of character. Consequently, it is not meant to be embodied by a dramatic agent other than by way of allegory. In the second part of the play Woyzeck does speak and act in the name of *virtue,* despite his poverty. This can be analyzed by comparing *Woyzeck* and *Danton's Death,* where wealthy and licentious Danton speaks against *virtue* and for "the nature of man." In *Woyzeck* we find a conflict between love and jealousy within the protagonist's soul, the same as we saw in Othello's soul: "Do you feel cold, Marie? But you're warm, your lips are hot. Hot breath, harlot's breath. Yet I'd give heaven to kiss them again" (129). But this is certainly not the drama's major conflict and its tragic essence is not rooted in it.

There are also those who believe the play's tragic essence is in the suffering that results from Woyzeck's poverty. It is not inaccurate to see *Woyzeck* as a social play, since such a level does undoubtedly exist, but to view this precise aspect as the central tragedy seems to deflate the play far too much.

Thus, the tragic essence in *Woyzeck* may stem, as seen in *Othello,* from the Aristotelian peripaty experienced by Woyzeck, and the same goes for the Hegelian tragic conflict that engulfs the protagonist. But, as also seen in *Othello,* these essences originate in a much deeper and comprehensive tragic essence, which finds clear expression in *Woyzeck.* In *Othello* the most intense tragic essence stems from the gap between *being* and *seeming*—between that which is and that which seems to be. In *Woyzeck* the most profound and comprehensive tragic essence comes from the fact that beyond what *seems* to be, there is merely *Nothing*. From the fear of *Nothingness* and *Void*, in which Man is doomed to exist, he finds shelter in the mask of Eros represented in the play by the individual who acts according to his Nature, as opposed to living by Morality and the *Virtues*. Their collapse bares Man to the terrors of *Nothingness* and *Void*.

VI. Conclusion

In our effort to answer the question of how to reconcile the affinity in the plots of *Othello* and *Woyzeck* with the extreme difference that exists between the tragic heroes, two different approaches yielded two different answers. In spirit, if not literally, each play in its own way fits in with the aesthetic criteria established by Aristotle and Hegel. According to Aristotle, the plot similarity leads to a similar interpretation for both plays. In both, the action is based on the tragic passing from happiness to misfortune and on the loss of bliss in love. The tragic error of both Othello and Woyzeck is marrying beyond the conventions acceptable to their social environment. The moment that each in his own way discovers the infidelity of the woman on whom their happiness depends, coincides with the tragic turning point in their fates, which leads them to murder, suicide, and to their ultimate destruction.

The fact that Woyzeck has also experienced a degree of success and happiness in life, and that the universality suggested by his figure, his suffering and his fate greatly adds to his enhancement, serve to reconcile the great difference between both tragic protagonists. The outstanding difference in the action of both plays, concerning the false betrayal of Desdemona as opposed to the true betrayal of Marie, can be resolved by explaining that the jealousy that possesses both Othello and Woyzeck arises from discovering the potential for betrayal in each woman and not from the actual unfaithfulness, and in this respect Othello's discovery of Desdemona's imaginary betrayal is in no way different from Woyzeck's discovery of Marie's true betrayal.

By Hegelian criteria, on the other hand, the plays differ substantially. The tragic conflict in *Othello* stems from the powerful feelings of Love and Jealousy, which reach the point of collision in the figures of Desdemona and Othello and within the soul of

Othello. Hence, the tragedy in *Othello* fits the Hegelian description of a *modern* tragedy, one that is based on a tragic conflict where the hero is a torn figure, and where the major tragic concern deals with the subjective emotions of the protagonists. *Othello* does not fit Hegel's definition of a *classic* tragedy, which depicts the confrontation and collision of life values personified in the tragic protagonists. In *Woyzeck*, on the other hand, life values reach the point of tragic confrontation—the desire to live according to values and needs dictated by Man's Nature collides heads on with the demands of Morality and the *Virtues*. However, in comparing *Woyzeck* with the tragedy of *Danton's Death*, also by Büchner, where a conflict similar to that in *Woyzeck* reaches resolution as a *classic* Hegelian tragedy, the conflict in *Woyzeck* takes on a different shape that is expressed in the peripaty and in the tragic hero being tossed between the conflicting tragic polarities that engulf him and impel him toward his own destruction.

The major difference in the action of *Woyzeck* and *Othello*, namely Marie's real betrayal as opposed to Desdemona's imaginary betrayal, as well as the different dramatic structuring of the protagonists, were found most significant in analyzing the plays according to the various tragic conflicts in them. Whereas loyalty is essential in Desdemona, for she represents the intensified emotion of Love, which stands in opposition to Othello's intensified jealousy, Marie provokes Woyzeck's jealousy because she acts "according to Nature" and thus her real betrayal is essential to the very nature of the conflict that engulfs them. Whereas Othello needs to be huge and powerful, to emphasize his being torn by the powerful opposing emotions that rage within his soul, Woyzeck—from the outset not at ease with the values that guide his existence—is merely a simple mortal caught between opposing life values that toss him back and forth between them.

An Aristotelian analysis of *Othello* and *Woyzeck* emphasizes the significant similarity between them for, according to Aristotle, the tragic essence in both is in the passing from happiness to misfortune. Analysis of the plays according to Hegel stresses the fundamental difference between them, for the conflicts of essence and structure in each are completely different from the other despite the great similarity of their plots. This is not a basic difference between two esthetic approaches. If we were to conduct a detailed comparison and contrast between *Woyzeck* and *Danton's Death*, for example, the Aristotelian approach would emphasize the differences in action, whereas the Hegelian approach would highlight the similarity between the tragic conflicts in both tragedies.

However, neither of these esthetic approaches fully succeeds to clarify the tragic essence that underlies each of the tragedies here analyzed. Each focuses only partially on the tragic essence of each play. The deeper and more comprehensive essence must be found in each by going beyond the theories of Aristotle and Hegel. In *Othello* the tragic essence is in the limitations of Man, his inability to distinguish between *Seeming* and *Being*, and to choose *Good* over *Evil*. Büchner goes even further and sees the tragic in the terror of *Nothingness* and *Void* in which Man exists, where his survival is only possible under the fickle and transient patronage of Eros or that of *Morality* and the *Virtues*.

Shakespeare in fact seems to anticipate Büchner in his approach, and, in turn, the latter foreshadows the approach of the Absurd, which is woven into twentieth century drama, despite the essential difference of the theatrical models in the Absurd.

Notes

Translation, Ruth Pancer 1994.

1. All quotations of *Poetics* are from the translation by Ingram Bywater.
2. See, for example, Kaufmann 1969, 270–74; and Steiner 1961.
3. See S. Johnson (1915, 473) on *Othello*, and how it fits Aristotle's classic norms: "Had the scene opened in Cyprus, and the preceding incidents been occasionally related, there had been little wanting to a drama of the most exact and scrupulous regularity." See also Coleridge's response to Johnson's observation (Coleridge 1959, 17). Kaufmann, on the same subject: "It is one of the ironies of history that some of Aristotle's ideas about tragedy seem to apply rather better to Shakespeare than to Aeschylus or Sophocles" (Kaufmann 1969, 317). Kaufmann then proceeds to analyze several Shakespearean plays according to the Aristotelian theory.
4. All quotations from *Othello* are from the Arden Shakespeare edition, 1969.
5. This version has been negatively criticized, following Lehmann's research and critical edition of Büchner's works (1972). However, the essence of our analysis is still valid, even according to Lehmann's version. On different versions of *Woyzeck*, manuscripts and their editing, see Lehmann 1972; also Bergemann 1965, 242–45; Price 1971, 133–36, and others.
6. In Bergemann's version. In Büchner's manuscripts and Lehmann's version, this is scene 5. All quotations are from Bergemann's edition, Ibid, according to the translation by Price 1971.
7. See Bergemann 1965, *Paralipomena* 264, and Bergemann's commentary, 133.
8. In the German original, *Die Tugend*. There is no word corresponding exactly to this in other languages; it more or less means morality with a degree of humility, in a Christian and feudal hierarchy of values.

BIBLIOGRAPHY

Bradley, A. C., 1950, "Hegel's Theory of Tragedy," *Oxford Lectures on Poetry* (London: Macmillan).

Büchner, Georg, 1965, *Werke und Briefe,* ed. Bergemann Fritz (München: Deutscher Taschenbuch Verlag).

―――― 1971, *The Plays of*―, translation and introduction by Victor Price (New York: Oxford University Press).

―――― 1972, *Sämtliche Werke und Briefe, Historisch-Kritische Ausgabe,* Hg. von Werner R. Lehmann (München).

Coleridge, Samuel Taylor 1959, *Coleridge's Writings on Shakespeare,* ed. Terence Hawkes (New York: Capricorn).

Eliot, T. S., 1969, "Shakespeare and the Stoicism of Seneca," *Selected Essays* 3rd ed. (London: Faber & Faber).

Frye, Northrop, 1970, *Anatomy of Criticism* (New York: Atheneum).

Hegel, 1962, *On Tragedy,* ed. and introduction by Ann Paslucci and Henry Paslucci (New York: Doubleday).

Johnson, Samuel, 1915, *Johnson on Shakespeare: Essays and Notes,* ed. Walter Raleigh (New York: Oxford University Press).

Kaufmann, Walter, 1969, *Tragedy and Philosophy* (New York: Doubleday).

Shakespeare, William, the Arden Shakespeare 1969, *Othello,* ed. and introduction by M. R. Ridley (London: Methuen & Co Ltd).

Steiner, George, 1961, *The Death of Tragedy* (London: Faber & Faber).

Coriolanus and the Compulsion to Repeat

SHULI BARZILAI

I. SIGMUND FREUD, AUTHOR OF *THE TRAGEDY OF CORIOLANUS*

INVITED to report before the patricians and tribunes of Rome "A little of that worthy work perform'd / By Martius Caius Coriolanus," the general Cominius describes his deeds in battle:

> His sword, death's stamp,
> Where it did mark, it took; from face to foot
> He was a thing of blood, whose every motion
> Was tim'd with dying cries.
> (*Coriolanus*, 2.2.45–46, 107–10)

Already at age sixteen, Cominius reminds his audience, Coriolanus "fought / Beyond the mark of others," "[s]lew three opposers," and was "brow-bound with the oak" (2.2.88–89, 94, 98). Ever since he has reaped death for Rome; "as weeds before / A vessel under sail," men fall beneath his sword (2.2.105–6). Likewise Volumnia, anticipating her son's oak-garlanded return from war, praises his violent progress:

> Death, that dark spirit, in's nervy arm doth lie,
> Which, being advanced, declines, and then men die.
> (2.1.160–61)

Death and Coriolanus are words often paired in the play.

In contrast to the famous conundrum of *Hamlet*—Why does he refrain from moving in for the kill?—*Coriolanus* thus provokes an opposite concern. The hero kills too much. To put into question that which Cominius commends: What makes Coriolanus "[r]un reeking o'er the lives of men" (2.2.119)? Why does he go forth into every field of battle like "a harvest-man that's task'd to mow / Or all or lose his hire" (1.3.36–37)? And as if enemies outside the walls of Rome were in scant supply, Coriolanus also cultivates hostility within. In the words of an officer-witness to his conduct in the Capitol, Coriolanus seeks the common people's "hate with greater devotion than they can render it him, and leaves nothing undone that may . . . discover him their opposite" (2.2.18–21). Yet why should he solicit the title of "chief enemy to the people" (1.1.7–8) and disdain to plead for the consulship?

Explanations of his relentless aggression are not hidden in some corner of the play. In this respect as well, Coriolanus resembles Hamlet with an inverted symmetry. If, as Sigmund Freud suggests, the text provides no reasons or motives for Hamlet's hesitations, the riddle of Coriolanus' zeal is posed and a solution offered at the very outset.[1]

> *Second Citizen.* Consider you what services he has done for his country? . . .
>
> *First Citizen.* Though soft-conscienc'd men can be content to say it was for his country, he did it to please his mother, and to be partly proud, which he is, even to the altitude of his virtue.
> (1.1.30, 37–40)[2]

The plebeian answer evidently holds a widespread appeal. It is a critical commonplace that the downfall of Coriolanus demonstrates the consequences of bad mothering. Critics look to information given about the hero's early childhood and upbringing, information mainly supplied by his mother, for evidence to condemn her. Here is a sampling of judgments:

> The ultimate view of the man as victim . . . is given in *Coriolanus*. Wives and mistresses may have great influence, but it is nothing like the shaping control that the dominating mother can have over [her] son; . . . and Volumnia provides Shakespeare's most blood-chilling study of the destructive consequences of a woman's living out at someone else's expense her fantasy of what manhood should be. (Harding 1969, 252)
>
> Volumnia . . . is seen to be an extremely unfeminine, nonmaternal person, one who sought to mold her son to fit a preconceived image gratifying her own masculine (actually pseudo-masculine) strivings. (Hofling 1970, 292)
>
> [H]er envy of men is evident first in her unequivocal usurpation of as much of the masculine role as she can manage and later in her

living through Coriolanus to enjoy what she cannot seize for herself. (Smith 1970, 319)

> For such a mother, a son is the literal embodiment of her phallus which from infancy she had wished to attain by one means or another. . . . She relentlessly incites him to a state of sustained tumescence, of virile achievement, from which he is permitted no relief. Volumnia never stops prodding this swollen battering ram to keep it at full salute. It comes as no surprise that she directly incites him to his doom. (Stoller 1966, 266, 271)[3]

In presenting Volumnia as the model of the manipulative woman who uses all available resources to achieve dominance through her son, these studies disclose the extent to which she has become the focus for strongly negative feelings about maternal possession (or "usurpation" as Gordon Ross Smith calls it) of power and influence.[4] Robert J. Stoller thus congratulates Shakespeare for having had the "good sense" not to produce a father for Coriolanus: "Such a father would have only cluttered the stage as he scurried around trying to avoid being eaten by his wife" (Stoller, 270–71). Janet Adelman also stresses Volumnia's role as a deadly consumer of vital male energies: "The cannibalistic mother who denies food and yet feeds on the victories of her sweet son stands at the darkest center of the play" (Adelman 1980, 140).

Yet these appraisals of Volumnia entail a double erasure. First, they partially or fully ignore the sociocultural context of a male-oriented world (such as Coriolanus' Rome and Shakespeare's England) in which aggression and militarism are preeminent values. Plutarch, whose *Life of Caius Martius Coriolanus* in Thomas North's translation (first published in 1579) is the main source for the play, establishes at the outset the Greco-Roman cult of military as opposed to moral or contemplative virtue:[5]

> Now in those days, valiantness was honored in Rome above all virtues, which they call *Virtus* by the name of virtue self, as including in that general name all other special virtues besides. So that *Virtus* in Latin was as much as valiantness. But Martius being more inclined to the wars than any other gentleman of his time, began from his childhood to give himself to handle weapons. . . . (Plutarch 243)

Cominius echoes this ancient ideal of active warring heroism: "It is held / That valor is the chiefest virtue, and most dignifies the haver" (*Coriolanus*, 2.2.83–84); and in the same vein, Volumnia explains the ethos of valor and glory that guided her son's education: "I, considering how honor would become such a person . . . let him seek danger where he was like to find fame" (1.3.9–13). The motif of honor, like the citizen's "he did it to please his mother," again derives from Plutarch's *positive* description of the filial devotion Coriolanus displays in his moments of martial triumph: "nothing made him so happy and honorable as that his mother might hear everybody praise and commend him, that she might always see him return with a crown upon his head, and . . . embrace him with tears running down her cheeks for joy" (Plutarch 246). As Coppélia Kahn observes, the women in Shakespeare's plays "did not contrive their ideals of manliness out of whole cloth; they took them from a world managed by men" (Kahn 1981, 152n). Nonetheless, when Volumnia affirms the *virtus* upheld by Cominius and by other valiant (male) Romans, commentators find her altogether "morbid," "repulsive," and "inimical to [Coriolanus'] development as an individual" (Hofling 1970, 301; Putney 1962, 377; Wilson 1968, 239).

Second, to consider the destructive or hypermasculine behavior of Coriolanus primarily as a consequence of pathogenic mothering is to assume a cause-effect relationship obtains among literary characters analogous to "real" life relationships. Bad or inadequate mothers produce problem children. The motif of mother blame, however, disregards the fact that Volumnia is not the mother-next-door but rather a character who is, as Kenneth Burke shrewdly suggests, "derivable" from Coriolanus. If historical context and plot requirements are taken into account, it seems more accurate to reverse the cause-effect relationship: that is, "instead of viewing Coriolanus as an offspring of his mother, we view her role as a function contributory to his" (Burke 1966, 85). This approach abrogates the critical attitude that reduces Coriolanus from the status of tragic hero to that of victim of his mother's voracity or a case of infantile neurosis. "All told, in being the kind of characters they are, the other figures help Coriolanus be the kind of character he is" (Burke, 87).

In readdressing the question of the play—"What makes Coriolanus run?"—I want to propose a reading that does not point to the woman (however satisfactory and even time-honored such a gesture might be) as blameful origin and cause of the hero's fall. For the repetitive, almost monotonous predictability of his actions and reactions throughout the play suggests a single-minded purpose and wish. Of the polar possibilities "To be or not to be," Coriolanus reveals a marked predilection for the second. An understanding of the complications attendant upon his relentless aggressive activity requires, as I hope specific examples will make clear, a consideration of its inward counterpart: namely, the impulse silently pressing for dissolution of the self. Hamlet often talks about self-slaughter, but Coriolanus does something about it.

The Tragedy of Coriolanus thus delineates, after its own fashion, the correlation between the compulsion to repeat and the death instincts articulated in *Beyond the Pleasure Principle* (Freud 1920). The two works, Shakespeare's and Freud's, may be shown to intersect or gloss one another at several cardinal points; that is, the play will not be read here as a proof-text that validates the psychoanalytic theory. Without disregard for rhetorical modes and other constituitive differences, it can be suggested that *Beyond the Pleasure Principle* and *Coriolanus*—possibly drawing on a common store of experiences or observations—enter into a dialogue. In what follows, then, I do not follow Freud (and other psychoanalytic readers) in regarding the literary text as an exemplum, or as a hook upon which to hang a theoretical assumption. Such a reading tends to cast the text conceptually, and often graphically by means of a footnote, in a marginal role; conveniently, the literary footnote is subordinate to the analytic statement it presumably upholds. The graphic correlative for my presentation of Shakespeare's warrior-protagonist as an embodiment of the impulsion designated *Todestriebe* in Freud's writings would be a juxtaposition, a side-by-side arrangement rather than a hierarchical positioning of texts.

There is, however, another motive for my method. In considering the correspondences between *Coriolanus* and *Beyond the Pleasure Principle,* this analysis repeats and recapitulates the conditions of my initiation into the worlds of these two works. First, as a student at the Hebrew University in the seventies, I had the privilege—and the pleasure too—of attending Ruth Nevo's seminar on Shakespeare. Her teaching challenged, provoked and, at the end of the course, elicited from me a paper on *Coriolanus.* I present the main argument and several details of that paper here. Although psychoanalytic theories were generally in the air, and no doubt enabled me to argue for the protagonist's "death wish," I was still innocent enough; that is to say, I had not yet read a word Freud wrote. I persisted in this state of nonknowledge for about ten years until I attended Harold Bloom's seminar on Freud at Yale University.

The influence of the two seminars, so many years apart and yet inextricably intertwined in my mind, has left me with a certain souvenir: I sometimes say "Freud" when I want to say "Shakespeare" or, conversely, say "Shakespeare" when I want to say "Freud." It occurs especially in between a blackboard and a classroom full of students. The students, alerted and unexpectedly entertained, soon become adept at sorting out the names but occasionally someone shyly tells me that her notebooks have become infected (and I imagine to what interesting effect) by my symptom. The moral of this prologue is not intended, I think, to caution against the coming of what Freud allegedly called the "plague" but, rather, to situate my discussion within a context of recurrences.[6] On rereading *Coriolanus* today, long after first reading *Beyond the Pleasure Principle*, I retain a strong impression of Freud's meditative essay as an instance of *apophrades* or the return of the dead:

> [T]he uncanny effect is that the new poem's achievement makes it seem to us, not as though the precursor were writing it, but as though the later poet himself had written the precursor's characteristic work. (Bloom 1973, 15–16)

II. Visions and Revisions

The problem of repetition—what produces unchecked or involuntary repetition? what factors motivate and sustain the compulsion to repeat?—engaged Freud's "metapsychological" and clinical attention throughout his work. The prevalence of repetitive reactions in the analytic situation, of patients who symptomatically replayed unpleasant or painful experiences constituted a difficulty that challenged his therapeutic ambition. Could the compulsion to repeat be cured or, at least, be arrested through the psychoanalytic process? At different times Freud offered definite but different answers to this two-pronged problematic: the questions of the cause and the cure. To clarify the radical nature of the conceptions introduced in *Beyond the Pleasure Principle*, I want briefly to compare Freud's speculative hypotheses in "Remembering, Repeating and Working-Through" (1914) with his later formulation of an indissoluble connection between compulsive repetition and the death instinct.

According to Freud's 1914 essay, the compulsion to repeat (Wiederholungszwang) is an expression of the lost personal past. It originates in repressed conflicts and experiences, more or less unique to the individual; memories are replaced or, more accurately, displaced by repetitive activity. Reenactment wards off recollection:

> ... the patient does not *remember* anything of what he has forgotten and repressed, but *acts* it out. He reproduces it not as a memory but as an action; he *repeats* it, without, of course, knowing that he is repeating it. ("Remembering," 150)

The task of the analyst is to translate repetition into remembrance. The patient's behavior may be compared to a broken record that mindlessly repeats what was uttered in the past. By successfully handling such repetition automatism in the course of the treatment, the analyst "can bring it about that something that the patient wishes to discharge in action is disposed of through the work of remembering" ("Remembering," 153). Thus a coming to terms or a reconciliation with the traumatic sources of the compulsion can be accomplished. Freud envisions the reality of a cure.

Six years later Freud reopens the questions his earlier discussion had closed. In *Beyond the Pleasure Principle,* he tentatively sets forth the idea of the conservative nature of repetition that, followed out with consistency, points to the existence of a death instinct: "What follows is speculation, often farfetched speculation, which the reader will consider or dismiss according to his individual predilection" (*Beyond the Pleasure Principle,* 24). Subsequently however, his initial expressions of supposition and doubt disappear. In *The Ego and the Id* (1923) and in later writings, Freud unhesitatingly asserts: "I have lately developed a view of the instincts which I shall here hold to and take as the basis of my further discussions" (*Ego and Id,* 40.)[7] The 1920 theory of instinctual dualism not only alters but reverses aspects of his earlier conceptualization of repetition phenomena. Principally, the revision entails four interrelated factors: the cause, direction, and extension of the repetition compulsion, and the possibility of a cure.

A. The compulsion to repeat is no longer viewed as unconsciously motivated by a failure of reminiscences but rather by the compelling attraction of an inorganic state of stability.

B. Instead of a turning away from the past, the repetition compulsion signifies a turning back, a propulsion toward a past prior to any lost or repressed memory.

C. Repetition is a phylogenetic necessity and not an ontogenetic tendency; in other words, it is a fundamental expression of an instinctual trend extending to all living organisms and not merely an accident of individual human histories.

D. The physician cannot heal this ill. This point, though derived from those preceding it, is not presented with the same degree of explicitness in Freud's essay.[8]

Beyond the Pleasure Principle remains to a large extent outside the canon of Freud's own psychoanalytic writings. The theory of the death instincts, in particular, is "still one of the most controversial of psycho-analytic concepts" (J. Laplanche and J.-B. Pontalis 1983, 97).[9] Perhaps foremost among the factors that have made these ideas difficult to accept is the last reversal just mentioned. Evidently hope is not so easily abandoned. Or, as Ernest Jones wryly observes, "Our narcissism makes it very hard to admit that our vital processes have their own inherent limitation" (Jones 1957, 3:278). Moreover, the practical consequences of acknowledging the impossibility of a cure would be to undercut the branch on which the analyst remuneratively sits.

Yet another factor might enter into the overall resistance, if not aversion, aroused by Freud's revised hypothesis. For the dark corollary of the death instincts is the inevitability of aggression and destructiveness. Primary masochism or the innate self-destructive trend is channeled into action against objects outside the self. Ten years after the appearance of *Beyond the Pleasure Principle*, Freud summarily restates these ramifications of his theory:

> ... a portion of the [death] instinct is diverted towards the external world and comes to light as an instinct of aggressiveness and destructiveness. In this way the instinct itself could be pressed into the service of Eros, in that the organism was destroying some other thing, whether animate or inanimate, instead of destroying its own self. (*Civilization and Its Discontents*, 119)

In Freud's thought, the elemental force of the death or destructive instinct within each organism becomes inseparable from its displacement outward: "the two kinds of instinct seldom—perhaps never—appear in isolation from each other" (*Civilization and Its Discontents*, 119).[10] Because the death instinct is biologically encoded in every organism, any attempt to eradicate aggression is doomed to failure. Our favorite banner words—Give Peace a Chance, or No More War—are hopelessly deluded. War will be forever more. It is hardly surprising, Freud argues quite combatively himself, that the idea has encountered strong opposition in analytic circles; for "'little children do not like it' [*Denn die Kindlein, Sie hören es nicht gerne.—*Goethe] when there is talk of the inborn human inclination to 'badness'" (*Civilization and Its Discontents*, 120).

Nevertheless, even as I recapitulate these views, I find myself wanting to contain them. Such containment could be effected by recalling the contingent conditions that accompanied Freud's increasing insistence on the validity of his new vision: the death of his beloved grandchild, the knowledge of the disease he bore within himself, and the specter of a world at constant war. Recollection in this instance, however, could be accounted a resistance and not a working-through. It enables the reduction of a powerful though irrefutable, that is, "nonscientific" analysis of how our world came to be the ravaged place it indisputably is to the vagaries of a private, subjective destiny. Thus, after listing personal factors (as I have just done) and claiming these factors motivated (whereas in fact they belatedly reinforced) Freud's theories in *Beyond the Pleasure Principle*, Arnold Wilson and Carol Malatesta speak of "the unhappy theoretical relationship between the death instinct and the repetition compulsion" and argue that, if the concept of repetition had not been "tied to an eccentric cosmology," namely, Thanatos, then it "could have been brought into the mainstream of psychoanalytic theory" (274).[11] Wilson and Malatesta's words of objection ("unhappy . . . relationship," and "tied"), as well as their subsequent attempt to affix "primal repetition" to a different cause, namely, preverbal and presymbolic human development, are helpful in highlighting another crux of the theory.

It would appear arbitrary, even willful on Freud's part to insist on an essential connection between the actuality of repetitive activities (which lend themselves to a wide range of interpretations) and the highly abstract notion of instinctual regression. From a strictly logical viewpoint, the common characteristic said to link the repetition compulsion and death instincts, namely, the conservatism of these disparate phenomena is not a sufficient one. The difficulty is that recognition of "conservative instincts which impel towards repetition" (*Beyond the Pleasure Principle*, 37) draws upon the type of knowledge not easily accessible through step-by-step or deductive reasoning. This is not to suggest that such knowledge requires a leap of faith but, on the contrary, a pragmatism born of lived (whether actual, clinical or, say, literary) experience. Freud acknowledges as much at the outset of his meditation on the death instinct. "It is of no concern to us," he writes, "to enquire how far . . . we have approached or adopted any particular, historically established, philosophical system. We have arrived at these speculative assumptions in an attempt to describe and to account for the facts of daily observation in our field of study" (*Beyond the Pleasure Principle,* 7).

III. HIS DOUBLED SPIRIT

Reuben A. Brower, after citing an instance of "dramatic foreshadowing" in *Coriolanus,* parenthetically comments on the prominence of this technique:

> One characteristic of the play is the number of scenes that have close parallels, in which Coriolanus goes through the same routines, but under changed circumstances which he alone seems not to notice. Hence the odd *déja-vu,* almost nightmarish quality of much of the action in the latter part of the play. (Brower 1971, 378)

Foreshadowing, as Brower's observation implies, entails a kind of repetition; later or foreshadowed scenes duplicate and recall earlier ones. The play thus exhibits a formal, repetitive tendency ("close parallels") dramatized by and through the actions of Coriolanus ("same routines"). As the Volscian general Tullus Aufidius says, Coriolanus' nature is "no changeling" (*Coriolanus,* 4.7.11). He replays old moves, retraces roads already taken, or inscribes the past within the present moment until a particular condition is met. In related psychoanalytic terms, Coriolanus is the embodiment of a compulsion to repeat that distinguishes the structure of his tragedy.

In saying the governing principle of the play is a repetition compulsion, I am not trying to shift the focus from the unconscious of the protagonist to the unconscious of the text or the author. However, I do want to talk about what happens in *Coriolanus* without ignoring the hero's function as part of an overall dramatic construct. Events or situational positions involving Coriolanus, on the one hand, frequently parallel a previous event or situation and, on the other, proceed toward the final resolution. Such scenes as his fight with Aufidius (1.8.), for example, occurred more than once in a past prior to the play's beginning and prepare for a future fatality. Complex progression toward a regressive aim constitutes the tragic trajectory of Coriolanus. "It is as though the life of the organism moved with a vacillating rhythm" (*Beyond the Pleasure Principle,* 41). The play is structured, then, as a knot rather than as a string of episodes. Its linear succession of events is also recursive. The plot pattern as a whole can only be grasped retrospectively.

The bifurcations at various points in the story—the two-directional pull to the past and to the future—correspond or keep time, as it were, with the celebrated deeds of Coriolanus. For his actions are almost invariably marked by a double destructive impulse.[12] One part of his destructiveness, directed toward the external world, is immediately manifest, for the play spasmodically erupts and moves forward according to its promptings. Less evident is the inward directed, primary component of his aggressiveness. Its movement is also forward but only for the purpose of turning back. The difficulty in demonstrating the existence of this retrograde impulse is compounded by its noisy diversionary tactics. "It is then called the instinct of destruction, of mastery, the will to power" (Freud "Masochism," 260). However, if destructive replay may be viewed as an expression of instinctual conservatism, then *Coriolanus* is replete with sounds of the silent death instinct. The desire for death has its complex representation in the play through reverberative action and language.

Perhaps more than any other Shakespearean hero, Coriolanus is the sum of his actions.[13] It is not, as has been suggested, that "Coriolanus is the least articulate of Shakespeare's tragic heroes" (Charney 1970, 80). He rarely lacks a voice with which to vent his feelings and opinions. A series of vituperative outbursts against the plebeians and other less confrontational speeches demonstrate an elocutionary force above the common measure. As distinct as "thunder from a tabor," so is "the sound of Martius' tongue / From every meaner man" (*Coriolanus*, 1.6.25–27).[14] That Coriolanus nonetheless produces an inarticulate impression seems to derive from a dramatic design that largely precludes moments of extended introspection. The highlighting of action, the emphatic insistence on "the deeds of Coriolanus" (2.3.82), is consonant with the play's paucity of soliloquies and their accompanying self-exploratory movements.

In fact, Coriolanus has only the three short soliloquies (2.3.112–24, 4.4.1–6, and 12–26) throughout the play, and yet, in every one he invites the consummation of his life through death. "Better it is to die, better to starve / Than crave the hire which first we do deserve," he says proudly "in a gown of humility," all the while trying to bring himself to petition the common people for the consulship (2.3.113–14). Versions of the same situation reappear in the later scene. Once again "in mean apparel, disguised and muffled"—and about to request his enemy for asylum in Antium, he pronounces the words "slay me" in the final sentence of each soliloquy. Thus, when left alone on stage, Coriolanus expressly invites the end toward which his actions amid the crowds at home and enemies abroad, howsoever indirectly, advance him. His destructive deeds resemble his robes of humility in that they, too, cover up or disguise another, more compelling inclination. Structurally homologous to those circuitous proceedings that lead to a state of former stability, the heroic exploits of Coriolanus "give a deceptive appearance of being forces tending towards change and progress, whilst in fact they are merely seeking to reach an ancient goal by paths alike old and new" (*Beyond the Pleasure Principle*, 38).

Several dramatic and verbal sequences demonstrate the pattern just described. First, there is Coriolanus' precipitate and lone entry into an enemy city in act 1, a sequence completed by his return to the same city in act 5. Coriolanus exhibits extraordinary valor in plunging headlong into Corioles without any supporting forces: "He is himself alone, / To answer all the city" (*Coriolanus*, 1.4.51–52).[15] His chances of emerging alive are so unlikely (*All.* "To th' pot, I warrant him") that his comrade-in-arms, the general Titus Lartius, immediately delivers a eulogy: "Thou wast a soldier / Even to Cato's wish" (1.4.47, 56–57). The speech is interrupted when its subject suddenly emerges—"Enter Martius bleeding"—from the city gates that had enclosed him. Because cities are archetypes of the female body-vessel and gates of the entrance into the womb, a symbolization reinforced by explicit equation between the city-state of Rome and Volumnia's womb (5.3.122–24), the scene at Corioles has been read as a rape and a rebirth: "the underlying fantasy is that intercourse is a literal return to the womb, from which one is reborn, one's own author" (Adelman 134; see also Kahn 1981, 160–61). However, the city-womb is also traditionally a symbol of darkness, of the regions of death. Corresponding to the life-bearing side of the city image, as Erich Neumann points out, is "the negative death-bringing belly-vessel": "The opening of the vessel of doom is the womb, the gate, the gullet" (Neumann 1963, 171). Insofar as enclosure within the city walls represents a return to the womb, it signals a transitional stage in Coriolanus' journey back to the tomb. Already in the first act of this return, he seems to have chosen Corioles (in Cominius' suggestive phrase) as the "grave of [his] deserving" (*Coriolanus*, 1.9.20). The bloody figure of Coriolanus, newly emergent from the gates of a walled city, is not merely embryonic; it also conjures the image of a living corpse.

Throughout the play the hero's spectacular or, at times, spectral appearances correlate with repetition and death. As Coriolanus repeatedly performs valiant feats (Cominius. "And in the brunt of seventeen battles . . . / He lurch'd all swords of the garland" [2.2.100–101]) and imposes defeats (Aufidius. "Thou has beat me out / Twelve several times" [4.5.121–22]), he exudes for his observers an aura of inhuman or superhuman power. Cities give way where he irresistibly presses forward: "Alone he ent'red / The mortal gate of th' city," and then "with a sudden reinforcement [he] struck / Corioles like a planet" (2.2.110–11, 113–14). Later, in bringing the Volscian army to the gates of Rome and thus repeating in reverse his earlier destructive expedition, Coriolanus retains a more *and* less than human visage:

> He is their god; he leads them like a thing
> Made by some other deity than Nature,
>
> (4.6.90–91)

and:

> This Martius is grown from man to dragon: he has wings; he's more than a creeping thing. . . . The tartness of his face sours ripe grapes. When he walks, he moves like an engine, and the ground shrinks before his treading. . . . He wants nothing of a god but eternity and a heaven to throne.
>
> (5.4.12–24)

"The manifestations of a compulsion to repeat," according to Freud, "give the appearance of some 'daemonic' force at work" (*Beyond the Pleasure Principle*, 35). This observation is one of the nodal points at which Shakespeare's text and Freud's intersect; or, to borrow from Bloom's revisionary formulation, "the tyranny of time is almost is overturned, and one can believe, for startled moments, that [Freud is] being *imitated*"—by Shakespeare (Bloom 1973, 141). Hints of demonic possession run through the play. First in war and last in peace, Coriolanus is exalted or denounced time after time as an elemental, uncontrollable force. Thus, Cominius recalls how directly after the conquest at Corioles, he did not pause to "ease his breast with panting" as men of ordinary flesh might do but, rather,

> straight his doubled spirit
> Requick'ned what in flesh was fatigate
> And to the battle came he, where he did

>   Run reeking o'er the lives of men. . . .
>   (*Coriolanus*, 2.2.122, 116–19)

The word "doubled" is annotated as "renewed" here (*Riverside Shakespeare*, 1410 n.). However, in the light of later developments, "his doubled spirit" also suggests the duality of what might be called Coriolanus' "object-choices," that is, a predisposition to destroy one's self and its substitutive selection of objects outside the self.[16] Cominius, who comes to praise Coriolanus, complexly sums up: "[he] rewards / His deeds with doing them, and is content / To spend the time to end it" (*Coriolanus*, 2.2.127–29). The *Riverside* note expounds: "finds reward for his feats in the satisfaction of doing them, and asks no payment for the time so spent beyond the pleasure of passing it in such a fashion" (*Riverside Shakespeare*, 1410n). Yet another gloss of these lines swiftly reads: "in killing time, the hero is killing himself" (Brower 1971, 358).

Duality also marks Coriolanus' ongoing rivalry with Tullus Aufidius. The odd nature of their enmity is intimated at the very outset. In the play's opening scene, Coriolanus describes the compelling allure of his foe: "And were I any thing but what I am, / I would wish me only he"; and again, "Were half to half the world by th' ears, and he / Upon my party, I'd revolt, to make / Only my wars with him" (*Coriolanus*, 1.1.231–32, 233–35). Coriolanus, whose statements are mostly declarative and often imperative, projects himself here into conditional improbability. In the scenes leading up to the confrontation between the rivals, the stage is set for a fight-to-the-finish. As Aufidius says:

>   If we and Caius Martius chance to meet,
>   'Tis sworn between us we shall ever strike
>   Till one can do no more.
>   (1.2.34–36)

When actual engagement takes place however, Aufidius' expectations of victory or death are defeated; for Coriolanus overpowers but does not kill his adversary. Shortly after, Aufidius discloses the routine, almost ritual nature of their confrontation. What seems to be a singular occurrence or accident at first sight is, as it turns out, a bad habit. Coriolanus has made a practice of defeating him and, then, letting him go:

>   Five times, Martius,
>   I have fought with thee; so often hast thou beat me;

> And wouldst do so, I think, should we encounter
> As often as we eat.
>
> (1.10.7–10)

Thus the battle of the generals in act 1 is a repetition. The critics of *Coriolanus* have overlooked the frequency of this event, although it takes place at least five (or "twelve several") times in the story and is mentioned several times in the text.[17] It even recurs in dream-time as revealed in Aufidius' confessional greeting at Antium: "Thou [Coriolanus] hast beat me out / Twelve several times, and I have nightly since / Dreamt of encounters 'twixt thyself and me" (4.5.121–23). In the fourth act comic interlude, three servingmen attached to the house of Aufidius gossip about these encounters in terms that bring out, like the gravediggers' scene in *Hamlet*, the grotesque aspects of the fate they portend:

> *Third Servant.* Why, here's he that was wont to thwack our general, Caius Martius.
>
> . . . .
>
> *First Servant.* He [Coriolanus] was too hard for him, directly to say the troth on't, before Corioles; he scotch'd him and notch'd him like a carbinado.
>
> *Second Servant.* And he had been cannibally given he might have boil'd and eaten him too.
>
> (4.5.178–89)

A strikingly analogous pattern of pursuit and appetitive violence appears in the often-quoted passage about Coriolanus' son and a butterfly. Lady Valeria describes young Martius at play:

> I saw him run after a gilded butterfly, and when he caught it, he let it go again, and after it again, and over and over he comes, and up again; catch'd it again; or whether his fall enrag'd him, or how 'twas, he did so set his teeth and tear it. O, I warrant, how he mammock'd it! (*Coriolanus*, 1.3.60–65)

Volumnia promptly responds, "One on's father's moods"; and it does seem apt to say so. *Comme père, tel fils:* a filament of blood connects father and son. The boy's chase after the butterfly provides one possible explanation of his father's adversarial relations with Aufidius. For Coriolanus, combat with someone almost his equal affords a sense of mastery and pleasure that he cannot find in other human relations. Hence this catching, letting go, and after it again. But what is, after all, only a game for young Martius becomes a deadly sport for Coriolanus. His species of "gilded butterfly" conceals beneath a noble exterior—to the extent that Coriolanus "sin[s] in envying his nobility" (1.1.230)—a ruthless and treacherous intent. However, bred in Rome to equate brute strength with moral worth (*virtus*), Coriolanus is blinded by the glitter of a well-wielded sword. A rival his near equal on the battlefield enters the ranks of his peers in all else. His hatred for the common people derives to a considerable extent from their reputed cowardice in battle, while his misplaced appreciation of Aufidius is born of the opposite cause. The world of Coriolanus is neatly divided into the brave and the bad. Above all, he says, "brave death outweighs bad life" (1.6.71).

Yet from another standpoint, the dynamic and repetitive interplay between Coriolanus and Aufidius seems overly influenced by a different division. Coriolanus' hatred for his specular rival ("I would wish me only he") is, at one and the same time, self-inflected and all-consuming. He compulsively seeks out Aufidius, "scotching" him thoroughly and setting him free, up until his own banishment from Rome. In exile he renews rather than ends their bond because, "like one that means his proper harm" to whom Cominius compares him (1.8.57), Coriolanus is secretly loathe to destroy the anticipated source of his own destruction, the gilded object toward which his darkest regressive instincts blindly turn. Long "before Corioles" as the servingman says, Coriolanus picked out the means whereby his aim of death would be achieved: "I'll fight with none but thee," he promises his foe (1.8.1); and Coriolanus is a constant man. The pattern of his aggressive (re)play with Aufidius exhibits from the first scene to the last a primary wish for a way out.

In the closing sequence of this retrograde progress, Coriolanus puts an end to the idle pursuit of butterflies by turning his back on safety ("For my part / I'll not to Rome" [5.3.198–99]) and returning once more to Aufidius' stronghold. He voices awareness of the fate awaiting him—

> But let it come,
>
> (5.3.189)

and then actively incites it:

> Cut me to pieces, Volsces, men and lads,
> Stain all your edges on me.
>
> (5.6.111–12)

In this manner, not unlike another "flower of warriors" (1.6.32)—Othello in act 5, Coriolanus brings his own death upon himself as surely as he puts one foot in front of another.[18] His call to the Volsces resonates with his earlier imperative to the people of Rome: "Let them pull all about mine ears, present me / Death on the wheel, or at wild horses' heels, / Or pile ten hills on the Tarpeian rock" (3.2.1–3) reiterated shortly after: "Let them pronounce the steep Tarpeian death," and so forth (3.3.88). In a different tone—"Longer to live most weary" (4.5.99), he similarly offers up his services or life to Aufidius at Antium: "[I] present / My throat to thee and to thy ancient malice; / Which not to cut would show thee but a fool" (4.5.99–101). Repetition in ever more dangerous circumstances is the essence of Coriolanus. He does not learn. He repeats himself ("Cut me to pieces") once more at Corioles.

IV. POSTSCRIPT

In September 1930, Freud's mother, Amalia Nathansohn, died at the age of ninety-five. She predeceased her famous son by only eight years. Sigmund Freud died in September 1939. "It was strange to a young visitor," Ernest Jones recalls, "to hear her refer to the great Master as *'mein goldener Sigi'* and evidently there was throughout a close attachment between the two" (Jones 1953, 1:3). More distant and cautious, Peter Gay writes that "there is no evidence that Freud's systematic self-scrutiny touched on this weightiest of attachments, or that he ever explored, and tried to exorcise, his mother's power over him" (Gay 1988, 505). Perhaps for this reason Freud was wont to say "his chief fear was the haunting thought that he might die before his mother" (Jones 1957, 3:279). His concern, Freud explained to Jones, was that such news would cause her great pain. This thought was not unduly morbid given Freud's own prolonged illness. It is noteworthy, nonetheless, that Freud claimed he felt no grief or pain when his mother died but, rather, a deep relief at his release from the distressing fear (or a wish?) that she might live to mourn him. Jones concludes his account of Freud's thoughts about death, which is a part of his discussion of *Beyond the Pleasure Principle,* with an uncharacteristically ambiguous sentence: "Altogether his attitude was a rich and complex one with many aspects" (Jones 1957, 3:279). In context, this statement could refer to either the paragraph subject, "Freud's attitude toward the topic of death," or the directly antecedent description of Freud's relationship with his mother.

In September 1608, Shakespeare's mother, Mary Arden, died and was buried at the Stratford churchyard.[19] She predeceased her famous son by only eight years. William Shakespeare died in April 1616. The death of Shakespeare's mother the same year in which *Coriolanus* was probably written serves several "pathogenic mothering" critics as evidential reinforcement of their readings. The argument runs that his mother's death seems to have triggered or retriggered in Shakespeare a latent hostility toward her and, possibly, toward women in general. But it would seem at least equally valid to conjecture that Shakespeare was closely, even if complexly attached to his mother. Perhaps he mourned her passing. And perhaps as a part of the process of mourning, Shakespeare became preoccupied more than ever by thoughts about his own mortality.

But, and here art parts with life, Coriolanus' mother survives him. The entire play veers toward the death of the hero. No other character falls with Coriolanus. Moreover, he ensures his mother's position as "patroness, the life of Rome" (*Coriolanus*, 5.5.1) by agreeing to spare his natal city in spite of the fatal and foreseen cost to himself. That is, to take what is given at face value, Coriolanus is a highly devoted and protective son. The final scenes of the play are illuminated, as G. Wilson Knight writes, with "love's filial fire" rather than with the bright heat of a burning Rome or her raging son (Knight 1951, 196). In this view of the mother-son relationship, Coriolanus' story becomes a vehicle for the expression of a twofold longing: the desire to grant his mother the gift of life as she once gave life to him; and no less compelling, the desire to die before her so that she might grieve (and care all the more) for him.[20] "I shall be lov'd when I am lack'd," Coriolanus says to his friends before he departs for exile (*Coriolanus*, 4.1.10). In *Coriolanus*, Shakespeare reverses the actual succession of death. He fashions a son strong and vital enough to remove the shadow of his mother's death and to determine the order of his own going. Thus he blunts the keen edge and triumph of devouring time.

Notes

1. Freud's inaugurating discussion of Hamlet and the psychoanalytic causes of his inhibition can be found in *The Interpretation of Dreams* 4:264–66. For a different approach to Hamlet's hesitation, considering it not a result of his iden-

tification with his uncle Claudius but of his evolving position in relation to Ophelia, see Jacques Lacan's "Desire in *Hamlet*."

2. The martial connotations of the word "virtue" in Shakespeare's play are discussed on p. 233.

3. For further exemplification of this critical orientation, see Janet Adelman, David B. Barron, Rufus Putney, and Emmett Wilson Jr.

4. On the effects of predominantly female responsibility for childrearing and the ambivalences it provokes, see Nancy Chodorow's *The Reproduction of Mothering: Psychoanalysis and the Sociology of Gender* and esp. Dorothy Dinnerstein's "The Rocking of the Cradle and the Ruling of the World," in her *The Mermaid and the Minotaur: Sexual Arrangements and Human Malaise*, 28–197.

5. In his *Hero and Saint: Shakespeare and the Graeco-Roman Heroic Tradition*, Reuben A. Brower presents an illuminating study of the Homeric image of military heroism in the works of Shakespeare and of his contemporaries.

6. Freud's designation of psychoanalysis as the plague is reported by Lacan who claims to have heard it from C. G. Jung: "Thus Freud's words to Jung—I have it from Jung's own mouth—when, on invitation from Clark University [in 1909], they arrived in New York harbour and caught their first glimpse of the famous statue illuminating the universe, 'They don't realize we're bringing them the plague,' are attributed to him. . . ." (Lacan 1977, 116). Though widely accepted as having been uttered in fact, this statement turns out to be a fiction invented by Lacan for his own partisan purposes. On Lacan's motives and the acceptance of this legend as history, see Elisabeth Roudinesco's *Jacques Lacan & Co.: A History of Psychoanalysis in France, 1925–1985*, 177.

7. For example, in *Civilization and Its Discontents* (1930) Freud writes that "in the course of time they [his views on the death instincts] have gained such a hold upon me that I can no longer think in any other way" (Freud, 119). At the outset of *Beyond the Pleasure Principle*, however, he still expounds a view of repetition as mastery, especially in his famous description of the *fort-da* game. Traces of the hypothesis presented in "Remembering, Repeating and Working-Through" thus remain in the later work.

8. However, in the later paper "Analysis Terminable and Interminable" (1937), Freud specifies the death instinct as an insurmountable impediment and source of resistance to analytic treatment: "we must bow to the superiority of the forces against which we see our efforts come to nothing" (Freud, 243).

9. For an account of the mixed reception of Freud's new theory among his colleagues, see Jones 3:276–78 and Peter Gay 402–3.

10. In *Beyond the Pleasure Principle* and other works, Freud uses the terms *death instinct* and *destructive instinct* synonymously, interchanging frequently between them or using both ("death or destruction") together. In his 1932 correspondence with Albert Einstein, however, he makes the following distinction: "The death instinct turns into the destructive instinct when, with the help of special organs, it is directed outwards, on to objects" ("Why War?" 211).

11. It has been established that *Beyond the Pleasure Principle* was composed four years before the death of Freud's grandson Heinele and the onset of his cancer. Freud completed and circulated the manuscript among his colleagues several months before the sudden death of his daughter Sophie, the child's mother. See Jones, 3:280, and Gay, 395.

12. The major exception is Coriolanus' decision not to destroy Rome. This decision suspends the outward directed pole of his aggressivity, leaving only

the self-destructive tendency that leads him back to Corioles. In analyzing the relations between class hatred and war in *Coriolanus*, Zvi Jagendorf observes: "War, for Rome, is a kind of relief, in the form of fighting others, from the obsessive rigors of internal strife" (Jagendorf 1990, 457). This reading suggests a continuity between the interplay of conflictual forces within the private world of Coriolanus and the body politic of Rome.

13. Terry Eagleton makes a similar point: "Whereas Hamlet falls apart in the space between himself and his actions, Coriolanus is nothing *but* his actions" (Eagleton 1986, 73). My analysis tries to show what is left over or exceeds those actions.

14. In this respect as well Shakespeare's representation of Coriolanus closely follows that of Plutarch's *Lives:* "So Martius was called forth who spake so excellently in the presence of them all that he was thought no less eloquent in tongue than warlike in show" (Plutarch 1579, 279).

15. Cf. Plutarch: "But [Martius] looking about him, and seeing he was entered the city *with very few men* to help him . . . did things, then, as it is written, wonderful and incredible" (Plutarch, 251; italics mine). Coriolanus' isolation at Corioles is stressed in act 1, scene 4 and later in the play: "Alone I fought in your Corioles walls" (1.8.8); "Alone he ent'red / The mortal gate of th' city (2.2.110–11); and "Alone I did it! Boy!"(5.6.115). According to Kahn, this emphasis signifies his denial of human bonds, especially "the wish to separate himself as violently and bloodily from Volumnia as from his antagonists" (see Kahn 1981, 160–61). Other patterns in the play suggest, however, withdrawal not only from the mother-son bond but from life itself.

16. The term *object-choice* usually designates the "act of selecting a person or a type of person as love object" (Laplanche and Pontalis 1983, 277). I would like to recall by using this term here that, in Coriolanus' vocabulary of action, violence and warfare are not devoid of erotic elements. For detailed examples of the connection between sexuality and military activities in *Coriolanus*, see Ralph Berry 1978, and Wilson 1968.

17. See, for instance, *Coriolanus*, 1.1.239–40; 2.1.126–30; and 3.1.13. On the distinction between story-time and text-time in relation to narrative frequency, see Shlomit Rimmon-Kenan 1983, 43–58, esp. 56–58.

18. Brower emphasizes the contrast between the deaths of Coriolanus and Othello: "in *Coriolanus* there is no terrible recognition by the hero, as there is in the final scenes of *Othello*, that simple soldiery and simple justice have not been enough, that they have indeed brought chaos again" (Brower 1971, 373). My comparison points to the common suicidal end of both heroes but, as Brower suggests, Coriolanus dies without any words of insight or self-revelation upon his lips. His inside is not turned outside even at the play's close.

19. Mary Arden's date of birth remains unknown. She was born in the parish of Aston Cantlow, where registry records do not begin until 1560. See Schoenbaum 1970, 19.

20. The fantasy of authoring or granting life to one's own mother has been read otherwise: as an expression of the wish to erase all traces of former dependency. In Adelman's view, Coriolanus is acting out "the child's fantasy of reversing the roles of parent and child, so that the life of the parent is in the hands of the omnipotent child. The child becomes . . . in effect the author of his mother, so that he can finally stand alone" (Adelman 1980, 140–41). In my view, the parent-child role reversal enacted in the final scenes is not motivated by a wish for

separation from the mother but, on the contrary, for sustained connection between the living and the dead.

Bibliography

Adelman, Janet. "Anger's My Meat": Feeding, Dependency, and Aggression in *Coriolanus*." In *Representing Shakespeare: New Psychoanalytic Essays,*" edited by Murry M. Schwartz and Coppélia Kahn. Baltimore and London: Johns Hopkins University Press, 1980, 129–49.

Barron, David B. "*Coriolanus:* Portrait of the Artist as an Infant." *American Imago* 19 (1962): 171–93.

Berry, Ralph. "Sexual Imagery in *Coriolanus.*" In *The Shakespearean Metaphor: Studies in Language and Form.* London: Macmillan, 1978, 88–100.

Bloom, Harold. *The Anxiety of Influence: A Theory of Poetry.* Oxford: Oxford University Press, 1973.

Brower, Reuben A. *Hero and Saint: Shakespeare and the Graeco-Roman Heroic Tradition.* London: Oxford University Press, 1971.

Burke, Kenneth. "*Coriolanus*—and the Delights of Faction." In *Language as Symbolic Action: Essays on Life, Literature, and Method.* Berkeley: University of California Press, 1966, 81–97.

Charney, Maurice. "The Dramatic Use of Imagery in Shakespeare's *Coriolanus.*" In *Twentieth Century Interpretations of Coriolanus,* edited by James E. Phillips. New Jersey: Prentice-Hall, 1970, 74–83.

Chodorow, Nancy. *The Reproduction of Mothering: Psychoanalysis and the Sociology of Gender.* Berkeley and Los Angeles: University of California Press, 1978.

Dinnerstein, Dorothy. *The Mermaid and the Minotaur: Sexual Arrangements and Human Malaise.* New York: Harper, 1977.

Eagleton, Terry. *William Shakespeare.* Oxford: Basil Blackwell, 1986.

Freud, Sigmund. "Analysis Terminable and Interminable (1937)." Vol. 23 of *Standard Edition.* London: Hogarth, 1964, 211–53.

———. *Beyond the Pleasure Principle* (1920). Vol. 18 of *Standard Edition.* London: Hogarth, 1955, 1–64.

———. *Civilization and Its Discontents* (1930). Vol. 21 of *Standard Edition.* London: Hogarth, 1961.

———. "The Economic Problem in Masochism (1924)." Vol. 2 of *Standard Edition.* London: Hogarth, 1956, 255–68.

———. *The Ego and the Id* (1923). Vol. 19 of *Standard Edition.* London: Hogarth, 1961.

———. *The Interpretation of Dreams* (1900). Vol. 4 of *Standard Edition.* London: Hogarth, 1953.

———. "Remembering, Repeating and Working-Through (1914)." Vol. 12 of *Standard Edition.* London: Hogarth Press, 1958, 145–56.

———. *The Standard Edition of the Complete Psychological Works of Sigmund Freud.* 24 vols., ed. and trans. James Strachey. London: Hogarth, 1953–74.

———. "Why War? (1932)." Vol. 22 of *Standard Edition.* London: Hogarth, 1964, 199–215.

Gay, Peter. *Freud: A Life for Our Time.* New York and London: Norton, 1988.
Harding, D. W. "Women's Fantasy of Manhood: A Shakespearian Theme." *Shakespeare Quarterly* 20 (1969): 241–53.
Hofling, Charles K. "An Interpretation of Shakespeare's *Coriolanus.*" In *The Design Within: Psychoanalytic Approaches to Shakespeare,* edited by Melvin D. Faber. New York: Science House, 1970, 289–305. Orig. pub. *American Imago* 14 (1957): 407–37.
Jagendorf, Zvi. "*Coriolanus*: Body Politic and Private Parts." *Shakespeare Quarterly* 41 (1990): 455–69.
Jones, Ernest. *The Formative Years and the Great Discoveries: 1856–1900.* Vol. 1 of *The Life and Work of Sigmund Freud.* 3 vols. New York: Basic, 1953.

———. *The Last Phase: 1919–39.* Vol. 3 of *The Life and Work of Sigmund Freud.* New York: Basic, 1957.

Kahn, Coppélia. "The Milking Babe and the Bloody Man in *Coriolanus* and *Macbeth.*" In *Man's Estate: Masculine Identity in Shakespeare.* Berkeley: University of California Press, 1981, 151–92.
Knight, G. Wilson. "The Royal Occupation: An Essay on *Coriolanus.*" In *The Imperial Theme: Further Interpretations of Shakespeare's Tragedies Including the Roman Plays.* Oxford: Oxford University Press, 1931; London: Metheun, 1951, 154–98.
Lacan, Jacques. "Desire and the Interpretation of Desire in *Hamlet,*" trans. James Hulbert. *Yale French Studies* 56/57, 11–52. Reprinted in *Literature and Psychoanalysis: The Question of Reading—Otherwise,* edited by Shoshana Felman. Baltimore: Johns Hopkins University Press, 1982.

———. *Ecrits: A Selection,* trans. Alan Sheridan. New York and London: Norton, 1977.

Laplanche, J., and J.-B. Pontalis. *The Language of Psycho-Analysis,* trans. Donald Nicholson-Smith. London: Hogarth Press, 1983.
Neumann, Erich. *The Great Mother: An Analysis of the Archetype,* trans. Ralph Manheim. New Jersey: Princeton University Press, 1963.
Plutarch. *The Life of Caius Martius Coriolanus.* Vol. 2 of *The Lives of the Noble Grecians and Romans,* trans. Thomas North. 8 vols. New York: Limited Edition Club, 1941.
Putney, Rufus. "Coriolanus and His Mother." *Psychoanalytic Quarterly* 31 (1962): 364–81.
Rimmon-Kenan, Shlomit. *Narrative Fiction: Contemporary Poetics.* London and New York: Methuen, 1983.
Roudinesco, Elisabeth. *Jacques Lacan & Co.: A History of Psychoanalysis in France, 1925–1985.* Chicago: University of Chicago Press, 1990.
Schoenbaum, Samuel. *Shakespeare's Lives.* New York: Oxford University Press, 1970.
Shakespeare, William. *The Tragedy of Coriolanus. The Riverside Shakespeare,* edited by G. Blakemore Evans. Boston: Houghton Mifflin, 1974, 1396–1440.
Smith, Gordon Ross. "Authoritarian Patterns in Shakespeare's *Coriolanus.*" In *The Design Within: Psychoanalytic Approaches to Shakespeare,* edited by Melvin D. Faber. New York: Science House, 1970, 309–26.
Stoller, Robert J. "Shakespearean Tragedy: *Coriolanus.*" *Psychoanalytic Quarterly* 35 (1966): 263–74.

Wilson, Arnold, and Carol Maltesta. "Affect and the Compulsion to Repeat: Freud's Repetition Compulsion Revisited." *Psychoanalysis and Contemporary Thought* 12 (1989): 265–312.

Wilson, Emmett Jr. "*Coriolanus:* The Anxious Bridegroom." *American Imago* 25 (1968): 224–41.

Shakespearean Re-Generations in Hebrew: A Study in Historical Poetics

Harai Golomb

I. Translation as Revenge, or: Living Shakespeare and Dead Hebrew

Isaac Edward Salkinson (1820–83) was responsible for the text of the first complete Shakespearean play ever printed in Hebrew. This was a version of *Othello*, published under the title *Ithiel Ha-Kooshi* [*Ithiel the Moor*] [Vienna, 1874]). Although Salkinson had converted to Christianity (and has to his credit, *inter alia*, a church-authorized Hebrew translation of the New Testament), he never interrupted his vigorous Hebrew activity, maintaining the literary posture of a nineteenth-century Hebrew scholar and man of letters. His translations from Shakespeare are a case in point. In the two tragedies that he translated (the other one being *Romeo and Juliet*, whose Hebrew title is *Ram ve-Yael* [*Ram and Yael*]), he strictly adhered to a practice prevalent in several nineteenth-century Hebrew versions of non-Hebrew works: all characters were de-Christened, receiving new biblical-Hebrew names. Thus, Othello is Ithiel (Prov. 30); Iago is Doeg (I Sam. 22); Desdemona is Asenath (Gen. 41); and so forth. These versions of the two tragedies were, once again, the first **complete** texts of Shakespearean plays in Hebrew, but they had been preceded by quite a few fragments out of plays: thus, several Hebrew versions of the famous soliloquy "To be or not to be" (*Hamlet*. act 3) had been devised and published by various Hebrew enthusiasts prior to Salkinson's *Ithiel*.[1]

The Hebrew author Perets Smolenskin (1842?–85) was the proud publisher of this pioneering endeavor. His publisher's preface begins as follows:

> Come let us inflict our vengeance this day upon the sons of Albion! They have taken unto themselves our Holy Scriptures and done

with them as with their own, transcribing them into their own tongue, dispersing them unto the four corners of the earth. Now we too shall pay them in their own coin, taking unto our bosom what they deem holy, the theatricals of Shakespeare, transcribing them into the idiom of our holy tongue. Is not this the sweetest manner of revenge?

This is a day of triumph to our beloved holy tongue. . . . Such gems as Shakespeare's theatricals will bestow upon her their charm and rejuvenate her today, to spite those who despise her, saying: "she is old and decrepit; let us bury her . . . and commit her name to oblivion."[2]

The attitude expressed in these words is indicative of the cultural and mental climate surrounding the work of Hebrew translators of classical literature in the nineteenth century.

Today it is hard to contemplate, let alone justify, treating translation as revenge. Even if we—native users of modern Hebrew in late twentieth-century Israel—adopt the view that the activity of translating Shakespeare into Hebrew reciprocates the translation of the Hebrew Bible into English, we would tend to regard this reciprocity in more affirmative and benevolent terms, as "rewarding" the English-speaking world for its contribution to the worldwide distribution of the Hebrew Scriptures, by exposing readers of Hebrew to the greatness of Shakespeare's works, thereby enabling them to join the admirers of his genius. In contrast, Smolenskin's view of translation as being our revenge for acts of violence, robbery, and usurpation committed against us, is typical of a Hebrew tradition deeply rooted in the Jewish culture developed under conditions of persecution and humiliation throughout centuries of Diaspora and exile.

Hebrew had an almost two-thousand-year-long period of "clinical death" as a **spoken** language, nonetheless kept alive artificially, as it were, by a constant simmering activity in **writing.** This activity was carried out in most generations by an elite consisting of a handful of scholars and poets, often alienated not only by the Gentile world surrounding them, but also by large segments of their Jewish environment, with which they shared very little in terms of cultural values and outlook. For centuries, the mainstream of Hebrew writing was predominantly liturgical and religious. Using the language for any secular purpose, including nonreligious poetry and artistic prose fiction, was generally considered by orthodox Jewish establishment as profaning the holy language of the Scriptures. This language, one has to remember, is supposed to have been chosen by God Himself for the pronouncement of the Creation (which, according to the Bible, began with the Hebrew words *Yehi or!* [= "Let there be Light"]), and was used by Him as a vehicle for revealing His message through the text of the Torah and the words of the prophets. The language was indeed used in everyday life before the destruction of the Temple, but then the Divine Presence had not yet left the Jewish people. In exile, with the Temple having been destroyed, it was considered preferable that secular discourse be conducted in a non-Hebrew language: either the one used by the local Gentiles, or the Jewish non-Hebrew vernacular (for European Jews this meant Yiddish). However, the Hebrew-writing elites believed in the preservation of Hebrew through emancipating it from its exclusively religious function. They were not content with confining Hebrew to the role of a language suited solely for the expression of the sacred and the divine. For them the Hebrew Bible served as a constant reminder and a living monument of the glories of Hebrew in the proud days of yore, when used by divine, royal, and prophetic speakers, and during the Divine Service and holy rites of sacrifice in the Jerusalem Temple, and so forth. It was inseparably linked with memories of cultural and religious pride and national liberty. The sharp contrast between these ancient glories and the pitiful state of the language in their own time was for them a source of envious frustration. Motivated by a deep sense of torchbearers' mission, and regarding Hebrew and the Bible as the true common source of all monotheistic civilizations, Hebrew elites of most generations developed a mixture of inferiority- and superiority-complex in their attitude toward foreign tongues and cultures. The recurring image describing the factual superiority of foreign tongues to Hebrew was that of the "handmaid that is heir to her mistress" (Prov. 30, 23). In the original biblical context ("For three things the earth is disquieted, and for four it cannot bear: for a servant when he reigneth . . . and an handmaid that is heir to her mistress") this phrase means, in addition to its modern sense of inheriting after death, that the "handmaid" takes **immediate** possession of the "property," thereby dispossessing the **living** "mistress," as a cuckoo fledgling does to the "rightful owners" of the nest. In the metaphoric use of the phrase, the "dispossessed mistress" is, of course, Hebrew, whereas the usurping "handmaid" is the foreign tongue of the relevant time and place, including Yiddish.

Such a mental climate makes the attitude of the Hebrew elite toward translation in general, and translation from the great classics of foreign cultures in particular, very complex and ambivalent. Most Hebrew translators of the time were painfully aware of Hebrew's inferiority to the modern, vital languages of the original texts, whose normal development had never been hindered (see Salkinson's "complaints" in this context, sec. III). This awareness encouraged them (a) to engage as much as possible in translating, in order to strengthen and enrich Hebrew language and literature; and (b) to adhere to the original text as faithfully as possible. On the other hand, their conviction that Hebrew was the genuinely superior language, queen of all tongues, made some of them (a) reluctant to translate in the first place, in order to preserve Hebrew's purity; and, (b) while translating, prone to look up to ancient Hebrew tradition itself for solutions to their translation problems. In "intra-Hebrew" terms, the translators' dilemma can be described as a conflict between the desire to make Hebrew vital and modern and the desire to "freeze" it in order to remain faithful to its biblical heritage (which was the main ideological and emotional reason for making the effort to write in Hebrew in the first place). In Hebrew, then, clashes between the powers of archaism and of innovation (to use Yuri Tynianov's terminology) were of special magnitude. Under these circumstances, a Hebrew translation of a great work of verbal art was considered not only as a challenge to the translator's individual talents and ability, in the same way that every translation of a masterpiece is, but also—and mainly—as a challenge to Hebrew itself, as a test-case for its vitality as a vehicle for the creation and transmission of literary greatness.

This uniquely complex state of affairs[3] was, and to some extent still is, at the core of all translations of classical masterpieces into Hebrew. Only in recent years does the grip of this heritage, oppressing and enriching at the same time, show some signs of loosening.

It is against this background that any evaluation of the inception of Hebrew Shakespearean translation has to be made. Thus, it serves as background for the present essay, which is a study of two topics in the historical poetics of Hebrew translations of Shakespeare's tragedies; namely (a) the translators' choice of vocabulary ("poetic diction" and the historical origin of the chosen words, phrases, and grammatical forms); (b) their choice of versification systems designed to shape the translated text's prosodic contours. These are two major literary intersections in which the various heterogeneous forces that operate in this complex situation interact. By closely looking at these interactions one can assess the contribution of each of the major colliding forces to the final result.

II. THE *HASKALA* ("ENLIGHTENMENT") PERIOD

The enterprise of translating classical works of Western literature into Hebrew started during the *Haskala* ("Enlightenment") period in nineteenth-century central and eastern Europe[4] (even Salkinson, who spent most of his creative life in England, had been born in Russia, and published his *Ithiel Ha-Kooshi* in Vienna, where he eventually was to die). It was in this period that the first systematic attempts to translate Shakespeare into Hebrew were made. The self-image of *Haskala* poets was that of "men of the world," opposed to what they viewed as self-imposed Jewish seclusion in a religious, cultural, and lingual ghetto. Their attempts to write original secular poetry in Hebrew and to translate foreign classics served similar purposes.

By and large, the *Haskala* period produced a rigid neoclassical poetry. Its vocabulary ("poetic diction") was usually 100 percent purely biblical, as was its grammar. On the other hand, its meters (following an internal Hebrew development described by Hrushovski 1971) were syllabic.[5] As is often the case in neoclassical epigone literature, the representation of biblical language is often distorted in the *Haskala* poetry's attempt "to out-Bible the Bible itself": several ancient syntactic and morphological practices, rare and obsolete in the Bible, are frequent in this poetry: it may well happen that a strange, cryptic, undecipherable word, appearing only once in the entire Hebrew Bible (*hapax legomenon*), signifies nothing several times in a single *Haskala* poem. At any rate, these poets' dependence on the Bible was extreme: the quotation of complete biblical phrases was adopted by them as common practice. In fact, the act of reading an "original" text involved incessant quotation and reference hunting.

The first *Haskala* translators of Shakespeare were great admirers of the Bard. However, out of the two conflicting tendencies—i.e., reproducing the features of the original Shakespearean text on the one hand and perpetuating the features of biblical Hebrew on the other hand—the latter usually prevailed. It seems that most *Haskala* translators—with the exception of some, notably Salkinson, one of the most gifted among them—did their utmost to fill their texts with what is termed in Hebrew tradition *shibbutsim*—near-mosaics composed of fragments of **identifiable** biblical verses—as substitutes for the Shakespearean original. Obviously, this resulted in removing the Hebrew texts further away from the original meaning, let alone the original dramatic function, of the original texts and the major components interacting within them (diction, syntax, imagery, prosody, figurative language, etc.). In fact, many of these nineteenth-century Hebrew "Shakespearean" texts were not even designed to meet the requirements of modern standards of **adequacy** in translation (for a discussion of this term see Toury 1980); rather, they were conceived of as "Imitations" in the Renaissance sense, or as studies and exercises in expressing a Shakespearean argument in the most biblical phraseology practicable. According to such norms and standards, the translator's challenge is to show that he can make biblical Hebrew express Shakespearean thought; only thought, rather than poetic art, was of any interest to such a "translator," with the inevitable result of distorting the thought as well. His achievements were judged not by his ability to recapture and respond to the original subtleties and complexities, but by his ability to demonstrate his biblical erudition while "imitating" Shakespeare. This hierarchy of values was shared by the writers-translators and by the community of lovers and scholars of Hebrew, who constituted their small and select readership. In other words, their prospective audience actually expected them to produce texts prescribed by the said guidelines.

Thus, for instance, Y. L. Gordon, or "Yalag" (1830–92), a leading *Haskala* poet, in his 1884 version of the "To be or not to be" soliloquy (*Hamlet*, Act 3), translated the phrase "the undiscovered country" as "*erets lo yeda'ah ish*" (= A country no man knew), which, in biblical phraseology, has an **exclusively** sexual meaning (in the Hebrew Bible the phrase "no man knew" is **always** used as a literal reference to a virgin). Since one cannot doubt Gordon's Hebrew erudition, one must conclude that he was consciously ready to sacrifice semantic fidelity to the original, in order to attain biblical authenticity. For him, it was almost unimportant what the words exactly say, as long as they sound biblical, thus enchanting the nineteenth-century reader with the cherished aroma of phrases he had memorized since childhood, which for him constituted the very essence of the Hebrew experience. For us, users of modern Israeli Hebrew, it is inevitable that such pseudo-Shakespearean texts should sound ridiculously cumbersome and obsolete; yet, we have to bear in mind the cultural and historical conditions in which they were produced, and the almost unsurmountable difficulties which faced anyone trying to write in Hebrew in those days. Taking into account what makes those early endeavors culturally heroic, we may be more lenient in our judgment of those who produced them, though the texts themselves remain, of course, outdated curiosities.[6]

III. "Classical" versus "Contemporary" Ideals of Translation

After the *Haskala*, at the turn of the century, most of the period's aesthetic and ideological values were rejected, and new approaches to the Hebrew language and its biblical and postbiblical sources emerged. H. N. Bialik (1873–1934), the major poet of the next generation, was a literary giant towering above the entire postmedieval Hebrew poetry, and his status in Hebrew cultural consciousness almost parallels that of Shakespeare, Goethe, and Pushkin in their respective English, German, and Russian cultural consciousnesses. In his essay "Our Young Poetry" (1907) he made a distinction, which I shall paraphrase as follows: whereas in his generation's (including his own) poems, biblical quotes functioned as [a dog] "wagging its tail behind" its master [i.e., the poet using the quotation], the poet of the *Haskala* generation had used those quotes as "a blind man's stick," without which he could not make a move. In other words, a *Haskala* poet was the slave of his biblical quotes; Bialik (or his contemporary) was their master. This difference is borne out by any analysis of the relevant texts.

And indeed, from Bialik's time and onward, one can notice internal conflicts in Hebrew writers' approaches to their idiom: writers began to feel that they have a stylistic choice, enjoying a wide range of historic strata, with numerous combinations, at their disposal. So far as our topic is concerned, two abstract ideal models of translating Shakespeare emerged. I have named them the "classical" and the "contemporary."

The "classical" model is based on the following implicit premises:

1. Shakespeare is great and classical.
2. No contemporary use of language can function as great and classical.
3. The only Hebrew idiom that conveys a sense of greatness and classicism is the language of the Bible.
4. Consequently, Shakespeare's greatness is better served (in terms

of conveying it adequately to the Hebrew reader) by making the translation as biblical, rather than as Shakespearean, as possible. This, as we have seen, is the *Haskala* model.

The "contemporary" model, conversely, is based on the following premises:

1. As every genuine creative artist, Shakespeare wrote, at his time, **contemporary** literature; no literature can exist, survive, and attain recognition as "classical" unless it was originally written as contemporary.
2. No use of language can convey greatness unless it is perceived as "contemporary," at least to a certain degree, in terms of communicability.
3. A contemporary fusion of various historical strata of Hebrew should convey the desired effect of **communicative** great poetry.
4. Shakespeare's greatness is better served by making the translation as **our** "contemporary" as possible, both in the sense of communicability *vis-à-vis* a modern reader, and in the sense of meeting the requirements of our contemporary standards of "adequacy" in translation.

The conflict between these two abstract and polar ideals was usually implicit, inferable from the translators' practices, but sometimes more explicit. Thus, Salkinson takes his readers into his confidence in discussing his difficulties in translating the personal idiom and language-idiosyncrasies of Juliet's Nurse (in *Romeo and Juliet*, i.e., his *Ram ve-Yael*), in the absence of colloquialisms, let alone slang, in the Hebrew that was at his disposal. He concluded his presentation of the problem by saying that he had opted for "the proper manner of the language, rather than the proper manner of faithful rendition." However, in Salkinson's time there was no real choice, because there was no viable alternative to the stylistic practices adopted by Hebrew writers. "Classical biblical Hebrew" and "contemporary *Haskala* Hebrew" were virtually the same: the language of the original poems and of prose writings of this period was shaped in biblical moulds, or even in hyperobsolete, "overbiblical" ones. Yet, in some cases, as in Gordon's, the conscious effort to produce "biblical mosaics" of identifiable allusions is apparent in Shakespearean translations even more than in the same poets' original poetry.

However, nowhere is the difference between *Haskala* poets' practices as authors and as translators more apparent than in the field of prosody: while syllabic meters prevailed in their original works, some of them tried to make Shakespeare sound more biblical (and, consequently, less Shakespearean!) than their own verse, by replacing syllable-count with purely accentual biblical metrics.[7]

Now the pattern dictated by the "classical" ideal in Hebrew translation of Shakespeare is quite clear: an adherent of this ideal would translate Shakespeare into a poetic language, and set of poetic norms, that in his view would produce the "classical" effect, both for himself and for his prospective readers. This usually means **translating into the poetic language and norms of a previous generation of Hebrew poetry,** whether immediately preceding the translator's own generation, or historically further removed. At any rate, when strictly implemented, the ideal precludes the employment of the translator's own practices as a poet (inasmuch as he can help it). As we have seen, in the *Haskala* the distinction between the two models is blurred, since this was a unique period, in which the "classical" ideal governed original writings as much as translations from classical literature. Since in most fields, with the notable exception of prosody, poets adhered in their own work to biblical precedents, the "contemporary" model hardly existed. It is only in later generations of Hebrew literature, especially after the revival of Hebrew as a spoken language, that original poetry departed from the lingual and normative tyranny of the Hebrew Bible, and fresh styles emerged, based on the fusion of historical strata of Hebrew drawn from biblical and postbiblical sources. These styles included types of prose (spoken, written fiction, and written nonfiction) and poetry, all of which were unprecedented in Hebrew's peculiar history. Thus, a normal gap between the ancient and the modern opened, making a conflict between "classical" and "contemporary" models possible.

IV. The "Classical" Ideal at Work: The Case of Bialik

The next phase in this historical outline is a very short specimen—H. N. Bialik's version of act 1 of *Julius Cæsar* (published 1929). Bialik (see the beginning of Sec. III) lived through the transitional period of the revivification of Hebrew as a spoken language: although he learned it and wrote much of his oeuvre when it was still unspoken, his writing was inseparably linked with the revival process, inspired by it and inspiring it. His abrupt and largely conscious break from *Haskala* style has already been mentioned. For these reasons it is of special interest that his single attempt at Shakespearean translation is perhaps the purest implementation of "the classical ideal": the almost total rejection of the poet's own norms in favor of his predecessors', in spite of the fact that he had dissociated himself from those norms not only implicitly, in his practice as a poet, but also explicitly, in outspoken essays (see sec. III).

Bialik's original poetic diction, to be sure, is predominantly biblical; however, his treatment of his biblical sources is diametrically opposed to that of the *Haskala* poets: it is free and imaginative, even manipulative, deliberately changing and distorting those sources, mingling them with elements derived from Mishnaic, modern, and even Yiddish origins (e.g., turning a Yiddish noun into a Hebrew verb by the use of suffixes, and subversively transplanting it into a pseudobiblical context.). This mixture, or blend—anathema to purist *Haskala* poetics—creates the unmistakable "Bialik idiom" in the history of Hebrew poetic language. In his prosodic practices Bialik was a real innovator, being the first **great** accentual-syllabic poet in Hebrew (this versification system is much more compatible with most traditions of spoken Hebrew).[8]

Bialik's fragment-translation of Shakespeare, though, has none of these qualities: the language is biblical after the *Haskala* fashion already described, both in grammar and in diction. In this single act, some of the rarest, most cryptic and most obsolete biblical forms are used more frequently than in the entire Hebrew Bible. The *Haskala* nature of his text is even more apparent in his treatment of prosody: accentual-syllabic Shakespeare is translated by accentual-syllabic Bialik (with the help of mediating accentual-syllabic German and Russian translations) into biblical-accentual (and occasionally, perhaps by accident, into "*Haskalaic*" purely syllabic) Hebrew verse. Bialik's case shows, then, how powerful "the classical model," ostensibly motivated by reverence for the Classical, can be: it can bring its adherents to the point of literary and stylistic self-denial. This may be one of the hidden reasons why Bialik did not continue this endeavor: he never completed the translation of *Julius Cæsar* beyond its first act, nor did he try his hand with any other Shakespearean text. It has to be noted that Bialik did not command real knowledge of the English language, and must have based his version on German and/or Russian translations of the play.

V. After Bialik, I: "The American Group"

In the history of Hebrew translations of Shakespeare after Bialik one can speak of two "groups" or "schools."[9] The first to be described is the so-called American group of Hebrew translators of Shakespeare. These were writers of Hebrew verse, who grew up and spent their formative years in the United States, though most of them had been born in Europe, and some of them later settled in Israel. These poets—most of them contemporaries of Palestine/ Israel's Shlonsky generation (see sec. VI)—matured as Hebrew readers and writers in relative isolation from spoken Hebrew emerging in the Yishuv (i.e., the Jewish community in pre-Israel Palestine); that is why they rarely experienced the natural give-and-take between written and spoken forms of verbal expression, that is one of the major characteristics of a living language. Inasmuch as one can generalize, the "Americans" (e.g., S. Z. Davidowitz, I. Efros, R. Grossman-Avinoam, and E. A. Lissitzky) tended, as poets, to use the Hebrew poetic idiom of Bialik and his generation, whereas as Shakespearean translators the Hebrew they used can be placed somewhere between the *Haskala* and Bialik's original poetry. An extreme case is Reuven Grossman-Avinoam's: having immigrated as a young adult to Israel, where he lived and worked for decades, as a poet he hardly ever went beyond Bialik's Hebrew idiom. In fact, his Shakespearean translation, published in the Israel of the '50s, exhibits basic traits of pre-Bialik *Haskala* poetry.

However, there are important features distinguishing the translations of "the American group" from Bialik and the *Haskala*. First of all, unlike most members of other "groups" of Hebrew translators, "the Americans" were native or virtually native speakers and writers of English. Consequently, their translations are much more accurate semantically, with fewer mistakes stemming from misunderstanding. Second, their basic idea of translation in general was much closer to modern ideals of adequacy than to *Haskala* ideals of Bible-inspired imitations, curiously adopted also in Bialik's fragment. This difference is apparent in all facets of their texts. Though their vocabulary drew heavily on the Bible, there were hardly ever quotations of complete, identifiable biblical phrases and verses. Their effort to achieve maximum semantic fidelity cannot escape the modern reader's eye: though frequently unsuccessful, the endeavor is always apparent. Their erudition was equally English-Shakespearean and Hebrew-biblical: fully aware of Shakespeare's art of language, poetry, and drama, they tried their utmost—to the best of the limited abilities of their individual talents and of the crippled Hebrew at their disposal— to render the original text with all its artistic values and complexities. They also tried their best to reproduce Shakespearean rhythms, basically adhering to the original iambic pentameter. However, the results were usually poor; in certain cases, when they use by-now outdated, bookish Ashkenazi pronunciation of Hebrew (involving changes in the location of phonemic stress in most words), a modern native speaker of the language cannot sense that the text is metered. The very attempt to preserve the original meter in translation, however, is one of the novelties introduced by the "Americans" into the field of Hebrew Shakespearean translation.

VI. After Bialik, II: The "Shlonsky-Alterman-Goldberg Group"

With the rebirth of spoken Hebrew, patterns have become more complex, and translators' individual traits more apparent. However, the dilemma of the two ideal models in Shakespearean translation remained more perplexing in Hebrew than in languages with "normal" history.

The "Shlonsky-Alterman-Lea Goldberg Group" (henceforward SAG-group; see my reservation in n. 9) in the Hebrew poetry of the 1930s, 1940s, and 1950s began publication of their Shakespearean translations in the 1940s. In cultural, literary, and personal terms, this was a generation-group, which—despite inevitable personal differences, and tensions—showed strong bonds of partnership and resemblance, some of which were conscious. Looking back from our vantage point of several decades later, the traits of the group as such, shared to a greater or lesser degree by its three leading "members" and their lesser followers and "groupies," seem even more uniform than they did at the time. The three poets shared roughly similar cultural, lingual, and even political characteristics. All of them, though not to the same extent, had a Russian literary background from early childhood, which was a decisive factor in the formation of their concepts of poetry, poetic language, prosody, and so forth: their practices often echoed modernistic early-twentieth-century trends in Russian poetry. All of them had some knowledge of Yiddish poetry, later reinforced by a French cultural component. Alterman (1910–70) and Lea Goldberg (1911–70) later acquired a good command of English; Shlonsky (1900–1973), however, never did, and he translated two Shakespearean tragedies through mediating translations (most probably Russian and French), checking the final texts against the original with Israeli Shakespeare specialists. All of them were central figures in the literary scene of their time, and engaged in genuine interaction between their personal poetic idiom and the rapid growth that they witnessed in the development of spoken and written Hebrew: the development of the language, of course, had a decisive effect on their personal styles, but their writing—much more than the writing of most great individual authors in normally functioning languages—had a formative effect on the development of the language as a whole. Moreover, they consciously regarded translation as one of their foremost cultural tasks, and they were influential through their literary and stylistic choices as translators just as through their original writings. It was no accident, then, that Hebrew theaters turned to them (and sometimes to comparatively second-rate "members" of their "group") for up-to-date versions of Shakespeare's plays. And, indeed, theirs were among the earliest Hebrew-Shakespearean texts to be commissioned and performed by the central theaters of Tel-Aviv. This in itself made an impact on the nature of the end product. The text had to be as stage-speakable and as performance-failure-proof as possible. It could not afford to sound ridiculous in the ears of youngsters and young adults, the first native speakers of modern Hebrew (and, indeed, the first native speakers of any kind of Hebrew in many centuries). The tests were severe, and the results very impressive, not only relatively, within their historical context, but also in absolute terms, insofar as anything "absolute" can be established from the vantage point of today.

In June 1963 Prof. Dan Miron published a series of six articles in the literary supplement of the Israeli daily *HA'ARETZ*, on the occasion of the eight-volume collective publication of a selection of SAG-group Shakespeare translations. Miron's was the first attempt, unrivaled to the present, to evaluate critically the SAG-group's contribution to Hebrew Shakespearean translation. In spite of sometimes harsh criticisms against the group's poetics of translation, Miron hails the creation of a genuine Hebrew-Shakespearean idiom, which combines stately classical eloquence with everyday fluency (my paraphrase). This idiom, says Miron, was the joint result of objective conditions (the rapid growth of colloquial Hebrew and Hebrew-speaking theater) and the individual talents of Israel's major poets. Unlike the present essay, however, Miron's series of articles is based on the assumption that the SAG-group poets created their Shakespearean idiom after the mould of their own original poetry. Indeed, they did not adhere to "the classical model" with the same rigor as Bialik had done; however, it can be demonstrated that, at least so far as the "grand style" of the tragedies' rhetoric is concerned, central sections in Bialik's original poetry, much more than their own, constitute the stylistic groundwork for their Shakespearean versions. In other words, this is the second generation applying "the classical model," preferring their predecessors' idiom to their own in translating Shakespeare.

It has to be noted that the original poetry of the SAG-group was very distinct from Bialik's in almost every conceivable respect; they were the modernists of Hebrew poetry, importing the diction, sound, and general poetics of symbolism, acmeism, imagism, and other modernistic trends, into Hebrew, discarding the predominance of the Bible as a major source of poetic language. They openly challenged the poetic authority of the norms established by Bialik and his epigones and followers. However, just as Bialik had rejected the *Haskala* as a poet and adopted it as a translator, so the SAG-group rejected Bialik as poet and adopted him as translators of Shakespeare. As translators of more recent texts, which directly inspired their own poetry (e.g., Baudelaire, and modernist and Russian poetry), however, their translations resemble their own poetry to a greater extent, because they did not regard the original poems as "classical" in the sense just proposed (see Even-Zohar 1975 for an analysis of such translations in this context). At any rate, the combination of the predominantly freebiblical component in their Shakespearean vocabulary, with a modern syntax, and an occasional mixture of postbiblical and even genuinely contemporary elements, is indicative of a strong Bialik influence.

As regards prosody, the SAG-group invariably adopted iambic meters; usually reproducing the original pentameter, with greater or lesser rigor (with the notable exception of Shlonsky's translation of *Hamlet*, where iambic hexameter is used). It has to be borne in mind in this context, that while English is a predominantly monosyllabic language, an average Hebrew word is about 2.8 syllables long (according to statistics by Prof. David Tene). It is very hard, then, to convey the semantic content of an English tensyllable line (e.g., "Thoughts black, hands apt, drugs fit, and time agreeing" in *Hamlet*, or "You blocks, you stones, you worse than senseless things" in *Julius Cæsar*) in a Hebrew ten-syllable line. The tricks adopted by translators to get around this problem are varied and versatile; one of them involves some lengthening of the text. Shlonsky opted for adding one iambic foot throughout *Hamlet*, thus turning the play's meter into iambic hexameter. In *King Lear*, however, he made the effort to reproduce the pentameter, as did almost all of his contemporaries in other plays. The results are sometimes dazzling in their virtuosity, but sometimes rigid and mechanical.

The SAG-group showed much reverence for Shakespeare's formal meters, much less for his rhythms and implied intonation contours. In general, Hebrew poetry tends to be more rigid than English in the rhythmic application of its meters: thus, for instance, in Hebrew iambics there are hardly ever inverted feet (a trochaic foot in an iambic poem, as in the beginning of the second line in the "To be or not to be" soliloquy in *Hamlet*: "**Whether** 'tis nobler in the mind"). As Dan Miron has demonstrated, the SAG-group often went "beyond the call of duty" in sticking to iambic pulse, disregarding Shakespeare's freedom in applying it. In this way fine points of rhythmic characterization of individual persons and scenes are lost, and metric uniformity prevails. This is especially apparent in the aforementioned Shlonsky translation of *Hamlet*. Replacing the original pentameter, with its odd-numbered feet, with even-numbered hexameter, almost inevitably leads to the widespread occurrence of symmetrical lines, divided right in the middle by a strong caesura into two equal hemistichs (3:3). The rhythmic-intonational result is fundamentally different from the original, not only in the obvious sense of language-difference, but also in being much more rigid, repetitive, uniform, and evenly flowing, without the polarity of harsh versus smooth and heavy versus light, which is typical of many speeches in Shakespeare.

Yet, one has to give the SAG-group credit for what may be the most important achievement in poetic translation: they—especially Shlonsky and Alterman—produced the first, and in certain instances the only, genuinely poetic renditions of Shakespeare's plays. Leaving aside isolated components of the text—such as prosody, vocabulary, syntax, and above all semantic fidelity in any given instance—one has to address the overall problem of whether the text as a whole reads as a great work of art, the brainchild of a poetic and dramatic giant. If a Shakespearean translation is accurate in every detail, and fails to leave the impression of greatness, it has not fulfilled its major mission. In my view, the achievements of Alterman and Shlonsky in meeting this challenge—which is a real one, however difficult to define—have set for later generations a model that is impossible to imitate and hard to surpass.

VII. Latest Developments

The Hebrew language has changed and developed unbelievably rapidly over the last hundred years. Just imagine a leap from Shakespearean to present-day English in one century, to grasp the pace of this revolution. Though SAG-group translations can still be used and enjoyed today as reading material for schools and Shakespeare lovers, they can hardly stand the test of stage performance without any updating. Thus, for instance, Avraham Oz, the editor of this volume and an eminent Shakespearean scholar and translator of the new generation, had to work hard on adapting Alterman's version of *Othello*, which—though widely acknowledged as a classic—was found unsuitable for the Hebrew stage of the 1980s and 1990s. Conversely, Rina Yerushalmi—a highly original theater director—staged an experimental workshop production of *Hamlet*, curiously preferring Shlonsky's version of the play to more recent ones by the poets T. Carmi and David Avidan, commissioned for previous theater productions. She made a point of preferring the poetic and archaic effect of that translation to the more recent, everyday effect of the later versions. In fact, she opted for the "classical model" in language, and the "contemporary" in theatrical production. The clash between these two ideals produced one of the production's unique effects. In a certain sense, it can be compared with Peter Sellars's productions of Mozart/Da Ponte's operatic trilogy, where Mozart's music and Da Ponte's Italian original texts are followed to the letter, while the theatrical production, time of action, set design, and identity of the characters are modernized and Americanized beyond recognition. Yerushalmi did not go so far, but there is some similarity in the clash between the choice of by-now-outdated text and up-to-date pretense in staging. However, this production is an exception.

Modern Hebrew theater, as a rule, keeps looking for new translations, commissioning them from Hebrew poets and Shakespearean scholars active today. An interesting case, involving a loud controversy, was the commissioning of a new translation of *Othello* by our National Theatre, Habimah. The previous artistic director of the Theater, Omri Nitzan, had intended to direct a production of the play, for which he commissioned a translation from the late T. Carmi, an eminent poet and Shakespearean translator. Carmi indeed translated the play, and published it late in 1991 in the series of new Shakespearean translations edited by Oz. The production, however, was postponed, and in the meantime a new artistic director (Hanan Snir) took office at Habimah, and decided to produce *Othello*. The role of director was assigned to Gdaliah Besser, who did not like Carmi's text, although it had been completed and paid for by the theater. Snir decided not to impose the translation on the director, and commissioned another version, this time from Nissim Alloni, who is a major Israeli playwright and director, but not a poet. Besser explicitly preferred a prose translation. A row ensued, involving poets, translators, actors, theater directors, and scholars, who wrote articles and "Letters to the Editor" in the press, gave interviews in the media, etcetera. Apart from personal and financial considerations, which need not concern us here, the controversy revolved around the question of whether Shakespeare's plays should be translated for the Hebrew stage in verse or in prose. The various views echoed the "classical" versus "contemporary" dichotomy, *inter alia* (though without using this terminology, of course). I have told this story in order to demonstrate the cultural viability of interest in Shakespeare in the literary and theatrical scene of present-day Israel, and the awareness of the problems emanating from the poetic and theatrical complexity of his plays.

To make this controversy more concrete, I have compared four Hebrew versions—by Salkinson, Alterman, Carmi, and Alloni—of two passages from *Othello*, both being speeches of Othello himself: "Her father lov'd me" (*Othello*, I.3.128–70), and "Soft you, a word or two" (5.2.339–57; references are to the Arden Shakespeare edition, ed. M. R. Ridley). The detailed analysis of this comparison is included in an article to be published in Hebrew. For the purpose of the present essay, though, suffice it to say that some of the results are surprising. Salkinson's text (1874) justifies Alterman's expression of envy (see n. 6): the translator manipulates his exclusively biblical vocabulary in a masterly way, that lends an aura of poetic majesty and greatness to the text, purging its obsoleteness from any vestige of the ridiculous effect that a modern reader senses in most other *Haskala* texts. Alterman's version (1955) is poetic, majestic, fluent, and flexible; however, some phrases are outdated and cannot be used without updating. Surprisingly, Carmi's text (1991) is metrically rigid, sticking mechanically to iambic pentameter, thereby creating contrived, cumbersome enjambments. Carmi solves the problem of Hebrew's polysyllabic nature by increasing the total number of lines rather than lengthening the single line. Whereas in Alterman the line is a syntactically, semantically, and intonationally viable unit, many of Carmi's lines exist only graphically, and reflect technical syllable count. Alloni's version (1992/3, unpublished) is supposed to be prosaic, but it is divided into poetic lines. Most of his text has a basically iambic meter, but not pentametric, the various lines differing considerably in length. Hence there are no enjambments at all. Moreover, Alloni is not committed to any kind of metrical consistency, moving freely between metrical and nonmetrical lines. In diction, too, unlike Alterman's and Carmi's poetic consistency, Alloni's style oscillates between the poetic and the colloquial, thereby often weakening the text. In my view, Alterman is still unrivaled in getting relatively nearer to the original's greatness.

VIII. Interim *Finale*: Exit the Classical/Contemporary Dichotomy?

Of course, it is too early to view the most recent developments with the perspective necessary for balanced academic research. A thorough analysis of these developments will be possible in the first decade of the next century, at the earliest. However, one observation can be made, with caution. Some of the most recent translations still maintain the "classical model" approach, whereby they produce texts reminiscent of SAG-group original poetry. I have found such examples in the work of Oz, Carmi, Dan Miron and others, though much less consistently than in the work of the SAG-group in producing Bialik's style, or in Bialik producing *Haskala* style. However, in certain other cases the Shakespearean texts tend to resemble the poet's own original poetry. In other words, the process may have come full circle: recent poets seem increasingly to resemble the *Haskala* generation in using their own style as translators.

David Avidan (1934–1995) is a case in point: his version of *Hamlet* is often reminiscent of his own poetic style. It has to be pointed out, though, that Avidan cannot serve as a model example: he developed a language of his own, with peculiar stylistic traits easily recognizable by attentive and informed readers, much more idiosyncratic than most of his contemporaries. It is no wonder, then, that such a poet would tend to impose his personal "idiolect" on his translations. Indeed, Avidan's case is extreme, yet not unique. The tendency to make Shakespearean translations resemble the translator-poet's own style can be found elsewhere, as in the case of Meir Wieseltier. Yet, as I have just stressed, it is too early to reach any clear-cut conclusions.

Moreover, the similarity between the *Haskala* and the most recent generation of translators is somewhat misleading. True, on both extremes of the historic scale so far, original and translated styles by the same poets look alike. But whereas in the work of *Haskala* poets the contemporary was turned into "classical," in the work of Avidan and other recent translators the "classical" is turned into contemporary. The circle is perhaps closed, but reopened in the opposite direction.

As regards prosody, once again, recent translations waver between iambic verse, free verse, and rhythmic prose. One solution, though, has never been tried. I am referring to a strong preference for anapest and amphibrach in metrical Hebrew poetry, a logical result of the many polysyllabic words in the language. Free, flexible anapestic meter, with sporadic omission of syllables here and there (Hrushovski 1971, calls this practice "The ternary net"), is almost as natural to Hebrew as iambic pentameter is to English. If Hebrew translators tried to listen to Hebrew's own prosody with the same attentiveness that they try to apply to Shakespeare's original—who knows?—perhaps some of the problems (including the number of syllables per meaningful word) would be solved. The problems are complex, and creative ideas are called for.

* * *

Hebrew's attempt to come to grips with the greatness of Shakespeare's poetry and drama highlights the abnormal nature of the language's history. Yet it is precisely this history that makes the phenomena discussed in this essay so fascinating to observe and challenging to study.

Notes

This is an updated and considerably revised and enlarged version of an article published previously (Golomb 1981). Both versions discuss the tragedies only; problems of translating Shakespeare's comic style require separate treatment. I am gratefully indebted to Prof. Dan Miron for his constructive criticism.

After submitting this essay for publication in 1994, I read Prof. Benjamin Harshav's stimulating book (Harshav; 1993). Unfortunately, it was too late to include explicit references to this brilliant analytical account of the revival of Hebrew in my essay.

1. Dr. Dan Almagor—*inter alia*, a Hebrew translator of Shakespearean comedy and the Israeli correspondent of the *Shakespeare Quarterly* Annual Bibliography—has published two comprehensive and richly documented bibliographical surveys of the history of Shakespearean activity in the Hebrew language and in the State of Israel (translations, research, stage productions and press critiques reviewing them, etc.): Almagor 1966, in English, and Almagor 1975, in Hebrew.

2. I am indebted to Chaya Amir for her help in producing this English version of Smolenskin's nineteenth-century hyperbiblical *Haskala* Hebrew. See sec. II of this article.

3. For a broader view of this intricate, multicultural state of affairs in the activity of the Hebrew writer in the Diaspora in previous centuries see Hrushovski, [Harshav] 1971.

4. In this, as well as in several other respects, developments in Hebrew literature lagged behind comparable ones in European literature. That the *Haskala*, supposedly the Hebrew equivalent of European "Enlightenment," should occur in the nineteenth century (roughly, the era of European "Romanticism"), rather than in the 18th century (to coincide with its European namesake), is a case in point. Needless to say, there are other fundamental differences between the various "Enlightenments." The discussion of these differences, and the reasons for the prevalent nomenclature which stresses the analogies and minimizes the differences, are outside the scope of the present study. Incidentally, the word *Haskala* itself means, literally, "learning" or "erudition," but its use to denote the Age of Enlightenment is so deeply rooted in Hebrew terminology, that the translation inaccuracy hardly ever comes to mind. In Jewish-Hebrew terms, however, the terminology is no mere coincidence, because the concepts of knowledge and ignorance are inseparably linked with those of light and darkness, respectively. This imagery corresponded to the way the *Haskala* poets viewed the difference between themselves and their rivals in the Jewish world.

5. It should be noted that syllabic meters are fundamentally alien to Hebrew, which has a stress-dominated phonology; the conditions of an unspoken language, however, contribute to the potential acceptability of clashes between norms of poetic versification on the one hand and the phonology of the language on the other hand.

6. In the translator's afterword concluding his 1955 translation of *Othello*, the great Hebrew poet Natan Alterman (1910–70), one of the major translators of Shakespearean plays into Hebrew, had this to say about Salkinson's *Ithiel Ha-Kooshi*:

> Any [completion of a] new Hebrew translation of *Othello*—including future translations, that will follow this one—is an opportune occasion to return with amazement to one of the cherished treasures of Hebrew art of translation: that wondrous, immaculate gem—Salkinson's *Ithiel Ha-Kooshi*. . . . even today it is still shining to us, not only as from a museum. . . . As regards **the translator's craft** [emphasis in the original] itself, that subtle and attentive artist [i.e., Salkinson] achieved something beyond the means and limitations of the Hebrew of his time. . . . One reads it today, and quite often hears the vitality—let alone the poetry—of the original. Here Biblical phraseology is the only work-tool, but what capable hands are holding it! Time and again, when one encounters the all-round, beautiful solutions of that artist-translator, one is envious; and after all,

envy [in Hebrew the same word denotes envy and jealosy] is not irrelevant to *Othello*. . . .

7. See Hrushovski 1971, for a thorough discussion of the unique and fascinating history of Hebrew prosody from the Bible to the present.

8. Hrushovski 1971, and Shavit 1983, discuss this phase in the history of Hebrew poetry and prosody in great detail.

9. The quotation marks around these words reflect the uneasiness and caution which one has to sense whenever, for the sake of one's justified quest for convenience and expediency in research, one groups together several highly individualistic artists. Of course, artists who live in the same time and place, having had similar education and shared social and cultural background, tend to produce works of art that include similar traits. However, one has to stress that terms like *group* or *school* seldom refer to an experience of belonging to a collective sensed by the artists themselves; rather, it usually reflects a need for such qualities as order, clarity, hierarchy, classification, and systematicity, in research. Yet, in the history of Hebrew literature, perhaps more than in other literatures, there were cases of collective awareness in groups of creative artists, rallying behind a literary journal, a publishing house, a political-cultural outlook an authoritative mentor, etc.

Bibliography

Almagor, Dan. "Shakespeare in Israel: A Bibliography, 1950–1965." *Shakespeare Quarterly* 17, no. 3 (1966): 291–306.

———. "Shakespeare in Hebrew, 1794–1930: Monograph and Bibliography." In *For Shimon Halkin* (Jerusalem, 1975), 721–84 (in Hebrew).

Even-Zohar, Itamar. "Decisions in Translating Poetry." *Hasifrut/Literature* 21, 32–45 (1975): ii (in Hebrew; English summary).

Golomb, Harai. "'Classical' vs. 'Contemporary' in Hebrew Translations of Shakespeare's Tragedies." *Poetics Today* ("Theory of Translation and Intercultural Relations" Issue) 2, no. 4 (summer/autumn 1981): 201–7.

Harshav [Hrushovski], Benjamin. "Prosody, Hebrew." *Encyclopedia Judaica* 13, (1971): 1195–240.

———, 1993. *Language in Time of Revolution*. Berkeley, Los Angeles, and London: University of California Press.

Shavit, Uzi. *The Rhythmic Revolution*. Tel-Aviv: Ha-Kibbutz Ha-Meuchad Publishing House, 1983 (in Hebrew).

Afterword: "Prosper Our Colours:" A Case/Noncase for National Perspectives on Shakespeare and his Contemporaries

AVRAHAM OZ

THE present volume forms part of an intriguing, if not problematic project: it is designed to provide the English-speaking reader with samples of studies of Shakespeare and his contemporaries grouped and arranged by the nationality of their authors. As such, it is by definition a double-edged project, and though no further requirement than the national affiliation of the authors was given as a guideline to the editors of this series, the mind is naturally intrigued by the question as to whether any further connections, ideological and others, do exist between the subject matter, namely early-modern English theater, and the various approaches to it represented by a given "national" essayistic, mainly academic, body of writing. History lends the issue an enhanced acuteness, if one is to bear in mind that the series as a whole (though this does not necessarily apply to every essay included in this volume) is published in times readily alert to the complex reemergence of the question of nationalism: times that, following the collapse of the Cold War and the significant changes in the ideological global picture, give rise to acute conflicts erupting in various geopolitical foci, old-new crises that many would like to read as a sudden resurgence or invigoration of allegedly dormant forms of nationalism; and when the various predictions pretending to enunciate a "new world order" raise a host of old and new ideological questions concerning the national issue and nationalist project everywhere.

The case presented in this volume raises a particularly intriguing question. Whereas no "national" consideration was given to either content or methodology in the selection of the essays included here but for the general qualification rigorously imposed on the editor regarding the nationality of the authors, one cannot ignore the contextual significance inherent in a group of essays all originating within a common intellectual discourse, highly pregnant with a particularly charged collective memory, one that plays an active role in an ongoing process of building a national culture. For a Jew in the twentieth century, the very fact of residing in Israel, or formerly Palestine (as all the contributors to this volume do) is at least an existential, if not a deliberately political statement; it means partaking, at least passively, in the working of a constantly emerging Israeli national identity, gradually formed and shaped even before the official foundation of the State of Israel in 1948, from the very outset of the Zionist project in the last quarter of the nineteenth century. It is hardly fortuitous that the almost premeditated, procedural agenda of appropriating Shakespeare into the emerging national culture promoted by the Zionist project, first by means of translation and then by lending it a local polemical, essayist, and academic habitation, overlaps that span of time in which a new national discourse negotiated its novel deployment on the geopolitical array of late nineteenth-century nationalism, its official narrative informed by invigorating rituals of self-assertion, often supported by aggressive tropes of cultural belligerency (even though seasoned mildly by a touch of humor): "Come let us inflict our vengeance this day upon the sons of Albion," the nineteenth-century Hebrew writer Peretz Smolenskin introduces Salkinson's pioneering 1874 translation of *Othello* as *Ithiel the Negro*:[1] "They have taken unto themselves our Holy Scriptures and done with them as their own. Now we too shall . . . [take] unto our bosom what they deem holy, the theatricals of Shakespeare . . ." (see Harai Golomb's essay for a fuller translation of this passage). The appropriation of cultural assets may be construed here as a frivolous gesture of legitimate piracy (in times where "colonization" bears a positive, avant-garde meaning within major European nationalist discourse), an act of ameliorative and corrective discrimination, an integral part of constructing a national culture. The stress on artificial, manipulative construction of some aspects of national narrative is significant in this context, bearing in mind the old Renanian argument concerning the wrong reading of a nation's history being an inevitable condition for constructing its national identity—a contention that may implicate not only Elizabethan writers of fictional drama, but also their interpreters writing from a distance of time and cultural perspectives. If it is true, as Philip Edwards, Robert Weimann, Walter Cohen, and many others have so competently suggested, that the Elizabethan theater should indeed be considered first and foremost as a pioneering project of a theater of a nation, then the very analogous processes undergone by Shakespeare and his contemporaries and their audience on the one hand, and the authors of the present essays (as well as their implied Israeli readers, whether or not intended as the major readership of these mostly academic essays, produced within an academic industry the very geocultural location of which has a bearing on its cultural orientation) on the other, may bear witness to the charged presence of cultural phenomena to which this brief afterword, if not necessarily the essays themselves, would like to attest.

The seemingly artificial interrelation between these two historical junctures, represented in the current collection by the observing subject and by the object of her/his observation, may look less than arbitrary when some contextual points are carefully drawn and contemplated. Not only are some general historical events curiously associated, as demonstrated, for instance, by the wide, knowing smile spread upon the faces of my students whenever I speak of a sweeping military victory, won in a few days of battle, that sends the nation into a euphoric state of mind lasting several years (1588 and 1967 are thus well intertwined within both collective memories), just to converge thereafter into a sense of national confusion, or even depression. Nor only the respective invocation of common practices generally related with the enforcement of nationalism, like the insistence on naming places by allegedly indigenous names ("Judea," Samaria") that bring up ideological recollections and call for one-sided ideological conclusions. There exists, however, a more solid point of intersection between the two national narratives—more solid, since it involves material existence (or sometimes absence, for that matter) rooted in place and time that affects in turn cultural transformations and collective memories. This latter point of attachment manifests itself when one bears in mind that the immediate locus of the later of the two analogous national projects—apart from having served, almost by accident and then again not altogether so, a territorial meeting point of the two national, or colonial, enterprises in the twentieth century, which brought about a political and cultural clash leaving its marks on both nations' recent collective memories—appropriates an ideological space indirectly shared with the collective memory of the earlier one, a fact alluded to by the seemingly innocent, yet charged in context, title of this volume. It is a juncture sanctified by a narrative well rooted in both national discourses, in which various degrees of materially geographic presences conveniently intervene with symbolic meaning.

Benedict Anderson's distinction between the emergence of Zionism and the birth of Israel in that "the former marks the reimagining of an ancient religious community as a nation . . . while the latter charts an alchemic change from wandering devotee to local patriot" (Anderson 1991, 149) falls into two inaccuracies: first, faithful to his contention that nationalism is exclusively a modern phenomenon, he fails to recognize national features in the pre-Zionist Jewish community; and second, he fails to stress the strong element of local patriotism inherent in the very idea of Zionism. A major feature that the Zionist project appropriated from earlier messianic movements in Jewish history is the centrality of its territorial claim on the biblical locus informing the Jewish national myth. All those forerunning movements were doomed to failure partly because they were historically premature, but partly because of their lack of a pragmatically material appropriation of the mythical locus in which their dreamed reality was planted to counterbalance their Utopian mysticism. From its inception, the historical narrative inherent in Zionism constituted the collective memory in regarding three phases in the romance-like national biography of the Jewish people: the ancient period, stretching from the biblical version of its myth of origin and emigration into its sacred territory to the series of unsuccessful rebellions against the Romans that ended with the fall of Jerusalem; the long exile period in which the Jewish people retains its national identity even when dispersed in the diaspora; and, finally, the return to Zion, a dream of centuries materializing since the late nineteenth century. Territory plays a dominant role in that conception of nationhood, as an ultimate answer to assaults on Jewish nationality both by foreign enemies (e.g., aggressive anti-Semitism) and internal factors (the yearn for assimilation, conceived as self-denial as a separate nation). The secularization of Zion (i.e., Jerusalem), allowed to Zionist thinking from its very inception by late nineteenth-century Enlightenment and by the modern European idea of nationalism, brings evenly together myth and history, and national ideology and political pragmatism. Naming the entire nationalist movement of the Jewish people after one particular geographical locus, be it of that highly symbolic value as it always had been, inevitably exposed the abstract potency inherent in the symbol to ongoing processes of social and political dynamics.[2]

The major Shakespearean instance in which Jerusalem is invoked by the hegemonic voice in order to manipulate the subjected classes into a belief in, and hence the construction of, an imagined community, may be contextualized by a more recent political moment in Israel, where the agenda of constructing a nation, collective memory and all, is still an ongoing process. It may be argued that the 1996 elections results in Israel marked the death of a century-old national project aimed at constructing a unified imagined community, comprising religious and secular nationalist constituents, and the first blunt assertion of the birth of a multicultural community, still acconted for, in the absence of a clear term, or rather precisely owing to its inherent vagueness and looseness, as "a nation." Benjamin Netanyahu, whose image was presented to the public during the election campaign as a recycled virtual-reality emblem, hovered elusively in the virtual space constructed and distributed by American cultural colonialism, substituting any single, genuine, constituent Zionist ideology may have constructed since its incipient phases. A product of the yuppie image of an American executive, Netanyahu seemed at his most ludicrously out-of-place position whenever donning the traditional Jewish *kippa* when stooping to seek the blessing of an aged mystic, posing as praying at the sacred wailing wall in Jerusalem, or adopting the frequent verbal mannerism "God willing" into the verbal fabric of his speeches. Formerly married to a non-Jewish American, choosing to live in the United States, and rushing to the media to confess of an allegedly exposed affair to save his political career by saving his current, third marriage, his career seemed to contradict any single signifier of the set of values the Zionist imagined community has appropriated in its present phase of existence. In campaigning for being elected for his envisaged position as leader of the Zionist nation-state, a vision modeled on the stereotypical image of the American presidency, Netanyahu, devoid of any articulate long-term alternative to the other party's policies, opted, like Bolinbroke, to mystify his hollow ambition by clinging to a sacred symbol. Thus, the issue of a unified Jerusalem became the focal issue of his campaign. When his opponent, Prime Minister Peres, fell into the trap, failing to indicate that for all practical matters Jerusalem was already divided, at least since the eruption of the Palestinian *intifada*, but angrily denying any intent to divide the sacred city, Netanyahu was heard to refer to his opponent by citing "the lady doth protest too much." Thus, projects of constructing a national agenda by a hegemonic voice as a manipulative device are forged in a similar shape in distant periods, using cultural monuments such as Jerusalem or Shakespeare to crown or preside over the common agenda.

On some levels, the biblical sacredness of Jerusalem, informing the Christian collective memory since its inception, provided political ideology in the Middle Ages with a comparable ideological tool, whereby material distantiation could paradoxically disalienate a local national narrative, rendering the heavenly Jerusalem of the New Testament (e.g., Revelation 21: 2, 10) real up to a convenient extent. The destruction of the earthly city by Titus in A.D. 70 was regarded by Christianity as the fulfillment of Jesus' prophecy predicting the destruction of the Temple. In this, the Christian view read probably correctly the Roman intention in destroying the major shrines of Jewish culture (see Smith 1991, 32): the territorial locus of faith thus loses its validity. "Thus saith the Lord, the heaven is my throne, and the earth is my footstool;" (Isaiah 66:1) is cited in the letter attributed to Barnabas from the second century: "where is the house that ye build unto me? and where is the place of my rest?" The bishops of Nicea accorded the city of Jerusalem, a provincial town within the Roman political system and renamed by Hadrian as Aelia Capitolina, a special spiritual stature within Christianity, which was given a political emphasis by the convenor of Nicea, the converter of the Roman empire to Christianity, Emperor Constantine, who marked the site of Jesus' sepulcher by building above it the *Anastasis* ("Resurrection"), a monumental rotunda-shrine: "So on the monument of salvation itself was the new Jerusalem built," says Eusebius (*Life of Constantine,* III, 33; see Peters 1985, 136). Christian pilgrims in the fourth century regarded Jerusalem as Christian in spirit, and conceived the failure of the anti-Christian emperor Julian's project of restoring the Temple mount a divine intervention designed to prevent the falsification of Christ's prophecies. The proclamation in 451 of the Bishop of Rome, Leo I, as the successor of Peter, established the papacy in Rome in imitation of the High Priesthood of the Temple in Jerusalem, a migration read allegorically into Virgil's *Aeneid,* where the travel of Aeneas (suggesting St. Peter) from Troy to Rome portended the transfer of the Holy City from Jerusalem to the seat of the papacy. Since the Muslim conquest of Jerusalem in 638 by Caliph Umar, a special attention was paid to constituting the city, and especially the Temple mount, as a religious center, with the al-Aqsa mosque and the Dome of the Rock erected as the major shrines of worship. Christianity regarded the fall of Jerusalem as a chastisement for falling off from the Christian ideal. Architecturally, however, the Muslim shrines begin to affect Christian places of worship: what starts with the influence of the Dome of the Rock on the shape of the Church of the Ascension on the Mount of Olives, will later on affect church building in Europe when the crusaders will mingle the actual view of the earthly city with the allegorical images of the heavenly Jerusalem. The practical interest of European Christianity in Jerusalem gains a significant momentum with Charlemagne, who acquires some authority over the Church of the Holy Sepulcher, and his son, Louis the Saint, who prescribes an annual tax of one dinar for the maintenance of the Christian holy places in Jerusalem. The ninth-century Muslim writer, AlJahit, testifies that the Muslim society appreciated the Christians more than the Jews and the Persians, since the former were supposed to be the subjects of an Emperor reigning outside the borders of the Muslim kingdom: national government was a God-given gift to what otherwise would have been considered merely a religious group. This kind of attachment of the Christian contingency in Jerusalem to the West is typical of the basic conception leading in the late eleventh century to the crusades, emanating from ideological developments in medieval Europe (see, e.g., Erdmann 1977, and Baldwin's notes; or Gilchrist, 1985, for a dissenting view). Indeed, there is much evidence regarding the persecution of Christians—both residents and pilgrims—in Muslim Jerusalem: news was spread about pilgrims having been robbed and arrested, and the Church of the Holy Sepulcher was razed ninety years before the first crusade reached the city. And yet, the proclamation of the first crusade by Pope Urban II in 1095 has to do with European religious and secular politics rather than a mere rescue operation. The convenient conditions developing in the Middle East were matched by the polarization of social discrepancies in feudal western Europe: the crusades, proclaimed ideologically as religious enterprises, concealed economic and social motives. Above all, perhaps, the sacred image of Jerusalem serves the Church as a tool to exert ideological unity on its European flock, otherwise scattered and divided between conflicting national, economic, and class identity. Though left aside by the initial wave of the crusading zeal, a similar motivation may apply to the policies of the English throne, attempting since the Norman Conquest to foster a national identity in order to separate territorial feudalism from the political sphere. For the inhabitants of that sea-walled garden, detached in many ways from direct Mediterranean interests, Jerusalem could hardly incite the common imagination as a target point of territorial expansion. Thus, any involvement of

England in the actual crusading project was indirect and sporadic, since William Rufus's financing the crusading enterprise of his brother, the Duke of Normandy, as a settlement of feudal conflict, or since the short participation in the first crusade of Stephen of Blois, who was to regard England as a piece of territorial inheritance, to the individualistic undertaking of Richard Coeur-de-Lion to join the third crusade.

With the years, however, and especially since the crusaders' loss of Jerusalem and the Holy Land, material Jerusalem stopped playing a significant role in the crusading enterprise: a shelter for Christian malefactors who had to run away from England or the rest of Europe to save their skin, as Burchard of Mount Sion describes it in 1280 (see Burchard 1896, 102; and see Peters 1985, 462–64), it stood no chance to attract any more massive collective undertakings on behalf of further English rulers. The crusading activity might then be dissociated from material Jerusalem and confine itself to Europe (See, e.g., Housley 1992). Whereas Christopher Columbus may have still urged his sovereigns (as he writes in his diary by the end of 1492) to spend all the profits of his enterprise "on the conquest of Jerusalem," the laughter of his sovereigns at his suggestion, saying "that it would please them and that even without this profit they had that desire" (Columbus 1989, 291) hardly betrays a serious undertaking. Rather, Stephen Greenblatt tells us in the name of Alain Milhou and other historians, "while the references in Columbus to the rebuilding of the 'arx Sion' and the restoration of the 'Casa Santa' may be meant literally, this literal sense, in the context of Columbus's Joachite Messianism, may serve as a metonymic reference to Christian holy places far from Jerusalem" (Greenblatt 1991, 165). From the fourteenth to the sixteenth centuries, Milhou observes, "millenarian movements frequently translated the struggle to retake Jerusalem into a national campaign against the enemies of the people: the crusading rhetoric was adapted for very different social ends" (Ibid., 158). This new attitude toward the crusading activity made the enterprise more accessible for the English kings who wished to wage "holy" wars against the opponents of the Angevin dynasty: backed by their papal ally, those champions of Plantagenet rule "sought to sanctify their respective causes and came to harness the sentiment, vocabulary, and symbols of crusade;" moreover, already contemporary observers have noted "that the royal cause was indeed sublimated as a crusade," using (in Powicke's words) the "prestige" of a crusade, with those having taken the crusader's vow for the fifth crusade being absolved from the duty of fulfillment as long as they fought for Henry (Lloyd, 113). A similar case applies to the ventures of the historic Henry Bolingbroke, the Earl of Derby, whose two expeditions of 1390–91 and 1392 took him up to Prussia, with Danzig and Vilnius substituting Jerusalem as an ideological goal. It is doubtful what part devotion played in such entrprises. The national churches in both England and France respectively took part themselves in accounting for battles partly designed for the assertion of national supremacy, such as the Anglo-French war, in terms not incompatible with those that had been used for the crusading enterprise. When reflected in Shakespeare's histories, then, such particular ventures into geography have gone a long way since Stephen of Blois participated in the conquest of Jerusalem, or even since Richard I, who never actually saw Jerusalem, but gained pilgrimage rights to it at the negotiation table in Jaffa. Earthly Jerusalem, now under Mamluk rule and inhabiting a small minority of Roman Catholics, was irrelevant to any Christian military enterprise, but visited sporadically by a few Latin pilgrims, by sufferance of the pope (who issued special pilgrimage license) and the Mamluk sovereigns and Muslim population (Peters, 430–31). A report by an anonymous English traveler to Jerusalem in mid-fourteenth century regards the Muslim domination as a constant situation and betrays no hope for an imminent crusading project (Hoade 1948, 65–70). Related in Shakespeare to Bolingbroke, now Henry IV, the crusade experience, still officially proclaimed under the pretext of liberating Jerusalem and the Holy Sepulcher, is appropriated into manipulative use by English hegemonic ideology, having much to do with the growing interest in the concept of nation in its particular English mould, for the promotion of which even the obsolete battle for Jerusalem may be revived and ideologically recruited.

The myth of the nation, in general, is based on continuity: preserving the constancy of a human collective; it shuns new beginnings, for innovation calls for Utopianism or eccentricity (Said 1975, 32) rather than that kind of self assurance depending on widely accepted norms, well-trodden paths of common experience, and lasting patterns of ritual and collective behavior. "Going to Jerusalem" as material act and symbolic gesture combined, involving temporary travel or constant migration, serves Jewish, Christian, and Islamic "imagined communities" (Benedict Anderson's telling phrase, deliberately stressing the inherent vagueness of the shared attributes implied by any concept of 'nation') as an integrative ritual supported by pragmatic consequence. Whereas literary moves of communal migration typical of pastoral literature are exclusively Utopian, the tangible sense of personal commitment informing communal myths such as Jewish "return to Zion," the Christian crusade, or the Islamic Jihad consolidate ritual constancy by involving locus with action and enunciate that *"locality* of culture" that, for Homi Bhabha, "is more *around* temporality than *about* historicity" (Bhabha 1990, 292). Its inevitable dependence on travel and migration serves, under any circumstance of nationness, to break with an alienating sense of exile (whether *from,* or *in* the sanctified territorial center informing the particular myth of nation) and to celebrate a material and symbolic sense of naturalization.

The complementary presence of both material and symbolic levels is crucial here: the myth of nation is about material ownership no less than about self-transformation and communal cohesion. European invasions of the Holy Land from the eleventh to the thirteenth centuries, which on the level of material commodity gained the Italian city-states Mediterranean maritime routes, later adorned the titulature of the House of Habsburg, which assigned a special significance to the King of Austria's being "King of Jerusalem,"[3] or the old Duke Reiner of Anjou, Queen Margaret's father, "writyng hymself," as Hall reminds us, "kyng of Naples, Scicile, and Jerusalem" (Hall 1548, 194), or, closer to Shakespeare's time, Queen Mary, who, jointly with King Philip of Spain, styled themselves "by the grace of God kyng and quene of England, Franse, Napuls, Jerusalem, and Ireland, deffenders of the fayth, and prynsses of Spayne and Ses[ily,] archdukes of Austherege, dukes of Melayn, Burgundye, and Brabantt, contes of Haspurge, Flandurs, and Tyrole" (Machyn 1848, 34). Towards the end of *1 Henry VI,* Suffolk brings up Margaret's father's title as "The King of Naples and Jerusalem" as a crucial argument in favor of her becoming Queen of England (5.5.40; and cf. *2 Henry VI,* 1.1.48), a "type" clearly devoid of any material substance, as the tortured York will not forget to mention derogatorily when spiting his tormentress:

> Thy father bears the type of King of Naples,
> Of both the Sicils, and Jerusalem,
> Yet not so wealthy as an English yeoman.
> (*3 Henry VI,* 1.4.121–23)

For Margaret herself, however, that part of her father's title is far from an object of derision, nor an empty signifier. Charging the type with its inherent symbolic significance, she conjures at her final defeat "the holy city, new Jerusalem, coming down from God out of heaven, prepared as a bride adorned for her husband" (Revelation 21: 2), thus commanding her inherited title to appropriate a transcendent resort to which she, more than the rest of Christianity, is privileged both by divine and secular right:

> So part we sadly in this troublous world,
> To meet with joy in sweet Jerusalem.
> (3 *Henry VI*, 5.5.7–8)

Bereft of all her worldly powers and wealth, Margaret may still cling to the one asset left of her initial dowry: the symbolic standing she claims on a heavenly city through an earthly title.

The identification with scriptural models in the English Renaissance informs not only dramatic texts, from early humanist ones, still affected by the tradition of the Corpus Christi plays to Jacobean plays such as Elizabeth Cary's *The Tragedy of Mariam*, but also many contemporary voyage narratives. It is the sense of material travel such texts exert that appropriates signifiers from the realm of rhetoric to the ideological context of collective rituals. The actual sensation of touching a myth, such as seeing the spots of the Virgin's milk upon the stones of Bethlehem or the step of Jesus' left foot on the Mount of Olives, as John Mandeville testifies to have done (Greenblatt 1991, 39), or merely such that friends coming to Israel today often vouch for when first encountering place-names like Jerusalem, Cesarea, or Nazareth on plain road-signs, may provide for national cohesion in any "imagined community" partaking to some extent in that myth. This will occur when such a symbolic touch is replaced by a sense of material possession, when owning a myth is translated into a collective property and added to some collective repository of both material and cutural treasure, supported by an appropriate narrative. The possibility for such a move to partake in the constitution of a national myth is enhanced in the sixteenth century, when the discovery of non-European cultures is accommodated with the European experience in Utopian writing (see, e.g., Anderson 1991, 68–69), and may, on another level of collective consciousness, provide for a complex sense of nationality constructed on multiple narratives complementing each other not solely on the symbolic level but also on material grounds. Such a multiplicity of narratives constitutive of one, more or less integrated national myth may be similarly found in both early modern England and in modern Israel.

It is in such a vein that the notion of a holy land (as symbolically represented by The Holy Land) figures as a notable presence behind the dynastic procedures and the national consolidation accounted for in Shakespeare's history plays, written within an era in which "England's past became an issue in England's present to a degree unknown elsewhere in early modern Christendom" (Cressy 1994, 61). It may be significant that the ascent of the Tudor dynasty to the English throne almost exactly coincides with the printing of the first realistic map of Jerusalem (by Bernard von Breydenbach, Maintz, 1486), which marks a departure from that Jerusalem that for Sir John Mandeville had been "the center of a symmetricallly distributed set of continents, a center whose perfect mid-point are the sacred rocks" (Greenblatt 1991, 42), and is until then commonly conceived as placed by the Lord "in the midst of the peoples and the circuit of her lands." Henry VII, who professed at his ascent to lead a crusade, did not manage to collect at court more than eleven guineas for that noble cause, but the symbolic value of such a venerable gesture must still have been considered viable. Shakespeare, careful enough not to embarrass his Queen with awkward details from the reign of the first Tudor monarch, nevertheless made use of an analogous royal gesture in writing about an earlier English king: beside the various occasional allusions connecting English history to biblical themes, such a notion is manifestly deployed when *the first part of Henry IV* opens by a Royal ceremony in which an act of the Crown's interest is presented as a national issue allegedly comprising religious and national concerns—in this case serving the typical Lancastrian policy of aggressive nationalism (more commonly directed against neighboring France). Urged, as later admitted by himself, by internal pressures caused by the "giddy minds" (2 *Henry IV*, 4.5.213)[4] of his aristocratic peers, King Henry proclaims his pious intention to sacrifice lately and precariously achieved peace at home to wage a sacred war "in stronds afar remote." His chosen strand, however, is not fortuitous. When Sidney "urges national renewal through poetry" in quest for military enterprise, Edward Berry reminds us, his desire "is less an expression of disinterested nationalism than of class solidarity," pertaining to "the crisis of the aristocracy" (Berry 1991, 1,2). For such an exclusively aristocratic, elitist brand of nationalism (inspired to a great extent by the international pressures on England in the political atmosphere of the 1580s) any war, anywhere, will do (Berry 1989). But for Henry to gather his vassals of all ranks in the feudal hierarchy under the banner of a common cause at a time of no immediate danger to the crown, such a project can hardly fall short of launching a spectacular crusade in the Holy Land, an illustrious pageant whereby a universal Christian cause will turn into national enterprise:

> a power of English shall we levy,
> Whose arms were moulded in their mothers' womb
> To chase these pagans in those holy fields
> Over whose acres walk'd those blessed feet
> Which fourteen hundred years ago were nail'd
> For our advantage on the bitter cross.
> (1 Henry IV, 1.1.20–27)

Contrary to the assumption by Anderson and other authorities on nationalism who argue that unifying forms of collective identification in the early modern era consisted on narrower (civic) or larger (religious) communities (see, e.g., Anderson 1991, 12–22), Henry's stress on "a power of English" here suggests a manipulative use of a Christian cause to strengthen national cohesion. Obviously, pertaining to a great extent to what for Anderson is "dynastic identity," and for Anthony Smith "possessive state," this creation of a combined Christian and national discourse, containing what in Mandeville's accounts is "a blend of estrangement and familiarity" (Greenblatt 1991, 44), betrays Henry's rather shaky claim to the Crown, and hence to the "pure" prerogative of symbolic representation of national interests. Such a claim requires a reinforced validity by an ideologically sound, harmonious image of cohesion, a heroically transcendental narrative whereby the English powers are devoutly ordained to remedy the predicament suffered by the entire Christian universe at the hands of the heretic other. This very trope, combining universal and local concerns, irrespective of the actual implementation of its promised contents, forms a speech-act exemplifying national myth in the making. Henry's invocation of a supreme mission in which his subjects may join him as an integrated nation is primarily designed to initiate a new national entity; and it is done in the biblical spirit of the Genesis prophecy, as later transported by Cranmer to account for the sacred vocation of the English Crown to "make new nations" (*Henry VIII*, 5.4.52).

Thus, nation in the making in early modern drama often turns out to be a product of a manipulative gesture, a "calculated use of national memory" (Cressy 1994, 61), initiated by a hegemonic party whose political or cultural interests such an act are designed to protect. This propagated ideological unity is presented as a social ritual that, as Mary Douglas puts it, creates "a reality which would be nothing without [it]. For . . . it is impossible to have social relations without symbolic acts" (Douglas 1966, 62). King Henry's Holy Land is an ideological construct cleverly disguised as a symbolically charged locus. When, however, his intentions are frustrated by the sudden intervention of a genuine, unforged external reality in the shape of the more acute news from Wales and the north, Henry "must neglect [his] holy purpose to Jerusalem" (Ibid., 99–100). Ironically, the destiny he prophetically wished to forge for his nation as a whole in the shape of a social ritual is eventually to play a personal trick on him on the verge of his death by way of an age-old prophecy, itself adopted from a general Christian source to serve as an English national myth:

> King   Doth any name particular belong
>   Unto the lodging where I first did swoon?
> Warwick   'Tis called Jerusalem, my noble lord.
> King   Laud be to God! Even there my life must end.
>   It hath been prophesied to me, many years,
>   I should not die but in Jerusalem,
>   Which vainly I suppos'd the Holy Land.
>   But bear me to that chamber; there I'll lie;
>   In that Jerusalem shall Harry die.
>
> (2H4, 4.5.231–40)[5]

This little personal ritual set by the king for his own death retains the symbolic meaning of Jerusalem for Shakespeare's audience, ranging from an accessible locus to a transcendental concept. A universally revered symbol, Jerusalem may equally stand pejoratively for London when William Proctor preaches against the latter's iniquity (Chandos 1971, 250–51) or positively for Virginia, when William Crashaw would set it as an ideal model for the builders of that New World colony (Ibid., 141); or, better still, as in Donne, may be at once sanctified and the bosom sister of Sodome as Babylon, "that Church of Confusion" may nevertheless be our sister too (Donne 1958, 375). Seeing themselves as the heirs of ancient Israel (Cressy 1994, 62), English Protestant preachers of early modern England adopted Jerusalem as their symbolic capital. Shakespeare's King Henry hits, then, a palpable point in the English collective memory. As has often been noted, Henry's initial announcement of his intended crusade echoes and challenges John of Gaunt's prophecy of despair in *Richard II*, in which he expresses his loss of faith in the English power's ability to redeem both Christianity and chivalry, and where Jerusalem and the Holy Land figure as the very image of its national impotence:

> This royal throne of kings, this scepter'd isle,
> This earth of majesty, this seat of Mars,
> This other Eden, demi-paradise,
> This fortress built by Nature for herself
> Against infection and the hand of war,
> This happy breed of men, this little world,
> This precious stone set in the silver sea,
> Which serves it in the office of a wall,
> Or as a moat defensive to a house,
> Against the envy of less happier lands,
> This blessed plot, this earth, this realm, this England,
> This nurse, this teeming womb of royal kings,
> Fear'd by their breed and famous by their birth,
> Renowned for their deeds as far from home,
> For Christian service and true chivalry,
> As is the sepulchre in stubborn Jewry,
> Of the world's ransom, blessed Mary's Son,
> This land of such dear souls, this dear dear land,
> Dear for her reputation through the world,
> Is now leased out, I die pronouncing it,
>
> (*Richard II*, 2.1.40–59)

The multiple reference to England as a throne, an Earth, a seat of gods, a demi-paradise, a breed, a little world, a blessed plot, a realm, or a womb, deliberately mixes locus with concept, a device "built by Nature" with a "breed of men." Yet the dizzy dance of the signifier between that host of signified meanings in Gaunt's speech never departs from viewing England as "built by nature." The many facets of that harmony the loss of which the speech laments is solidly rooted in some nostalgic normative order. There exists in the passage, however, one exception to that order, that stands out verbally as well as geographically and ideologically. The sepulcher of Christ is placed "in stubborn Jewry," an awkward phrase, for "Jewry" suddenly accrues an irregularly added meaning of communality on top of its inherent sense of locality suggested by the syntactic logic of the sentence. It is primarily to this added meaning that stubbornness is imported as a qualifying attribute. This community of "stubborn Jewry" is far from being "a breed of men" constituted by Nature. It represents a deliberately chosen moral orientation, devised and shared by a collective of people whose unifying parameters as a group are at best complex: religion seems to be the obvious suggestion, but then the sentence directs the mind to a territorial attribute, another concept often associated with national identity. But what reality figures beyond that territory? Is it that obscure "country" that, according to Jessica, rather enigmatically unites Shylock with Tubal and Chus (*The Merchant of Venice*, 3.2.284)? Presumably not (Chus, incidentally, here cited as a person's name, is the biblical Hebrew word for the land of Ethiopia): no territorial definition of nationality would possibly apply here. As opposed to Marx's reference to the "*chimerical* nationality" of Judaism as "the nationality of the merchant, of man of money in general," which may be read as a sociological or theological one (Marx 1975, 239), the reference to a Jew as a "countryman" is purely symbolic, implying absence rather than identity. Since Jews reached Europe through expulsion and through a process of gradual dispersion rather than through conquest, colonization, or mass migration, they could possess no economic positions that depended on hegemonic power or expropriation of lands:

> I must confess we come not to be kings:
> That's not our fault: alas, our number's few,
> And crowns come either by succession,
> Or urg'd by force.
> (*The Jew of Malta*, 1.1.127–30)

Even where the Jews could be in possession of lands, such as in Barabas's island, whose circumstances Marlowe appears to have studied carefully:

> Barabas.   . . . and I have bought a house
> As great and fair as is the Governor's;
> And there in spite of Malta will I dwell,
> Having Ferneze's hand . . .
> (2.3.13–16)

—they often preferred to deal in landed property not so much as "a form of family investment, as it was for the Christians in Malta as elsewhere, so much as a method of making money," since that tricky "mortgage" system served "to avoid the odium which the taint of usury brought with it" (Wettinger 1985, 40). With the continuing practice of the expulsion of Jews, which became widespread especially in Western Europe throughout the fifteenth century, such a prospect becomes a considerable factor in the Jewish investment policy (see Katz 1961, 47). The lack of lasting property, in Feudal and early modern Europe, meant a temporary status of citizenship and a perpetual state of alienation. Othello the Moor, another alien in Venice, is theoretically free to join his fellow countrymen in the realm of the Prince of Morocco. In *The Merchant of Venice,* all the characters are identified by local habitation: Portia's suitors are identified by their countries; there is a clear division, at the outset, between the Venetians and the residents of Belmont; Launcelot Gobbo defines himself as an Italian (*The Merchant,* 2.2.150), and his father, who owns a horse and brings a dish of doves as a present, must own a plot of land in the country. Even "a poor Turk of tenpence" such as Ithamore would season his fantasy of marrying the courtesan with the vision of settling in "a country":

> Content: but we will leave this paltry land,
> And sail from hence to Greece, to lovely Greece.
> I'll be thy Jason, thou my golden fleece . . .
> (The *Jew of Malta,* 4.2.92–94)

Whereas all the others may be referred to by their local habitation or country of origin, the Jew may cite a list of places where he visited for a purpose (Shylock's Frankfort, Barabas's Italy, France, etc.) or at best be related to his latest country of temporary residence, where, like in Venice, he was residing in "hell." Not even the ancient, spiritual locus of Jewish desire will do: "creep[ing] to Jerusalem" (4.1.62) is brought up by Barabas as a mode of penance only when he shams a wish to become a Christian. Calling their fellow Jews "countrymen," as does Jessica (who, whether she reports faithfully or lies about Shylock's particular talk with Tubal or Chus, probably quotes her father's regular terminology) and Barabas, betrays aliens' conspiracy rather than citizens' local pride or patriotism:

> Barabas   . . . let 'em combat, conquer, and kill all,
>   So they spare me, my daughter, and my wealth.
>   (150–51)

Territorial nationality is thus certainly dubious when it comes to Jews, which may partly account for the unpleasant silence by which Jessica's volunteered evidence is received. But it is also ambiguous, at best, in relation to Shakespeare's compatriots. Geographic conditions alone, Norbert Elias tells us, are far from accounting in full for established national traits. Further narratives, pertaining to historical development, are inevitable: lack of monopoly on physical power by King and Church contribute to a national character (Elias 1994, 540–41). Shylock, however, is closer in this particular respect to be a parable for indigenous Europeans than their binary opposite. His otherness thrust upon him no less than insisted upon by himself, he regularly refers to members of his community in the play as a tribe, a term of ethnicity, or a nation, a term the significance of which for early modern consiousness lay mainly in its diffusion.

The manipulative social rituals of Renaissance hegemony would not have been so effective, indeed, unless they were falling on a fertile ground in postmedieval consciousness. The dream of a nation was one of the strongest and most suggestive constituents of the powerful web of the Renaissance desire for self-fashioning. The yearning for a collective identity has became more and more acute with the loss of medieval forms of communal belonging to the newly acquired, relative independence of early modern individuality. Whereas the inclusion of humanity in the religious universe, its partaking in the body of Christ, is God-given, national affiliation is constituted by man. This gendered phrase is hardly fortuitous in context: man rather, not woman, whose participation in this constitutive process of procreation is considered passive, as ever. England, as we have seen, is conceived by John of Gaunt as a "happy breed of men," and the best ideological refuge offered, accordingly, to Parolles by his peers, upon his having suffered an irrevocable shame in the world of men, is to "find out a country where but women were that had received so much shame," so that he "might begin an impudent nation" (*All's Well That Ends Well*, 4.3.315–17). Again, the use of the exact term is crucial here: Parolles is not to begin a new race, nor an ethnic tribe, for these are considered natural phenomena. Only nation is manifestly a cultural, self-fashioned entity, and as such, is negotiable and exclusively human. The woman, who at man's will is freely married to the barbarous King of Tunis (Claribel in *The Tempest*) or the suspicious King of France (Cordelia in *King Lear*), or coopted to the English Crown property (Princess Katharine of France in *Henry V*), serves as a living token of that negotiability inherent in the very concept of nationhood. The new "impudent nation" to be bred by Parolles will be governed, no doubt, by patriarchal authority; otherwise it will have to be crushed and tamed, like Hippolyta's nation of Amazons, whose very existence calls for a special intervention from Theseus on behalf of male hegemony, unless they could be almost grotesquely transformed into male warriors and recruited at a time of emergency to serve the interests of united patriarchy in defending chivalrously "Dear mother England":

> For your own ladies and pale-visag'd maids
> Like Amazons come tripping after drums,
> Their thimbles into armed gauntlets change,
> Their needl's to lances, and their gentle hearts
> To fierce and bloody inclination.
> (*King John*, 5.2.154–58)

The Elizabethan theater, Robert Weimann asserts, flowered in an era of national awakening; yet it represented this new sense of nationalism supporting "widely divergent viewpoints" (Weimann 1978, 161, 169). Whereas the economic and political processes the English "nation in the making" (Elias 1994, 275) is undergoing at the time are theoretically traceable by hindsight, the cultural representation of its progress toward civility is far less tangible. If in the general history of nationalism in Western culture, "the Renaissance merely outlined the possibilities of future developments," and even those were confined to kings and some elite groups, while "the people themselves remained entirely outside the reach of nationalism" (Kohn 1951, 120, 124), the case of English nationalism in particular hardly betrays any solid notion of common national identity. Indeed, one finds evidence in Tudor England for pride of being English and hatred of foreigners; but such sentiments, which imposed severe restraints on, and eventually defeated, the prospects of Queen Elizabeth's marriage to the Duke of Anjou, hardly amount to any sense of nationalism proper. Orlando Patterson complains of the confused and overinclusive use of the term *nationalism*, which has come to label any expression of group solidarity. He does admit, however, that the Middle English usage of the term *nation* "referred simply to a collection of people from a special locality or simply an aggregation of human or animal individuals." Unlike the usage of the word on the continent, "the English, with respect to their own political order, have never found the term nation useful, because they have never developed the entity" (Patterson 1977, 67–68). Indeed, such frivolous use of the term *nation* by Dromio of Syracuse:

> methinks they are such a gentle nation that, but for the mountain of mad flesh that claims marriage of me, could find in my heart to stay here still and turn witch. (*The Comedy of Errors*, 4.4.151–54)

Hardly manifests a serious attitude for what it stands for. Given the ethnic history and social conditions of early modern England, the English throne never attempted to base its absolutist project on any consolidated cultural or ethnic traits. Rather it seems that the leaders of the crowd often attempt to foster national pride by insisting on forged parameters of cohesion. Though themselves aware that

> There is a law in each well-order'd nation
> To curb those raging appetites that are
> Most disobedient and refractory
> *(Troilus and Cressida,* 2.2.181–83)

none will refrain from stirring the mutinous emotions of the crowd to manipulate their national feelings as they see fit. In this there is no difference between the arguments of the tribunes of *Caesar's* Rome, who, opposing Caesar, urge the common citizens of Rome to consider their freedom as a token of their national identity:

> Marullus. Wherefore rejoice? What conquest brings he home?
> What tributaries follow him to Rome
> To grace in captive bonds his chariot wheels?
> You blocks, you stones . . .
> *(Julius Caesar,* 1.1.32–35)

and Mark Antony, who, mourning his beloved Caesar, would proclaim their nationality as heirs to Caesar's material possessions:

> Moreover, he hath left you all his walks,
> His private arbors, and new-planted orchards,
> On this side Tiber; he hath left them you,
> And to your heirs forever-common pleasures,
> To walk abroad and recreate yourselves.
> Here was a Caesar! When comes such another?
> (3.2.249–54)

"To the English king," Patterson argues, "the modern state was a political creation concerned strictly with . . . the lands, the laws, a well-stocked treasury, a strong loyal army, and dependable allies . . . it was in no way related to the idea of a common nationality . . . a distinct tribal or cultural heritage" (Patterson, 74). Shakespeare's major political concerns, Patterson goes on to argue, are well tuned with those of hs Tudor audience:

it was not the celebration of British cultural distinctiveness which was of central concern to Shakespeare but the nature and problems of power, the loneliness and deep unease of authority, the integrity of the state, and the legitimacy of the crown. (Ibid., 75)

Indeed, much of the narrative that builds a sense of a nation in the history plays depends on the invocation of Saint George, who, coupled with a kingly leader, is implored to "prosper our colours in [some] dangerous fight" (*1 Henry VI*, 4.2.55–56). And yet the very image of colors, a common token of national identity, is double-edged. That same image of solidarity that groups the English under a national flag also bears the very mark of individuality in solitary death:

> These eyes, that see thee now well coloured,
> Shall see thee wither'd, bloody, pale and dead.
> (4.2.37–38).

or, more clearly, in the very act of differentiating the other, be it a social malcontent marked by his "nighted colour" (*Hamlet*, 1.2.68), an ethnic outsider, rival to all "the wealthy curled darlings of our nation" (*Othello*, 1.2.68):

> A gentle riddance. Draw the curtains, go.
> Let all of his complexion choose me so.
> (*The Merchant*, 2.7.78–79)

a cowardly buffoon—

> Falstaff Sir, I will be as good as my word. This that you heard was but a colour.
> Shallow A colour that I fear you will die in, Sir John.
> Falstaff Fear no colours;
> (*2 Henry IV*, 5.5.85–88)

or a woman—

> your own ladies and pale-visag'd maids
> (*King John*, 5.2.154)

And, both nation and color are prone to deception. One is easily believed to be

> misled with a snipt-taffeta fellow . . . whose villainous saffron would have made all the unbak'd and doughy youth of a nation in his colour.
> (*All's Well That Ends Well*, 4.5.1–4)

It is important to note that issues related to the marked complexity of national unity did not go unnoticed in the work of Shakespeare and his contemporaries, as Patterson's argument might suggest. "It is only after one ceases to reduce public affairs to the business of dominion," says Hannah Arendt, "that the original data in the realm of human affairs will appear, or, rather, reappear, in their authentic diversity" (Arendt 1970). And Shakespeare, for all his concern with majesty and authority, never neglects the processes undergone by his individual and common characters. In that area of "original data," namely human attitude to its primary individual and social identity, with Henry VII's dubious ethnic descent and his granddaughter's problematic class origin, the Tudor dynasty could hardly set a model for a pure and unified brand of nationalism, based on ethnic or class solidarity. However, the very absence of customary national traits gave breed to a creative and intriguing tension between various potential notions of national distinctions, which find their way to the very core and tissue of dramatic conflict. The loss of both communal affiliation within the feudal unit and the comforting subordination to a medieval theocentric system imposed on early-modern individual consciousness in England a desire for some substitute sense of collective belonging, and the concept of nation was vague enough to satisfy this need without obliging one to a too specific commitment to what Andrew Hadfield, following Habermas, would call "a national public sphere" (Hadfield 1994, 5–6).

And yet the term does not readily avail itself as an obvious part of the popular emotional vocabulary in early modern England. Even after the Church of England is established, much of the popular sense of *nation* is still not in full conjunction with the clerical discourse. In texts of sermons delivered by the official clergy, the term is regularly avoided or supplanted by safer terms. Unlike the literary invocation of "England as of a new Israel, His chosen and peculiar people" (Lyly 1902, 205), of which Shylock's "sacred" nation (*The Merchant* 1.3.43) would be considered an unjust and blasphemous parody, official preachers of the Church barely refer to the concept of nation. Their references to forms of communality will range from the distinctly royal "realm" (which is not a far cry from Lyly's own concept of the term *people*), as in Rev. William Barlow's apology for the execution of Essex: "Himself a surfet to the realme, to be spewed out justly" (Chandos 1971, 119), to the more generally divine "Commonwealth," as in the Rev. Henry Smith's harangue on poverty: "every Commonwealth that letteth any member in it to perish for hunger, is an unnaturall and an uncharitable Commonwealth" (Chandos, 87). For the Rev. Bernard Gilpin, "England" is the location where "some terrible examples of God's wrath" have occurred (Chandos, 33). In the theater of the author of *Julius Caesar*, in which the citizens of Rome are driven to perform national functions without the actual term being mentioned even once, it still takes mainly manipulative social rituals and the forging of tendentious political myths on the part of some hegemonic élite to foster an action based on emotionally accepted national narratives.

Notes

1. Ithiel is a Hebrew name of a Biblical sound, the denotation of which is "with me God."

2. See, e.g., Menache 1990, 193: "When symbols become rooted in the mental climate of society, they often replace the abstract ideas that they had originally represented, giving to them a higher significance. In the process, the objects, words, and phrases that become social and national symbols often free themselves from the circumstances out of which they have evolved, and develop along lines of their own, which tend to follow the social process."

3. *See* Anderson 1991, 20.

4. All shakespearean quotations are from the New Arden editions. All Marlowe quotations are from *Complete Plays and Poems*, ed. Eric D. Pendry, London: Dent, 1976.

5. Shakespeare has probably borrowed the "Jerusalem Chamber" prophecy from Holinshed (3:541). The tradition, however, is older than the historical Henry himself, originating from a general Christian mythical stock. It may have been first introduced by Walter Map in his *De Nugis Curialium*, 4:11 ("De Fantastica Deceptione Gerberti"), where it is told of Gerbert—later Pope Sylvester II— to whom it is also assigned by William of Malmesbury in his *De Gestis Regum Anglorum*, §172. While retaining the equivocal "fulfillment" of this prophecy, Shakespeare makes Hotspur mock the notorious "Moldwarp" prophecy—which was actually used by the historical Percies in their rising against Henry IV.

Bibliography

Anderson, Benedict. *Imagined Communities: Reflections on the Origin and Spread of Nationalism*. Revised Edition. London & New York: Verso, 1991.

Anderson, Perry. *Lineages of the Absolutist State*. London & New York: Verso,1979.

Arendt, Hannah. *On Violence*. New York: Harcourt, Brace & World, 1970.

Berry, Edward. "The Poet as Warrior in Sidney's *Defence of Poetry*." *Studies in English Literature* 29 (1989): 22–34.

———. "Sidney's Poor Painter: Nationalism and Social Class." in Newey & Thompson, 1991.

Bhabha, Homi K. ed. *Nation and Narration*. London and New York: Routledge, 1990.

Burchard of Mount Sion. Translated from the Latin by A. Stewart. Palestine Pilgrims Text Society 12 (1896). New York: AMS Press, 1971.

Chandos, John. ed. *In God's Name: Examples of Preaching in England 1534–1662.* London: Hutchinson, 1971.

Cohen, Walter. *Drama of a Nation: Public Theater in Renaissance England and Spain.* Ithaca and London: Cornell University Press, 1985.

Columbus, Christopher. *The "Diario" of Christopher Columbus's First Voyage to America, 1492–1493.* Transcribed and translated by Oliver Dunn and James E. Kelley Jr. Norman: University of Oklahoma Press, 1989.

Cressy, David. "National Memory in Early Modern England," in Gillies, John R. ed. *Commemorations: The Politics of National Identity.* Princeton: Princeton University Press, 1994.

Donne, John. *The Sermons of John Donne.* eds. Evelyn M. Simpson and George R. Potter. vol. 9. 1958.

Douglas, Mary. *Purity and Danger: An Analysis of the Concepts of Pollution and Taboo.* London: Routledge & Kegan Paul, 1966.

Edbury, Peter W., ed. *Crusade and Settlement.* Cardiff: Cardiff: University College Cardiff Press, 1985.

Edwards, Philip. *Threshold of a Nation: A Study in English and Irish Drama.* Cambridge: Cambridge University Press, 1979.

Elias, Norbert. *The Civilising Process,* translated by Edmund Jephcott. Oxford, UK and Cambridge, USA: Blackwell, 1994.

Erdmann, Carl, *The Origin of the Idea of Crusade.* Trans. Marshall W. Baldwin. Princeton: Princeton University Press, 1977.

Gilchrist, John. "The Erdmann Thesis and the Canon Law, 1083–1141." in Edbury, 1985: 37–45.

Gillies, John. *Shakespeare and the Geography of Difference.* Cambridge: Cambridge University Press, 1994.

Greenblatt, Stephen. *Marvelous Possessions: The Wonder of the New World.* Oxford: Clarndon Press, 1991.

Hadfield, Andrew. *Literature, Politics and National Identity: Reformation to Renaissance.* Cambridge: Cambridge University Press, 1994.

Hall, Edward. *Chronicle: The Union of the Two Noble and Illustre Famelies of Lancastre & Yorke.* London, 1548.

Hoade, E. *Western Pilgrims.* Jerusalem: Franciscan Printing Press, 1948.

Housley, Norman. *The Later Crusades: From Lyons to Alcazar 1274–1580.* Oxford: Oxford University Press, 1992.

Katz, Jacob. *Tradition and Crisis: Jewish Society at the End of the Middle Ages.* New York: The Free Press of Glencoe, 1961.

Kohn, Hans. "The Genesis and Character of English Nationalism." *Journal of the History of Ideas* 1 (1940): 69–94.

———. *The Idea of Nationalism: A Study in Its Origins and Background.* New York: Macmillan, 1951.

Lasswell, H. D. "Nations and Classes: The Symbols of Identification." In Berelson, B. and Janowitz, M. eds. *Public Opinion and Communication.* New York, 1966.

Lloyd, Simon." 'Political Crusades' in England, c. 1215–17 ad c. 1263–5." in Edbury, 1985: 113–20.

Lyly, John. *The Complete Works*. Ed. R. Warwick Bond. Oxford: Clarendon Press, 1902.

Machyn, Henry. *The Diary of Henry Machyn, Citizen and Merchant-Taylor of London, from A.D.1550 to A.D.1563*. Ed. John Gough Nichols. London: Printed for the Camden Society, 1848.

Mandeville, Sir John. *The Travels of John Mandeville: The Version of the Cotton Manuscript in Modern Spelling*. London: Macmillan, 1900.

Map, Walter. *De Nugis Curialium*. Englished by Sir Frederick Tupper and M. B. Ogle. London, 1924.

Marx, Karl. "On the Jewish Question." In *Early Writings*, translated by Rodney Livingstone and Gregory Benton. Harmondsworth: Penguin, 1975.

Menache, Sophia. *The Vox Dei: Communication in the Middle Ages*. Oxford: Oxford University Press, 1990.

Newey, Vincent and Thompson, Ann. eds. *Literature and Nationalism*. Savage, MD: Barnes and Noble, 1991.

Patterson, Orlando. *Ethnic Chauvinism: The Reactionary Impulse*. New York: Stein and Day, 1977.

Peters, F. E. *Jerusalem*. Princeton: Princeton University Press, 1985.

Said, Edward. *Beginnings: Intention and Method*. New York: Basic Books, 1975.

Smith, Anthony D. *National Identity*. Harmondsworth: Penguin, 1991.

Weimann, Robert. *Shakespeare and the Popular Tradition in the Theater: Studies n the Social Dimension of Dramatic Form and Function*. Baltimore and London: Johns Hopkins University Press, 1978.

Wettinger, Godfrey. *The Jews of Malta in the Late Middle Ages*. Valletta, Malta: Midsea Books, 1985.

Wilkinson, J. *Egeria's Travels in the Holy Land*. Rev. ed. Warminster: Aris and Phillips, 1981.

Index

Acmeism, 268
Adelman, Janet, 81, 86 n. 28, 184, 191, 198 n. 6, 199 n. 23, 200 n. 29–30, 234, 243, 251 n. 20
Aeschylus, 230; Prometheus, 141
Aggression, 233, 236, 242
Aljahit, 282
Allen, D. C., 58, 61 n. 31
All's Well That Ends Well, 21, 113–37, 155, 293, 296
Almagor, Dan, 274
Aloni, Nissim, 271, 272
Alterman, Nathan, 266–70, 271, 272, 274
Amir, Chaya, 274
Anderson, Benedict, 279, 283, 286, 287
Antichrist, 168
Antony and Cleopatra, 18–19
Arden, Mary, 249, 251 n. 19
Arendt, Hannah, 297
Aristotle, 18, 85 n. 17, 152, 204–30
As You Like It, 51–61, 115, 151, 155; Jaques, 51–59
Aubrey, John, 200 n. 24
Auden, Wilfred H., 36 n. 2, 178
Augustine, Saint, 55, 60 n. 19
Austen, Jane, 17–18; *Pride and Prejudice*, 18; Mrs. Bennet, 18
Avidan, David, 270, 272, 273

Babb, Lawrence, 61 n. 27
Barber, C. L., 48 n. 2
Barker, Francis, 178, 198 n. 7
Barlow, William, 297
Barnet, Sylvan, 60 n. 16
Bartels, Emily, 49 n. 20, 50 n. 29, 176 n. 6, 176 n. 6
Barthelemy, Andrew, 50 n. 31, n. 34
Barthes, Roland, 84
Bataille, Georges, 185, 199 n. 20, 200 n. 33
Baudelaire, Charles, 268

Baudrillard, Jean, 151, 175
Bawdry, 17
Begin, Menahem, 153–54
Benjamin, Walter, 188, 193, 195, 201 n. 43, 202 n. 53, 203 n. 63
Bergmann, Fritz, 219, 223, 230, 231
Berry, Edward, 287–88
Besser, Gedalia, 271
Bhabha, Homi, 285
Bialik, Hayim Nachman, 261, 263–66, 268, 272
Bible, 187, 189, 190 201 n. 38, 255–60, 263, 264, 265, 268, 275, 281; Genesis, 26–27, 30, 36 n. 4, 255, 288; Isaiah, 281; New Testament, 225, 281; Proverbs, 255, 257, 267; Psalms, 53, 63, 65; Revelation, 281; I Samuel, 27–28, 255; Song of Songs, 19
Blacks on the English Stage, 42–50
Blazon, 79–82
Bloom, Harold, 236, 237, 244
Boccaccio, 87
Body, 31, 34–35, 72–84, 88, 154–55, 165, 167, 177–203
Booth, Stephen, 37 n. 8
Bosch, Hieronymous, 188
Bradbrook, M. C., 43, 49 n. 22
Braden, Gordon, 203 n. 65
Bradley, A. C., 208, 231
Braunmuller, A. R., 40, 48 n. 12
Brecht, Bertolt, 152; *Life of Galileo*, 152
Bernard, Saint, 53
Breydenbach, Bernard von, 287
Bright, Timothy, 187, 201 n. 40
Briseis, 100
Bronfen, Elizabeth, 91, 108, 111 n. 8
Brooks, Peter, 116
Brower, Reuben A., 241, 250 n. 5, 251 n. 18
Büchner, Georg, 204, 224, 230, 231; *Danton's Death*, 224–30; *Woyzeck*, 204–7, 218–30

Bulman, James, 48 n. 7
Burchard of Mount Sion, 283
Burckhardt, Sigurd, 39–40, 41, 42, 48 n. 2, n. 6, n. 10, n. 11
Burke, Kenneth, 235
Burkert, Walter, 198 n. 12, 199 n. 20
Bywater, Ingram, 230

Carmi, T., 270, 271, 272
Cary, Elizabeth, 286
Cathexis, 99
Cavell, Stanley, 178–79, 197, 198 n. 9, 200 n. 31, 203 n. 67
Cazani, Liliana, 72; *Night Porter, The,* 73
Chaplin, Charles, 117
Charlemagne, 282
Charnes, Linda, 110 n. 1
Charney, Maurice, 202 n. 50
Chaucer, Geoffrey, 51, 84, 87
Chivalry, 89
Chodorow, Nancy, 250 n. 4
Chryseis, 100
Clemen, Wolfgang, 201 n. 34
Clubb, Louise George, 59 n. 2
Cohen, Walter, 36 n. 3, 277
Coleridge, Samuel, 180, 199 n. 15, 230, 231
Colie, Rosalie, 86 n. 26
Colonialism, 277–80
Columbus, Cristopher, 283
Comedy, Comic, 31, 114–16, 117, 119
Comedy of Errors, The, 24, 294
Constantine, 281
Cook, Carol, 110 n. 1
Coriolanus, 166, 232–54
Courtly Love, 89
Crashaw, William, 289
Cressy, David, 287, 288
Culture, 11, 256, 257, 259, 261, 267, 271, 274, 275
Curtius, Ernst Robert, 51, 59 n. 2
Cymbeline, 136

D'Amico, Jack, 48 n. 1
Damned, The (Visconti), 73
Danson, Lawrence, 48 n. 16
Da Ponte, L., 270
Davidowitz, S. Z., 265
Death, Death Instinct, 44, 117, 156, 159, 163–64, 167, 170–71, 181–86, 194–96, 236–37, 239–40, 247, 250 n. 7–8, n. 10
de Certeau, Michel, 66
de Man, Paul, 65, 84, 164
Derrida, Jacques, 110 n. 4, 112 n. 16
Descartes, 152, 155
Desire, 62–86, 178, 189, 191, 193, 196, 199 n. 22, 292
Diction, Poetic: vocabulary, 258, 259, 260, 262, 264, 265, 268, 271
Disease, 110, 117, 118, 191
Donawerth, Jane, 48 n. 2
Donne, John, 289
Douglas, Mary, 289
Dryden, John, 86 n. 31
Duality, 245
Durand, Jean-Louis, 198 n. 12

Economy, Exchange and Market, 17–37, 60
Edwards, Philip, 277
Edwards, Robert, 60 n. 18
Efros, Israel, 265
Ekphrastic poem, 67, 69
Eliot, T. S., 180, 199 n. 17, 208, 231
Elizabeth I, 155, 199 n. 21
England, 38, 40, 48 n. 1, 190, 259, 282–84, 286–88
Engle, Lars, 36 n. 3
English (language, poetry), 256, 264, 265, 266, 267, 268, 273; Monosyllabic Nature of, 268; vs. Hebrew, 269, 273
Enjambment, 272
Enlightenment (Hebrew). See *Haskala*
Epicure, 174
Erdmann, Carl, 282
Europe, 38, 259, 282–83, 291
Evans, B. I., 48 n. 2
Even-Zohar, Ithamar, 268

Face, veiled face, 154–55, 158–62, 167–73, 192
Falstaff, 20
Felman, Shoshana, 164, 176 n. 12
Ferber, Michael, 50 n. 32
Ferguson, Margaret F., 65
Figures of Speech, Figurative Language, 260
Fineman, Joel, 37 n. 9
Foucault, Michel, 160
Frankis, P. J., 59 n. 4
Freedman, Barbara, 92, 111 n. 10

French (language, poetry), 267
Freud, Sigmund, 43, 49 n. 25, 88–112, 122, 182–83, 189, 194, 195, 199 n. 21, 201 n. 46, 202 n. 57, 233, 236, 242, 244; *Beyond the Pleasure Principle*, 88, 236, 237–39, 240–41, 243, 248, 250 n. 7, n. 10; *Civilization and Its Discontents*, 239, 250 n. 7; *Ego and the Id*, 238; Fort/Da Game, 88; *Interpretation of Dreams*, 189, 201 n. 46
Freud, Sophie and Ernst, 108
Freund, Elizabeth, 86 n. 32, 110 n. 1
Fried, Erich, 200 n. 25
Friendship, 21–28, 31
Frye, Northrop, 31, 59, 204–5, 231
Frye, Roland M., 59 n. 6
Fujimura, Thomas, 48 n. 2

Gardner, Helen, 57, 61 n. 26
Gaze, 67–82
Genette, Gérard, 176 n. 15
German (language, poetry, thought), 12, 261, 264
Gilchrist, John, 282
Gilman, Sander, 39, 48 n. 5
Gilpin, Bernard, 298
Girard, René, 86 n. 31
Goethe, J. W., 140, 239, 261; *Faust*, 140; Mephistopheles, 140
Goldberg, Leah, 266–70
Golomb, Harai, 11, 273, 277
Gordon, Yehuda Leib, 260, 262
Gorfain, Phyllis, 136 n. 6
Graham, Kenneth J. E., 48 n. 2
Green, Henry, 61 n. 29
Greenblatt, Stephen, 154, 156, 176 n. 7, 283, 286, 287, 288
Greene, Gayle, 86 n. 31, 110 n. 1
Greyerz, Georg von, 51–52, 59 n. 3
Grossman-Avinoam, Reuven, 265
Guigemar, 58
Gulf War (1991), 151

Ha'aretz (Israeli daily), 267
Habermas, Jürgen, 297
Habimah (Israel's National Theatre), 271
Hadfield, Andrew, 297
Hadrian, 281
Hall, Edward, 285
Hamlet, 57, 122, 139, 166, 177–203, 232, 255, 268, 269, 270; Claudius, 139, 181, 182, 184, 185, 186, 188, 191, 192, 193, 200 n. 27, 202 n. 51; Hamlet, 122, 149, 177–203, 233, 249; "To be or not to be," 255, 260
Harding, D. W., 233
Harington, Sir John, 175 n. 5
Harshav (Hrushovski), Benjamin, 259, 273, 274, 275
Hartman, Geoffrey, 62, 86 n. 31
Haskala [Hebrew Enlightenment], 259–64, 265, 268, 271, 272, 273, 274
Haviv, Shafiq, 176 n. 20
Hebrew (language, poetry); and Shakespeare Translation, 255–75 (*See also* Translation of Shakespeare into the Hebrew); Biblical 255, 257 260–66, 268, 271, 274; (*see also* Bible); "Death" and Revival of, 255–59, 263, 266, 274; grammar, 258, 260; influence of individual poets on development, 263–64, 267; modern (Israeli), 256, 260, 262, 264, 267, 268, 270; modernist poetry in, 266, 267, 268, 273; native speakers of, 256, 260, 267; poetic language, poetic generations, 263, 264, 265, 266, 268, 273, 275; poetry, 262, 266; polysyllabic nature of, 268, 273; sacred vs. secular language, 256–59; spoken, colloquial vs. written, 256–59, 262, 263, 265, 267, 268, 270, 272, 274; slang, 262; style(s), 262, 263, 267, 272; syntax, 260, 263, 268, 269, 272; theater and stage in Israel, 267, 268, 270; vs. English, 269, 274
Hegel, G. W. F., 206–18, 223–30, 231
Helsinger, Howard, 60 n. 8
1 Henry IV, 20, 287, 288, 296
2 Henry IV, 287, 289, 296
Henry V, 12, 293
1 Henry VI, 285
2 Henry VI, 285
3 Henry VI, 141–46, 285
Henry VIII, 288
Hercules, Herculean, 31, 44, 49 n. 27, 159
Hermeneutics, 179
Hoade, E., 284
Hofling, Charles K., 233
Holinshed, 298 n. 5
Homer, 84, 100, 107; *The Iliad*, 100

INDEX

Homosexuality, 20, 21, 24–26, 34, 189
Hooker, Deborah, 104–5, 111 n. 13
Housley, Norman, 283
Hrushovski, Benjamin. *See* Harshav (Hrushovski), Benjamin
Hunt, John, 197 n. 5
Hunter, G. K., 50 n. 31, 136 n. 5, 176 n. 18
Hussein, Saddam, 168, 175
Hutcheon, Linda, 48 n. 8

Iconography, 12, 51–61, 70–72
Ideology, 11, 13, 74, 152–53, 164–65, 167, 278–79, 282, 284
Ignatieff, Michael, 168
Il Pecorone, 28–29, 32
Impotence, 29
Inwardness/Interiority, 81, 177–97, 200 n. 30
Isolation, 138–50, 186
Israel, 256, 265, 270, 271, 274; Israeli culture, 11–12; Israeli politics, 11, 153–54, 170–71, 175, 278–80
Italian (language, poetry), 270

Jagendorf, Zvi, 50 n. 35
James, Caryn, 76–77
Jenkins, Harold, 58–59, 61 n. 32
Jerusalem, 276–300
Jew vs. Gentile, 26–27, 33–35, 50 n. 35, 290–92
Jewish Culture, 11–12, 255–59, 274, 277–80
Johnson, Samuel, 230, 231
Jones, Eldred, 50 n. 30
Jones, Ernest, 108, 248
Jonson, Ben, 21; *Epicoene, or The Silent Woman*, 21
Julius Caesar, 165–69, 171–74, 263, 264, 269, 295
Jung, Carl G., 250 n. 6

Kahlo, Frida, 198 n. 12
Kahn, Coppélia, 110 n. 1, 235, 243
Katz, Jacob, 291
Kaufmann, Walter, 206, 230, 231
King John, 190, 294, 296
King Lear, 65, 81, 269; Lear, 47, 139, 293
Kelsall, Lawrence, 176 n. 9
Klein, Melanie, 94, 106, 194, 203 n. 58
Knight, George Wilson, 197 n. 4, 249

Knights, L. C., 140
Kohn, Hans, 294
Kohut, Heinz, 194–95
Komisarjevsky, Theodore 48 n. 7
Kopper, John M., 94, 110 n. 6, 111 n. 7
Korman, Sarah, 49 n. 17
Kott, Jan, 51, 53–54, 59 n. 1, 86 n. 31
Krieger, Murray, 64
Kristeva, Julia, 112 n. 17

Lacan, Jacques, 89–90, 111 nn. 9 and 11, 168, 171, 176 n. 14, 183, 187–88, 199 n. 22, 201 n. 42, 250 n. 6
Laing, R. D., 189–90, 201 n. 47
Language, linguistic representation, 193–94
Lascelles, M., 60 n. 13
Lawrence, W. W., 113
Legalism, 17, 37 n. 8
Lehmann, Werner R., 230, 231
Leo I, Bishop of Rome, 281
Levin, Richard A., 136 n. 2
Lewalski, Barbara Keiffer, 36 n. 4
Line (poetic): line division, 272
Lissitzky, Ephraim A., 265
Lodge, Thomas, 59 n. 2
Lopez, Rodrigo, 48 n. 1
Louis the Saint, 282
Love, 18–23, 27–28, 34–35, 58, 126–27, 139–49, 158–59, 177, 184
Luther, Martin, 57
Lydgate, 84
Lyly, John, 297

McFarland, Thomas, 55, 61 n. 21
Macbeth, 139; Macbeth, 139
Madonna, 66, 72–77
Mahood, M. M., 48 n. 3
Mandeville, Sir John, 286, 287
Mansfield, Katherine, 113
Map, Walter, 298 n. 5
Mapplethorpe, Robert, 73
Marlowe, Christopher, 43–44, 154, 155, 156, 159, 164–65, 176; *The Jew of Malta*, 291–93; *Tamburlaine*, 43–44, 156–65, 166, 176 n. 10; Tamburlaine, 43–44, 156–65
Marriage, Courtship, 17–18, 31, 114–16, 118, 130, 135–36, 136 n. 6, 222
Marx, John H., 175 n. 4
Marx, Karl, 291
Mastery, 43, 68

Materialism, 178
Maus, Katharine Eisaman, 178, 197 n. 2
Measure for Measure, 113, 135, 172; Mariana, 135
Melancholia, Melancholy, 18, 182, 187, 194–95, 199 n. 21, 201 n. 40, 202 n. 57
Menache, Sophia, 298 n. 2
Merchant of Venice, The, 12, 17–37, 38–50, 291–93, 296, 297; Antonio, 18, 20, 21–26, 27–29, 30–31, 32–35, 41, 111 n. 14; Bassanio, 19–20, 21–26, 27–29, 30–31, 33–35, 36, 39, 43, 44, 111 n. 14; Gratiano,17, 22, 29–30; Jessica, 39, 50 n. 35, 292; Launcelot Gobbo, 48 n. 7, 292; Nerissa, 17, 30; Old Gobbo, 48 n. 7; Portia, 17, 19–20, 21, 28–29, 30–31, 32–35, 45–46, 111 n. 7, 292; Prince of Morocco, 28, 38, 42–50, 292; Shylock, 12, 20, 21, 26–27, 31, 32–35, 39–47, 50 n. 35, 292–93; Salerio, 22, 39, 46; Solanio, 18, 39; Solario, 22, 42; Tubal, 41
Meter(s), Metrics, 262, 263, 266 (see also Prosody); and Rhythm (rigidity vs. flexibility in the application of meter), 269, 272, 273; accentual (Biblical), 263; accentual-syllabic, 264, 272; amphibrach, 273; anapest, 273; hexameter (iambic), 268, 269; iambic pentameter, 266, 268, 269, 272, 273; syllabic; syllable count, 259, 262, 263, 264, 272, 274
Midsummer Night's Dream, A, 64–65, 169, 293
Milhou, Alain, 283
Militarism, Cult of War, 234–35, 250 nn. 2 and 5
Milton, John, 66
Miron, Dan, 267, 268, 269, 272, 273
Montrose, Louis, 167–68, 176 n. 13
Moody, A. D., 49 n. 21
Moor, 38–50
Mothering, 233–35, 249, 250 n. 3, 251 n. 20,
Mozart, W. A., 270
Much Ado About Nothing, 155
Mullaney, Steven, 199 n. 21
Murphy, James J., 49 n. 18

Nathansohn, Amalia, 248
Nationalism, 11, 276–300
Netanyahu, Benjamin, 280
Nevo, Ruth, 36 n. 5, 236
Neumann, Erich, 243
Newton, Helmut, 72
Nicol, Allardyce, 114
Nietzsche, F., 169, 174, 176 n. 19, 177, 179, 189, 195, 196, 197, 198 nn. 10–13, 200 n. 28, 201 n. 44, 202 n. 52
Nitzan, Omri, 271
Normand, Lawrence, 48 n. 9, n. 15
Norris, Christopher, 151, 175 n. 1

Opera, 270
O'Rourke, James, 110 n. 1
Othello, 50 n. 29, 204–30, 248, 251 n. 18, 255, 270, 271, 274, 275; Desdemona, 255; Iago, 138, 140, 171, 255; *Ithiel Ha-Kooshi*, or *Ithiel the Moor* [Hebrew], 255, 259, 274; Othello, 12, 45, 47
Other/other, 44, 49 n. 20, 168, 197
Oz, Avraham, 270, 271, 272

Paglia, Camille, 73–77
Palestine, 265
Palmer, D. J., 55
Paster, Gail Kern, 178, 197 n. 3
Pastoral, 52
Patterson, Orlando, 294–96
Peres, Shim'on, 280
Peter Pan, 24
Petrarch, 79–80
Phillips, Adam, 186, 201 n. 35
Pierce, Robert B., 59 n. 4
Plutarch, 234–35
Poverty vs. Richness, 18
Price, Victor, 230, 231
Primary Narcissism, 88–90
Proctor, William, 289
Prophecy, 151–76, 298 n. 5
Prose (prose fiction), 262, 263
Prosody, versification, 258, 260, 262–66, 268, 269, 273, 275
Prosopopoeia, 69–70, 73–74
Psychoanalytic Criticism, 13, 44, 87–112, 113–37, 232–54
Pushkin, Alexander S., 261
Puttenham, 65
Pygmalion, 62

Rabin, Yitzhak, 153–54, 175 n. 3
Rank, Otto, 136 n. 4

Raysor, T. M., 113
Reich, Wilhelm, 187, 201 n. 41
Reification, 156–57
Renaissance, 38, 40, 63, 154
Repetition, compulsion to repeat, 38–41, 236–38, 240–41, 244, 248
Representation, 62–86, 153–54
Rhetoric, rhetoricity, 37 n. 9, 38–50, 62–86
Richard II, 68, 289–90, 293
Richard III, 138–50, 152, 172–73
Ricoeur, Paul, 199 n. 21
Riddle, 130, 136 n. 6, 152, 159–64
Ridley, M. R., 271
Rivera, Diego, 198 n. 12
Rogers, Robert, 137 n. 7
Romanticism, 274
Rome, 232, 244
Romeo and Juliet, 12, 255, 262; *Ram ve-Yael* (Hebrew), 255, 262
Rosenzweig, Franz, 150; *Star of Redemption*, 138
Rossiter, A. P., 86 n. 23
Roth, Cecil, 48 n. 1
Russian (language, poetry), 259, 261, 264, 266, 267, 268

Said, Edward, 168, 175, 284
Salame, Ghassan, 175
Salkinson, Isaac Edward, 255, 258, 259, 262, 271, 274, 277
Scarry, Elaine, 187, 189, 193, 198 n. 12, 200 n. 30, 201 n. 38, 202 n. 54
Schiller, Gertrud, 60 n. 7
Scott, William O., 111 n. 12
Sedgwick, Eve Kosofsky, 36–37 n. 7
Self-reflexivity, 67
Sellars, Peter, 270
Seneca, 196–97
Shakespeare, William, 11–12, 154, 244, 278, 279, 295; comedies, 17, 31, 114, 115, 155; "Rape of Lucrece", 66–72; Sonnet 23, 65; Sonnet 129, 88; Sonnet 134, 30, 32, 37 n. 8, n. 9. *See also under separate play entries*
Shapiro, James, 48 n. 1, 49 n. 20, n. 24, 50 n. 35
Shavit, Uzi, 275
Shaw, George Bernard, 136 n. 4
Shaw, John, 61 n. 24
Shell, Marc, 39, 48 n. 6, 50 n. 35
Shipley, Joseph T., 176 n. 21

Shlonsky, Avraham 266–70. *See also* Translation, of Shakespeare into Hebrew: "SAG-Group"
Sidney, Sir Philip, 63–65
Smith, Antony D., 281, 288
Smith, Gordon Ross, 233–34
Smith, Henry, 297–98
Smith, James, 61 n. 30
Smolenskin, Peretz, 255, 274, 277
Snir, Hannan, 271
Socrates, 179, 197
Solitude, 138–50, 186
Sophocles, 230; *Antigone*, 141
Spurgeon, Caroline, 201 n. 34
Steiner, George, 230, 231
Stoller, Robert J., 234
Stress (prosody), 266, 274
Symbolism, 268

Taming of the Shrew, The, 155
Taylor, C. P., 164
Taylor, Michael, 56, 61 n. 23
Tel Aviv, 267
Tempest, The, 293
Tene, D., 268
Terence, 114
Tertulian, 55.
Theology, 12, 51–61
Timon of Athens, 139; Timon, 139–40
Titus Andronicus, 45, 199 n. 23; Aaron, 12, 45, 49 n. 20, 50 n. 27
Toury, Gideon, 260
Tragedy, tragic, 12, 27, 55, 83, 138–50, 155, 158–59, 168, 169, 204–30
Translation, of Shakespeare into Hebrew, 12–13, 255–75; adequacy, in translation, 260, 262, 265, 269; "American Group" of Shakespeare translators, 265–66; Americanization, 270; archaism (vs. innovation), 258; Ashkenazi (pronunciation, in Hebrew), 266; "classical" (vs. "contemporary") ideal/model of translation, 258; classical literature, as a challenge to translation, 258; innovation, (vs. archaism), 258; norms of, 260, 262, 263; as revenge, 255–59; "SAG-Group," 266–70, 272; verse vs. prose, 271, 272, 273
Traub, Valerie, 88, 110 n. 3
Troilus and Cressida, 12, 77–84, 87–112, 295

Tropes, and figures, 67
Twelfth Night, 115, 128; Feste, 120; Malvolio, 128; Olivia, 120; Viola (Cesario), 128
Two Gentlemen of Verona, The, 115
Tynianov, Yuri, 258

Uhlig, Claus, 57, 60n. 16
Umar, Caliph, 281
Urban II, Pope, 282
Ut Pictura Poesis, 67

Verse, verse drama, blank verse, 260, 264, 265, 266
Vickers, Nancy, 79
Vienna, 259
Violence, 156
Virgil, 281
Voice, 62–86

Waddington, Raymond, 49n. 28
Waith, Eugene M., 49n. 27
Weimann, Robert, 277
Wettinger, Godfrey, 291
Wheeler, Richard P., 115, 126
Wieseltier, Meir, 273
Wigham, Frank, 43, 49nn. 20 and 23
Wilcox, J. 59n. 5
Wilson, Douglas B., 110n. 1
Wilson, John Dover, 59n. 2, 190–91
Winnicott, D. W., 95–96
Winter's Tale, The, 57, 62

Yeats, W. B., 178
Yerushalmi, Rina, 270
Yiddish, 257, 264, 266
Young, David, 54, 60n. 13

Zionism, 11–12, 279–80